The American We

The American West

Competing Visions

Karen R. Jones and John Wills

Edinburgh University Press

© Karen R. Jones and John Wills, 2009

Edinburgh University Press Ltd
22 George Square, Edinburgh
www.euppublishing.com

Typeset in 11/13 pt Stempel Garamond by
Servis Filmsetting Ltd, Stockport, Cheshire, and
printed and bound in Great Britain by
CPI Antony Rowe, Chippenham and Eastbourne

A CIP record for this book is available from the British Library

ISBN 978 0 7486 2251 1 (hardback)
ISBN 978 0 7486 2252 8 (paperback)

The right of Karen R. Jones and John Wills to be identified as authors of this work has been asserted in accordance with the Copyright, Designs and Patents Act 1988.

Contents

List of Figures — vii

Introduction — 1

Part One: Old West

1. Lewis and Clark: Mapping the West — 11
2. Frontier Germ Theory — 39
3. 'The Gun that Won the West' — 60
4. Cowboy Presidents and the Political Branding of the American West — 87

Part Two: New West

5. Women in the West: The Trailblazer and the Homesteader — 121
6. Women in the West: The 'Indian Princess' and the 'Lady Wildcat' — 141
7. The Wild West Defiled: The American Indian, Genocide and the Sand Creek Massacre — 171
8. The Thirsty West: Grand Canyon, Hoover Dam and Las Vegas — 194

Part Three: Recreating the West

9. The Western Renaissance: *Brokeback Mountain* and the Return of Jesse James — 231

10. The Arcade Western	260
11. Turn here for 'The Sunny Side of the Atom': Tourism, the Bomb and Popular Culture in the Nuclear West	284
12. Re-creation and the Theme Park West	305
Bibliography	324
Index	338

Figures

I.1	Pioneertown Gun Store, 2006 (Karen R. Jones)	2
3.1	William R. Eyster, *The Lightning Sport; Or, The Bad Men at Slaughter Bar* (Beadle & Adams, 1882), front cover (Autry Library, National Autry Center, 89.141.175)	81
4.1	'The Charge of San Juan Hill: Wm. H. West Impersonating Col. Roosevelt, Leading the Famous "Rough Riders" to Victory, 1899' (Library of Congress, Prints and Photographs Division, LC-USZ62-26060)	96
4.2	'Playing the Last Card' (Monty Wolverton, 2006)	112
6.1	'Calamity Jane Carey [sic], Scout for Gen. Crook in Black Hills, 1880–1900' (Autry Library, Autry National Center, 90.253.1807)	150
7.1	In the White House Conservatory during the Civil War, Brady, New York (Library of Congress)	189
8.1	Three construction workers putting a coat of paint on a slanted wall of riveted-steel plates on the Hoover Dam spillway (Library of Congress)	208
8.2	Night Lights, 05/1972 (US National Archives)	216
9.1	Jesse James (Library of Congress, Prints and Photographs Division, Washington, DC)	248
9.2	Jesse James movies	253
10.1	*Boot Hill*, 1977 (courtesy of Midway)	267
11.1	Atomic mushroom cloud from Operation Buster-Jangle, as witnessed from Las Vegas downtown, November 1951 (Las Vegas News Bureau)	287
12.1	Frontier Village postcards, c. 1970s (courtesy of Gary Lenhart)	316

Introduction

Automobiles flash past giant wind farms in the Californian desert. Shining white guardians of new technology in the American West, the wind turbines turn kinetic energy into state electricity. Their airplane-like propellers revolve repeatedly, as if filtering the air adjacent to the highway, blasting aside the smog with clean ions. The cars and trucks meanwhile continue their way along 29 Palms Highway to Joshua Tree National Park, where the sunny palms turn to wizened trees and a desert wilderness beckons. Some vehicles turn off north of the small residential stretch of Yucca Valley into the desert hills, to visit Pioneertown, an historic 'ghost town' of wood cabins. The main street boasts a mine, a saloon, a jail and a motel. Cowboys and cowgirls wander its dusty confines. Stars mark the midnight sky, tumbleweed blows along the dirt street. Thanks to a lightning strike, a brush fire nearly engulfed Pioneertown in 2006, but most of this Old West remnant survives.

Pioneertown is a figment of imagination, a monument to fakery. Built in 1946 by a group of Hollywood investors that included actors Roy Rogers and Gene Autry, the ramshackle nature of the buildings and the rustic decor of their interiors represented a deliberate design aesthetic. Pioneertown was constructed as a film set. During the 1940s and 1950s, a number of television series were shot on location here, including *The Cisco Kid* (1950) starring Duncan Renaldo and *Annie Oakley* (1954) with Gail Davis. 'Singing cowboy' Gene Autry retained a room at the Pioneertown Motel. The frontier facades hid a range of conspicuously modern activities effectively, including a bowling alley where Roy Rogers took first aim at the pins and one cabin which served as an ice-cream parlour. With the demise of the Hollywood Western in the 1970s, Pioneertown scraped by as a tourist attraction and stop-off on the way to Las Vegas and the Mojave. Originally built

Figure I.1 Pioneertown Gun Store, 2006.

as a novel combination of a gas station and frontier cantina, Pappy & Harriet's Palace opened in 1982 as a restaurant hosting live music. Every Saturday, from April to October, the Old West Re-enactment Troupe (or Pioneertown Posse) still dress up, fire guns and play cowboys. On Sundays, 'Gunfighters for Hire' promise a 'wagonload of old-West style live action, wild-West excitement and fun for the entire family'. Their roster of entertainers currently includes Wyatt Earp, Weak Eyes Cody and Johnny Widowmaker. Such hokum and role-play ensures that the Wild West fantasy of Pioneertown endures far beyond its filmic days.

Pioneertown enacts a constructed vision of the American West. It offers an architectural simulation of a frontier boom town circa the 1870s, designed to make money from the entertainment business not to serve as a living museum or relic of a bygone era. The town plan was conceived to meet the expectations of movie directors, not western historians. On the nineteenth-century frontier, mines rarely exited directly onto Main Street, while bowling alleys in saloons proved even less common. Yet Pioneertown captures so much of what we understand as the 'mythic frontier', the popular land of cowboys and Indians. The 'old West' can be felt there almost as something tangible, dusty and momentous. Cowboys look rough and mean, and the rustic cabins creek with dilapidation. It seems almost real. At the same time, the vintage view is fractured by modern intrusions of technology, culture and society. The cars parked in the lot, electricity generators and motel wifi connections denote cultural signifiers of a different West: that of machines, modernity and mass consumption. Experimental art installations suggest a modish New Age aesthetic. The photographic image of a rough-hewn cabin with a plastic chair on its porch and classic automobile outside resonates with temporal distortion, ably conveying the West as a place party to competing images.

'Vision' represents a powerful motif in a twenty-first-century West shaped by electronic signs, billboard posters, computer monitors and Hollywood celluloid. It relates to the seen, the visual and the aesthetic. Sometimes the West literally challenges the way in which people see the world. The strange two-dimensional monumentalism of the Grand Canyon as seen from the South Rim makes psychological connection with the huge chasm a difficult prospect. The Los Angeles freeways swathed in a blanket of smog in the summer months renders driving a blurred and sometimes suffocating experience. Vision is also about clarity in seeing. To have 'vision' is to have foresight, to nurture a grand design or propitious plan. In the West, individuals such as Californian engineer and booster William Mulholland, Wovoka (Jack Wilson) of the Nevada Paiute, founder of the Ghost Dance movement, and cartoonist and film-maker Walt Disney all harboured creative imaginings. Visions often involve constructions of empire, utopia, the future or indeed the frontier. They are often mental images, transcribed onto existing landscapes, or manufactured into material structures (in Mulholland's case, water aqueducts). They can also be projected onto the past. At the 1893 World Columbian Exposition at Chicago, organised to commemorate the discovery of the 'new world' by Christopher Columbus, several visions of the West were explored. Keen to promote Chicago as a city to rival the very best of the urbane East Coast, the World's Fair was hardly the perfect vehicle to capture images of the old American West. Tellingly, at that point in time, the most famous vision of the West delivered at Chicago was located outside the Exposition ground, by scout and entertainer Buffalo Bill. Buffalo Bill, or William Frederick Cody, presented his Wild West as a stage show brimming with live action and colour. Cowboys, Indians, horses and gunfire dominated the performance. Bill's vision of the West enthralled and excited audiences. In retrospect, the more significant event was historian Frederick Jackson Turner introduction of his 'frontier thesis' to a small group of academics gathered one afternoon at the World's Congress on Literature. Turner broadcast the frontier as a process that made Americans American. White farmers, travelling westwards, taming the wilderness and crafting a civilisation, represented true national heroes. The audience hardly noticed the significance of the proposition. There were other visions of the West at the Exposition. State buildings in Jackson Park celebrated a region of agricultural endeavour, while other exhibits revelled in industry, technology and futurism.

Early in the twentieth century, the popular vision of the West captured and promoted by Buffalo Bill made its way onto film. The Hollywood Western dominated the 1930s to the 1950s. Audiences fell in love with the nostalgic, unambiguous pioneer spirit of the genre. It was not just film, however, which contributed to Western mythmaking. Disneyland opened in 1955 with its own fully interactive fantasy world of 'Frontierland'. Elias Disney, the father of Walt, had served as a construction worker at the Columbia World's Fair. Later, his son concocted a magic land to rival Chicago's best. Other visions of the West were fashioned from concrete and steel rather than plastic and cartoon. Los Angeles, Las Vegas, Phoenix, Denver all grew in population and business. Old frontier myths seemed moribund in a climate of skyscrapers, computer chips and espressos to go. With a buoyant Hispanic population in the southwest, lingering white hegemony came into question. By the late 1980s, the academic vernacular on the West had dramatically changed. Criticism of outdated frontier concepts had grown to the point of severance with the Turnerian West. Influenced by social movements of the 1960s, scholars such as Patricia Nelson Limerick and Richard White documented a different view of the region as a land of complexity, ambiguity, conquest, multi-ethnicity and environmental tragedy. 'New Western' history posed the greatest challenge to older visions. Progress read conquest, and the frontier became the 'f-word' in revisionist vocabulary.

With the rise of New Western scholarship, social activism and demographic changes in the West, clashes of interpretation proved to be unavoidable. At Little Bighorn Battlefield National Monument near Crow Agency in Montana, the number of signs and monuments at the tourist site provided aesthetic markers of the discrepancy between views. In 1879, just three years after the death of Custer, the War Department established a National Cemetery for the 7th Cavalry at the site. In 1881, a marble monument on Last Stand Hill marked the resting place of fallen troops. In 1946, the area earned the designation of the Custer Battlefield National Monument in honour of the US Army. However, in 1991, Congress ordered that the site be renamed the Little Bighorn Battlefield Monument, and mandated the construction of an Indian Memorial in order 'to express the Plains Indian legacy'. Newly furnished commentary by the National Park Service focused on the meaning of the place not for Custer, but for his foes, pointing out how 'This area memorializes one of the last armed efforts of the Northern Plains Indians to preserve their way of life'. This shift of emphasis from brave White loss to equally courageous Native American defence might be taken as a corrective process, an acknowledgement of what actually went on in the American West. According to revisionist logic, realism had won over myth. Equally, the change of name indicated a shift from one vision to another. Dedicated in June 2003, the Indian Memorial articulated the desire for 'peace through unity', and a more inclusive West. The new memorial sat opposite the old one, marking the National Monument as an uneasy alliance of images, where two very different meanings of history collide and compete. On the welcome plaque to the park, the Indian stands on one side of the message, Custer on the other. Some competing visions of the American West remain difficult to resolve.

As can be seen with the Little Bighorn Battlefield, discreet visions of the West compete over geographic boundaries and interpretative labels. They clash over historical meaning. Sometimes, the material environment provides formative influence. There is no doubt that the geologic characteristics of the Grand Canyon contribute to its cultural identity. Visions can also be the product of individual human engineering. As already mentioned, visionaries such as Mulholland, Wovoka and Disney all had specific plans for the West. For Mulholland, effective management of water supplies would lead to great metropolises such as Los Angeles. Wovoka's literal vision of an imminent return to pre-White civilisation served as a message of survivance for Plains Indians. Disney deputised his imagineers (Disney's own version of visionaries) to manufacture utopic playgrounds, such as EPCOT and Disneyland, as models for future society. The substance of visions both reflects and shapes popular sentiment. Ideas are often products of the time of their creation. Both Frederick Jackson Turner's thesis and Buffalo Bill's West-themed show precipitated a surge in pioneer nostalgia in the 1890s, as well as a search for nationhood through frontier gazing. Both views of the West reflected the dominance of White America in the period, and the corresponding marginalisation of ethnic minorities. Most visions draw on common cultural signifiers (or stereotypes) of 'westernness': 'items' such as the wagon, the cowboy, sage brush, gold and cabins. In the process, the 'West' becomes a fictive yet generic realm drawing on all manner of constructed legends, brands, products and folklore identities. Part of the joy of looking at such visions lies in the deconstruction of the cultural markers at play.

This work explores competing visions of the American West through a range of topics associated with the history and culture of the region. Part One tackles elements of what might be called the 'Old' or 'Turnerian West'. Here, in Chapters 1 and 2 the frontier thesis (1893) and the expedition of Lewis and Clark (1804–6) are revisited with the aim of assessing their worth in a post-revisionist climate. Chapter 3 considers 'frontier violence', a topic that fits well with Buffalo Bill and Hollywood's descriptions of a classically 'Wild West'. The selling of the iconic cowboy is discussed in Chapter 4 on politics, in which the cowpuncher personas of Presidents Roosevelt, Reagan and Bush Junior are unpacked. Part Two is firmly located within the spectrum of 'New West' thought, at least as its starting point. The issue of gender in the West is explored in Chapters 5 and 6 through case studies of four women: a trailblazer; a homesteader; an American Indian princess; and a lady wildcat. In terms of ethnic conflict in

Introduction

the West, there is no more controversial topic than Indian genocide, debated in Chapter 7. The environment, both natural and artificial, is examined in Chapter 8 through case studies of three intersecting locations: the Grand Canyon; Hoover Dam; and Las Vegas using the common current of water to link them. Part Three tackles the power of images in the West through film, digital culture and tourism. It considers the continual re-creation of the West (and its heroic past) via the conduit of recreation. The 'making' of the past for popular consumption is crucial here. The Hollywood Western, a format that once served as chief promoter of the 'Old West', is discussed in Chapter 9 with reference to two recent movies that together marked a minor renaissance for the genre, namely *Brokeback Mountain* (2005) and *The Assassination of Jesse James by the Coward Robert Ford* (2007). Many of us remember playing 'cowboys and Indians' at school. From the 1970s onwards, arcade machines replicated this type of behaviour on digital screens, giving players the chance to shoot each other (or a computer opponent) in arcades. Chapter 10 explores digital culture and its technological take on the American West and Chapters 11 and 12 tackle tourism. The first deals with the unusual but interesting interplay between nuclear issues, popular culture and recreation. Ever since the first atomic bomb was developed in the West under the auspices of the Manhattan Project, Americans have been drawn to atomic sites as conduits to apprehension of doomsday. Even a somewhat bizarre tourist industry has grown up around the atom. The concluding chapter considers Disney and the rise of a theme park West, illuminating the extent to which simulation and fakery shapes popular understanding of history.

There are, inevitably, gaps in coverage here. The most notable omission concerns Hispanic and Black contributions to visions of the West. This reflects a lack of comprehensive work on the topic, the dominance of White visions in American popular culture, and the focus of this project on testing visions of the old West. Readers are none the less encouraged to explore the ideas of labour leader César Chávez, Japanese narratives of Second World War internment and Black radicalism in Los Angeles in the post-1945 period as a few valuable starting points. The work is also biased towards image deconstruction, especially in terms of the frontier. Thus, practical issues of state economics and politics and legal recourse receive relatively short shrift. The aim of this work has always been to reach a new stage of scholarship, likely to be dubbed post-revisionism, by comparing competing visions of the American West and pondering if amalgams are possible. However, the authors are keen to point out that they do not refute the agenda of New Western history in this process.

The authors thank the Centre for American Studies and the School of History (especially the then head of department Professor Mark Connelly) at the University of Kent. The Templeman Library, particularly its interlibrary loan section, aided in locating project materials. Students enrolled on a variety of modules relating to the American West at both the University of Essex (2002–5) and the University of Kent (2004 onwards) provided stirring debate and quite remarkable insight into the western diaspora. David Johnson and Susan Wladaver-Morgan at the *Pacific Historical Review* and the University of California Press are gratefully acknowledged for allowing a version of a published article on videogames to be included in this study. The Historical Society of Southern California helped with financing one of several research trips to California, while the Montana Historical Society aided under the auspices of its Bradley scholar scheme. Thanks are due to the Autry National Center and the Southwest Museum of the American Indian, Los Angeles, as well as the Huntington Library, San Marino. In particular, Marva Felchlin, Liza Posas, Manola Madrid and Stephen Aron at the Autry and Peter Blodgett at the Huntington ventured invaluable advice and assistance. Nicola Ramsey at Edinburgh University Press enthusiastically supported the project, even when deadlines slipped. This work is dedicated to our parents.

Part One
Old West

Chapter 1

Lewis and Clark: Mapping the West

Across the United States, people commemorated the 200th anniversary of the Lewis and Clark Expedition (1804–6). History buffs watched re-enactors pose as nineteenth-century wilderness heroes in rustic venues from St Louis to Portland, hikers trod in the footsteps of the Corps of Discovery in Missouri and Montana, and armchair admirers from across the country purchased all manner of Lewis and Clark memorabilia in cyberspace. Meriwether Lewis and William Clark, co-captains of the Corps, inspired plaudits as 'our extreme founding fathers', outdoors junkies minus the Gore-Tex paraphernalia. They appeared as frontier diplomats without the cultural baggage of expansionism. The Corps of Discovery maintained an allure in a globalised society where industrial technology collapsed both distance and time: 8,000 miles eaten up comfortably on a long haul flight or courtesy of broadband connectivity. The Lewis and Clark mystique remained alive and well in the twenty-first century.[1]

The event most frequently analogised to the Lewis and Clark expedition in terms of significance for the American nation is the 1969 Moon landing. Both epitomised the restlessness of the time and the flight into the unknown of a confident nation. As Astronaut James Lovell explained:

> I think that the nature of America, how it was born, how it grew up, sort of exemplified the idea of exploration. We were a young country, we grew, and I think this idea of being explorers is ingrained in our psyche here in this country. I think we'll always be explorers.

Seen in this frame, the Corps of Discovery illuminated the American spirit of both geographical and cultural mobility. On Columbus Day 2001, President George W. Bush paid homage to stalwart American values embedded in both events – virtues of fortitude, adventurous spirit and risk-taking 'echoed down through history by some of America's greatest pioneers, from Meriwether Lewis and William Clark's daring explorations of our western frontier to the Apollo astronauts planting the American flag on the moon'. The experience of Lewis and Clark mirrored that of Armstrong, Aldrin and Collins in other critical ways. The Corps of Discovery travelled across a strange land, a terrain as alien to Americans in 1804 as the Moon was to their countrymen in 1969. Their 7,689-mile journey across the continental United States to the Pacific and back yielded all manner of peculiar artefacts and inaugurated the mapping of a blank region. The enterprise presented American science, diplomacy and imperial power as ascendant. Put simply, Lewis and Clark represented America's first astronauts, enshrined in popular memory as the makers of the West.[2]

From Flight Plan to Touch Down: The Mechanics of Exploration

In 1800 the trans-Mississippi West may as well have been Mars to most Americans. Scarcely anything was known about the region. Spanish traders had travelled from St Louis up the Missouri as far as the Mandan tribes living in present day Dakota, while American seafarer Robert Gray reached the mouth of the Columbia River in 1792. The territory in between remained a mysterious space, party to fantastical ideas (to Euro-American eyes at least). Learned scholars conjured the West as a landscape roamed by mammoths, giant beaver and other animals from prehistory: a land that time forgot. Narratives spoke of fierce volcanoes, ridges five miles high, 180-mile long salt deposits and a huge mountain from which all the rivers in the continent flowed. Rumours also abounded of blue-eyed Indians who spoke in a Welsh dialect, the vestiges of a visit from twelfth-century Welsh prince Madoc.[3]

The orchestrator of the 'first space race', the man at ground control co-ordinating the exploration of this wild frontier, was Thomas Jefferson. Jefferson had always entertained a keen interest in the lands beyond the Mississippi, even though he failed to stray more than fifty miles west of his Monticello home. For Jefferson, the region held the promise of a virtuous agrarian republic. It aroused his curiosity as a naturalist and a nationalist. Jefferson's library attested to this fascination – his collection contained more books on the West than any other in the world.

Lewis and Clark: Mapping the West

Throughout the late 1700s, revolutionary politics and economic matters prevented Jefferson from concentrating on exploring the West as a policy goal. He was involved in three separate attempts to mount expeditions, one led by George Rogers Clark (brother of William), but all failed to get off the ground. However, circumstances changed radically at the turn of the century. Jefferson assumed the presidency in 1801, affording him more power to advance expeditionary schemes. American settlers made their own inroads west, and by 1803 more than 500,000 people had made the trip over the Appalachians into the Ohio valley, aided by famous woodsmen such as Daniel Boone, trailblazer of the Wilderness Road through the Cumberland Gap. Land hunger and population dynamics thereby serviced Jefferson's project for a growing American 'empire of liberty'. The imperial ambitions of European powers also figured in Jefferson's consciousness. He feared Spanish encroachment from California and Texas, a revitalised Napoleonic France expanding along the Mississippi from New Orleans, British fur traders moving south from Canada and Russian pelt ships in the Pacific north-west – foreign nations jostling for control of the resources of the West. The exploits of Scottish fur trader and explorer Alexander Mackenzie crystallised Jefferson's thinking. In 1793, Mackenzie crossed the Rockies to reach the Columbia River, where he painted his name on a rock. That gesture, along with his published journal, *Voyages from Montreal* (1801), suggested an incipient British claim to ownership based on a lucrative fur trade and overland access. According to historian David Nicandri, Mackenzie's journals served as 'the functional equivalent of Sputnik in 1957', spurring Jefferson to facilitate American command of the West and the fruits it had to offer.[4]

In late 1802, Jefferson appointed Meriwether Lewis, his private secretary and ex-captain of the 1st US Infantry, to lead an expeditionary force. Lewis consulted the library at Monticello to synthesise the current state of knowledge on the West, its geography, flora and fauna. Subsequent training took him to Philadelphia for advice on science, medical training, use of instruments and biology. Jefferson meanwhile worked on the political dimension. The president sounded out diplomats from France, Britain and Spain, obtaining passports for travel from all but the last – Spanish ambassador, the Marques de Casa Yrujo, remained cynical of Jefferson's declared motive of 'literary pursuit'. Congress received a secret communiqué in January 1803, requesting authorisation and a $2,500 stipend to explore the headwaters of the Missouri for the purposes of commerce. Jefferson's aims appeared multifarious. Science, economics and realpolitik blended seamlessly into his flight plan. Commercial gain dominated considerations, in particular the search for a navigable waterway and trading route to the Pacific, the elusive 'Northwest Passage' that had captured the imagination of illustrious travellers for centuries. That said, Jefferson saw the West not only as a thoroughfare but also as intrinsically valuable. By exploring the region, he hoped to capture the fur trade and undermine European claims to the far West. Fur represented an instrument of empire and the West a repository of resources from which to build ambitions for American sovereignty. Land held a similar function with the acquisition of territory from American Indians on the banks of the Mississippi offering a potential bulwark against the resurgence of a French empire. To add to all this, the chance to find out about the West offered Jefferson his own Enlightenment Elysium – a place to acquire scientific knowledge and expand his own mental frontiers as a naturalist.[5]

The parameters of Jefferson's scheme changed drastically in July 1803. While sending diplomats to Paris in the hope of securing New Orleans from the French, the President found himself with the opportunity to purchase a far greater territory stretching from the Mississippi to the Rockies. Following Napoleon's defeat by the British, the French seemed eager to offload Louisiana Territory. At a price of $15 million, Jefferson procured 800,000 square miles of land under the deal, doubling the size of his country in one stroke. Historian Bernard DeVoto described the Louisiana Purchase as 'one of the most important events in world history', a decision that abetted American expansionism both practically and psychologically. The acquisition held significant implications for Jefferson's expedition. No longer travelling across a foreign land, Lewis and his cohorts would now be on home turf, albeit *terra incognita*. Matters of inventory and sovereignty loomed large. Revised instructions advised Lewis to gather evidence of the region's material value (and thereby justify its purchase) and inform indigenous residents of their new 'Great Father'. An expanded remit warranted more manpower, hence Lieutenant William Clark, with whom Lewis worked at Fort Greenville, joined the party as co-commander.[6]

Lewis and Clark met at Clarksville, Indiana in October 1803 to choose personnel from a roster of volunteers more than 100-strong. After winter training at Wood River, Illinois, the expedition set off up the Missouri on 14 May 1804. The party consisted of twenty-seven military personnel, two civilians (Clark's slave York and guide George Drouillard) along with Seaman, Lewis' dog. Two tonnes of supplies testified to the intricate planning process surrounding the journey and to the Enlightenment predilections of overseer Thomas Jefferson. Provisions included a keelboat and two pirouges (canoes), new Kentucky rifles from Harper's Ferry armoury, medical supplies (such as lancets, powders, pills and a penis pump to relieve gonorrhoea), ammunition, books (including tomes by Linnaeus and Mackenzie) and scientific instruments. Gifts for Indians were also included – scissors, knives, mirrors, tobacco, fishhooks and beads – together with an air rifle to ensure that the explorers captured tribal attentions.

Two critical pieces of paper accompanied the Corps. The first, a letter of credit, offered a promise of repayment by the United States government for services rendered. The dog-eared original remains with the Missouri Historical Society. The second contained Jefferson's official instructions for the journey. The primary object of the expedition lay in exploring the Missouri River in order to discern 'the most direct and practicable water communication across this continent, for the purposes of commerce' – in other words, find the 'Northwest Passage' and control the fur trade. Subsidiary aims spoke of gathering information on the geography, zoology, botany, geology and ethnography of the interior. As historian John Logan Allen noted, the instructions smacked of 'a lifetime's worth of imaginary geography', coloured by Jefferson's impressions of the West as a garden of verdure and American virtue. Meanwhile, the president's directives with regard to indigenous peoples appeared somewhat ambiguous. The Corps received orders to forward diplomatic relations with Indians, to adopt a 'friendly and conciliatory manner' and assure them of the 'innocence' of the trip. At the same time, Jefferson posited that the acquisition of knowledge about the western tribes including their customs, habits and territories would 'better enable those who endeavor to civilize & instruct them'. Such pronouncements illuminated Jefferson as a pragmatist – the expedition needed to tread carefully as it navigated alien territory – but also revealed his rationales as a politician, a scientist and an empire-builder.[7]

The party made good progress up the lower Missouri, racking up fifteen miles a day. By 25 May 1804 they reached La Charette, a small settlement sixty miles upstream. Sergeant Floyd described the stop as 'the last settlement of whites on this river', beyond which they entered Indian territory. Encounters with indigenous groups proved varied and eventful, betraying both the colonial vantage of the Corps and their dependence on native goodwill. On 3 August 1804, the Corps participated in their first official council with western Indians in which Oto and Missouri Indians received flags, friendship medals and presents from the soldiers. The Corps projected the magic of civilisation with a uniformed parade, displays of the air rifle and the compass in action, all washed down by copious quantities of whiskey. Lewis addressed the crowd as 'children' before talking of the new 'great father' in Washington, DC. A more fractious meeting occurred on the Plains in September, when the Corps spent four days feasting and brawling with the Teton Sioux. Already conditioned to perceive the Teton as warlike, and lacking sufficient interpretive skills, the encounter was marked by miscommunication. Clark's conclusion that: 'These are the vilest miscreants of the savage race, and must ever remain the pirates of the Missouri, until such measures are pursued, by our government, as will make them feel a dependence on its will for their supply of merchandise' (mis)guided official policy towards the Sioux for years to come. None the less, the winter of 1804–5 saw the Corps practising a policy of peaceful co-existence towards western Indians. From October 1804 to April 1805 they lived with the Mandan and Minnetaree Indians, buffalo hunting, writing up their field notes, listening to bear stories, feasting, dancing and contracting, in Clark's colourful spelling, 'Venerials Complaints'.[8]

The Corps packed out from Fort Mandan in April 1805, dispatching the keelboat down river with a compendium of artefacts and reports for presidential scrutiny. The amassed materials of more than 1,600 miles travel included sixty species of plants, sixty-seven mineral specimens, a sharp-tailed grouse and a live prairie dog which the Corps had spent an entire day capturing. For the Corps, the route instead lay westward, with three new recruits: French trapper Touissant Charbonneau; his wife Sacagawea, of the Shoshone; and their small baby. The gravitas of what lay ahead struck Lewis, who mused in his journal: 'We were now about to penetrate a country at least two thousand miles in width, on which the foot of civilized man had never trodden ... I could but esteem this moment of my departure as among the most happy of my life.'[9]

Navigating the Great Plains during the summer, the Corps recorded encounters with Grizzly bears, herds of bison, strange cliffs and stunning prairie flora. Lewis' journal entry for 13 June 1805 offered a blend of science and romanticism, the material and the imagined fused together in a powerful invocation to a mythic West. His scouting party set off at dawn after breakfasting on venison and fish. Lewis described a beautiful plain on which grazed 'infinitely more buffaloe than I had ever before witnessed at a view'. In the distance stood mountains of yellow clay akin to 'ramparts of immense fortifications'. A fifteen-mile stroll later, the scouts reached the Great Falls of the Missouri. Army analysis conjoined with the rapture of the naturalist as Lewis described how his 'ears were saluted with the agreeable sound of a fall of water'. This 'sublimely grand specticle' required classification according to the rubrics of rationalism *and* artistic appraisal. For Lewis, the responsibility of documenting such natural splendour raised serious interpretive questions:

> I wished for the pencil of Salvator Rosa or the pen of Thompson, that I might be enabled to give to the enlightened world some just idea of this truly magniffcent and sublimely grand object, which from the commencement of time has been concealed from the view of civilized man.

Lewis, always the more quixotic of the two captains, sat mesmerised before the 200-foot falls for four hours, before rejoining the camp for a supper of fresh buffalo and fine trout.[10]

Once the Missouri became un-navigable, the Corps proceeded on foot. After the harsh winds and sandstorms of the Plains, the explorers faced a different challenge in the form of the western mountains. Sacagawea proved to be a key negotiator in procuring horses for the party. As Clark noted, 'the wife of Charbonneau, our interpreter, we find reconciles all the Indians, as to... our friendly intentions. A woman with a party of men is a token of peace.' On 12 August 1805, Lewis trudged up Lemhi Pass, the Continental Divide, to view not a downhill stretch to the Pacific but more forbidding ranges. This, according to historian Dayton Duncan, represented his 'Neil Armstrong moment'. Six days later, on his thirty-first birthday, Lewis reflected on life so far, vowing – with resonances of Armstrong's famous lunar address – 'in future, to live for *mankind*, as I have heretofore lived *for myself*'. Through September, however, survival seemed a more pressing issue as the Corps struggled with rugged topography, a forbidding climate and dwindling food supplies in the Bitterroot Mountains. A chance meeting with the hospitable Nez Perce, armed with dried buffalo, camas and fish, proved critical in saving the explorers from starvation, although the rich diet caused less agreeable short-term effects. Leaving with directions and canoes crafted from burned logs, the Corps of Discovery rafted down the Clearwater, Snake and Columbia rivers to reach the Pacific on 3 December 1805. William Clark commemorated the moment by carving on a pine tree: 'William Clark, December 3rd, 1805, By Land, From the U. States', the nineteenth-century equivalent of planting the Stars and Stripes on the moon.[11]

The Corps of Discovery wintered at Fort Clatsop, named on behalf of the local Indians, before leaving the Pacific coast on 23 March 1806. After retracing the route back to the Nez Perce camp, they crossed 'the most terrible mountains', Patrick Gass's apposite description of the Bitterroots. There the expedition divided to cover more of the Louisiana Territory. Clark took a team down the Yellowstone River while Lewis returned to the Great Falls of the Missouri and the Marias River, where his party had an altercation with the Blackfeet. The two commanders rendezvoused at the mouth of the Yellowstone in August, before paddling down the Missouri for home. After twenty-eight months away – marked by arduous terrain, dysentery, mosquitoes, temperatures as low as −48 °F, not to mention capsized boats, sabre-rattling with the Teton Sioux and Pierre Cruzatte shooting Lewis in the buttocks after mistaking him for a deer – the Corps of Discovery touched down in St Louis on 23 September 1806. Only Sergeant Floyd failed to make it back, due to a fatal bout of appendicitis. Even Seaman managed the whole trip without injury.[12]

Small Steps and Giant Leaps: Lewis and Clark and the Making of the West

> In obedience to your orders we have penetrated the Continent of North America to the Pacific Ocean, and sufficiently explored the interior of the country to affirm with confidence that we have discovered the most practicable rout which dose exist across the continent by means of the navigable branches of the Missouri and Columbia Rivers.[13]
>
> Meriwether Lewis to Thomas Jefferson, 23 September 1806

Lewis exaggerated here. Perhaps he was trying to let Jefferson down gently, or had in mind that the expedition came in over budget at $38,722.35. Yes, the explorers had followed their mission plan. Yes, they had travelled up the Missouri, trudged 340 miles overland and paddled down the tributaries of the Columbia to the Pacific. However, their route hardly offered a 'practicable' one for the purposes of commerce. The 'Northwest Passage' remained undiscovered. There were, nevertheless, other achievements to report. The Corps of Discovery had gone where no *Americans* had previously done so: they had proved the possibility of continental traverse. Both in a practical and a symbolic sense, this placed Lewis and Clark in an esteemed position. As DeVoto noted, the Corps offered 'the first report on the West, on the United States over the hill and beyond the sunset, on the province of the American future. There has never been another so excellent and so influential.' Lewis and Clark thereby informed both the process and the mythology of westward expansion.[14]

The Corps amassed copious data on western ecology. They documented an impressive 178 new species of plants and 122 animals. Lewis and Clark described the floral and faunal curiosities of the West with romantic prose, documented them according to Linnaean classification, despatched them with rifle shot and carefully packed them in specimen boxes for shipping back East. Their findings advanced the frontiers of science and projected the West as a cornucopia of natural bounty. Empirical detail embellished imagination. Such visions of the West as a fertile paradise informed government policy for the next century and beyond.

Depictions of wide, open prairies teeming with game projected the West as a vast storehouse of resources waiting to be exploited. Prairies became agricultural lands, forests timber lots and mountains repositories of mineral wealth in the popular imagination – a catalogue of economic potential. Translation from the organic to the commercial appeared particularly evident with regard to fur-clad species. In his report to Jefferson, Lewis urged: 'we view this passage . . . affording immence advantages to the fur trade'. Exceptionalised as a paradise for pelts in the famous phrase: 'the Missouri and all its branches from the Cheyenne upwards abound in more beaver and Common Otter, than any other streams on earth', the Rockies witnessed a steady stream of trappers eager to make their fortune in the wake of Lewis and Clark.[15]

The Corps of Discovery also made first contact with more than fifty Indian nations, tendering tentative diplomatic and commercial links with Native Americans. They hunted, caroused, traded and even lived with native groups. In fact, at critical moments the survival of the Corps remained contingent on indigenous assistance. That said, the Lewis and Clark expedition cannot be read in isolation from the broader history of Indian assimilation. Although on an everyday level, the Corps communicated effectively with the majority of tribes encountered (only one violent encounter occurred during the entire expedition), they still represented agents of an imperial nation. Peace medals signalled a change of sovereignty, rhetoric spoke of 'savages' and 'children', while altercations with the Sioux and the Blackfeet shaped Indian policy later in the century.

As Lewis and Clark paddled, rode and trudged their way across the continent they forwarded a process of territorial mapping. Journal entries recorded geographic positions, tables, diagrams and maps with exactitude (Lewis' estimate of mileage matched GPS projections to within forty miles). According to historian Richard Francaviglia, maps serve as tools for storytelling and empire-building alike. William Clark's sketches of the American West ably performed both functions. In 1800, only the periphery had been charted, namely the mouth of the Columbia and the route up the Missouri to the Mandans. Over his twenty-eight-month journey, Clark charted the space in between, crafting a map so precise it remained in use for the next fifty years. Places along the route commemorated the expedition and its landmark moments. Floyd's Bluff marked the final resting place of Sergeant Floyd, Independence Creek indicated where the party struck their first Fourth of July camp and Pompey's Tower related Clark's fondness for the son of Sacagawea. This process denoted more than practical orienteering or sentimental reflection. Instead, the conferring of names on the landscape assumed both knowledge of and control over the terrain: the semantics of place erasing prior land title and assuming the right of dedication. Meanwhile, the footprints of Lewis and Clark on the Pacific shore, not to mention Clark's tree carving, provoked nascent interest in American territorial claims beyond the confines of the Louisiana Purchase. In the minds of American expansionists, the trails routed by Lewis and Clark left an 'American highway' for the taking.[16]

On crafting his memorandum, Lewis catered to the imaginings of his audience, the reader (in this case Jefferson) filled in the blanks. The expedition had been informed by visions of an imagined West, and on their return, the co-commanders helped to create a potent mythology of verdant open space, commercial potential, wild adventure and American dominion. The importance of the Corps of Discovery lay not in its failure to achieve the principal objective – finding the 'Northwest Passage' – but in other successes. The travels of Lewis and Clark signified promise, mystique and American power. Their significance rested on a symbolic level, much like the 1969 Moon landing. This reading helps to explain why Lewis and Clark remained icons of westward expansion: for Hine and Faragher 'the most illustrious exploring party in American history', for Bernard DeVoto, 'unequalled in American history and hardly surpassed in the history of exploration anywhere', even though the Spanish, French and British, not to mention Native Americans, got there first. It elucidates how the Corps of Discovery became the champions of Manifest Destiny even though forty years elapsed before farmers and gold-seekers travelled West in numbers, using trails far further south than the expedition in

1804–6. Lewis and Clark stand tall as symbols of American expansionism, the events surrounding their expedition reconfigured in the shape of a grand story of progress and posterity. In essence, their reputations remain inextricably linked to the bigger picture, namely the wholesale conquest of the trans-Mississippi. The West could have been won *without* them, but temporal convenience, the benefit of hindsight and the power of imagination, saw Lewis and Clark installed as the advance guard in the transformation of the West. As Roosevelt delineated in *The Winning of the West* (1889–96): 'Close on their tracks followed the hunters, trappers, and fur traders who themselves made ready the way for the settlers whose descendants were to possess the land.' Seen in this context, the Lewis and Clark expedition inaugurated a grand American fable. As Henry Nash Smith surmised: 'The importance of the Lewis and Clark expedition lay on the level of imagination: it was drama, it was the enactment of a myth that embodied the future.' In 1803, most citizens still looked eastward and two-thirds of them lived within fifty miles of the Atlantic Ocean. Although it may have been a slow-burn, Lewis and Clark helped turn the nation's eyes westward, to view the continental interior not as *terra incognita* but as an object of empire, economy and mythology, a place worthy of American title. In the words of DeVoto, the expedition 'satisfied desire and it created desire: the desire of a westering nation'.[17]

Remembering Lewis and Clark

In a 2002 issue of *Time* magazine dedicated to Lewis and Clark, journalist Walter Kirn motioned: 'There are so many lessons and morals to be drawn from the expedition of Lewis and Clark that each generation tends to pick a new one according to its temperament and needs.' Public interest in the Corps has waxed and waned over time, the exploring party and their exploits cast in various different lights. However, our proclivity for periodicity, the appeal of a simple narrative, stress on the activities of 'great men' in historical writing, together with the Teflon-coated mythology of the West ensured that the Lewis and Clark expedition consistently resurfaced in popular memory. Over the span of 200 years, the Corps of Discovery has been reinvented to cater for the social mores of Americans, the story of the trans-continental expedition appropriated to create a usable past that imparted lessons and values to the present.[18]

Back in 1804, Lewis and Clark had left St Louis to little flourish. Locals at St Charles hosted a ball to honour the explorers, but emphasis remained workmanlike. As the Corps traversed the continent, public awareness proved minimal. Jefferson himself knew nothing of the exploits of his employees beyond the Fort Mandan shipment. The first sighting of Lewis and Clark paddling down the Missouri in September 1806 prompted shouts of delight from settlers. Lewis wrote in his journal of arriving in St Louis: 'we Suffered the party to fire off their pieces as a Salute to the Town, we were met by all the village and received a harty welcom from it's inhabitants.' The Corps duly received three cheers and a party at Christy's Inn. Snacking on French pastries, revellers toasted the President, the Corps, the United States and 'Captains Lewis and Clark – Their perilous service endear them to every American's heart'.[19]

In an age before rapid travel and technological communications (only four roads crossed the Appalachians in 1800) the return of Lewis and Clark was first reported through local media. St Louis did not have a newspaper in 1806, but the story slowly found its way into the national press. Breaking news spoke of vigorous adventurers and a West full of Indians and faunal wonders. The Frankfort Kentucky *Palladium* commended Lewis and Clark on their safe passage as well as their 'courage, perseverance and prudent deportment' while pointing to the 'incalculable commercial advantage' of the western territory. The Boston *Columbian Centinel* reported 'curiosities' and 'numerous Indians'. At this stage, Lewis and Clark may not have been national heroes, but they were hailed as patriots by those they encountered. A trail of feasts and banquets ensued as the captains made their way east. Guests raised their glasses to the explorers and their intrepid journey into the wilderness. At Locust Hill, Virginia in November 1806, local dignitaries wined and dined Lewis, offering toasts to the safe return of their friend to 'civilized life' and praising 'the difficult and dangerous enterprise . . . pregnant with consequences' that he had undertaken. In Washington, DC, the captains delivered reports to the President, congressmen and various officials. One Senator commented that the furore surrounding the expedition was as if they had been to the Moon and back. In his sixth State of the Union address, Jefferson paid homage to the explorers thus:

> They have traced the Missouri nearly to its source, descended the Columbia to the Pacific Ocean, ascertained with accuracy the geography of that interesting communication across our continent, learnt the character of the country, of its commerce and inhabitants; and it is but justice to say that Messrs. Lewis and Clark and their brave companions have by this arduous service deserved well of their country.

In further recognition of their heroism, the two captains received double wages and 1,600 acres of land (other members of the party received double wages and 320 acres). Career promotions for both men carried westward expansion to its next phase with Lewis as governor of Louisiana Territory and Clark as Indian Agent for the West and Brigadier General of the Louisiana Territory militia.[20]

Jefferson's instructions to the Corps had stressed the written record as an essential part of the trip. Before he left for the Pacific, Lewis secured a deal with a Philadelphia publisher for a three-volume opus on the wonders of the West (a travel narrative, an account of western geography and the Indian tribes and a scientific report) to be produced in his own inimitable style. In 1807, Sergeant Patrick Gass published his account of the journey to some popular acclaim. The official record, however, remained unwritten as Lewis struggled to adapt to life back in civilisation. Suffering with work pressures, financial problems, alcoholism and depression, Lewis committed suicide in October 1809. Clark assumed responsibility for editing the notes, but his post in the Louisiana Territory left little time to write. Eventually, in 1814 a one-volume tome on the expedition appeared. Compiled by Nicholas Biddle, *The History of the Expedition under the Command of Captains Lewis and Clark* emphasised the Corps as patriotic heroes and romantic naturalists, but the 'moment of celebrity' in Patricia Nelson Limerick's parlance, had passed. Interest in the expedition, tangible in 1806, had dissipated eight years later. Only 1,417 books were sold, while distribution problems meant that Clark himself had not received a copy two years on. Foreign entanglements with the 'Old World' rather than the New represented the news of the day: war with Britain and not the promise of the West occupied public debate. A decade on from the feasts and songs of 1806, Lewis and Clark had become extraneous.[21]

This drift into obscurity continued through the mid-1800s. As John C. Frémont and John Wesley Powell blazed new trails for the United States and garnered fame as fearless explorers, the exploits of the Corps of Discovery faded into the background of popular memory. Notes and sketches compiled by Lewis and Clark gathered dust in the American Philosophical Society archive in Philadelphia. When Henry Adams wrote his *History of the Administration of Thomas Jefferson* (1890), he concluded that the expedition had 'added little to the stock of science and wealth'.[22]

However, Lewis and Clark were not ignored. Two events ensured a dramatic reversal of fortune for the Corps: first, the closure of the frontier by the Census Bureau in 1890; and secondly, Frederick Jackson Turner's famous articulation of his frontier thesis before the American Historical Association in 1893. Collectively, these developments suggested that the West had been won, and popular memory could now reflect upon the process of expansion as a complete and glorious one. The illusion of an 'ending' fostered a search for a beginning that placed Lewis and Clark at the front of a stream of Americans traipsing west through the 1800s. As Turner motioned 'stand at the Cumberland Gap, and watch the procession of civilization marching single file'. Filtered through a Turnerian teleology, Lewis and Clark garnered reinvention as standard bearers for the future: heroic Americans striking out across 'free land', vigorous, self-reliant, creative and patriotic.[23]

Historians served an important role in repackaging Lewis and Clark as American icons. In 1893, Elliot Coues edited a three-volume collection of the Lewis and Clark journals, described as 'our national epic of exploration'. In 1904–5, a further edition of the journals from Reuben Thwaites hailed the explorers as expansionist heroes, their story billed as the 'Original Record of the Winning of the West'. In Theodore Roosevelt's *The Winning of the West* (1889–96), Lewis and Clark earned plaudits as part of the 'honor role of American worthies' and 'wilderness veterans' – not only critical historical actors but outdoorsmen who spoke to a contemporary urban elite caught up in a craze for virile masculine sports. Frederick Jackson Turner had ignited a process of reflection and revisionism that comprehensively rewrote the historical canon. Where Henry Adams had deemed Lewis and Clark as irrelevant, historical accounts now placed the Corps as essential to the mythology of westward conquest. For J. W. Buel, author of *Louisiana and the Fair* (1904) the overlooking of Lewis and Clark by his predecessors smacked of 'partiality', their 'heroic deeds and beneficial accomplishments' events that 'every American should be ... familiar with'.[24]

Artists, too, participated in the revitalisation of Lewis and Clark in American popular remembrance. Renowned chronicler of the West, Charles Russell painted twenty or more canvases relating to the Corps of Discovery. Brought up in St Louis, Russell counted himself as somewhat of a Lewis and Clark buff. In October 1913, he took a 400-mile boat trip with Frank Linderman and others, retracing the route of the Corps along the Missouri from Fort Benton, accompanied by a copy of the journals, snow, rain and a rather less authentic outboard motor. Most of Russell's works situated Lewis and Clark in a romantic West dominated by wild nature and imposing Indians. His first published print, 'Lewis and Clark meeting the Mandans' (1896), appeared in the sporting journal *Field and Stream*. Painted the same year, 'Indians Discovering Lewis and Clark' projected an indigenous vantage of scouts atop a bluff, spying on the vulnerable Corps on the river below. In 1912, the Montana State legislature approached Russell to produce a piece for display in the Capitol building. Russell's suggestions – Indians attacking a wagon or Lewis and Clark with the Shoshones – were rejected in favour of a specifically Montanan scene: the Corps meeting the Flathead in the Bitterroot Valley. The massive twelve by twenty-four-foot canvas, 'Lewis and Clark meet the Indians at Ross' Hole' resonated with dramatic energy, of big sky, wide prairie and Indians on horseback, bestowing a sturdy frontier identity on the Treasure State.

Commemoration of the Lewis and Clark expedition crystallised around centennial celebrations. Public events established a fervent dialogue between past and present, lauding the Corps of Discovery as the inaugurators of a strident and glorious American expansion that marked the contemporary milieu. For Buel, the Corps planted 'sign posts of civilization' in a wild and fantastical land that now featured 'the merry hum of industry, prosperity and contentment'. In Portland, the Lewis and Clark Centennial and American Pacific Exposition opened on 1 June 1905 to a cavalcade of pomp and fireworks watched by 40,000 people. A parade wound its way from downtown to process under the gates of the fairground, over which the motto read: 'westward the course of empire takes its way.' Designed to be 'compact' – in the words of the official guide: 'to see the trail does not require a tiresome walk' – the 402-acre site contained attractions including the Agricultural Palace, Oriental Palace, Centennial park area, sideshow amusements and refreshment stalls. Statues depicted Lewis and Clark, Sacagawea and her baby, along with stock western motifs of Indians and pistol-packing cowboys. For Expo organisers, the idea seemed to be to look forward by looking backward, to see 'the success of the Lewis and Clark Expedition' and demonstrate the 'marvellous progress of western America . . . and the great possibilities for trade development in the Orient'.[25]

Yet, as in 1806, people soon forgot about Lewis and Clark once the festival gunpowder had been extinguished. The 1905 commemorative $10 coin with the two captains on one side and a bison on the other was filed away for posterity in a drawer and other stalwart citizens invoked to project American values. In the 1920s, when the state historian of

South Dakota proposed a monument memorialising the foremost icons of the West – Fremont, Red Cloud and Lewis and Clark – his nominations were rejected. The Mount Rushmore Monument instead featured presidential profiles deemed to be more significant to the nation at large.

The Cold War returned Lewis and Clark to the status of all-American heroes. Once again, the Corps of Discovery earned report as exemplars of core patriotic values: freedom fighters with a mission of civilisation and commerce, navigating a frontier between the worlds of capitalism and communism. In 1955, local community groups and historical societies in Washington worked together to construct a replica of the Fort Clatsop log cabin (based on a floor plan drawn by Clark in his elk-hide field notebook) to honour the Corps on their sesquicentennial. In 1963, Lewis and Clark provided the name of an intercontinental ballistic missile submarine, swapping the western theatre for a tour of the world's oceans. The era of Cold War conservatism also saw Lewis and Clark make their first appearance as subjects for the silver screen. Loosely based on the novel *Sacajawea of the Shoshones* by Della Emmons, *The Far Horizons* (1955) played havoc with the historical record. Directed by Rudolph Mate, the movie starred Charlton Heston as William Clark and Donna Reed as a childless Sacagawea, the two leads locked in a love triangle with Charbonneau, played by Alan Reed. In an age of civil rights unrest, York had been airbrushed out entirely while Sacagawea applied simpering 1950s domesticity to the wilds. A kind of *African Queen* on the Missouri, the weather was sunny, the scenery stunning and the good guys wore Stetsons. The Indians always instigated conflict, thereby projecting an inverted view of western conquest in which the Corps acted in self-defence and with moral compunction. Significantly, the major villain of the piece was Frenchman Charbonneau, representative of a dominant 'Old World' empire (that is, the Soviet Union), foiled by an American display of superior might and honour. *The New York Times* and *Variety* commended the western foliage, filmed in vibrant Vistavision, but deemed the story a 'slow and unimaginative safari' and 'a tedious tour of the Louisiana Purchase'.[26]

By 1992, the *Lewis and Clark* submarine lay in dry dock for decommissioning, and the Cold War was over, but the Lewis and Clark legend continued. New editions of the journals from Gary Moulton, Stephen Ambrose's *Undaunted Courage* (1996) together with Ken Burns' four-hour documentary (described by *New York Post* critic Marvin Kitman as seeming to last as long as the expedition itself) suggested that the Corps retained a sense of relevancy at the dawn of the twenty-first century. Meanwhile, the appearance of Lewis and Clark – albeit as a vaudeville double act – in the reduced Shakespeare Company's 'Complete History of America (Abridged)' (1995) situated the captains as firmly ensconced in the popular historical canon. 'Lewisandclark', the two captains conjoined into a single entity, represented part of the collective education of generations of Americans. Popular culture reflected this familiarity with the expedition, its key characters and their story, in various (sometimes hackneyed) ways. In the 1990s, Superman spin-off *Lois and Clark* slyly referenced the two commanders, while the rescue ship *Lewis and Clark* in *Event Horizon* (1997) took the Corps into sci-fi territory. The two hundred-year anniversary of the Corps of Discovery brought 'Lewisandclark' mania to a fever pitch. Historian Stephen Aron described them as the hottest historical celebrities around, while journalist writer Betsy Taylor analogised the pair to 'ageing rock stars on a comeback tour'. In July 2002, President George W. Bush presided over the hanging of a chalk and charcoal portrait of Lewis at his old haunt in the East Room of the White House, while a plethora of bicentennial events took place in the thirteen states passed through by the expedition. From Ohio Falls to Fort Clatsop, people attended exhibitions, historical re-enactments, statue dedications, guided trails and camps.[27]

As with earlier incarnations, the mythology of the Lewis and Clark expedition in the twenty-first century spoke to a particular audience. As David Plotz noted, 'our fascination with Lewis and Clark is much more about us than them'. The story of the Corps of Discovery had to dialogue with issues such as globalisation and post-9/11 terrorism, as well as providing a functional past dictated by the demands of contemporary society. Visions of the Corps in the twenty-first century proved to be complex – traditional motifs of morality, adventuring, patriotism and identity sitting alongside more recent designs of multiculturalism, environmentalism, celebrity culture and reality television.[28]

To be feted in 2006 meant different things than it did in 1806, 1893 or 1955, as was evident in portrayals of Lewis and Clark. Just as modern role models bear hallmarks of political correctness, green ethics and corporate team-building culture, so did the popular memory of the Corps of Discovery. In this vision, Lewis and Clark appeared as culturally sensitive diplomats making intimate contact with native nations. *Lewis and Clark: Great Journeys West* (2002), produced for National Geographic, hoisted the expedition as a grand and cinematic American adventure ideally suited for the IMAX screen. The trailer depicted the Corps as a hand-picked crew led by two far-sighted captains venturing into the domain of 'great nations of people already living in the West'. Their task: 'to catalogue for science the nature of the new land, to discover a waterway across it, and to survive to tell of what they had learned'. *Time* magazine presented Lewis and Clark as exemplars of sound corporate relations: 'commanding, cooperative, complementary . . . perfectly cast as co-CEOs'. The Corps of Discovery was also represented as a vibrant symbol of multicultural America: Euro-Americans, Africans and Indians operating together in a democracy in which all voices were heard. This utopian snapshot presented a roseate, comforting past where the strife of slavery, civil rights and gender inequality did not exist (apart from the tricky issue of York's return to slavery). Meanwhile, obsessions with celebrity culture demanded the presentation of the Corps as a group of individuals with particular character traits: Lewis the dreamer, drinker and melancholic military man; Clark his easy-going, dependable foil; Sacagawea (who appeared on a dollar bill in 1998 symbolising liberty) as a working mother (albeit enslaved). In a world influenced by animal rights and biocentric philosophy even Seaman the dog 'told' his story. On one level, the qualities projected onto Lewis and Clark and their cohorts – vigour, adaptability, equality and courage – bore a Turnerian hue. However, the presentation remained inextricably twenty-first century – the stress on emotional connection and outdoors challenge offering the Corps of Discovery as a kind of wilderness reality show where contestants, 'hand-picked . . . the best the American west had to offer', bonded as a team and got out alive. As Stephen Ambrose waxed lyrical, 'The number one story here is there is nothing that men can't do if they get themselves together and act as a team . . . And they had come to love each other'.[29]

Interpretations of Lewis and Clark framed them as incipient environmentalists finding community with nature. The mythology of the Corps had long traded in themes of wilderness versus civilisation, but in a post-industrial climate this construct acquired added resonance. Put simply, Lewis and Clark earned laurels as heroes of nature as well as nation. In one sense, the allure of the Corps could be described as that of an exotic travelogue, a thrill-ride into a primitive, sometimes dangerous, space offering an escape from the mundane and thoroughly charted pathways of modern living. The trailer for *Lewis and Clark: Great Journeys West* depicted the Corps crashing through woodlands, climbing rugged escarpments and paddling down river rapids. Over a stirring soundtrack, the narrator asserted: 'It has been called the greatest expedition in American history, perhaps it was also the most dangerous'. In this context, the appeal of Lewis and Clark might be analogised to *Around the World in Eighty Days* (1989) or *Long Way Round* (2004), modern-day televised searches for the undiscovered country. Significantly, the trip to primitive America offered by the Lewis and Clark expedition communicated ideas of environmental transformation and despoilation. The lost world of Lewis and Clark, of faunal plenitude and wide prairies, comprised part of an ecological narrative that stressed a modern West robbed of its wildness. In the comic strip *Wally's Woods* (2001), Goose and Beaver (the reincarnated souls of Lewis and Clark) spoke of dead water in place of vibrant rivers, mountains that appeared much smaller, highways of asphalt and the placement of the Nez Perce in 'prison camps'. For Sierra Club activist John Osborn, the landscape desperately required a 'Corps of Recovery' to re-animate the world seen by the Corps of Discovery. Whereas the audience in 1893 had looked back on westward expansionism with fanfare and triumph, a hundred years on their peers saw loss as well as gain.[30]

Elements of the Lewis and Clark mythology in the twenty-first century none the less retained a consistency with prior incantations. In the popular vernacular, the Corps of Discovery remained an epic American journey into the unknown led by Captains Lewis and Clark as Rooseveltian supermen. Their exploits appeared as part of a Turnerian history that brought the United States to its singular status as global superpower. Stephen Ambrose drew a direct line of ascent from the Corps to American world dominance: 'It has made us the greatest nation in the world. And it has made us a nation in which democracy extends from sea to sea. This is the number one result of the expedition.' The Lewis and Clark expedition continued to earn kudos as a story dripping with core American values and magnanimous destiny. In 2006, as in 1893 and 1955, the Corps of Discovery spoke to popular conceptions of identity, morality and global purpose. As historian William Lang explained: 'this is a story that befits a self-congratulatory nation at the end of the "American century"'.[31]

According to Walter Kirn, their strident journey into the unknown represented a perfect model for navigating a post-9/11 world:

> we sense that there's something enormous and strange ahead of us – in the darkness, over the mountains, through the trees – but we have no idea what it is or how far off. To find it, face it and live to write the story, we'll have to be resourceful, lucky, patient, flexible and observant, much as Lewis and Clark were.

Interpreted in this context, Lewis and Clark harboured a cathartic allure: the captains proffering a dependable presence in an uncertain world. Moreover, commentators touted the explorers as a galvanising force, their story uniquely equipped to unify a divided nation. As Stephen Ambrose declared: 'Lewis and Clark are the real thing. They're authentic heroes. And they provide us with a sense of national unity that transcends time, and distance, and place, and brings us together from coast to coast.'[32]

The notion of Lewis and Clark leading a process of national accord and community renewal none the less betrayed remarkable flaws. The Lewis and Clark narrative provided a comfortable and uncomplicated version of the western past, a frontier encounter in which the captains waxed lyrical about the monumental sights they encountered and Europeans and Indians interacted without violence. However, for those who regarded Lewis and Clark not as forebears of stalwart American values and progress but, in the words of Blackfoot activist Jim Craven, as 'frontmen for genocide' this reading appeared intensely problematic. Bicentennial events thus raised complicated ethical issues regarding the difference between commemoration and celebration. The responsibilities of public history – how to maintain the charm of the Corps and their national mythology in popular memory without reneging on the truth or misrepresenting the nature of European – Indian relations in the West – proved manifold. Given the plethora of 'official' and 'non-official' events, a range of interpretations seemed inevitable. With a Circle of Tribal Advisors sitting on the National Council and a narrative emphasising cultural interaction, 'official' events conveyed a sense of competing mythologies and historical revisionism. The $11 million Fort Mandan and the North Dakota Lewis & Clark Interpretive Center promised to bring tourist dollars to the reservation, allow the Mandan to tell the story from *their* vantage point, and use the occasion as a platform for promoting cultural renewal. However, the banner of 'mutual discovery' proved less enticing to other native nations. The Teton Sioux saw little to celebrate when greeted with plans for a Lewis and Clark scenic byway through ancestral territory. As Ronald McNeill commented, 'I am tired of playing Indian and not getting to be Indian.'[33]

If commemoration represented one buzz word of the bicentennial then authenticity was surely another. Chanting the mantra of 'bringing the past to life', re-enactors indulged in the cult of precision, preserving the specifics of historical detail from costumes to musical accompaniments. Lewis and Clark trekkers followed the trail of their heroes in historically accurate keel boats and ate representative fare by the camp fire. For David Jolles and Ritchie Doyle, stars of the 'Manifest Scrutiny' show that operated out of a Dodge van in Montana, punctiliousness proved essential. Their take on the Corps may have been strikingly revisionist – 'to set the historical record straight with a fresh perspective on everything from the places they really slept to whether they actually discovered anything at all' – but 'Clark' still imported sideburns from China and treated them with a particular dye to achieve an historically accurate hue. At other events, authenticity was conferred by the material presence of Lewis and Clark artefacts, the purchase of a direct connection to the past through the medium of ephemera. At the 'Lewis and Clark: The National Bicentennial Exhibition' that kicked off in St Louis before travelling nationwide, a 500-square foot exhibit promised 600 genuine period items including a compass, Clark's elk skin journal, bear claws and medical instruments. Such presentations not only told the story of the expedition but also indulged in object worship with specific artefacts elevated as symbolic of the frontier experience and imbued with the power to allow the visitor to 'join' the Corps via an osmotic process of historical displacement.[34]

Thus, at precise moments in time, the Lewis and Clark expedition offered a malleable creation story for the American nation. Robust themes of pioneer adventure and primitivism ensured that it remained relevant over a 200-year span. The story seemed familiar but also exotic; individual but also collective; it looked backwards and forwards simultaneously. Lewis and Clark proffered a pliable fictive in which to explore themes of progress, identity and nationhood – perennial favourites for American memory. Successive generations appropriated the extant epistemology, modified it according to their needs and bolted on modish additions. History eased gently into saga, with Lewis and Clark enlisted to provide a usable past.

Lewis and Clark go Post-modern: Simulation, Consumption and New Media

For philosopher Jean Baudrillard, America represented the ultimate simulacrum, a utopian land of construct and imagined reality. In *America* (1989), he wrote: 'Everything is destined to reappear as simulation . . . Things seem only to exist by virtue of this strange destiny.' This world of replication and imitation extends to the material culture surrounding the Lewis and Clark expedition, a realm that encompasses such disparate products as cartoons and comic strips, sea salt and virtual reality tours. Three issues are of particular relevance here: parody, consumption and digital technology, each suggestive of paths the Corps might take in the popular imagination in times ahead.[35]

For a culture obsessed with celebrity and celluloid (Baudrillard noted that 'the whole country is cinematic') the relative paucity of Lewis and Clark-related Westerns may seem surprising. That said, the Corps featured in the televisual world of *The Simpsons*, Lewis and Clark rendered in animate yellow and their story re-enacted by nuclear plant cronies Carl and Lenny. In the episode 'Margical History Tour' (2004), Bart and Lisa visited the library to prepare school reports. Thwarted by a lack of books, ever-resourceful Marge recited anecdotal stories of Henry VIII, Mozart and the Corps of Discovery in pop-history style. She conjured Lewis and Clark as buffoons carrying fake compasses, mistaking a puddle for the Pacific and getting excited about mermaid sex. In the vernacular of *The Simpsons*, the co-captains appeared as part-comics and part-colonisers. On meeting a group of Indians led by Chief Homer, Carl/Clark promptly remarked: 'Have a flag, and while you're at it, cover your nakedness and worship our Lord'. Bart, true to form, acted up as an Indian warrior with tomahawk and scalping fetish, while Sacagawea (Lisa) imparted indigenous knowledge of the landscape (how to frighten mountain lions by making herself appear larger) and became exasperated by her comedy duo companions. History was condensed, hybridised, satirised. At the end of the montage, Carl and Lenny turned to Lisa and wailed: 'we'll never forget you, Pocahontas'. The inclusion of the Lewis and Clark story in the Springfield universe attested to its cultural salience, place in national mythology and proverbial character. After all, you have to be famous to guest on *The Simpsons*. The success of the parody predicated on viewer understanding of the Corps, the satirical qualities of the piece contingent on knowing the terms of engagement. Moreover, for writer Brian Kelley, the saga of Lewis and Clark offered a chance to conjoin myth, history and cinema, reject meta-narratives and trade in the kind of irreverent, revisionist irony for which the show has become famous.[36]

If parody and simulation represented one direction for the Lewis and Clark myth then another route led firmly towards the mall. Jefferson's principal aim in despatching the Corps west in 1804 touted purposes of commerce, and while Lewis and Clark failed to locate a lucrative 'Northwest Passage', the legacy of their trip proved to be decidedly commercial. Not only did the nineteenth-century West serve as cash cow for the American nation, but two hundred years after their epic journey, Lewis and Clark represent a recognisable brand in their own right. The 'L&C' label exudes primitivism, adventure, American self-sufficiency and resolve, nature lore and brotherly bonding, all wrapped up in the mythology of the Wild West. After all, the Corps made it all the way to the Pacific and back with only minor calamities: who better to rely on for camping accoutrements? Products within the L&C stable take many forms: trinkets; mugs; coins; T-shirts; plush toys; board games. For some, buying into the label offers an exercise in patriotic acknowledgement, advertising the American creation myth of 1804–6, projecting a particular identity of nationhood and belonging. For others, 'Lewis and Clark' seems little more than an all-American travel brand, their antics in the West a pioneering exercise in tourism. On one level, the selling of the Lewis and Clark myth trades in heritage and authenticity – camp cook books, replica medals, 1803 leather-bound travel journals, seed collections – yet the packaging of the Corps as consumer icons often strays into the territory of generic western fantasy, kitsch and cash-in. In the first case, history earns report as popular myth, in the second, as adventure. Heritage, education and novelty became de-differentiated, the purchase of Lewis and Clark at the mall like buying a souvenir at the end of a theme park thrill ride. Lewis and Clark sea salt invites us to 'taste the adventure'. Camp fire grog comes courtesy of Lewis and Clark Expedition Reserve Beer. Lewis and Clark air fresheners bring a whiff of the West indoors. Such products deploy Lewis and Clark as signifiers of frontier simplicity and the great outdoors, attractive propositions to an audience harbouring a post-modern desire to escape from the constraints of urban, timetabled life, to embrace individualism by conjuring a mythic West of wildness and absolute freedom. Arguably, however, the Lewis and Clark label speaks more of the illusion of wilderness than its reality. Comfort remains *de rigueur* in the deployment of the Corps as purveyors of fine travel goods. Best Western hotels advertise their rooms with the tag line: 'Discover what Lewis and Clark missed . . . a good night's sleep', while other companies offer Lewis and Clark comfort eye masks and three-in-one travel plugs. The Corps brand may sell the myth of the wild frontier, but the automobile and a comfortable bed remain essentials.

For an event memorialised for its primitive credentials, the Lewis and Clark mythology appears remarkably at home in the ultra-modern, futuristic realm of digital technology. The Internet provides an opportunity for a multifarious, technicolor presentation of the

Corps courtesy of multimedia maps, digital exhibitions and interactive games. Websites offer vivid details of the expedition and its route, with photographs of key artefacts and extracts from the journals placed strategically along the trail. In that sense, the world of cyberspace affords a real-time glimpse into the realms of Lewis and Clark, technology offering the chance to retrace two hundred-year-old steps. Constraints of chronology and geography are rendered immaterial as virtual treks and field trips promise a time machine experience courtesy of web access. This opportunity is not entirely new. The existence of the Lewis and Clark Trail (1978) together with thirteen volumes of edited journals already allowed Corps buffs to relive the expedition and the landscape it encountered via physical and literary mediums. However, the dematerialisation of Lewis and Clark enables the opportunity to join the Corps more completely. Bombarded by a swathe of stimuli (maps, satellite imagery, texts, photographs, sound files) visitors to the digital realm encounter a virtual panoramic West. This digital re-invention of the Corps bears the imprint of the classic mythology, but technology allows a full-on sensory barrage and the airbrushing out of reminders of the contemporary world. The visual(ised) digital landscape of Lewis and Clark features herds of bison and nomadic Indians, and not a telegraph pole or car in sight. For the more intrepid armchair wilderness enthusiast a further step into virtual reality beckons: transportation into the shoes of Lewis and Clark courtesy of interactive games (*Lewis and Clark Into the Unknown*; *Go West across America with Lewis and Clark*) prompting the player to make critical decisions along the route west. Under a rubric of discovery, participants decide how to navigate different routes, engage with indigenous peoples and manage the camp. This process allows the public to 'live' the expedition, provides direct interface with popular mythology and facilitates a personal exercise in manifest destiny. Claiming blank spaces on the virtual frontier, Lewis and Clark buffs can live the fantasy life of the timeless explorer from pioneer to astronaut. Temporal and historic barriers collapse as the Corps of Discovery, the myth of the West, the American road trip and digital technology collide. In the words of the famous explorers themselves, the mythology of Lewis and Clark 'proceeded on'.[37]

Notes

1. David Plotz, 'Lewis and Clark: stop celebrating, they don't matter', *Slate Magazine*, 16 August 2002. Available online at: http://slate.msn.com/?id=1069382.

2. James Lovell, quoted in 'Lewis and Clark in Montana'. Available online at: http://lewisandclark.montanainfo.org/anecdotes.htm; Presidential Proclamation for Columbus Day, 8 October 2001. Available online at: http://www.whitehouse.gov/news/releases/2001/10/20011008-9.html.
3. On the imagined West, see James Ronda (ed.), *Thomas Jefferson and the Changing West* (Albuquerque: University of New Mexico Press, 1997) and David Lavender, *The Way to the Western Sea: Lewis and Clark Across the Continent* (New York: Harper & Row, 1988).
4. David Nicandri, quoted on the radio show, 'Unfinished Journey: The Lewis and Clark Expedition. Ep. 109: The First Space Race', Public Radio International, Oregon. Transcript available online at: http://www.opb.org/unfinishedjourney.
5. Quoted in Bernard DeVoto (ed.), *The Journals of Lewis and Clark* (Boston: Houghton Mifflin, 1953), p. xvii.
6. DeVoto, *Journals of Lewis and Clark*, p. xxiv. In his letter to Clark, Lewis noted 'what follows is secret' before talking of the importance of information gathering, science, Indian diplomacy and communicating the 'idea of the rising importance of the United States'. See Lavender, *Way to the Western Sea*, p. 56.
7. 'Jefferson's Instructions to Lewis', in DeVoto, *Journals of Lewis and Clark*, p. 482; John Logan Allen, 'Imagining the West: the view from Monticello', in Ronda (ed.), *Thomas Jefferson and the Changing West*, p. 16; 'Jefferson's instructions to Lewis', pp. 483, 484.
8. Charles Floyd, quoted in 'PBS: Lewis and Clark, a timeline of the trip'. Available online at: http://www.pbs.org/lewisandclark/archive/time. The meeting is evocatively described by Lavender in *Way to the Western Sea*, pp. 116–18; Gary E. Moulton, *The Journals of the Lewis & Clark Expedition* (Lincoln: University of Nebraska Press, 1983–2001), p. 3:418. Also see Jeffrey Ostler, *The Plains Sioux and U.S. Colonialism from Lewis and Clark to Wounded Knee* (New York: Cambridge University Press, 2004); Clark, quoted in DeVoto, *Journals of Lewis and Clark*, p. 90.
9. DeVoto, *Journals of Lewis and Clark*, p. 92.
10. DeVoto, *Journals of Lewis and Clark*, pp. 135–8.
11. See Clark's journal entry for 13 October 1805. Cited in 'Challenges and Achievements of the Sacagawea Golden Dollar Program', Hearing before a Sub-committee of the Committee on Appropriations, U.S. Senate, 107th Congress, 17 May 2002, Washington, DC, pp. 1–3; Dayton Duncan, quoted in 'Unfinished journey: the Lewis and Clark expedition. Ep. 109: the first space race'. Lewis' journal recorded concise, un-emotive prose at the Lemhi Pass, far removed from the lyricism at Great Falls: 'we proceeded on to the top of the dividing ridge from which I discovered immence mountains of high mountains still to the West of us'. For 12 August 1805 entry, see DeVoto, *Journals of Lewis and Clark*, p. 189; For Lewis' entry of 18 August 1805, see DeVoto, *Journals of Lewis and Clark*, p. 206.
12. Description of the Bitteroots offered by Gass in his journal of 16 September 1805. Cited in Gary Moulton (ed.), 'The Lewis and Clark journals'. Available online at: http://www.helenair.com/journals/journal.php?calendarMonth=September&day=16&calendarYear=1805.
13. Donald Jackson (ed.), *Letters of the Lewis and Clark Expedition with Related Documents 1783–1854* (Urbana: University of Illinois Press, 1978), pp. I: 319–25.

14. DeVoto, *Journals of Lewis and Clark*, p. lii.
15. Jackson, *Letters of the Lewis and Clark Expedition*, pp. I: 319–25; Lewis quoted in Lavender, *Way to the Western Sea*, p. 374. A few cut a direct trail from Lewis and Clark. John Colter, a member of the Corps, left the party directly to trap, stumbling across the bubbling mud pots and geysers of Yellowstone in the process; John Jacob Astor created the American Fur Company in 1811 after hearing of the exploits of the Corps and the prize of Louisiana; Clark himself became a partner in Manuel Lisa's St Louis-based Missouri Fur Company (1808).
16. Richard Francaviglia, 'Walt Disney's Frontierland as an allegorical map of the American West', *Western Historical Quarterly*, 30/2 (Summer 1999), p. 156.
17. Robert Hine and John Mack Faragher, *The American West: A New Interpretive History* (New Haven: Yale University Press, 2000), p. 137; DeVoto, *Journals of Lewis and Clark*, p. xliv; Theodore Roosevelt, *Winning of the West, selections*, H. Wish (ed.) (Gloucester: Peter Smith, 1976 [1889–96]), p. 235; Henry Nash Smith, *Virgin Land: The American West As Symbol and Myth* (Cambridge, MA: Harvard University Press, 1978 [1950]), p. 17; DeVoto, *Journals of Lewis and Clark*, p. lii. Equally significant was the fact that the Corps of Discovery was government-funded, Lewis and Clark the first in a long line of federal agents to enter the West for the purposes of expansion, acquisition, occupation and incorporation. As Milner notes: 'As expansion led to acquisition and as occupation led to incorporation, the initiatives of the federal government greatly shaped the history of the American West from 1803 to 1912 – and beyond'. See Clyde Milner II, 'National initiatives', in Clyde Milner II, Carol O'Connor and Martha Sandweiss (eds), *The Oxford History of the American West* (New York: Oxford University Press, 1994), p. 157.
18. Walter Kirn, 'The journey that changed America', *Time Magazine*, 30 June 2002. Available online at: http://www.time.com/time/2002/lewis_clark/lessay.html.
19. Quoted in Landon Jones, 'Leading men: commanding, cooperative, confident, complementary – why Lewis and Clark were perfectly cast as co-CEOs', *Time Magazine*, 30 June 2002. Available online at: http://www.time.com/time/2002/lewis_clark/lessay.html; DeVoto, *Journals of Lewis and Clark*, p. 478.
20. Frankfort Kentucky *Palladium*, 9 October 1806; Boston *Columbian Centinel*, 5 November 1806. Quoted in Joseph Mussulman, 'Consequences', in 'Discovering Lewis and Clark'. Available online at: http://www.lewis-clark.org/content/content-article.asp?ArticleID=1100. Thomas Jefferson, 6th State of the Union Address, 2 December 1806.
21. Conspiracy theories continue to surround the death of Lewis, with some Corps of Discovery buffs pointing to murder as a likely possibility. Limerick describes the West as enjoying 'its few moments of celebrity in mainstream American history as the necessary stage setting for the last big sweep of national expansionism'. See Patricia Nelson Limerick, *Legacy of Conquest: The Unbroken Past of the American West* (New York: Norton, 1987), p. 19.
22. Adams: quoted in Plotz, 'Lewis and Clark'.
23. Frederick Jackson Turner, *The Frontier in American History* (New York: Robert E. Krieger, 1976), p. 12.
24. Elliot Coues, *History of the Expedition under the Command of Lewis and Clark to the Sources of the Missouri River* (New York: Dover, 1964 [1893]), pp. 1: vi ; See

Gunter Barth, *Fleeting Moments: Nature and Culture in American History* (New York: Oxford University Press, 1990), p. 68; Roosevelt, *Winning of the West*, pp. 236, 234; J. W. Buel, *Louisiana and the Fair*, Vol. 3 (St Louis: World's Progress Publishing, 1804), pp. 1073–4.

25. Buel, *Louisiana and the Fair*, pp. 943–4. See: 'Official Guide to the Lewis and Clark Exposition, Portland, June 1–October 15 1905', Held at the Autry Library, Autry National Center, Los Angeles, CA; Carl Abbott, *The Great Extravaganza: Portland and the Lewis and Clark Exposition* (Portland: Oregon Historical Society, 1981), pp. 1–3.
26. *The New York Times*, 21 May 1955; *Variety*, 25 May 1955.
27. The 1967 buckskin boy band 'The Lewis and Clarke expedition' traded on the outdoors allure of the Corps to advertise their hippy infused 'frontier rock', while the *Sunshine Boys* (1975) saw George Burns and Walther Matthau starring as aging comedy team Lewis and Clark. See Stephen Ambrose, *Undaunted Courage; Meriwether Lewis, Thomas Jefferson, and the Opening of the American West* (New York: Simon & Schuster, 1997); Moulton, *Journals of the Lewis & Clark Expedition* (Lincoln: University of Nebraska Press, 1983–2001); Marvin Kitman: quoted in John Mack Faragher, 'The way to the West before Lewis and Clark', *Filson Newsmagazine*, 3/3. Available online at: http://www.filsonhistorical.org/news_v3n3_waywest1.html. 'Lewisandclark' concept noted by Stephen Ambrose in Dayton Duncan and Ken Burns (eds), *Lewis and Clark: The Journey of the Corps of Discovery* (New York: Knopf, 1997), p. 119; Band member Boomer Castleman: quoted in *MusicDish E-Journal*, 15 November 2004; Stephen Aron, 'The afterlife of Lewis and Clark', *Southern California Quarterly*, 87/1 (2005), p. 27; 'Lewis and Clark enjoy surge in popularity', *Associated Press*, 17 May 2004.
28. Plotz, 'Lewis and Clark'.
29. *Lewis and Clark: Great Journeys West* (Destination Films, 2002); See Landon Jones, 'Leading Men'; Stephen Ambrose: quoted on 'Lewis and Clark: The Journey of the Corps of Discovery: Living History'. Available online at: http://www.pbs.org/lewisandclark/living/idx_9.html.
30. As historian Walter Nugent explained, 'Americans have manufactured the mythology of an Old (or Golden, or Wild) West, the wide-open-spaced, manifestly destined, now-threatened West.' See Walter Nugent, *Into the West: The Story of its People* (New York: Vintage, 1999), p. 12; John Osborn, 'Protecting the lands explored by Lewis and Clark: 1805–1905–2005', *Ridgelines: The Newsletter of the Northern Rockies Chapter of the Sierra Club* (1: 2002); the Sierra Club, 'In the footsteps of Lewis and Clark'. Available online at: http://www.sierraclub.org/lewisandclark/thenandnow/osborn.asp. *Wally's Woods* creator Dean Norman noted of his comic strip: 'Everything in it is true (or possibly true), if you can accept the idea that Lewis, Clark, and members and friends of the expedition are reborn as wild animals.' In Norman's cartoon strip universe, Lewis and Clark had been reincarnated as a goose and a beaver, docile vegetarians bearing karmic responsibility for the animal-killing activities of their ancestors. After a tearful reunion, the critters went exploring – Clark/Beaver favoured Mars but the two settled on joining the crew of an historical re-enactment boat (with an engine) on the Lewis and Clark trail. On their way to the Pacific, Goose and Beaver recollected their earlier trip and re-acquainted

themselves with various faunal compatriots. Throughout, Norman toyed with the saga of the Corps, playing themes of mistaken identity, animal tomfoolery and authenticity for laughs. Underneath the humour, however, the piece contained a powerful revisionist–ecological message of transformation. See Dean Norman, *On the Lewis and Clark Trail: Wally's Woods*, vol. 2 (Cleveland: Beaver Creek Features and Trafford Publishing, 2002).
31. Ambrose quoted on 'Lewis and Clark: The Journey of the Corps of Discovery'; William Lang, 'Lewis and Clark and the American century', *Montana: The Magazine of Western History*, 48/1 (Spring 1998), p. 57.
32. Kirn, 'The journey that changed America'; Ambrose: quoted on 'Lewis and Clark: The Journey of the Corps of Discovery'.
33. Jim Craven's comments cited at Dotrez University, June 2002. Available online at: http://dotrez.com/dru.html; Ronald McNeill, quoted in Margot Roosevelt, 'Participate, profit or protest? Native Americans are sharply divided on the merits of the Bicentennial', *Time Magazine*, 30 June 2002. Available online at: http://www.time.com/time/2002/lewis_clark/ltribal.html.
34. Missoula *Independent*, 6 October 2005.
35. Jean Baudrillard, *America* (London: Verso, 1989), p. 32.
36. Baudrillard, *America*, 56; 'Margical history tour', *The Simpsons*, Season 15, episode 11, original air date 8 February 2004.
37. Examples of Lewis and Clark-related interactive games include *Go West across America with Lewis and Clark*, at: http://www.nationalgeographic.com and *Lewis and Clark Into the Unknown*, at: http://www.pbs.com. Both of these were aimed at an educational market. 'We proceeded on' denoted the most frequently utilised phrase in all thirteen volumes of Lewis and Clark's journals. See Duncan and Burns, *Lewis and Clark*, p. 231.

Chapter 2

Frontier Germ Theory

Putting Frederick Jackson Turner's Frontier Thesis under the microscope is no easy task. Gazing through the telescopic lens, it is difficult to probe beyond the folkloric integument enveloping America's most patriotic of theories. Blots of ink coagulate tales of national renown. Words mutate into elastic, freeform mythologies. Dissecting the frontier thesis is tantamount to pulling a legend apart. The task is hardly aided by the sweeping aims of the thesis itself. Gathered before members of the American Historical Association at Chicago's Columbian Exposition of 1893, Turner set out to explain the making of American character and nation through the westerly advance of Euro-American peoples. Written at the end of the nineteenth century, his paper 'The Significance of the Frontier in American History', reflected both fin-de-siècle anxieties and American aspirations of future greatness. Noting that the frontier had officially closed in 1890 (as recorded by the National Census), Turner described how a series of shifts westwards had taught Americans how to find themselves and claim their country. Before the assembled Chicago academia, Turner famously vociferated, 'The frontier is the line of most rapid and effective Americanization', and that 'The growth of nationalism and the evolution of American political institutions were dependent on the advance of the frontier'. Certainly the thirty-one-year-old historian from Wisconsin imbedded patriotic duty deep within his work. In their allegiance to the Turnerian view of history, later college tutors, politicians, academics and journalists kept with this tradition, fuelling the connection between national identity and frontier theory.[1]

Turner's thesis propagated a distinct kind of western vision: the West as a place of origin. The West provided a creation story for the American nation. Turner paid special attention to the trans-Mississippi region, an area he judged responsible for mass social, political and economic betterment. For Turner, 'The existence of an area of free land, its continuous recession, and the advance of American settlement westward, explain[ed] American development'. His paper asserted the primacy of the West in national history. Suddenly, the western frontier was where the real America was located, while the metropolitan East and the enslaved South faded into the backdrop. 'The true point of view in the history of this nation is not the Atlantic coast, it is the Great West', he stridently claimed. 'But when American history comes to be rightly viewed it will be seen that the slavery question is an incident', Turner affirmed on the matter of race and nation. While quietly received at the Chicago Exposition (Turner's own father commented not on the paper, but on his son's dutiful tour of the exposition shows), the Wisconsin academic had sneaked a home run. Turner promoted his frontier paper avidly, mailing out copies to fellow scholars and professionals, and his reputation grew accordingly. In a variety of guises, the thesis re-emerged in issues of the *Atlantic Monthly*, *Public Opinion* and the *International Socialist Review*. By the 1920s, Turner's frontier thesis dominated thinking about the West. His paper served as the starting point, the American ground zero, for all scholarship on the region. Generations of historians subconsciously swore their allegiance to the master by crafting works that stayed true to Turnerian mentality and logic. In the 1960s, Ray Allen Billington crafted a number of monologues and biographies sympathetic to his academic forbear. However, the prominence of the thesis left it open to detractors. In sporadic episodes, critics took pot shots at Turner's linear tale of White men travelling west, overcoming the wilderness and emerging as new Americans in the process. By the late 1980s, Turner's frontier thesis no longer held complete authority over western academia.[2]

This chapter grapples with notions of legitimacy and utility surrounding the frontier thesis. First, it explores the rise of an anti-Turnerian view of the West and the growth of historical criticism. Secondly, it tackles one of the key aspects of the frontier thesis: its service as a socio-environmental theory. Thirdly, the chapter turns to how the 'frontier' word was used in Turner's time. Conventional opinion suggests that Turner's ideas proved so successful because they represented American consciousness at the turn of the century. But did the frontier thesis perfectly surmise how Americans felt about the frontier and the westering experience?

Critical Moments

While Turnerian ideas dominated understandings of the West for almost a century, it is wrong to claim that universal support ever existed for the frontier thesis. Criticism of Turner goes back a long way. In his edited collection of frontier debates, George Rogers Taylor, writing in the 1970s, opened with the line: 'Ever since the late 1920s scholars have been arranging a decent burial for the Turner thesis'. Ray Allen Billington dated criticism even earlier, right back to 13 July 1893, the very occasion of Turner's address before the American Historical Association. That few audience members welcomed the Turner thesis on its first airing reflected not only their endurance of four lengthy academic papers beforehand, but also that Turner himself engaged in 'heresy' (to borrow Billington's words) by going against 'germ theory', a popular approach that explained American character as rooted in European antecedents (or antibodies). No wonder then, that Turner's missive went unmentioned in scholarly reports of conference proceedings.[3]

However, the first truly difficult period for the frontier thesis came in the 1930s, several years after the death of Turner. Political science professor Benjamin F. Wright Jr from Harvard questioned Turner's notion of institutions being reshaped on the frontier, becoming in the process something new and distinctly American. For Wright, the frontier was no transforming agent. Staying loyal to earlier American historiography, Wright insisted that 'Old World' democracy influenced both western and national schools of thought. By mimicking eastern systems (rather than rejecting them), western governance was in fact 'imitative not creative'. Turner had failed to note the similarities between state administrations on both coasts.

Yale scholar George Wilson Pierson, meanwhile, took issue with semantics and theory. To be truly useful, a thesis required precise language and logic. Rather than minor oversights, Pierson judged Turner's inexactitude in defining key concepts such as the 'frontier' to be catastrophic, commenting that: 'By what it fails to mention, the theory disqualifies itself as an adequate guide to American development'. Turner's theoretical approach received further criticism from Professor Fred A. Shannon from the University of Illinois. Shannon took hubris with Turner's concept of the frontier as an effective safety valve for over-population and industrial over-employment in the East: to him, the safety valve hardly worked when violent strikes dominated the 1870s and 1880s. In the estimation of Shannon, it was obvious that

'Steam escaped by explosion and not through a safety valve of free land'. Farmers were more likely to become city workers than vice versa, thus going against Turner's ideal of an agrarian West. Deeming the frontier thesis unproven and misleading, Professor Louis Hacker from Columbia University put in his oar by denouncing the Turnerian school of history as deadwood in the Depression era. In a feisty piece for *The Nation* in July 1933, Hacker asserted the past tense status of the frontier thesis, harping that 'Turner and his followers were the fabricators of a tradition which is not only fictitious but also to a very large extent positively harmful'. The significant effects of capitalism and class went ignored in favour of a misplaced focus on the romantic image of the lone pioneer in the wilderness.[4]

Such sentiments reflected not just academic rigour, but a broader review process taking hold in American society in the 1930s. Scholarly criticism intersected with the Great Depression and new directions in social thought and mass politics. Upbeat stories detailing the rise of a great nation lost their footing amid stock market collapses and dust clouds sweeping across the country. The frontier thesis had little to say to a nation wracked by economic turmoil. The Dust Bowl, in particular, shattered the bucolic image of a rural West, something that the frontier thesis hinged on (Turner, with an agricultural background, keenly projected the farmer as frontier maker and national saviour). Turner's concept of the safety valve seemed equally inapplicable when the mid-West offered little reprieve for millions of destitute and unemployed. Moreover, by promoting individualism and isolationism, the frontier thesis hardly seemed a useful guide to the socio-political movements of the 1930s. Collective work programmes and internationalism (with the rise of Nazi Germany) appeared far more apposite.

Emergent in the 1960s, a fresh spate of scholarly discourse highlighted the variety of technical problems with the frontier thesis, as well as pointing out its suspect social applicability. Frontier investigators included Marvin Mikeshell, professor of geography at the University of Chicago. Mikeshell deemed 'the principal failing of Turner, his followers, and most of his critics' to be 'a neglect of comparative research'. Accordingly, the frontier thesis needed to be tested abroad in order to fully understand its workings and to affirm or refute Turner's claims of American exceptionalism. Mikeshell himself took up the challenge by making forays into settlement patterns in Australia, Canada and South Africa. Empirical gaps similarly bothered Allan G. Bogue, professor of history at the University of Wisconsin, Turner's old academic haunt. Hoping to avoid the 'blood-drenched field of debate' surrounding the frontier thesis, Bogue none the less nicknamed the frontier thesis an 'alchemic process' that by magic turned ordinary people into exceptional Americans out on the frontier. Bogue attempted to unlock the mysteries of Turner's 'frontier society' using the tomes of sociologists and anthropologists. The sense of mythology surrounding the Turner thesis further intrigued Pulitzer prize-winning historian Richard Hofstadter. Hofstadter sought to disentangle hyperbole from history in Turner's work, and in the process raise the bar of American historical scholarship as a whole.[5]

Coined in 1893, the frontier thesis, somewhat predictably, appeared out of touch with the pressing social issues of the 1960s. Turner's White frontier farmer had little to say to a Black southerner relegated to the back of a bus in apartheid Alabama. That Turner had downplayed racial issues in his work hardly made him a voice for the baby boomer generation. As Jack D. Forbes noted, Turner was guilty of promoting an ethnocentric frontier, a one-sided take on American history where only the Anglo-Saxon mattered. Turner himself had stated how the frontier, as a process, was far more important than slavery. It was not just race that Turner omitted. As William Cronon and his colleagues later observed, 'the issues of the twentieth century that loomed largest in the minds of historians after World War II – communism, the atom bomb, civil rights, urban poverty, racism, feminism – seemed to have no obvious connection to the rural past of the western frontier'. With its agrarian patina, the Turner thesis seemed out of sync with modern America. The frontier thesis no longer appeared fundamental to an historical understanding of nationhood, demographics or identity.[6]

Yet, in the public sphere at least, the 'frontier' word still carried resonance. John F. Kennedy eagerly alluded to a 'new frontier' in a crowd-pleasing speech for the presidential election of 1960. The space race forwarded the persuasive idea of a fresh area for America to explore – an idea given voice, by among others, William Shatner as James T. Kirk, who at the beginning of every episode of *Star Trek* (1966–9) subtitled space as the 'final frontier'. Atomic developments in the period similarly reflected a strong belief in striding beyond scientific and technological frontiers: of turning swords into ploughshares and promising electricity too cheap to meter. Such positivism drew on the historic frontier ideal, but rejected the farmer's implements in preference for the scientist's rockets and missiles. The frontier looked forward, not backward, for inspiration. The one exception lay in entertainment: at Disney's Frontierland (1955) in Anaheim, California,

Turnerian nostalgia played centre stage with its rustic cabins and Mark Twain steamboat.

However, it took several decades for historians to fully ally themselves with new social trends and movements. In the late 1980s, criticism of the frontier thesis emerged from an alignment of scholars that came to be labelled 'New Western' historians. Chief among them, Patricia Nelson Limerick, from the University of Colorado railed against Turner for his ignorance of minorities and his artificial narrative of White Americans triumphing over the 'wilderness'. Limerick viewed the West as a place of colonisation and conquest, not free land, milk and honey. New Western historians researched areas that Turner (and his followers) deemed insignificant, but by the 1980s appeared crucial to any understanding of region or place. Glenda Riley worked on the gendered frontier, or the women's West, Richard White highlighted the role of the federal government (or federal West), while Donald Worster explored the hydraulic (and environmental) West. Some of the criticisms hurled at Turner were hardly new. That Turner offered a poor working definition of the frontier, that he was ethnocentric and that he ignored the input of women, were all issues already known. However, the breadth and cohesiveness of New Western history gave it a strength and power. For the first time, a complete list of past errors and omissions emerged *at the same time* as innovative research filled the gaps. New Western scholars also recognised the deleterious effect of Turner on the discipline. Limerick lamented that, 'to many American historians, the Turner thesis *was* Western history'. Richard Etulain quipped that the frontier thesis amounted to an 'interpretative straitjacket'. By breaking free from Turner, Western scholars found fresh open range to discover, and set themselves the task of re-documenting a region's history. They also faced the challenge of winning over the rest of the nation. Not everyone appreciated the sudden loss of confidence in the classic tale of frontier progress, a formula that had dominated text and celluloid for over a century. Huntington scholar Martin Ridge still referred to the Turner thesis as 'a masterpiece', and others like him clung to the idea of national destiny through frontier process.[7]

Accessing environmental, racial and gendered discourses dating back to the 1960s, New Western historians succeeded in forging a more rounded and socially relevant history of the West. While never overt or codified, scholars operated by a new post-modernist gaze. New Westerners shot down the Turnerian grand narrative: the popular explanation for where the West had come from and where it was heading. They deconstructed the 'old' ways of seeing the region and offered multiple images, ambiguities and approaches in its place. Their work reflected contemporaneous shifts in American society and politics. Once again, the interests of Western historians coincided with those of mainstream America at a fin-de-siècle moment. The ending of the twentieth century corresponded with national anxieties over the collapse in community spirit (see, for example, Robert Putnam's *Bowling Alone*), a deteriorating environment, an immigration boom and fears over America's place in a post-Cold War world. This time Turner remained silent, but New Western historians had plenty to say.

Clearly, the frontier thesis provided America with a triumphal tonic when it was most needed back in the 1890s. The thesis won over a nation looking for its roots and seeking forward momentum. When the thesis fell out of step with the mood of the country, only then did its popularity falter. The less the frontier thesis fitted with current affairs, the less it could be trusted. In this way, critical chatter became louder at times of national doubt and crisis. Opponents of Turner judged him not just by his oversights in the 1890s, but also by his failure to provide answers one hundred years on.

A Socio-Environmental Theory

Despite its myriad flaws, the frontier thesis forwarded an ambitious socio-environmental theory. In a relatively short paper (and, by some accounts, only finished the night before delivery), Turner stitched together a variety of concepts: social Darwinism; germ theory; environmental determinism; political science; 'melting pot' mechanics; and demographic theory. The resulting body of work, the frontier thesis, aimed to fill a void in national understanding. Turner's fusion of ideas proved exceptional. His work represented a storehouse of aspirations and modes of thinking.

Frederick Jackson Turner alluded to the American continent as a growing and evolving body. Once just an outline shape, a basic form, the country had gone through meteoric changes in the 1700s and 1800s thanks to the process of expansionism. By waves of people moving west, a nation had been gradually brought to life and nurtured. 'Civilization has followed the arteries made by geology', explained Turner as he mapped out the pathways of settlement. Ever-expanding commercial enterprises and sprawling cities uprooted the pristine wilderness and primitive aboriginals before them. The Wisconsin historian understood frontier development as 'like the steady growth of a complex nervous system for the originally simple, inert continent'. The American body had been born long ago: now it had life, vitality and the possibility of maturation. Native Americans, the first residents of America, belonged firmly to the old, inert country. Such articulations of natural succession, the inevitability of growth, the assured death of the indigene and the linearity of progress reflected the values of an Enlightenment scholar. Turner drew on popular predilections for modish scientific thought. America would be great because it was destined to be so: not just by divine ordinance in the guise of manifest destiny, but by scientific sanction, in the form of (accelerated) evolution. Turner proved so keen to link the country's development with natural progression that he put out a challenge in his Chicago paper: 'In this progress from savage conditions lie topics for the evolutionist.' Clearly, Turner had the work of Herbert Spencer, Charles Darwin, John Wesley Powell and William Graham Sumner in mind.[8]

Victorian philosopher Herbert Spencer's theory of socio-biology (Spencer coined the term 'survival of the fittest') ably suited the Turnerian landscape. For Spencer, evolution provided the only rational explanation for the multiplicity of species and variety of social systems around the world. Simple organic forms became complex (and matured) through processes of modification. As early as 1862, Spencer defined evolution 'as a change from an incoherent homogeneity to a coherent heterogeneity'. Such a principle applied to both man and beast. For the former, a poorly organised family of savages had the potential to become a sophisticated and interactive set of independents, given due time and process. The same pathways existed in Turner's frontier thesis. 'Complex society is precipitated by the wilderness into a kind of primitive organization based on family', noted Turner. Europeans could not help but be primitives in the wilderness, before being modified by (and in turn modifying) their frontier experience. Only then did they emerge as more complex and sophisticated beings. Both scholars saw an important role for individual agency in their meta-narratives. Spencer's 'heterogeneity' granted humans (and other species) significant roles and freedoms. Turner argued, 'the frontier is productive of individualism', that individual liberties, while sometimes taken to excess on the frontier, were ultimately conducive to a healthy, functional democracy. Despite the implicit suggestion in evolution of never-ending transformation, both men believed in an equilibrium of sorts, an ultimate endpoint. Once fully adapted, both Spencer and

Turner's subjects hit a plateau. For Turner, the puzzle came with what could possibly follow the frontier experience.[9]

Turner was also influenced by germ theory. In the 1860s, Louis Pasteur tackled the brewing problems of a Lille industrialist, M. Bigot, by finding unwelcome micro-organisms in his fermentation tanks. The French chemist subsequently discovered that micro-organisms were often the cause of disease, and could be combated by such means as clean hospitals, pasteurisation and vaccines. Pasteur revolutionised medicine and surgery with his germ theory of disease, as well as helping to debunk spontaneous generation theory (whereby living organisms were assumed to emerge from the non-living). In sociohistorical circles, germ theory was rendered applicable to the evolution of peoples, nations and races. Advocates pointed to the rise of a sophisticated Germanic race predisposed to self-government out of ancient Teutonic forested environments in Europe as evidence of this phenomenon. With his eyes fixed on the eastern seaboard of America, Turner originally fell into line with germ theory scholars by stating, 'Our early history is the study of European germs developing in an American environment.' However, the consummate patriot went on to reject the notion that 'Germanic germs' travelled extensively in the New World. According to Turner, they failed to mirror the workings of real biological colonialism as found in the spread of horses and non-native grasses across the West. Instead, once the frontier drew people away from the East Coast, a new wilderness experience took root with dramatic results. As Americans moved west, forced to 'return to primitive conditions', life started anew and dynamic cultures emerged. As Turner related, 'Little by little he transforms the wilderness, but the outcome is not the old Europe, not simply the development of Germanic germs . . . the fact is, that here is a new product that is American.' Turner thereby refuted the idea of European germs taking hold of America, and instead utilised the theoretical underpinnings of 'germ theory' to argue for a national rite of passage. In effect, he replaced the Germanic forest with an all-American variety.[10]

Giving such weight to the wilderness experience, Turner might easily have been labelled an environmental determinist. The relationship between humans and nature in his work was decisive: after all, Americans were made through their working of the land, discovering their individualism in barbarous soil. The brush with nature, with the primitive, is what distinguished nineteenth-century Americans from their European counterparts. Certainly, Turner, like other scholars of the time, sought comparison and linkage between the natural world and social developments. Organic references eminently suited the mantra of evolutionism. Herbert Spencer saw 'civilisation' as 'a part of nature; all of a piece with the development of the embryo or the unfolding of a flower'. Likewise, Turner cast the wild frontier as a place from which 'the American intellect owes its striking characteristics'.[11]

Turner's focus on concepts such as evolution and natural progression allowed him to leave behind traditional understandings of American history based on slavery, conflict and European antecedents. As Richard Slotkin pointed out, his thesis amounted to a rejection of racial origins and war as the defining forces in shaping the national experience. For Ostrander, despite the Wisconsin historian's subtle biases, 'Turner evidently was one of the least race-conscious historians of a thoroughly race-conscious generation'. The frontier thesis seemed, at least on the surface, fresh, pure and idealistic. The nation had been forged from processes of movement, exploration and transformation rather than civil war, ethnic struggles or European class systems. Turner seemed confident that the frontier produced a stock of freedom-loving, capable, vigorous and responsible individuals. As he put it, 'first, we note that the frontier promoted the formation of a composite nationality for the American people.' Herbert Spencer exuded similar confidence in the 'coherent heterogeneity' of evolved species.[12]

Despite their efforts, neither Spencer nor Turner formulated perfect theories. Spencer was attacked for his anti-statism and his (to some) unconvincing coupling of biology, cosmology, politics, linguistics and social evolution. For Turner, his view of the frontier, while striking in its scope, betrayed significant omissions. Along with his ignorance of class, gender and non-Whites, how exactly did democracy emerge from the forests of America? Where did the East and the South truly fit into a theory of national development so dependent on the West? And lastly, where did the frontier begin and end?

The 'Frontier' as Word

Turner was not the first American to employ the concept of the 'frontier'. The word boasts a colourful and variegated history of its own. During the colonial period, easterners employed the term to denote disputed borderlands. European psychology shaped the early American experience, and the frontier label occupied no special place in the colonial vernacular. In the 1780s, naturalist William Bartram wrote of his travels through the American South, referring to the 'depredations and murders', Indian skirmishes and pioneer trades on 'the utmost frontier of the white settlements on that border'. With national ascendancy, the frontier gradually emerged as a line of discovery, movement and continental expansion. By the time of the California Gold Rush, the meaning of the frontier was firmly imbued with patriotic overtones and based around the notion of free land in a variety of travel guides. The western frontier was said to provide a safety valve for immigration and criminality, a Garden of Eden, a ground zero for the great metropolis and an agrarian honeycomb. It served as an optimum vessel of 'wish projection'. This is the world of the frontier that Frederick Jackson Turner entered and diligently promoted.[13]

In 1893, Turner hung his frontier concept on extant terminology, namely the strict definitions of land ownership set down by the Census Bureau. The frontier only existed outside 'the margin of . . . settlement which has a density of two or more to the square mile'. In 1890, the Census recorded higher population figures across the whole nation: the frontier was no more. Turner linked this demographic tabulation to the closure of a mythic, national story. In a sense, he transformed the 'frontier' from the statistical to the spectacular. It was 'the meeting point of savagery and civilization' lying at 'the hither edge of free land', an engine of independence and a promoter of democracy. Despite the academic setting of his paper, Turner imbued the frontier with emotive language and temporal poise. The ending of the great frontier was something happening about the country, people just had to open their eyes. Calling witness at Cumberland Gap, Turner beseeched his Chicago listeners to gaze on the frontier vanishing before them.[14]

Although this frontier may have been lost, Turner made sure it was not forgotten. Throughout the twentieth century, the Turnerian frontier was synonymous with the American West and westward movement. The word 'frontier' had special poise and historic dominance. Then, in the late 1980s, New Western historians attempted to derail the Turnerian frontier, re-labelling it offensive, partisan and reductive. They deleted the word 'frontier' from book indexes. Patricia Nelson Limerick substituted 'conquest' for 'frontier' in her work (she later expanded her post-frontier dictionary with a c-based lexicon of 'continuity', 'convergence', 'conquest' and 'complexity'). Turner's 'frontier' had apparently outlasted its usefulness. In entertaining style, Kerwin Lee Klein at the University of California nicknamed Turner's famous axiom 'the f-word' due to its taboo status in new academic circles.[15]

By such actions, New Western scholars miscalculated. They unintentionally perpetuated the significance of frontier vernacular in

American history (to paraphrase Turner) by assuming it to still be an icon, if not the icon, of the Old West. If anything, the Turnerian frontier had faded from popular culture by the time New Western historians came on the scene. They took Turner on his word that his frontier *was* fundamental to American thinking. Rather than test how far Turner's 'elastic' definition reflected fin-de-siècle thought, they took for granted his status as the period's foremost spokesman. In this literal war of the words, they even misread Turner and wrongly associated the 'frontier' solely with the West. Turner himself had identified a series of frontiers that started on the East Coast – this approach gave him the legitimacy to argue that the frontier existed as a *national* phenomenon. They also judged Turner by today's standards. By his preference for the term 'free land', Turner went accused of ignoring Native Americans. Yet Turner covered the Indian frontier in his paper, and arguably used 'free land' as a neutral, legalistic term, common parlance in the period. The frontier word also had different connotations in the 1890s to the 1990s. In the 1890s, the label harboured naturalistic (read wilderness) and geographical variegations. One hundred years on, and associated with space travel and even the Internet, it sported a decidedly technological veneer. The fluidity of the frontier term perhaps, more than anything else, made the old Turnerian configuration moribund in the modern period.[16]

To gain a better sense of his efficacy as period spokesman, it remains useful to test how far Turner's frontier truly reflected American thought of the time. Turner and the nomenclature of the frontier have been inextricably linked for over a century, but did the historian ever hold complete monopoly over the term? Was the 'frontier thesis' his sole invention, or a reflection of greater chatter? The 1890s period elucidates a concept in the throes of refinement and negotiation across a wide range of popular platforms. At both the Chicago Expo, and in period literature, the frontier was under discussion. This section now turns to consider the meaning of 'frontier' at the end of the century, and whether or not Turner captured a moment in time.

In 1893, Theodore Roosevelt famously congratulated Frederick Jackson Turner for putting together 'ideas that had been floating around loosely'. Certainly, Turner never operated in a vacuum. His work reflected contemporary feelings, which undoubtedly included his own experiences growing up on a farm in the mid-West. Ideas were written in the same ink as other western authors. Turner fell into line with the frontiersman narrative, most identified with the *Leatherstocking* novels of James Fenimore Cooper, as well as Francis

Parkman's writings (Parkman described how 'contact with the wilderness endowed Europeans with a "rugged independence"'). Biographers James Bennett and Ray Allen Billington both argued that receptivity towards the frontier thesis had something to do with a social climate welcoming of American exceptionalism. For Richard Etulain, Turner 'spoke for many of his contemporaries' with 'a nationalistic, patriotic perspective that echoed the attitude of many Americans at the beginning of the twentieth century'.[17]

This sense of Turner perfectly capturing the sentiments of the period was tested by his visit to the Columbian World Exposition. The quiet reception of his paper questioned the influence of the frontier in American life. Moreover, the world outside the conference hall tested Turnerian logic. Turner was a man with his gaze cast firmly backward, only peeking into the future with some worry. With its festival atmosphere and technological exuberance, the Columbian Expo imparted none of his anxieties. A celebration of Columbus' visit to the continent, the Chicago site showcased a healthy and dynamic country on the cusp of international greatness. America faced the future powerful and with pride. By definition, the World Expo was outward looking, and did not seek to understand one nation's destiny in isolation. To a large degree, it represented a post-frontier environment, at least according to Turner's rationale. Exhibits pointed to new frontiers, technological and international, rather than older rural and insular versions. On display were icons of the future: the first foreign car, the Mercedes Benz; the Ferris wheel; the hamburger; and Thomas Edison's Kinetoscope. A ménage of inventiveness, consumption and amusement, the Columbian Exposition suggested a great future ahead for the West and the world as a whole.[18]

The 'real' West of the Exposition, the state exhibits of Jackson Park, proved closest to Turner's frontier. A series of state buildings set out the products and character of the nation at the century's end. Many western exhibitors chose to promote the peaceful and productive agrarian frontier, an agricultural kingdom consistent with the sentiments of both former President Thomas Jefferson and contemporary visionary Frederick Jackson Turner. North Dakota sported an impressive wheat frieze, while 1,200 bushels of corn and nearly four carloads of cereal decorated Iowa's central hall. On Missouri Day, state representatives organised a parade of livestock through the park. The exposition hall of Nebraska boasted grain specimens arranged by county and a sugar beet exhibit. Mottos of 'Corn is King' and 'Sugar is Queen' were made of state grasses. However, Jackson Park also highlighted the variety of life on the frontier, mapping out a place far richer than Turner ever projected. Most state exhibits explored the contributions of women, especially in their handicraft displays, to western industry. California's art gallery included female crafted art, music and literature. Displays of the 'cowboy artist' Charlie Russell's paintings in Montana's state building presented a very different West to that of Turner: all action, gunfire, animals and Indians. State buildings themselves declared European architectural influences, from the colonial verandas of the Dakotas to Montana's Romanesque marble and numeral inscriptions.

The entertainment section seemed even less in tune with Turner. The Midway Plaisance featured a kaleidoscope of internationally themed attractions for the curious visitor. Lodged as a staple of the amusement zone, and the chief American ingredient in the complement of attractions, the American West seemed all about entertainment, action and danger. On the same street as Carl Hagenbeck's dioramic Animal Show played an American Indian show, reasserting the idea of the other and the savage. Sitting Bull's cabin, identified as 'original', nestled between a military encampment (somewhat appropriate) and a Californian ostrich farm. Relics from Custer's Last Stand resided close by. A working model of a 'Colorado gold mine', complete with mountain, shaft and water flume, tantalised those eager to see the West from a Chicago stage. A fully operational model of a mineshaft included its own mountain (cut in two) and a processing plant. No doubt impressive, it none the less paled before the gigantic show-stopping Ferris wheel and a twenty-foot model of former Exposition steward, the Eiffel Tower. Midway's exhibitionists cast the frontier as exotic, not native, more a freak of nature than an experience of national and historic proportions.

The most obvious clash came when the 'World's Congress of Historians and Historical Students' met the 'World's Congress of Rough Riders', namely when Frederick Jackson Turner rubbed shoulders with Buffalo Bill Cody. Turner declined an invitation to see the Wild West Show on the afternoon of 12 July in order to finish his conference paper. He thus missed an opportunity to gaze upon a West in competition with his own: an historical reality show to rival, if not undermine, his frontier thesis. The Buffalo Bill live stage recreated western skirmishes, Indian raids and dazzling pieces of horsemanship all before an enraptured audience. It was part history, part circus and part rodeo. On Bill's frontier, conflict and honour ruled, with the bullet continually in evidence. This vision clashed loudly with Turner's frontier of sodbusters and, for the most part, peaceful progress. Two of the dominant figures of western interpretation stood together, but not alongside, at the Chicago Exposition. Each offered something different to their audience.[19]

Neither did Turner's presentation of the frontier perfectly match that of American authors and diarists of the time. In contemporary literature, the 'frontier' had a variety of uses: as a synonym for life in the West; a place of hardship and adventure; as a social partner to wilderness; as a military (or other type of) border; as an indicator of movement and progress; and as a fading memory. Some of these 'frontiers' sat well within the canon of Turner, others did not.

In 1902, Methodist preacher Reverend Charles Wesley Wells published his autobiography, *A Frontier Life: Being a Description of my Experience on the Frontier the First Forty-two Years of my Life*. For Wells, along with other writers of the time, the frontier denoted an intimate, life-changing experience. During the 1860s and 1870s, Wells spent significant time in Kansas and Nebraska. He diligently recorded buffalo hunts, Indian raids and a 'snowstorm' of grasshoppers that regularly decimated Nebraska cornfields. For the Methodist pioneer, the West signified first and foremost a religious frontier, a realm where the word of God was desperately needed. Wells noted his need to Christianise the Indian of the West, to bring her 'under the influence of the gospel'. The preacher relayed this, the 'real frontier work in the ministry' that drew him across the Mississippi, to a life far harder than that of 'the city pastor . . . sitting in his cozy study at home'. However, throughout his trials, Wells always found solace in 'the glory there is in laying the foundation of our Church in new fields'.[20]

Along with his farming impulses, Wells' dedication to the Church sat well with Turner's notions of civilising the West. In his Chicago paper, Turner acknowledged the role of religion in developing the region. Perhaps cognisant of the tendency of frontier writers to embolden and exaggerate their tales, Wells also committed himself to historical accuracy, declaring at the outset, 'I shall strive in every particular to give the facts' (in a similar vein, author W. J. Maltby claimed to present 'a vast storehouse of information relating to frontier life' in his book on Texas pioneering, published in 1906). However, such men saw the frontier as a living and real place, rather than a distant and removed academic process. The frontier represented their life, their foundational experience. While Turner went for the macro study of westward expansion, generalising over frontier processes and immigration waves, Wells focused on the personal, micro and even the mundane. For the dedicated parishioner, the only broader force at work in the West was the hand of God.[21]

For Wells, religious positivism vastly improved the frontier life. Others proved not so fortunate. William MacLeod Raine, a London journalist who travelled to the south-west in 1881, presented his frontier as a decidedly dangerous place. The grim reality of the place seemed to be marked by death, hard work and fear. First and foremost, westerly pioneering challenged survival instincts. Relaying his admiration for those who stood fast on the frontier, faced off Indians with guns and took on the challenge, Raine lamented at the drab stock of Euro-American colonists that also entered the region, all hardly matching up to Turner's (or even Buffalo Bill's) standards. As Raine described it, 'Unfortunately the frontier did not attract only good citizens. It was also a sink into which drifted much of the riff-raff of the country.' Raine was by no means on a par with French intellectual Alexis de Tocqueville in his erudite social analysis of the American character, but the outsider did, at least, show the frontier to be not all progress and fortitude as Turner claimed.[22]

For other writers, the frontier served as a storyboard, a backdrop for grand stories and startling yarns. This sat uncomfortably with scholars such as Turner and Theodore Roosevelt, who valued the concept of the frontier as a serious historical phenomenon. Works such as J. S. Campion's *On the Frontier: Reminiscences of Wild Sports, Personal Adventure and Strange Scenes* (1878) highlighted the popular attachment of the frontier axiom with escapade. Like Raine, Campion portrayed the frontier as a dangerous place. Prior to departure, he was warned, 'Do not go. In the present state of the frontier you will be killed.' None the less, outfitted for adventure, in his eminently fine 'frontier rig' of buckskin and pistols, Campion committed to the westerly experience wholeheartedly and without reservation. His readers, in turn, encountered a literary frontier analogous to the visual feast set out by Buffalo Bill: all show, action and violence.[23]

Part of the fear, adventure and challenge of the frontier was undoubtedly the wilderness quotient. Faced with Indians, wild animals, falling rocks and poor weather, Joseph Meek, an Oregon mountain man, struggled to lead parties West. According to biographer Frances Victor, Meek felt that 'Death sought his victims in the wilderness', and that the frontier proved a trial by fire (and other energies). Trepidation about the frontier coupled with European anxieties over savage nature, red in tooth and claw. Wolves and bears became colourful villains (and unconscious partners to Indians) in many travel diaries. At the same time, the frontier wilderness acted as a proving ground. In alignment with Turner's notion of men being made on the frontier, many diarists witnessed their own evolving survival skills. Frank Triplett, a colonel in the US Army, titled his work *The Conquering of the Wilderness* (1883). Meek argued that 'The law of self-preservation is strong in the wilderness', with men bettering themselves on the frontier. Such individualist vigour served to overcome existing cultural anxieties over nature's threat. Advertising images of the western wilderness as a hallowed ground also helped. The *Crofutt's Guide to California and the West* of 1874 glorified the abundant nature of the kingdom, waxing lyrical that the wilderness would indeed 'blossom like the rose' and the West rise as a 'land of the golden fleece'. While Turner avoided such romantic prose, he too recognised the centrality of nature in the frontier experience.[24]

Ever since the Turner thesis, the word 'frontier' has carried special meaning, an exceptional status, in American popular culture. Yet most authors at the time of Turner employed the 'frontier' in a neutral manner, bereft of any conscious emotion or political axe to grind. Only a prefix (the military border, colonial frontier) or addendum (such as the frontiersman) identified a greater scheme at work. Along with 'border', the 'frontier' proved an everyday noun of the travel vernacular. Both phrases served as simple descriptions of lands west of the Mississippi, signifiers of place. Most of the time, idioms of border and frontier were interchangeable in diaries and other publications. Hence, the words gained equal billing (like competing actors on a movie billboard) in Charles H. L. Johnston's *Famous Frontiersmen and Heroes of the Border* (1913). Numerous 'frontiers' littered the text of Colonel R. B. Marcy's *Thirty Years of Army Life on the Border* (1866). While 'border' was more liable to be coupled with the southwest, or with military–Indian conflict, it rarely meant anything tangibly different from 'frontier'. The *California Mercantile Journal* of 1860, for example, headlined border rather than frontier for its sketch of 'camping out' in the state. Authors of the *Journal* proclaimed adamantly that, 'life on the borders of civilization, in the forest, among the mountains, has its pleasures as well as pains, difficulties and inconveniences'. According to them, a tasty flapjack and evening coffee presented just rewards for the hardships and difficulties of the pioneering day. Such choice of setting imparted that the border, rather than the frontier, could easily have been Turner's 'meeting point' of 'savagery and civilization'.[25]

Border or frontier life always involved movement, whether the travel of pioneers across different states, or the rise and fall of frontier communities. Often movement had a positive slant. The West as 'the making of America' was commonly understood and translated into optimistic trail books and personal memoirs. Like Turner, many authors identified in the frontier a form of process, although they struggled to give it definition. Published six years prior to the Turner thesis, Frances F. Victor's biography of Meek amounted to a pre-Turnerian tale of individual progress. The frontier calling exercised a profound effect over Meek. According to Victor, 'Manifest destiny seemed to have raised him up, together with many others, bold, hardy, and fearless men, to become sentinels on the outposts of civilization.' Meek and his brethren duly emerged as 'the hardy frontiers-men' of the West. However, Victor's story of individual bravado proved unremarkable as a piece of frontier literature. Unexceptional exceptionalism, Meek warded off wolves, bears and buffalo, traded with Indians, like every other man caught up in romantic trail stories of the period.[26]

Likewise, Colonel Frank Triplett saw the frontier as responsible for a production line of proud American stock. A fine example of celebratory literature of the period, Triplett's account had nothing but admiration for the pioneers: 'Bold, dashing, adventurous and patriotic; loyal to friends, to country and to the interests of society, their work was singularly effective in the advancement of American civilization.' According to him, the frontier assumed responsibility for the 'moulding of the character of the whole American race'. However, Triplett struggled with the finer details, at one point confusing Buffalo Bill and Wild Bill Hickok. Colonel Marcy, writing in the 1860s, displayed a startling pre-Turnerian edge to his prose. Marcy felt that his work amounted to:

> the truthful history of a condition of men incident to the advance of civilization over the continent – a condition which forms peculiar types of character, produces remarkable developments of human nature – a condition, also, which can hardly again exist on this or any other continent, and which has therefore especial value in the sum of human history.

Such promotions proved hard to substantiate, and, once again, the frontier author disappointed in terms of content.[27]

Like the melancholic finale of Turner's paper, western diaries of the time spoke of moving on and the capture of a moment in time. Frontier closure loomed large in their narratives as authors expatiated on the romantic end of an era and its grand adventures and dioramas.

Frontier Germ Theory 57

Most books operated on some level as records of a passing age, providing idiosyncratic itineraries of frontier travel and the accoutrements of survival. Daniel Shipman's survey of fifty-eight years in Texas amounted to a catalogue of surveys, settlement, schools and Indian skirmishes. Alexander Majors grouped together outfitting, trapping, Indians, 'frontier telegraphy' and the dog ('most thoroughly the comrade of those who dwell upon the frontier') as key features of Missouri. As early as the 1860s, writers claimed to have witnessed the end of the frontier. Calling witness in 1866, Colonel Marcy presented his chapters 'as records of a fast vanishing age'. Reminiscent of George Catlin's artistic freezing of Native Americans on canvas, Marcy forwarded his prose as 'preserving the memory of the people and the customs of the West in the middle of the nineteenth century. The wild animals that abound on the great plains to-day will soon be as unknown as the Indian hunters who have for centuries pursued them. The world is fast filling up.' Wells noted the huge change occurring about him:

> On first coming to this country, I found Indians, buffaloes, deer, antelopes, turkeys, thousands of prairie dogs, and a few white men with their families. What a change has taken place in that country in so short a time! Then it was new, wild, and desolate; now it is a well-settled, rich, and fertile country, with schoolhouses and churches, fine residences have taken the place of the dug-out, the sod-house, and the log-cabin.

Frederick Jackson Turner could not have said it any better.[28]

Notes

1. Frederick Jackson Turner, *The Frontier in American History* (New York: Henry Holt, 1921), pp. 3–4, 24.
2. Turner, *The Frontier in American History*, pp. 1, 3, 24. See, for example, Ray Allen Billington, *Frederick Jackson Turner: Historian, Scholar, Teacher* (New York: Oxford University Press, 1973).
3. George Rogers Taylor (ed.), *The Turner Thesis: Concerning the Role of the Frontier in American History*, 3rd edn (Lexington: D.C. Heath, 1972), p. vii; Ray Allen Billington, *The Genesis of the Frontier Thesis: A Study in Historical Creativity* (San Marino: The Huntington Library, 1971), p. 3.
4. Benjamin F. Wright, Jr, 'Political institutions and the frontier' (1934), Taylor, p. 64; George Wilson Pierson, 'The frontier and American institutions: a criticism of the Turner theory' (1942), Richard Hofstadter and Seymour Martin Lipset (eds), *Turner and the Sociology of the Frontier* (New York: Basic Books, 1968), p. 39; Fred A. Shannon, 'A post-mortem on the labor-safety valve theory', (1945),

Hofstadter and Lipset, p. 184; Louis M. Hacker, 'Sections – or classes?' *Nation*, 26 July 1933; Taylor, p. 51.
5. Marvin W. Mikeshell, 'Comparative studies in frontier history' (1960); Hofstadter and Lipset, p. 152; Allan G. Bogue, 'Social theory and the pioneer' (1960); Hofstadter and Lipset, pp. 93n, 73. See: Richard Hofstadter, *The Progressive Historians: Turner, Beard, Parrington* (New York: Vintage, 1968).
6. Jack D. Forbes, 'Frontiers in American history', *Journal of the West*, 1 (July 1962), pp. 63–71; William Cronon, George Miles and Jay Gitlin (eds), *Under an Open Sky: Rethinking America's Western Past* (New York: Norton, 1992), p. 4.
7. Patricia Nelson Limerick, *Legacy of Conquest* (New York: Norton, 1987), p. 20; Richard Etulain (ed.), *Does the Frontier Experience Make America Exceptional?* (Boston: St. Martin's, 1999), p. 108; Martin Ridge, 'The life of an idea: the significance of Frederick Jackson Turner's Frontier Thesis', *Montana: The Magazine of Western History*, 40 (Winter 1991), p. 2.
8. Turner, pp. 14, 15.
9. Herbert Spencer, *First Principles*, 2nd edn (London: Williams and Northgate, 1867), p. 127; Turner, p. 30.
10. Turner, pp. 3, 2, 4. See also: Gilman M. Ostrander, 'Turner and germ theory', *Agricultural History* 32/4 (1958), p. 260.
11. Herbert Spencer, *Social Statics* (New York: Augustus M. Kelley, 1969 [1851]), p. 65; Turner, p. 37.
12. Richard Slotkin, *Gunfighter Nation: The Myth of the Frontier in Twentieth-Century America* (New York: HarperCollins, 1992), p. 55; Ostrander, p. 261; Turner, p. 22.
13. William Bartram, *Travels Through North & South Carolina, Georgia, East & West Florida, the Cherokee Country, the Extensive Territories of the Muscogulges, or Creek Confederacy, and the Country of the Chactaws* (Philadelphia: James and Johnson, 1791), pp. 515, 20; 'wish projection' idea: see Richard Slotkin, *The Fatal Environment: The Myth of the Frontier in the Age of Industrialization, 1800–1890* (Middletown: Wesleyan University Press, 1985), p. 40.
14. Turner, pp. 3, 12. See also: Richard White, 'Frederick Jackson Turner and Buffalo Bill', James R. Grossman (ed.), *The Frontier in American Culture* (Berkeley: University of California Press, 1994), p. 13.
15. For example, the 'frontier' is noticeably absent from the index of Richard White's 684-page tome, *'It's Your Misfortune and None of My Own': A New History of the American West* (Norman: University of Oklahoma Press, 1991); Patricia Nelson Limerick, *Something in the Soil: Legacies and Reckonings in the New West* (New York: Norton, 2000), pp. 18–22; Kerwin Lee Klein, 'Reclaiming the "F" word, or being and becoming postmodern', *Pacific Historical Review*, 65 (May 1996), pp. 179–216.
16. Elastic definition: Turner, p. 3; Indian frontier: Turner, pp. 12–15; 'free land': Billington (1973), pp. 77–9. Limerick (2000) noted the 'wonderfully ironic side effect' of New Western history in terms of Turner: 'It restored his celebrity', p. 143.
17. Roosevelt to Turner, 10 February 1894, Frederick Jackson Turner papers, The Houghton Library, Harvard University, cited in Ray Allen Billington, *America's Frontier Heritage* (Albuquerque: University of New Mexico Press, 1974 [1963]), p. 13; Parkman quote: James D. Bennett, *Frederick Jackson Turner* (Boston: G.

K. Hall, 1975), p. 41; Bennett (1975), pp. 52–5; Billington (1971), p. 66; Etulain (1999), p. 17.
18. Descriptions of fair taken from Hubert Howe Bancroft, *The Book of the Fair* (Chicago: The Bancroft Company, 1893).
19. Billington (1971), pp. 162–6; White (1994), pp. 7–12, 45–55.
20. Reverend Charles Wesley Wells, *A Frontier Life: Being a Description of my Experience on the Frontier the First Forty-two Years of my Life* (Cincinnati: Press of Jennings & Pye, 1902), Huntington Library, pp. 67, 59, 193, 196, 196.
21. Wells (1902), p. 5; W. J. Maltby, *Captain Jeff or Frontier Life in Texas with the Texas Rangers* (Colorado: Whipkey Printing, 1906), Autry Museum, p. 79.
22. William MacLeod Raine, *45-Caliber Law: The Way of Life of the Frontier Peace Officer* (Evanston: Row, Peterson, 1941), Huntington, p. 23.
23. J. S. Campion, *On the Frontier: Reminiscences of Wild Sports, Personal Adventure and Strange Scenes* (London: Chapman & Hall, 1878), Huntington, pp. 2–3, ii.
24. Stories of Joseph Meek related in Frances V. Victor, *Eleven Years in the Rocky Mountains and Life on the Frontier* (Hartford: Columbia Book Co., 1879), Huntington, p. 59; Colonel Frank Triplett, *Conquering the Wilderness* (New York: N. D. Thompson & Co., 1883), Huntington; Victor (1879), p. 60; *Crofutt's Trans-Continental Tourist*, VI (New York: Geo. A. Crofutt, 1874), Huntington, preface.
25. Charles H. L. Johnston, *Famous Frontiersmen and Heroes of the Border* (Boston: L.C. Page, 1913), Huntington; Colonel R. B. Marcy, *Thirty Years of Army Life on the Border* (New York: Harper & Brothers, 1866), Autry; David M. Gazlay (ed.), *The California Mercantile Journal*, I (San Francisco: George Elliott, 1860), Huntington, p. 263.
26. Victor (1879), pp. x, 41.
27. Triplett (1883), p. v; Marcy (1866), p. x.
28. Daniel Shipman, *Frontier Life: 58 Years in Texas* (1879), Huntington; Alexander Majors, *Seventy Years on the Frontier* (Chicago: Rand, McNally, 1893), p. 78, Autry; Marcy (1866), pp. ix, x; Wells (1902), p. 197.

Chapter 3

'The Gun that Won the West'

Dodge City, Kansas, 4 July 1876: in a centennial rifle shoot, quick-drawing frontiersman Lin McAdam wins a 'one in a thousand' Winchester rifle as a prize. Ambushed on return to his hotel room, McAdam loses the rifle to his nemesis Dutch Henry Brown, a nefarious character responsible for the murder of his father. However, Brown soon becomes desperate for hard currency and ammunition, and in a foolish card play with an Indian trader, forfeits the weapon. The rifle later passes to an Indian chief, a highwayman and a professional gunfighter. McAdam follows the coveted Winchester across the country as it passes from one illegitimate owner to the next.

Director Anthony Mann cast the gun as a pivotal force in the 1950 Hollywood Western *Winchester '73*. Inanimate, one-dimensional and more wooden than an actor in a B-Western, the rifle none the less dominated the film narrative. Heroes and villains alike obsessed over its 'just perfect' manufacture. A reviewer for *The New York Times* asserted the scale of technological fascination at play: 'They've got a new angle for Westerns. It's no longer cowboy loves girl, a motivation which is widely frowned upon as sissy stuff. This new dramatic angulation might be labeled cowboy loves gun, and it provides quite as much inspiration as any cowboy-horse romance.' The Winchester proved a hearty symbol of masculine affection, a consummate rival to the busty heroine or the trusty equine. The movie situated the American West as a realm shaped by conflict, especially over firearms. Everything turned on the click of the trigger. *Winchester '73* appropriately began with screen text heralding 'The Gun that Won the West'.[1]

The focus on the 'one in a thousand' rifle in *Winchester '73* marked it as a distinctive feature film. Guns proved a staple of the Hollywood Western, but rarely did the firearm serve as an individual character. Instead, firearms were important for stock action scenes.

They provided visual indicators of danger and death. They fitted in a broader celluloid frontier that emphasised themes of adventure, masculinity and contest. Colts and Winchesters rested on poker tables in bars populated by sassy prostitutes and restless cowboys, the wooden rickety saloons part of a pioneer townscape surrounded (like wagon trains) by wilderness and Indians. Despite their relative anonymity, firearms remained crucial to the filmic code of the Western. They set the speed and the tone of a scene. They dictated the action, ending the lives of good and bad. They also performed a broader mythological function. Put simply, guns explained how the West was made.

The majority of Hollywood Westerns forwarded the gun as a technological harbinger of victory on the frontier, the tool that facilitated the simultaneous conquest of savage natives, nature and lawless renegades. Guns fed into a distinctly violent myth, a Wild West imagining whereby out of conflict came civilisation. The climax of Western history, the closing of the frontier (and the beginning of a new society), came with a suitably visceral bullet-ricocheting showdown. Akin to fireworks heralding the New Year, one period of Western history ended and another began with a rain of bullets. Substituting the gun for the plough, Hollywood promoted a carbine version of Frederick Jackson Turner's 1893 frontier thesis. As with Turner's thesis, the creation of the West allied to the formation of national character. Where Turner had envisaged the farmer as hero, Hollywood instead forwarded the gun-toting cowboy as a symbol of Western (and national qualities) of individualism, justice, freedom and self-reliance. As Will Wright observed, in this myth-making process, 'the frontier defines the cowboy, and the cowboy defines individualism'. Moviemakers encouraged audiences to see their heritage through a cowboy's gun barrel. According to gun culture theorist Abigail Kohn, ever since the first Western, 'Shooters in general, and cowboy action shooters in particular, are literally "performing" their status as native sons and daughters, claiming their identity as authentic American citizens.' The gun, western history and nation all seemed inseparable.[2]

The inspiration for the gun-toting Hollywood cowboy, for *Winchester '73*, is multifarious. Dime novels, Wild West shows, fictions by Zane Grey and Owen Wister's *The Virginian* (1902) all propagated the allure of the gun-toting frontiersman. Frontier violence served as a marketable commodity in literature going back to James Fenimore Cooper's *Leatherstocking* novels of the early 1800s. This trend continued through the twentieth century; *45-Caliber Law*

(1941) by journalist and writer William MacLeod Raine being just one example of how the West continued to be portrayed as a savage land where only a gun served as a man's best friend. For Raine, 'before the law had come in and subdued the bad man and the killer, the life of a citizen was his own private affair and not that of the community. The only protection he had was his own character and the Colt revolver he carried on his hip.' The cowboy walked the line between savagery and civilisation.[3]

On the real nineteenth-century frontier, the firearm attracted some interest. In towns such as Dodge City and Ellsworth, according to popular images of the time, violence spread like wildfire on the prairie, with the absence of law and order a flaming match. Violence even became a spectator event promoted in period newspapers. It was claimed that one foreign tourist left Virginia City disappointed on not seeing a man murdered before breakfast. The gun skills of outlaws Kit Carson, Billy the Kid and Jesse James made national folklore. A popular maxim of the day read: 'There is more law in a Colt Six Gun than in all the law books.' It is little wonder that, as historian Richard Hofstadter claimed, 'it was the frontier that gave this country one of its central images of justified violence and some of its archetypal heroes of violence'.[4]

Common imaginings of the West as a realm of violence par excellence took hold in American popular culture. Images of violence made the West more American than anywhere else. As W. Eugene Hollon stated, 'America has always had a violent past, and the frontier in a way has stood for this country at its most violent.' Through its mythic gunfighter lore, the West connected with the Civil War and the American Revolution, and became part of a national teleology of violence. This chain was hardly regrettable – after all, the gun had been involved in the fight for freedom from the tyrannical British in 1776. It provided a romantic symbol of conflict. The gun was not an American invention, but its use in freedom fights and frontier showdowns made it a very different commodity from the pistol present at a gentrified duel in the Old World. Viewed as an equalising agent, a tool of democracy, the weapon could be used to subdue any enemy. This notion of a nation founded on firearm justice eminently suited the needs of later twentieth-century gun lobbyists. Gun culture linked with positive historic images of individualism, vigilante justice and pioneer settlement, rather than mass riots, homicides or lynchings. Behind legal justifications for gun culture based on the Second Amendment resided sentimental mythologies of America's armed frontier, the notion of 'taking the law into your own hands' and the gun-toting cowboy. The gun demonstrated social, historical and political values.[5]

It also exorcised guilt. The myth of 'good' violence, with the gun-toting cowboy as its minister, remade the conquest of the West in the popular imagination. The lone gunfighter became an American hero overcoming Indians and the wilderness. The invention assuaged rather than highlighted frontier guilt. Such a myth cemented positive ties between the West and firearms lore. For a gun culture to prosper, something more was needed than the gun itself. Sanction came through associations with the protection of life, liberty or family. Such purposes were then spelt out for the larger public through the framework of mass communication. Advertising by gun manufacturers, dime novel literature and, later, the Hollywood Western, all did this. Such steps ensured that the frontier endured as a triumphal endeavour. Concepts of 'beneficial violence' meanwhile served as a distraction from the real violence that occurred in the West, including domestic abuse and even instances of Indian genocide.[6]

This chapter has two aims. In the first section, the story of the West as the story of the gun is tested. What were the true manifestations of gun culture in the trans-Mississippi region during the nineteenth century? How significant were they? In the second section, the myth-making process that helped forge the 'Wild West' is questioned. The dime novel, commonly understood as one significant populariser of the 'gun-toting cowboy' image, is deconstructed and studied. Together, the two sections explore the role of history and myth in the making of a violent West.

The West and the Gun

Built into the common vision of the frontier is a predilection for violence. Gun conflict happened with some regularity at locations across the West. Contrary to popular belief, not just cowboys carried guns, and gunfights were not restricted to downtown duels and Indian ambushes. National events, in particular the Civil War and Mexican War encouraged a boom in firearms sales from the 1850s onwards. Indian skirmishes and military expansion fuelled weapon receipts. Weapons served as agents of westward expansion, and gun ownership become widespread. According to Albert Klyberg and Nathaniel Shipton, 'The cotton gin, the steamboat, the steel plow, the reaper, the telegraph, and the railroad were all developments that contributed to the transplanting of culture across America, but the initial advantage the European settler had over the American environment was his firearm.' Historians have gone so far as to suggest that the firearm was the key factor in Western settlement, a crucial piece of technology in the taming of the frontier.[7]

Guns certainly contributed to the development of an early Western economy. During the fur trade, most hunters carried rifles as necessary equipment for the gathering of pelts. Traders sold or exchanged firearms with Indian nations in return for well-prepared hides and fur for export to the East Coast and Europe. Guns (along with liquor and metal goods) were popular items at trading outposts. The American Fur Company used European guns for trade with Native Americans who preferred the quality of European goods. Frances Victor, writing in 1879, noted the utility of the firearm as trading tool and the recklessness it brought: 'The great desire of the Indians for guns and ammunition led to many stratagems which were dangerous to the possessors of coveted articles.' Firearms serviced a Western industry of animal enterprise. Bison hunting in the 1870s and 1880s rested, quite naturally, on successful shooting. More a tourist hunter than a professional bison killer, Chas Youngblood related his exploits on the Great Plains. He boasted that equipped with his trusty rifle, 'Old poison slinger', 'I have killed buffalo with it at a mile'. Youngblood vouched for his honest report of Western life, 'if you do not consider it sufficiently romantic and exciting, please remember that it is not a dime novel, but, so far as it goes, a true history of my life on the plains'. Other bison hunters saw no point in recording their tales or testing their target skills. They instead homed in on massive herds and fired without a second thought, cognizant that many animals would die in the process. For a time, mass carnage coincided with significant profit.[8]

To meet growing demand for firearms on the frontier (and also to encourage business), gun stores opened on both East and West coasts as the trans-continental exodus gathered speed. In the East, sales increased as people planned their overland wagon trains. In response to the 1849 California Gold Rush, Congress voted for the sale of guns at cost prize in order to facilitate the arming of trailblazers. Colt noted a corresponding rise in demand for its Frontier revolver. One émigré went so far as to claim that overland parties started out their journeys as 'walking arsenals'. Guns were hardly obvious mining instruments, but they represented tools of self-defence on the route to westerly mining camps. Travellers held on to their guns and serviced them on arrival. Preparing for new business, one gunsmith trader, Jules Francois Bekeart, a friend of John Sutter, moved shop from Coloma to

San Francisco to expand his enterprise. Set up in the 1850s, the Curry family business was positioned on Sansome Street, San Francisco up to 1886. The Curry sales catalogue from 1884 featured a range of rifles and revolvers, as well as tasteful decorative powder flasks with pictures of hunters and their dogs, Indians and buffalo.[9]

Mining camps could be harsh places. Bodie, California, a gold and silver town that prospered between 1877 and 1883, suffered a range of vices that included drinking, gambling, wrestling, drug-taking and prostitution. Muggings and stagecoach raids persisted. Roger McGrath described Bodie as 'a rough and rowdy town'. Conflicts erupted over mining and land claims, sometimes with racial dimensions (Chinese and Indian workers provided frequent targets). In such cases, guns hardly reflected the perfect antidote to violence. Firearms instead made enmity more deadly than it needed to be. There were undoubtedly episodes of concentrated violence against people and property. Gangs as well as individuals perpetrated gun crime. The Daly Gang of Aurora, Nevada, worked for the local mining company with the remit of intimidation. The gang was certainly gun-equipped, but hardly fitted a cowboy aesthetic. McGrath noted how 'They wore freshly laundered shirts and tailored suits and ate at Aurora's best restaurants'. Frontier violence did not need to be dirty.[10]

Guns proved to be big business in the West. In the mid-nineteenth century, coinciding with the Civil War and western expansion, a competitive market emerged between Colt, Smith & Wesson and Winchester. The Civil War led to a significant domestic industry for firearms. In 1860, Colt had the largest factory in the country in Hartford, Connecticut. Technological innovation, in the form of factory machinery and firearm design, spurred the competition. In response to a saturated market after the war, gun manufacturers looked for novel ways to boost sales, and marketing strategies became more sophisticated. Colt recognised that guns could be highly prized and collectable items, and offered services that included personal inscriptions and elaborate decoration. Presentational cases accompanied the most expensive models. Guns were naturally judged not just by their aesthetics, but also by their ultimate function: how well they could kill. One writer with the nickname Cimarron explained in a letter to Smith & Wesson, 'I have been shooting your make and find it a perfect revolver. I can kill a man at 100 yards with my revolver every time. I like all frontiersmen like the Smith & Wesson better than Colt's.'[11]

Colt was none the less a firm favourite in the West. Colt had pioneered the revolving cylinder firearm and the single-action shooter.

The company garnered a quintessentially westerly reputation: 'God created men, Colonel Colt made them equal', went the 1870s adage. Easy to operate, commonly available revolvers promised to level the playing field between rival westerners. Colt's 'Peacemaker' certainly suited the vigilante tradition of frontier justice. It could have been dubbed 'myth-maker', given its near godly status in the West. Folklore boosted sales, as did unexpected salesmen. Buffalo Bill Cody's Wild West shows promoted the gun as a perfect machine. Showmanship cemented the bonds between firearms, entertainment and progress. Cody himself owned a double-action Frontier Colt. He was not alone: 51,000 were made between 1878 and 1905, excluding sheriff and storekeeper variants (a John F. Kennedy-inspired 'New Frontier' gun was manufactured in 1961). Colt billed the single-action Frontier as a firm favorite. In one promotional piece, Colt elaborated, 'No story of winning the West is complete without mention of the Colt Frontier model.' It seemed as though in the process of westward conquest, the frontier opened and closed with the sound of a Colt revolver.[12]

'The law of the Colt became the law of the frontier – and a good law it was', recounted one Colt booklet. Exceptional stories of sheriff bravado, such as maverick Wyatt Earp's gunfight at the OK Corral in October 1881, presented the West as the land of swift justice. Not restricted to the West, vigilantism none the less thrived in lands beyond the Mississippi thanks to the fledgling judicial system. Challenges of distance, transport and resources (including a lack of jails) held back development of a comprehensive legal system, while instability, criminality, class and ethnic clashes facilitated the emergence of vigilante justice in its place. Over 300 groups formed in the West. Each one typically boasted a few hundred members. Organisations were especially active in Texas, California and Montana, where historian Richard Maxwell Brown calculated the meting out of 729 death penalties. The West San Francisco Vigilance Committee proved to be one of the most significant vigilante forces of the period. Formed in 1856 and led by Ted Coleman, a 32-year-old importer, the Bay Area group blossomed to between 6,000 and 8,000 members. Businessmen dominated the organization and many were well armed. Clearly, vigilante committees exercised power over more than just renegade criminals – they signified popular sovereignty, conservatism, property and business interests, and thrived in a climate of fear. However, Western vigilantism rarely abided by the cowboy stereotypes of Hollywood. Some observed leniency for first offenders, while hangings were the preferred system of punishment, with the rope getting more use than the gun.[13]

A sense of expeditious and popular justice aligned with notions of the West as a realm of action rather than words. On a basic level, violence appeared to be an uncomplicated, instinctive answer to emergent problems of ethnic interaction, land competition and class divisions. Notions of self-redress and individualism were sometimes used to justify such aggression. Firearms were thus associated with purposeful and retributive violence. An unwritten 'Code of the West' also had room for violence. Filling the void of established law and justice, the 'code', more a suggestion of appropriate behaviour than legal charter, focused on issues such as privacy, politeness, loyalty and courage. Within this code of Western social norms, issues of self-defence legitimised gun use. Whether or not any formal rubric existed, certainly it became a useful summary of frontier meaning. Later incarnations of the 'Cowboy's Code' by actors Roy Rogers and Gene Autry focused more on patriotism, God and kindness than frontier justice.[14]

As well as justice enforcer, the gun served a valuable recreational purpose in the West. European tourists on hunting trips across the 'wilderness' clocked up stupendous kill tallies with their coveted rifles. The aptly titled Sir George Gore from Sligo, Ireland, brought with him a carpet and forty servants on his hunting trip to Montana in 1854. Crow Indians complained to the Superintendent of Indian Affairs based in St Louis over the 105 bears, more than 2,000 bison, not to mention elk and deer dispatched by Gore in their region. Gore sported a fiery temper as well as trigger-finger: he burnt his hunting outfit, including wagons and carts, in a giant bonfire when the American Fur Company reneged on purchase. With the growth of organised gun clubs in the late nineteenth century, the firearm served as a tool of social bonding and quiet politicking in emerging Western towns. Los Angeles City Gun Club hosted tournaments in the late 1890s and early 1900s. Advertising 'Ammunition and refreshments on the grounds', with entrance fees including the price of birds, a largely male fraternity coalesced to shoot skywards and bolster the fortunes of the fledgling metropolis.[15]

Arguably, on a basic level, Western life suited gun culture. A number of factors made gun use seem more likely than elsewhere: basic food acquisition through hunting; fear of Indians; isolated living; the attractiveness of the West to criminals and misfits; competition between settlers; a lack of an effective justice system; and the lure of alcohol. The absence of women and families in some fledgling communities was further cited as fueling aggressive tendencies. Incidences of frontier violence reflected expressions of masculine power and freedom. But female pioneers were not averse to brandishing weapons. Alongside Calamity Jane and Annie Oakley, everyday pioneers had to know how to shoot, as well as cook, sow, plough and clean. William Fowler in 1880 noted the willingness of women to use 'The axe and the gun, the one to conquer the forces of wild nature, the other to battle against savage man and beast'. Fowler went against the idea of the docile, subservient female, claiming, 'We know that women could handle the gun and ply the axe when required to do so.'[16]

However, the gun-toting cowboy became the classic image of Western gun culture. The cowboy appealed as the frontier 'everyman' willing to take the law into his own hands. David Kopel related how 'The cowboy, the archetypal American hero, came from an indifferent family background, and fought – not with an exquisite samurai sword – but with a mass-produced Colt .45 that cost ten dollars.' This sense of the cowboy as free from elite heritage or big money made him all the more attractive. What evidence existed for the connection between cowhands and firearms? Given that the work was based around animal haulage, did cowboys need guns? Writing in 1898, C. C. Post claimed that 'while there is really far less lawlessness and disregard for human life among the cattle men and cowboys along our frontiers than the blood and thunder stories told of them would lead people to suppose', in case of Indian attack or 'reckless characters', 'of course, they had to go well armed'. Along with the rope, boots and neckerchief, the gun proved a familiar (and identifying) element of cowboy attire. Given their wide availability, some Texas ranchers fretted that the accessibility of firearms to cowboys would wreck their businesses. The movement of cattle across vast swathes of land also incited conflict. Competition for land, water and grazing spurred the range wars of the 1880s and 1890s between ranchers and settlers. Lawmen, hired guns and sometimes Indians became involved. Most famously, the Johnson County Range War in Wyoming (1892), pitted a group of small-time ranchers and farmers against powerful stockmen. Hired guns under the direction of the Wyoming Stock Growers Association set out to target rustlers and smaller ranchers alike (the latter organised under the banner of the Northern Wyoming Farmers and Stock Grower's Association). Following a raid on Nate Champion's KC Ranch, the WSGA outfit was intercepted at the TA Ranch near Fort McKinney by a 200-strong, sheriff-led posse aided by the US Cavalry.[17]

Stopping points along cattle trails also generated violent associations. Key 'cow towns' such as Dodge City, Kansas and Abilene, Texas garnered reputations as reckless, rowdy places. Cowboys used such towns to 'let off steam' after long journeys hauling cattle. With liquor on tap, wages to spend and gambling to entertain, brawls and minor skirmishes inevitably followed. However, weapon use or injury was not always deliberate: firearm accidents were said to be a greater cause of injury than duels. The adage of 'shooting yourself in the foot' maintained some currency in the frontier West. Rituals of violence were not always pretty or glorious affairs.

Envisioning the West as an eminently violent domain none the less ignores a wide range of evidence that points to a more peaceful and complex frontier experience. The number of recorded shootouts falls some way short of the fictive roll-call. While firearm ownership, especially after the Civil War, was common on the frontier, possessing a gun did not equate to gunning down all and sundry. The availability of guns often encouraged greater awareness of the need for common sense and sometimes codes of conduct. Safety proved important. Writing in 1879, Frances Victor related how fur traders that he met in the Rockies often prohibited the firing of guns at camp, insisting that all weapons were fully cleaned and taken care of. Neither were cattle towns exceptionally violent places. Many townships exercised strict controls over the use of firearms. Men handed in their guns on entry to Wichita, with metal tokens rather bullets the common exchange currency. During the 1870s and 1880s, supposedly the peak of frontier violence, settlers emphasised peacekeeping and the establishment of law systems in fledgling townships. Cattle towns were first and foremost about successful markets, commerce and growth, not simply existing as six-shooter alleys. The average settler entertained fears over disease, agricultural production, stock prices and poor winters, rather than the spectre of downtown duels. Yes, disagreements occurred between ranchers and settlers, but such conflicts rarely escalated into full-blown gun war.[18]

Violence proved the exception not the social norm. However, press reporters honed in on the most sensational stories to grab the attention of readers, and in the process, inventing frontier towns as hotbeds of bloodshed. Cheekily described as the 'wicked little town' by the *Evening Star* in 1878, Dodge City fell short of its devilish epithet by some margin. A meeting point for bison hunters, Indians, soldiers and the Santa Fe railroad, Dodge had some potential for conflict. In its first year, the boom town recorded fifteen deaths – a significant figure given its low population. Pistols could be purchased from local trader Frederick C. Zimmerman, and, with sixteen saloons by 1877, the popular vices of drinking and gambling were well catered for. However, the 'wicked little town' lacked straightforward wickedness. Above all, Dodge residents wanted to 'make' the city, not shoot it to shreds. The buffalo boom of the 1870s meant plenty of gunfire, but largely at animals not people. Dodge was a place of hard work and hope. By the late 1870s, most incidents of violence had died out. On a visit to Dodge in 1878, town founder Robert Wright felt relieved to find a town ordinance forbidding firearms, and that his 'party, on landing, instead of being received by a howling lot of cowboys, with six-shooters and Winchester rifles rampant, were received by a delegation as gentlemanly and courteous men as can be found in the state'. While staying at Dodge, Wright discovered a church and a courthouse. At night, he took solace from the fact that 'any noisy whisky demonstrations are promptly checked by incarceration in the lock-up'. 'The Beautiful, Bibulous Babylon of the Frontier' was for this visitor no worse than metropolitan Chicago, with Wright imagining a great future for Dodge now that the killing had stopped. 'Beautiful for situation, cosily nestled on the "beach" of the turbid Arkansas, while on the north the palisades rise above the busy little city, which in the near future will be ornamented with cozy cottages, modern mansions, and happy homes', Wright wrote, somewhat optimistically. His ornate prose seemed more fitting to a travel brochure than a report on frontier travel. Unexpectedly, given his initial fears, Wright came to the conclusion 'from a careful observation, that Dodge is a quiet and orderly as any town its size in Kansas'. Visitors seemed more likely to choke on their breakfast sausages than witness the shooting of a 'man before breakfast'.[19]

Dodge City boosters none the less realised the utility in fostering a reputation of the town as wild and dangerous. Closed in 1878 and opened to development, Boot Hill cemetery at Dodge found new use as a tourist dollar and myth-making machine. In 1932, town residents constructed a mock graveyard, complete with headboards, on the grass outside City Hall. They later added a hanging tree. Violence made an ordinary town exceptional, it placed the town on the map. Historian Richard Dykstra, a skeptic of frontier violence, explored the real Dodge behind this image. He claimed, 'The Kansas cattle trading center or "cattle town" of the 1870s and 1880s has up to now belonged more to the imagination than to history. The lively rendezvous of cowboy, cattleman, gambler, and city marshal is currently a theatrical image only tenuously connected with tradition.' The false image sold none the less.[20]

Gun manufacturers similarly advertised a violent West. The low density of law officers across western states gave some credence to the image of lawlessness. However, as one of the panoply of frontier tools in wagon trails heading West, the gun was far less useful than the stove, shovel or axe. Certainly, other items got more use in the everyday affairs of setting up camp, planting fields and building townships. The essential, practical qualities of the rifle and pistol were thus overstated. However, where the gun excelled was in its storytelling potential. An overriding purpose to kill and maim made it a tool to be reckoned with and respected – such reverence came not just from common sense but from elaborate myth-making. As if etched onto each gun casing, stories told of weapons that had tamed the West, saved an honourable man's life or seen off an Indian attack. The hard steel body came to embody values of self-reliance, individualism and self-determination. The gun was raised as a symbol of Western endeavour. Weapon manufacturers were complicit in making every gun seem special. Perhaps more significant than technological innovation, 'What Colt invented was a system of myths, symbols, stagecraft and distribution'. According to William Hosley, Henry Colt personified the 'Marlboro Man' of his day. Colt signed a picture deal with Indian artist George Catlin to promote his weapons. Presentation guns proved potent promotional tools. That the Texas Rangers used Colts provided another marketing opportunity. 'Texas and the West may not have generated the majority of Colt's sales, but its aura and associations were soon adopted as key elements of Colt's marketing strategy', noted Hosley. At Colt headquarters, the gun appeared more moneymaker than peacemaker. Manufacturers tapped a national market in making the gun a symbol of the Western conquest. Colt sold well in the East too thanks, in part, to this iconography.[21]

Such grandiose imagery did not always translate into far-sweeping western sales. The self-proclaimed 'permanent, cheap and desirable advertising medium' of the *California Mercantile* catalogue, the yellow pages of the 1860s, only carried one entry under 'Guns and Pistols' out of more than 200 entries. This compared unfavourably alongside five business listings for musical instruments, three for sewing machines, two for baths, two for pickles and two for undertakers (the latter surely affected by the dearth of gun sellers). The one armament advertiser, A. F. Brown of San Francisco, indeed sold Colts, along with other pistols and rifles, but hardly depended on their sales for survival. Brown also offered 'fancy goods', cutlery and perfumery. A feature article in the *Mercantile* catalogue entitled 'Duels and Duelling' demonstrated a mild disdain for gun culture of any kind. Labelling traditional pistol duels 'a barbarous relic of a barbarous age', the magazine combined an attack on hoary European custom and the entry of firearms into the West. According to the *Mercantile*, a total of twenty gun-related skirmishes in the state seemed already too many. Available in newsstands, bookstores and at railroads, *Crofutt's Trans-Continental Tourist* guidebook offered valuable advice to people thinking about heading westwards. While the 1874 edition offered descriptions of the territory, and ten handy hints before leaving the East (such as 'never purchase your tickets from a stranger'), it made no mention of firearms, either for the journey or after.[22]

The potent image of a lawless West reached its apogee with the all-American cowboy. Western mythology made the cowboy synonymous with frontier violence. However, real cowboys lacked both six-guns and freedom. They lived in a less than romantic landscape, marked by the grim daily routines of herding and riding rather than fantastical Indian raids and flashes of gunfire. Rather than a gun-toting hero, David Courtwright instead forwarded 'a realistic image of the cowboy as a hired hand with a borrowed horse, a mean streak, and syphilis'. Cowboys were more involved with the trail, the stampede and hungry cattle than with frontier justice. As low-paid hired hands, they signified the lowest rung in an expansive market economy. Their livelihood rested, often insecurely, on the fortunes of entrepreneurial ranchers, their bosses (whose own success depended on good market exchange rates), competitive bank credit lines, low storehouse provision prices and the occasional political friendship. Cowboys remained under the control of others. They were locked into a national economy, and had little ammunition to change it.[23]

The familiar image of gun-toting cowboys thus sits somewhat uneasily with a more realistic, complicated and often drab frontier experience. Viewing the West through a gun barrel inevitably focused attention on themes of justice and death, but filtered out other key elements of frontierism, ignoring greater roles played by capitalism, resource extraction, home building, agriculture and schooling. The story of the gun made for an interesting and exceptional West, but left little room for peaceful expansion. Life in cattle towns never revolved around the revolver. The dramatic vision of the American West as a realm of perpetual violence rarely reflected historic incidences. Instead, it elucidated the victory of fiction over circumstance.

Deconstructing the Myth: Manufacturing the Story of the Gun in Dime Novels

On a basic level, the story of the gun heralded from a simple desire for frontier folktales. Stories of Western adventure, chivalry and revenge all became popular in the late nineteenth century and early twentieth century through the formats of Wild West shows, songs, even poetry. Robert Carr's cowboy poem 'The Gun Fight' (1908) described a 'tender, loyal, western knight', fighting for 'Woman's honor, clean and spotless'. Romance combined with nostalgia for the 'lost' frontier at the outset of a new century and a period of uncertainty. Businesses made use of the frontier as a well-loved realm. Gun manufacturers continued to exploit the interface between firearm and frontier well into the twentieth century. In 1926, Colt produced a marvellously indulgent synthesis of gun production and nineteenth-century conquest entitled *Makers of History*. The short booklet whizzed through the fur trade, Fremont, Mormons, Jim Bridger, gold and the Pony Express at breakneck speed. All and sundry favoured the Colt revolver, especially cowboys. 'Indian infested country or nearness to the Mexican border where trouble brewed, were reasons for the cowboy's Colt proclivities', the book explained. Colt situated its gun as pivotal to the rising myth of the West, 'The cr-rack of the Colt had become a part of the voice of progress westward'.[24]

Publishing entrepreneurs also homed in on the quick buck to be made from Western myth-making. The dime novel emerged as the dominant form of public literature between the 1860s and 1890s. Typically costing between 5 cents and 25 cents, dime novels (named after the original purchase price of ten cents), contained short, self-contained stories (sometimes featuring serial characters), with attractive front covers depicting action scenes, and sporting ludicrous double titles. In 1860, Irwin Beadle & Co. based in New York City introduced the format. Beadle (late Beadle and Adams) used the steam printing press, cheap paper, a standard size for all publications (at first 6.5 by 4.25 inches(15 by 11.5 cm)), and advertising posters to highlight the fortnightly and monthly volumes. Competitors such as George Munro, Frank Tousey and Street & Smith copied the process. The most popular stories involved detectives, romance, sea adventure, city-based mystery or the frontier West. Much has been made of how quickly stories were produced. Prentiss Ingraham authored over 600 stories, some at breakneck speed. The writing of dime novels compared to industrial production, with William Wallace Cook managing one whole story in twenty-four hours. He called his autobiography *The Fiction Factory*, a wonderful epithet for the dime industry as a whole. The 'fiction factory' was not the easiest place to work: writers found their skills rarely acknowledged, pay could be low and their craft derided as monetary-based. Quantity won over quality. All this suggested a standardised product that offended intellectual sensibilities. None the less, the dime novel encouraged a wide audience to engage in reading. Albeit a reprint of an article in *The Ladies Companion* magazine in 1839, the first Beadle dime, *Malaeska; the Indian Wife of the White Hunter* (1860) by Ann S. Stephens hardly stood by convention with its challenging subject and female author. Bill Brown made the point that, 'These texts, which are responsible for perpetrating, or at least perpetuating, so many stereotypes – of savage Indians, helpless maidens, and self-reliant desperadoes – have themselves routinely been reduced to a mere stereotype'.[25]

The dime novel captured a growth market in the United States for cheap, disposable fiction. Rising educational standards and literacy rates combined with a new era of mass consumption. Richard Slotkin related how, 'The potential market for cheap fiction was as large as American democracy itself'. Between 1860 and 1865, Irwin Beadle published four million dime novels. The Beadle advertising line 'Books for the Million' attested to the wide target audience and impressive sales figures. Dime novels could be purchased from news-stands or by mail order. Americans read them at home and at work, children after school. Their eminent portability suited the new age of transport, with rail travellers procuring copies of Deadwood Dick's exploits before embarking on their own adventures. Dime novels even invaded the battlefield, with Civil War soldiers taking respite from the fighting with a tall story. As Merle Curti saw it, the dime novel amounted to 'a true proletarian literature, that is, a literature written for the great masses of people and actually read by them'. The *Atlantic Monthly* declared, 'From Beadle's days onward most of the dime tales have been American . . . In reading them the American boy's soul soared and sang.' By their mass accessibility, patriotism and frontier spirit, dime novels amounted to an authentically American product.[26]

Although the appeal of the dime novel proved widespread, titles sold particularly well to the working class. Alongside P. T. Barnum shows and Coney Island, the dime novel contributed to a new age of leisure for the poor. The American middle and upper classes exhibited some concern over such displays of bawdy recreation. Taken as a ribald challenge to Victorian gentility, the dime novel offended by its sensationalism, lack of sophistication and stock roster of grotesque characters and violent plot devices. A symptom of a cultural divide between classes, it became a target of derision by the American elite. Fears grew over the glamorization of outlaws and the common depictions of murder that might inspire real-life copycats. In the late 1870s, moral crusader, biblical literalist and secretary of the New York Society for the Suppression of Vice, Anthony Comstock began a campaign against the abject evil and rife sexuality of the dime novel. Declaring 'that some of the so-called boys' papers published in this city are pregnant with mischief', Comstock targeted dime novels as a key source of juvenile crime and delinquency. The *Atlantic Monthly* presented a more informed sense of the dime novel as crime maker, imparting how 'Nearly every sort of misdemeanor into which fantastic elements enters, from train robbery to house-burning, is laid to them'. Akin to an encyclopedia of criminality, the dime novel hardly educated the masses in high-class social etiquette. Many described dime novels as simple 'blood and thunder' stories. This mass popular indulgence, coupled with an apparent lack of intellectual merit, led Edmund Pearson to describe the dime novel as a 'social phenomenon rather than a matter of artistic achievement'. The success of the dime novel showed popular culture outside the control of elite culture, and as such, a cause for concern.[27]

The dime novel proved one of the key promoters of a fictive, violent West, and helped establish the modern Western formula of cowboys and Indians. The fascination of dime novelists with Western plotlines can be explained partly by timing. The creation of the 'Dime West' perfectly aligned with the chronology of settlement. The heyday of the dime novel, between the 1860s and 1890s, corresponded with the Homestead Act (1862), the ranching era and the closing of the frontier. Authors observed these historic moments, felt themselves on the cutting edge of the frontier experience, and related to all and sundry their excitement about westward conquest. The *Atlantic Monthly* claimed that, 'The aim of the original dime novel was to give, in cheap and wholesome form, a picture of American wild life'. With the lure of mineral rushes, the creation of new states and the danger of Indian wars, 'wild life' was best found on the frontier. Drawing on newspapers, theatre, Wild West shows and casual conversation, novelists furnished generalist accounts of frontier expansion. The dime novel reflected a popular expression of a nation coming to terms with its sudden growth westwards and a new phase of history. The novelty of the West compared only with the novelty of urban industrialism. Dime novelists wrote about both with enthusiasm.[28]

However, with many writers and publishers based in the East, actual experience of Western life proved rare. As Pearson noted, 'Some of the most popular of the Wild West stories were written by authors whose nearest acquaintance with the great plains was in White Plains, New York.' Novelist Edward Wheeler travelled as far west as Illinois, but generally resided in Pennsylvania. Rather than revealing the true West, dime novels showed what the East wanted the region to be. In the process, the West became a commercial property, a 'story' to be sold, a product of a burgeoning Eastern economy. The 'frontier' was imagined, generalised, but not visited. Authenticity thus proved a sticking point. Dime novels were of little use to those hoping to comprehend a normative, functioning region of the United States. The Dime West instead relied on caricatures and symbols. The stories of Deadwood Dick related more about concepts of 'social banditry' than actual frontier experience. Bruce Allmender grouped dime novels with later pulps and Hollywood Westerns as essentially 'non-cowboy texts': 'Their works exploit cowboys as metaphors: not interested in "real" cowboys, the work that they did, or the art that they made, the books use cowboys only as symbolic springboards for diving off into discussions of wide-ranging issues, most of which have little or nothing to do with real working cowboys.' For Allmender, writing about the West entailed realism and self-representation. However, most dime stories amounted to borrowed tales. Writers drew on the work of others, taking their inspiration from fellow dime novelists or from staples of classic literature such as the *Leatherstocking* series of James Fenimore Cooper. They used work contacts and family acquaintances. Dime novel scholar Albert Johanssen saw few problems with this: 'The writers of the novels, if not themselves pioneers, were often familiar with Indian, hunter, and trapper adventures from tales told by the older men of their communities, and their stories had all the earmarks of verisimilitude.' They recycled popular understandings of the West and kept them current. The lack of originality in dime novels also reflected tight writing schedules and storyboard conventions.[29]

Novelists proved selective in their coverage of the frontier experience. The Dime West covered only very small sections of the actual West. The dime map excluded farms, prairies and schoolhouses, but it included mining towns, cattle towns and mountain passes. This selectivity was far from accidental. The dime novel existed for a reason: to offer people fantasy and escapism at a cheap price. It promised a temporary diversion from the drudgery of city work, from the horrors of conflict, from the tedium of the classroom. The formula succeeded because of its distance from the real, not because of its close resemblance to it. As an enduring reference point for escape, both historic and in literature, the American West represented an ideal tableau for fictional 'fleeing'. Corresponding with an actual push westwards by settlers, dime literature reflected and participated in a mass fairytale.

The dime novel offered a roster of western caricatures that included the Mexican bandito, the rusty old timer, the Robin Hood-type social do-gooder, the Indian warmonger and the beautiful, innocent daughter. Rarely did the cowboy feature as the hero. Instead, frontiersmen, marksmen, scouts and hunters assumed the role of the gun-toting lead. The marginal status of the cowhand countered the assumption that dime novelists fleshed out the modern cowboy image, although the relative absence of the cowpuncher folk hero can be explained partially by the timing of the dime novel genre. Early novels predated the ranching West by several years, while the romanticising of the cattle industry reached its apogee in twentieth-century Hollywood. At the time of the earliest dime novels, the term itself lacked cultural significance: 'cowboy' denoted a ruffian, thief or worker. Other trade epithets such as the cowhand, puncher and vaquero were just as common.

The gradual emergence of dime cowboys coincided with the gradual rise in range folklore throughout the late 1870s and early 1880s. Boys stories and Wild West shows, in particular the inauguration of Buffalo Bill's productions from 1883 onwards, contributed to a rising interest in cowboy life. Dime cowboy authors came to include Joseph Badger ('Laughing Leo' novels), Frederick Whittaker, Prentiss Ingraham and William Patten (responsible for 'Cowboy Chris'). Stage player Buck Taylor, the 'King of the Cowboys' (1884), had a dime novel written about him by Prentiss Ingraham in 1887. Recycling the royal title, Ingraham granted Taylor a lead role in the West. The dime character of Taylor proved especially adept with firearms. As Ingraham explained, 'It was no easy task to load that long rifle on the back of a wild horse, but Buck managed it, and turning his saddle, again sent a bullet flying toward his pursuers.' That Ingraham promoted his work as a biography far from ensured historical accuracy. As Warren French related, Ingraham 'did not attempt to present a valid picture of the West; cattle are hardly ever mentioned in his works'. Even with such boosters as Ingraham, the cowboy rarely dominated dime literature. In a sample survey of 100 *Beadle* covers between 1881–3, only two featured characters easily identifiable as cowboys. Into the 1890s, novels continued to display a lack of command over the cowhand stereotype. For example, in *Dead-Shot Ralph's Drop* (1894), a group of 'cowboy smugglers' raided the Pacific Coast, their attire 'half-sailor, half frontier dress'. Their schooner was similarly unconventional in terms of its armaments, as 'around the masts were their rifles'.[30]

Unlike cowboy folklore, gun culture permeated the dime novel. Firearms were exposed as common pieces of frontier paraphernalia. In the same survey of cover images, a total of fifteen showed revolvers drawn and eleven featured rifles (while six covers featured knives and just one an arrow). More significant than the individual title of a novel, cover illustrations of explosive weaponry captured readers attention and set the tone of each tale. Guns were essential props to scenes of dangerous Indians and fair maidens in distress.

The gun proved a capable tool for the dime novelist. On front covers and inside text, guns relayed motion (such as gunfire), suspense (gun pointing and trigger cocking), surprise (the revealing of a gun underneath a dress or behind a jacket) and death (the explosion of a shell into a chest). Each weapon could be utilised as a focal point for denouements: an agent for sudden change; a device of pain; an instrument to kill off villains; and a tool to reaffirm the skills of a hero. Dime writers commonly granted nicknames to their fictive protagonists. Several went by their gun-toting reputations, such as Pistol Tommy and Gold Trigger, men defined by their firearms. Typical events in the Dime West included saloon fights, hijacks, jailbreaks and murder. The urgent pace of each scene needed translation for the reader. As Charles Harvey revealed, 'Dime novel horses never trot or walk – they always gallop'. Similarly, guns rarely resided in locked armories – they always had a purpose. Rifles and pistols provided a crucial signifier of action, with gunfire the most common of exchanges in the Dime West. Six-guns blasted with high speed. Firearms imparted the dramaturgy of the West, its noise, speed and feel. Rifles 'cracked' with a 'blinding flash', bullets 'whistled', gunfire caused a 'rattling thunder', and 'smoke' filled the open sky. In *Dashing Diamond Dick* (1898), Tombstone was defined by its noise: the music; chatter; laughter; drunks; and, most of all, 'the report of the ever-ready revolver and the shriek of its victim'.[31]

Erstwhile dime readers were exposed to continual gunfights and serial(ised) violence. For Edmund Pearson, dime novels 'dealt in violent action; in sudden death and its terrors'. Dashing Diamond Dick's Tombstone seemed on the edge of descent into primeval savagery. The report of the revolver indicated such a fine line, the frontier edge. Guns provided a cultural motif of the lawless frontier, of an unstructured society so different from the East. Mining towns in the Dime West were rowdy, violent places, havens of criminality and full of bars where revolvers settled all the scores. The gun served as a mediator between savagery and civilisation, with heroes thrown into a (intrinsically violent) state of nature, surviving only by their trigger finger. Novelists thus situated gun culture as a reflection of instability in the West, a cultural signifier of a region in transition. Some characters struggled to adapt to this climate, as in the case of General Gleason, a character in *Little Quick-shot* (1883) desperate to cling to time-honoured, respectable customs, even in conflict. When faced with a threatening situation, Gleason declared, 'We will settle our differences by swords, as Southern gentlemen do; not with pistols, as Western desperadoes do.' Others felt very comfortable caught in the melee.[32]

Occasionally, novelists cast the gun as being in perfect synchronicity with the wild nature of the West. In *Kit Carson, Jr.* (1878), Major S. Hall described a Ranger Camp in Texas:

> A dozen campfires burned brightly, casting their brilliant, pointed rays through the brackets of the oaks, flickering through the masses of Spanish moss – rich draperies of nature's chambers. By the trunks of these trees lean rifles of every make and caliber, and hanging from the branches are saddles, bridles, lariats, horns, pouches, canteens and tin cups, with all the accoutrements of war pertaining to men and beast – each and every article ready to slip from its twig for immediate use in case of sudden alarm.

When danger appeared, both technology and nature equally came alive: 'Men upon the ground leap to their feet and run for their rifles; revolvers are drawn quickly from scabbards; horses and mules are snorting, and the guard calling one to another.' The gun seemed at home in the West, ready to defend frontier country.[33]

According to dime logic, different guns suited different character types. The old timer always carried a trusty but archaic rifle, the Eastern gentleman a new and expensive revolver, and the gusty female a couple of dainty pistols. The presence of female gun-holders challenged a sense of the Old West as a masculine domain. Popular culture theorists have suggested that a range of male signatures, including the gun, left women with 'their ostensible power . . . negated' in (representations of) the West. Mary Stange and Carol Oyster argued that the gun rested as 'the symbol par excellence of masculinity: of power, force, aggressiveness, decisiveness, deadly accuracy, cold rationality'. However, dime novels occasionally told a different story. Tales of 'Hurricane' Nell showed the buckskin outlaw heroine to be a 'deadshot' with her rifle, in one scene dispatching three foes with just three bullets. In *Old Eclipse* (1883) by T. C. Harbaugh, the hero Thunder Sam hazarded upon a group of Apache attacking a trail party. Ready to 'carry mournon to more than one cursed Apache wigwam', Thunder found himself sidetracked by a female: 'At that moment, to the rough's amazement the door of the hut flew open and, despite the scanty starlight, Thunder Sam saw the beautiful girl who appeared on the threshold with an elegant repeating rifle in her hands.' This scene depicting an armed woman was taken as both unorthodox and titillating. The combination of guns and women proved eminently attractive in dime novel lore. Thunder Sam was dazzled by the accuracy of the lady shooter, witnessing how, 'Every bullet fired by the mountain girl seemed to prove effective, for the half-naked butchers fell from their horses'. Another novel, *The Lightning Sport* (1882) described 'little Lide' decidedly 'lively on the shoot', while *Gold Trigger, the Sport* (1880), also by T. C. Harbaugh, featured a female shooter. One of the most famous dime characters, Deadwood Dick even faced a female gunslinger, Pistol Polly, in a shootout (Dick did, however, win).[34]

Dime novelists also toyed with issues of racial identity. In *Ebony Dan: Or, The Rival Leagues of Silver Circle* (1880) by Frank Dumont, two rival Colorado gangs led by Ebony Dan and Bully Bolton competed for territorial dominance. Exploiting slurs on African Americans as devilish, Dumont described Ebony Dan's gang as a 'mysterious league of black ruffians', gifted with supernatural powers that included the ability to neutralise bullets. Dumont limited the language of Ebony Dan to racially-defined terms such as 'dis' and 'dat'. Dan none the less proved capable of great heroic deeds, including the rescue of Eleanor, the stereotypical maiden in distress, from the clutches of Bolton. In a final scene, Dumont revealed the true identity of the Ebony Dan as a boot-painted white hero: 'You have been hunted like a wild beast and you have doubtless transgressed the laws, you are not as black as you have been painted.'[35]

The best shooters proved to be those closest to their guns. Dime novelists imparted a sense of seamlessness between man and tool, with the firearm cast as a near extension of the human body. In *Gold Trigger*, the hero Murell Anton boasted: 'I never miss when I handle the gold-triggered boys.' In *Ebony Dan*, the power of Bolton rested very much on keeping his firearm close at hand: 'Bolton amused himself by examining the chambers in his pistol' to overcome anxiety

'The Gun that Won the West'   81

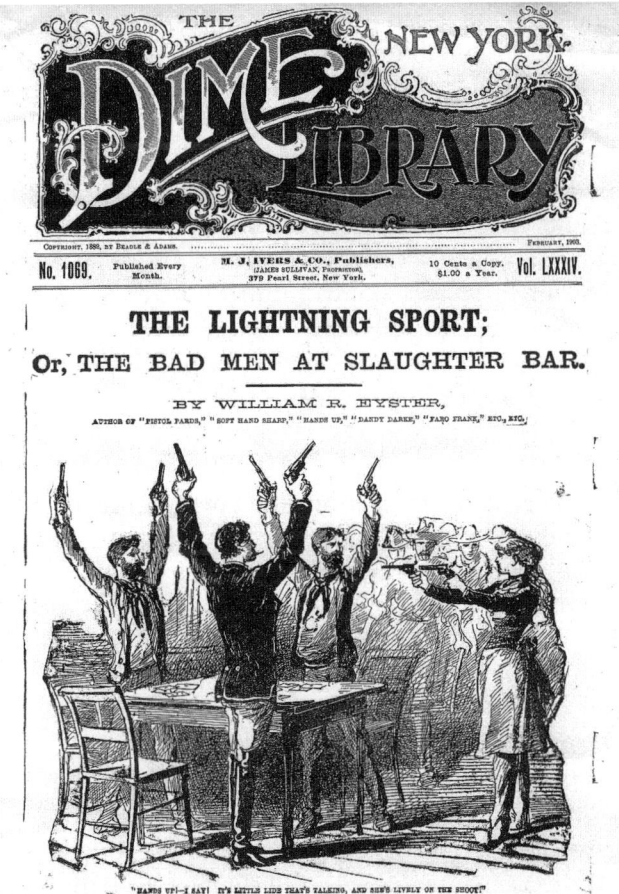

Figure 3.1 William R. Eyster, *The Lightning Sport; Or, The Bad Men at Slaughter Bar* (Beadle & Adams, 1882), front cover.

and demonstrate malice. The affinity between man and gun had few boundaries. In some stories, guns served as the best friend of the protagonist. In *Old Bull's Eye, the Lightning Shot of the Plains* (1878), the veteran shooter regularly conversed with his rifle, which he called Ebenezer. The firearm seemed to have a life of its own. In the opening scene involving a horseback ambush, Old Bull's Eye related his struggle to control his gun: 'Thar–I'm glad he's out o' range, fer I couldn't hold back old Ebenezer much longer. The bullet in its in'ards was a-kickin' like ge-mently, tryin' to git out after the reptile o' its own a'cord.' On meeting a group of Kiowa Indians, Bull's Eye again referred to the desire of the gun to come into action: 'Old Ebenezer's got the stomach-ache fearful, nor her wont be easy ontel he's knocked over one o' them rapscallions out yender.' Old Bull's Eye's compromised vernacular (which included the frequent use of 'cheese it') along with his frequent conversations with Ebenezer proved symptomatic of an old timer's quirks and eccentricities. Such personalised discourse also situated the gun as far from a neutral technology in the West. Instead, Ebenezer was granted its own volition – the rifle proving to be pivotal to the plot, as if a fictive precursor to *Winchester '73*. The gun also made the man. The accuracy of Bull's Eye rested on his long-term relationship with, or dependence on, Ebenezer. Ebenezer dictated events, Bull's Eye almost reneging on his own responsibility for killings by granting his gun chief agency and licence. The old timer passed on such duties with lines such as, 'Sock it to 'im, old Ebenezer! 'F ye miss him now I'll never fergive ye!' This allowed Old Bull's Eye to be a colder, more technical and rational killer (in one scene he dispatched a group of riders due to his 'coolly leveled' rifle winning against their horses dashing 'madly' across the range). However, Old Bull's Eye also recognised the essential truth of such occasions – that the technology itself had a purpose to kill and maim. As he rightly imparted, Ebenezer 'holds death in its chamber'.[36]

Heroism often rested on legendary gun skills in the Dime West. In *The Pilgrim Sharp; or the Soldier's Sweetheart: A True Story of the Overland Trail* (1888), author William F. Cody, aka Buffalo Bill, cast the gun as the crucial agent in making a Western hero. Deadly pistol skills suggested a man not to be messed with. The cover image depicted a number of firearms drawn, with Pilgrim Sharp warning, 'Say, strangers, I drives this huss and its dead folks through on this trail, or I'll make a graveyard right here.' Dime novelists also made 'real' heroes. Richard Aquila claimed that Ned Buntline and, with greater consistency, Prentiss Ingraham manufactured Buffalo Bill himself into the perfect 'imperialist frontier hero' by their work. Dime novelists exaggerated and romanticised Western notables, turning them into national folk heroes. Kit Carson became the 'Crack Shot of the West' on the cover of a magazine.[37]

Dime novelists rarely supplied information on the guns themselves. Arguably this reflected the lack of the descriptive throughout the format, but it also showed the gun as an instrument of good or bad, the same for both sides, and thus a fundamentally democratising agent. On one level, it might be argued that firearms were so widespread in the United States so as not to require elaboration. However, individual writers frequently glamorised gun culture. Firearms acted as prominent status symbols in the Dime West. Dead Shot Dandy and 'ranger, hunter, and Indian-fighter' Cimarron Jack were both presented as attractive dime characters, the former noteworthy for carrying gold revolvers and his penchant for shooting cigars from teeth, the latter a rifle expert and self-professed 'cock of the walk'. The buckskin hunter 'Gold Rifle, the Sharpshooter' carried with him a 'gold-plated Remington repeating rifle', that he brandished with skill, 'in a moment he had sighted it, fired, and somersaulted back upon his feet'. Dime novels defined the cultural identity of the gun as a status piece. They furnished an elaborate fiction about tools without the need ever to offer exquisite detail.[38]

One of the lasting impacts of the dime novel lay in its capturing and promoting a mass vision of the nineteenth-century West, broadcasting a coded mythology of the frontier for mainstream America to absorb. J. C. Dykes suggested that a range of Texas-based dime novels were responsible for forging an identity for the southwestern state in popular culture. Ingredients for this 'Dime novel Texas' included Mexicans, Indians, rangers, cattle, wagon attacks, ransoms, wars and hunts. Equally, the huge sales of dime novels ensured that the gun-toting frontiersman retained a wide audience. Dimes enshrined the West as the story of the gun. Generic tales of good versus evil, of romance and speed, set the template for future Western fictions of similar simplicity (and duplicity). Pulps later recycled the same stories and appealed to the same audience, with Western writers obediently following 'dime-like' formulas. As Bill Brown contended, 'the popularity of the dime version of the West – the shootin' and the stabbin' – has sustained countless films, radio programs, TV shows, and computer games, to the point of making the Western the quintessential American genre.' The dime novel may have died by the 1900s, but pulps, magazines, Hollywood and television kept the vision alive.[39]

On the success of *The Virginian* (1902), the Wild West novel by Owen Wister, David Davis claimed that, 'Wister had, in fact, liberated the cowboy hero from the Dime novels and provided a synthetic tradition suitable for a new century'. However, the contribution of the dime novel to the cult of the gun-toting cowboy has been exaggerated. If 'cowboy' is read liberally as a collective label for all 'frontier westerners', then dime novelists did, indeed, promote the cowboy brand. But taken more literally, it can be seen that the Dime West never had a cowboy at its core. Instead, he was one of many heroes of the fictive West. Dime novels promoted the region as a violent realm occupied by all manner of characters; many of whom brandished firearms. The gun took centre stage in the Dime West, but rarely was there a cowboy's hand on it. This powerful alliance came later. With the 'reel' West and Hollywood, the myth of the cowboy became more singular and more refined. Cowboys showed up on Hollywood film sets having just put on clean boots and fresh clothes, ready for 'action'.[40]

Notes

1. 'Just perfect': *Winchester '73* (Universal, 1950); Bosley Crowther, 'Winchester '73', *The New York Times Film Reviews*, 8 June 1950, 38:2. See also the *Variety* review, 7 June 1950.
2. Will Wright, *The Wild West: The Mythical Cowboy and Social Theory* (London: Sage, 2001), p. 7; Abigail Kohn, *Shooters: Myths and Realities of America's Gun Cultures* (Oxford: Oxford University Press, 2004), p. 39.
3. William MacLeod Raine, *45-Caliber Law: The Way of the Frontier Peace Officer* (Evanston: Row, Peterson, 1941), p. 16.
4. Richard Hofstadter and Michael Wallace, *American Violence: A Documentary History* (New York: Vintage, 1971), p. 12.
5. W. Eugene Hollon, *Frontier Violence: Another Look* (New York: Oxford University Press, 1974), p. vii.
6. Michael Bellesiles, *Arming America: The Origins of a National Gun Culture* (Brooklyn: Soft Skull, 2003 [2000]), pp. 5–8, 432.
7. Albert Klyberg and Nathaniel Shipton, *Frontier Pages and Pistols: A Guide to an Exhibition in the William L. Clements Library* (Ann Arbor: University of Michigan Press, 1966), p. 5.
8. Frances Victor, *Eleven Years in the Rocky Mountains and Life on the Frontier* (Hartford: Columbia Book Co., 1879), p. 30; Chas Youngblood, *Adventures of Chas L. Youngblood during Ten Years on the Plains* (Boonville, 1882), pp. 24–5, 198.
9. 'Walking arsenals': Alexander Deconde, *Gun Violence in America: The Struggle for Control* (Boston: Northeastern University Press, 2003), p. 81; Philip Bekeart, *Three Generations, 1837–1949* (Oakland: Westgate, 1949); N. Curry & Bro., San Francisco, Price List (1884) [Huntington].
10. Roger McGrath, *Gunfights, Highwaymen & Vigilantes: Violence on the Frontier* (Berkeley: University of California Press, 1987), p. 184, 87.
11. 'Cimarron' Beach, quoted in Norman Wiltsey, 'Smith & Wesson 3', *True West* (August 1964), p. 13.
12. *Colt on the Trail* (Hartford, Colt, 1936), p. 29.
13. Colt, *Makers of History* (Fromer, 1926), p. 8; Richard Maxwell Brown, *Strain of Violence: Historical Studies of American Violence and Vigilantism* (New York: Oxford University Press, 1975), p. 110.
14. Codes: See Peter Squires, *Gun Culture or Gun Control* (London: Routledge, 2000), p. 37 and Brown (1975).
15. Olga Roat, 'Nimrod from Ireland', *Great Falls Tribune*, 22 September 1957; LA Gun Club: see Matfield Family Collection Box 3 (folder 4) and Box 2 (folder 8) 'Second Semi-Annual Tournament of the LA City Gun Club' programme (March 1900) [Huntington].

'The Gun that Won the West' 85

16. William Fowler, *Woman on the American Frontier: A Valuable and Authentic History* (Hartford: S. S. Scranton, 1880), p. 79.
17. David Kopel, *Samurai, the Mountie and the Cowboy: Should America Adopt the Gun Controls of Other Democracies?* (Amherst: Prometheus, 1992), p. 382; C. C. Post, *Ten Years a Cowboy* (Chicago: Rhodes & McClure, 1898), p. 72.
18. Victor (1879), pp. 54–5.
19. *Evening Star*, 1 January 1878, see also: Odie B. Faulk, *Dodge City: The Most Western Town of All* (New York: Oxford University Press, 1977); Rob Wright, *Dodge City: The Cowboy Capital* (1913), pp. 148–9.
20. Robert Dykstra and Jo Ann Manfra, 'Contesting Boot Hill: the saga of metaphorical Dodge City', in Liza Nicholas, Elaine Bapis and Thomas Harvey (eds), *Imagining the Big Open: Nature, Identity, and Play in the New West* (Salt Lake City: University of Utah Press, 2003), p. 227; Robert Dykstra, *The Cattle Towns* (New York: Atheneum, 1976), p. 5.
21. William Hosley, *Colt: The Making of an American Legend* (Amherst: University of Massachusetts Press, 1996), pp. 54, 55, 64.
22. David Gazlay (ed.), *The California Mercantile Journal*, vol. 1 (San Francisco: George Elliot, 1860); *Crofutt's Trans-Continental Tourist*, 6 (New York: Crofutt,1874) [Huntington].
23. David Courtwright, *Violent Land: Single Men and Social Disorder from the Frontier to the Inner City* (Cambridge, MA: Harvard University Press, 1996), p. 88.
24. Robert Carr, *Cowboy Lyrics* (Chicago: W. B. Conkey,1908); Colt (1926), pp. 14, 6.
25. Bill Brown (ed.), *Reading the West: An Anthology of Dime Westerns* (Boston: Bedford Books, 1997), p. v.
26. Richard Slotkin, *Gunfighter Nation: The Myth of the Frontier in Twentieth Century America* (New York: Atheneum, 1992), p. 126; Merle Curti (1937) quoted in: Michael Denning, *Mechanic Accents: Dime Novel Accents and Working-Class Culture in America* (London: Verso, 1987), p. 2; Charles Harvey, 'The Dime novel in American life', *Atlantic Monthly* 100 (1907), p. 45.
27. Mark West, 'The role of sexual repression in Anthony Comstock's campaign to censor children's dime novels', *Journal of American Culture* (Winter 1999), pp. 45–9; Harvey (1907), p. 37; Edmund Pearson, *Dime Novels: Or, Following an Old Trail in Popular Literature* (Boston: Little, Brown, 1929), p. 9
28. Harvey (1907), p. 42.
29. Pearson (1929), p. 44; Blake Allmendinger, *The Cowboy: Representations of Labor in an American Work Culture* (New York: Oxford University Press, 1993), p. 12; Albert Johanssen, *The House of Beadle and Adams and its Dime and Nickel Novels: The Story of a Vanished Literature*, vol. 1 (Norman: University of Oklahoma Press, 1950), p. 4.
30. Warren French, 'The cowboy in the dime novel', 30 *Texas Studies in English* (1951), pp. 231, 229; survey of 100 consecutive 1/2 dime novels by Beadle and Adams, June 1881–April 1883, held by the Huntington Library; Prentiss Ingraham, *Dead-Shot Ralph's Drop, or, The Cowboy Smuggler Smash-Up*, 867 (New York: Beadle & Adams, 6 March 1894).
31. Of course, other names with little to do with firearms also proved commonplace, for example, when the popular dime character of Deadwood Dick, social bandit,

meets 'Bug Juice Bob'. See Edward Wheeler, *Deadwood Dick in Dead City*, 16/405 (New York: Beadle & Adams, 28 April 1885), p. 4; Harvey (1907), p. 41; W. B. Lawson, *Dashing Diamond Dick or The Tigers of Tombstone*, 104 (New York: Street & Smith, 8 October, 1898).

32. Pearson (1929), p. 8; Edward Wheeler, *Little Quick-Shot, the Scarlet Scout; or, The Dead Face of Daggersville*, 13/330 (New York: Beadle & Adams, 20 November 1883).

33. Major S. Hall, *Kit Carson, Jr., the Crack Shot of the West*, 1/3 (New York: Beadle & Adams, 1878). It also emerged as a tool of recreation and sportsmanship, a source of competition between men, as in the case of the opening scene of *Winchester '73*.

34. Richard Aquila, *Wanted Dead or Alive: The American West in Popular Culture* (Urbana: University of Illinois Press, 1998), p. 28; Mary Stange and Carol Oyster, *Gun Women: Firearms and Feminism in Contemporary America* (New York: New York University Press, 2000), p. 22; Nell: Edward Wheeler, *Bob Woolf, the Border Ruffian; or the Girl Dead-Shot*, 2/32 (New York: Beadle & Adams, 1878); T. C. Harbaugh, *Old Eclipse, Trump Card of Arizona, or Little Snap Shot's Horse Hunt*, 316 (New York: Beadle & Adams, 14 August 1883); William R. Eyster, *The Lightning Sport; Or, The Bad Men at Slaughter Bar*, 84/1069 (New York: M. J. Ivers [reprint of Beadle & Adams], February 1903 [1882]); T. C. Harbaugh, *Gold Trigger, the Sport; or, The Girl Avenger*, 6/155 (New York: Beadle & Adams, 13 July 1880); Edward Wheeler, *Deadwood Dick, Jr's Dead-Sure Game; or Pistol Polly of Nuggetsville*, 35/891 (New York: Beadle & Adams, 21 August 1894), p. 13.

35. Frank Dumont, *Ebony Dan: or, The Rival Leagues of Silver Circle*, 7/171 (New York: Beadle & Adams, 2 November 1880).

36. Harbaugh (1880); Dumont (1880); Joseph Badger, *Old Bull's-Eye, The Lightning Shot of the Plains*, 131/1043 (New York: M. J. Ivers [reprint of Beadle & Adams], December 1900 [1878]).

37. Buffalo Bill, *The Pilgrim Sharp; or, The Soldier's Sweetheart: A True Story of the Overland Trail*, 19/243 (New York: Beadle & Adams, 20 June 1888); Aquila (1998), p. 25.

38. Frederick Dewey, *Cimarron Jack, the King Pin of Rifle-Shots, or the Phantom Tracker*, 13/313 (New York: Beadle & Adams, 24 July 1883); Edward Wheeler, *Gold Rifle, The Sharpshooter*, 3/69 (New York: Beadle & Adams, 1878).

39. J. C. Dykes, 'Dime novel Texas; or, the sub-literature of the Lone Star State', *Southwestern Historical Quarterly*, 49/3 online edition, p. 6; Brown (1997), p. 6.

40. David Davis, 'Ten-gallon hero', *American Quarterly*, 6/2 (Summer 1954), p. 115.

Chapter 4

Cowboy Presidents and the Political Branding of the American West

On 17 September 2001, President George W. Bush fielded questions at the Pentagon relating to the terrorist attacks of 9/11. Asked whether he wanted Osama Bin Laden dead, Bush responded: 'I want justice. There's an old poster out West, as I recall, that said, "Wanted: Dead or Alive".' Such choice of words drew criticism from his wife Laura, who felt the statement made her husband sound more like a hot-headed cowboy than an elder statesman: 'Bushie, you gonna git 'im?' she reputedly whispered in his ear. Marital admonishments aside, Bush's rhetorical flourish suggested an enduring role for the Old West in political vernacular. Far from a hoary mythology, rendered disdainful and embarrassing by revisionist critiques, the traditional West of showdowns, shoot-outs and tough-talking lawmen seemed alive and well more than 100 years after the closure of the frontier.[1]

In the same speech, Bush fleshed out his role for the twenty-first century. He pledged to commit the resources of the government to track down the 'evil-doers', to 'smoke 'em out of their holes' and hold them to account. The 'terrorists who have no borders' were caught in a heady folklore of frontierism in which Bush, as the upstanding sheriff, promised retribution. Redemption would be secured, in true Western style, by frontier justice and recourse to violence. Indeed, while some criticised Bush's bellicose parlance, many among the American public took solace from situating the uncertain and complex world of terrorism into the predictable mould of traditional Western mythology. After all, Bush's Texas lawman pose bespoke familiar codes with which anyone who watched Western movies or played 'Tin Can Alley' with their toy Winchester could identify. The sheriff with the white Stetson always prevailed over black-hatted outlaws and feather-dressed Indians. The American West – a landscape resonant with national pride and emblematic of a teleological and exceptional destiny – was used by Bush as a metaphorical call to arms (wrapped in a comforting (saddle) blanket).

Bush's portrayal of a cowboy hero backed by a superpower six-gun mystique was hardly revolutionary. From Buffalo Bill Cody's shows to *The Assassination of Jesse James By the Coward Robert Ford* (2007) – not to mention several thousand movies, comics and pulp novels in between – the cowboy swaggered tall as a totemic character of national folklore. Brave, self-reliant and exuding machismo from every rugged pore, he personified the all-conquering American hero. According to the 'cowboy code' of 1930's singing-cowboy star Gene Autry, the cowpuncher upheld a patriotic and moral stance, kept his word, told the truth, behaved with respect and never shot first. Here stood an ideal champion, an Arthurian knight on horseback riding in with rites of honour and all guns blazing to save innocents from danger. This motif acquired considerable purchase in the twentieth-century marketplace as a signifier for masculine power complete with its own 'portable western atmosphere'. In the early 1910s, cartons of dried fruit depicted range hands roping steers, while later in the century, cowboys could be found roaming across the plains in 'Marlboro Country' attired in Wrangler or Levi jeans, and smelling of Ralph Lauren cologne. The cowboy brand transported its fans to a past age where freedom, rugged individualism and the lure of the frontier prevailed. As the tag line for 'Chaps' aftershave expounded: 'The West . . . Its an image of men who are real and proud. Of freedom and independence we all would like to feel . . . Chaps, it's the West. The West you would like to feel inside of yourself.'[2]

The winning formula that sold prunes could also sell presidents. In the waning years of the nineteenth century, Theodore Roosevelt deployed the myth of the West to his advantage as a self-styled 'cowboy soldier'. With the image of the cowpuncher hero firmly cemented by Hollywood, Ronald Reagan utilised his screen persona as an everyman of the range to win two presidential terms in the 1980s. A century on from cowboy Teddy, the same iconography became part of the presidential patina of George W. Bush. On one level, the fashioning of the cowboy into a political icon spoke of the broader saliency of the frontier fictive. As Richard Slotkin noted, the ideological potency of the mythic West serviced national unity as well as 'explaining and justifying the use of political power'. Kennedy's vocalisations of a 'new frontier' in his acceptance of the Democratic presidential nomination in 1960 elucidated his power to conjoin an inspirational past with an aspirational future. Moreover, the cowboy brand proved an appealing, secure and entirely marketable commodity well suited to the mantle of the commander-in-chief. A man of action and a home-grown luminary (an amalgam of idealised masculinity in the folk hero tradition) the cowpuncher tendered potent political capital. John Wayne, the ultimate cowboy, was encouraged to run for political office in the 1960s, and in 1979 received a Congressional Gold Medal for his celluloid renditions of American grit and valour. As Glenna Finney, tour guide at the John Wayne Birthplace Museum in Winterset, Iowa, proudly asserted: 'There's nothing so wrong with America that John Wayne couldn't fix if he was president.'[3]

The escapades of the cowboy president during the twentieth century illustrated an important disparity between the temporal specificity of the imagined West and a region party to widespread transformations since the 1890s. In its mythological guise, the West of the cowboy brand spoke of a place frozen in time, an imaginary realm doomed forever to replay well-worn tropes of pioneer action and gunplay, chronologically situated sometime between the Civil War and the Battle of Wounded Knee. However, as a geographical space, the twentieth-century West witnessed seismic changes (both literally and figuratively) that irrevocably altered its economic, demographic, environmental and political landscapes. Rural areas experienced a 'boom and bust' succession that pitted the revolutionising impulses of agri-business, federal subsidy and irrigation techniques against Dust Bowl storms, falling market prices, credit repayments and misplaced agrarian dreams. The population of the rural West fell from 785,000 in 1940 to 172,000 in 1990 – a demographic shift so significant that it effectively re-opened the frontier in some districts. Set against this story of a desert neither blooming nor booming, stood the rise of a metropolitan West marked by service industries and unbridled suburbanisation. *Time* magazine touted Los Angeles as 'the new Ellis Island' – a moniker which signalled a buoyant Latino demographic as well as pointing southwards towards a new frontier that rivalled Frederick Jackson Turner's occidental model. Where the West sent sixty congressmen to Washington, DC in 1900, by 1980 it dispatched 127. The region boasted a wide spectrum of political interests – red, blue, green, psychedelic and Technicolor – and served as home base for a wide range of causes – the Montana Freemen, the Diggers of San Francisco, the Mormons, Cesar Chavez's United Farmworkers Union and Earth First! Seattle sported a statue of Lenin (one of the few remaining upright in the world), Camp Verde Arizona favoured one of Kokopelli, the Navajo Indian God of Wealth and Fertility, while Butte,

Montana chose to memorialise in bronze a shaggy dog called 'Auditor' who lived at the Berkeley mine superfund site. Underneath this variegated ideological and cultural patchwork, however, lay broader congruities. Citizen concern with accountability and democracy (in the guises of populism, progressivism and the militia movement), dependence on outside capital, continuing wrangles over resources and, of course, the looming presence of the federal government, colourfully dubbed by historian Richard White as like a 'scratchy wool shirt in winter' – necessary but darn itchy – all marked the twentieth-century West. The cowboy president, then, faced a task as thorny as the cacti on his western White House spread: how to keep alive the mythology of the frontier while convincing modern interest groups that their voices were being heard. In other words, speaking up for the cowboy as well as playing one.[4]

Theodore Roosevelt and the Invention of the Cowboy President

Born in 1858 to a well-established Dutch family that presided over a successful banking empire in New York, Theodore Roosevelt experienced an elite Eastern upbringing. As a child he struggled with asthma and poor eyesight, but two and a half hours a day boxing at Harvard convinced him that the 'strenuous life' represented a veritable tonic to his sickly constitution. Roosevelt left Columbia Law School in 1881 to enter the New York State Assembly on a Republican ticket, where he gained a reputation as an activist legislator and anti-corruption campaigner. Inspired by visions of the American West as a paradise of agrarian adventure (and keen to bag a trophy before the bison disappeared), Roosevelt journeyed to the Dakotas on a hunting expedition in September 1883. As he confessed to his sister, this trip represented the realisation of a childhood fantasy, the chance to perform as 'frontier hunter in good earnest'. The spree also excited in Teddy an impulse to play absentee rancher, and he, along with two friends purchased the Maltese Ranch and the Hawley and Wadsworth brand for $14,000. Founded in 1882 (the year in which the beef bonanza finally reached north-west Dakota), the cattle-raising outfit was the first ranch of any size in the region.[5]

Teddy planned to visit the ranch intermittently, but the tragic death of his wife and his mother on Valentine's Day 1884 saw his plans change radically. Eschewing politics and erstwhile associations, Roosevelt relocated to the West for solace and reflection. For him, the journey was a direct response to dramatic changes in personal circumstance, filtered through a sense of the region as geographically and expressively distinct. The landscape of Dakota – its starkness, harshness and raw appeal – ably matched Roosevelt's search for isolation. As he remarked:

> Nowhere does a man feel more lonely than when riding over the far-reaching, seemingly never-ending plains; and after a man has lived a little while on or near them, their very vastness and loneliness and their melancholy monotony have a strong fascination for him . . . nowhere else does one seem so far off from all mankind.

The excursion afforded an escape from the East and its connotations, both painful and prosaic, and serviced cognitive reflections on individual purpose and identity. As Roosevelt wrote to his friend Henry Cabot Lodge, 'The Statesman (?) of the past has been merged, I fear for good, into the cowboy of the present.'[6]

Based at his ranch, Roosevelt swiftly decided to don the garb of an authentic frontiersman. Out went the pressed jacket and tie, which inspired such descriptions of Teddy as a 'pale, slim young man with a thin piping voice and a general look of dyspepsia about him . . . the typical New York dude', and in came a suit of fringed buckskin. Irish rancher Lincoln Lang recalled riding twenty-five miles with Roosevelt to nearby Maddox to collect his new outfit. Teddy glowed with pride at his new gear, hailing it:

> the most picturesque and distinctively national dress ever worn in America. Daniel Boone was clad when he first passed through the trackless forest of the Alleghenies and penetrated into the heart of Kentucky . . . the dress worn by grim old Davy Crockett when he fell at the Alamo.

When Roosevelt travelled back East a year later he modelled the buckskin ensemble, complete with dagger and rifle, timberline diorama and steely-eyed huntsman stare in a New York photographic studio. Such a performance proved edifying; first, in assuming that a bona fide rancher required a particular 'look', and, secondly, in judging a rawhide tunic to be the best fit. In reality, Roosevelt's captivations with the buckskin aesthetic spoke more of the pioneer hero of Eastern literature than the actual apparel of the Western cowpoke. Locals in Dakota certainly poked fun at the greenhorn rancher and his fanciful eccentricities. As the *Badlands Cowboy* newspaper gleefully reported, 'Mr Roosevelt is still at Ferris and Merrifield's ranch, hunting and playing cowboy. It seems to be more congenial than reforming New York state politics.'[7]

During Christmas 1885, a plains photographer snapped Theodore Roosevelt fresh from a bighorn sheep hunt. The image of a tanned, confident cowboy wearing a broad-brimmed hat, spurs, cowhide boots and chaps (Teddy dutifully removed his glasses) attested to Roosevelt's metamorphosis from effete Easterner playing the fantasy of the wilderness frontiersman to a genuine rider of the range. The man dubbed 'our own Oscar Wilde' by New York legislators was converted into a self-assured, fully-fledged Westerner courtesy of the regenerative forces of the frontier. As Roosevelt commented to sister Bamie, 'I now look like a regular cowboy dandy.' Although his ranch holdings were modest – some 5,000 head of cattle compared with the 40,000–60,000 that contemporaries sported – Teddy learned the ropes of the working cowboy, and earned his spurs within the ranching community. Along with serious saddle time at the round-up, sharp-shooting skills, skilful horsemanship and a tenacity of purpose he convinced the cattle folk of Dakota that he deserved the cowboy brand. The *Pittsburgh Dispatch* keenly noted the change in Teddy's disposition – the West having put an extra 30 lb (13.6 kilos) on him and giving him a voice 'hearty and strong enough to drive oxen'. Meanwhile, Roosevelt firmly embedded himself in local politics by assisting in the creation of the Little Missouri River Stockmen's Association (1884), an outfit that facilitated co-operation between cattlemen on salient issues (disease, rustling, predatory animals, Indian attacks) as well as despatching 'justice' in an area lacking law enforcement. The *Badlands Cowboy* proved a hearty advocate of Roosevelt's leadership style: 'Under his administration, everything moves quickly forward and there is none of that time-consuming fruitless talk that so invariably characterises a deliberative assembly without a good presiding officer.' Outside the meeting hall, Roosevelt garnered a similar reputation as a sponsor of 'big stick' wielding frontier fair-dealing. In April 1885, Teddy floored a man shooting off his guns and his mouth in a Mingusville saloon. A year later, desperado Mike Finnegan and his gang stole Roosevelt's boat. He responded by tracking them downstream, pulling a gun on the assembled posse, and marching them fifty miles to the sheriff's office in Dickenson. Deputy Teddy kept alert during his round-the-clock guard by reading Tolstoy and a Jesse James dime novel confiscated from one of the outlaws. Such a display of rugged individualism confirmed Roosevelt's credentials as an accomplished outdoorsman and his adherence to a distinctly western code of personal redress. As he vociferated:

> In any wild country where the power of law is little felt or heeded, and where every one has to rely on himself for protection, men soon get to feel that it is the highest degree unwise to submit to any wrong without making an immediate and resolute effort to avenge it upon the wrong-doers.

Teddy later recounted his exploits for *Century* magazine, complete with staged photographs of the arrest of Finnegan and his crew.[8]

In common with many ranchers, Roosevelt's cattle-raising outfit suffered significant losses during the winter of 1886–7. Extreme weather coupled with overstocking of the range left 75 per cent of Dakota herds dead. Accordingly, Teddy hung up his spurs and headed back to New York. However, this proved to be far from the end of his cowboy adventure. Instead, Roosevelt emerged as a keen promoter of the cowboy as an up-and-coming folk-hero. As Owen Wister pertinently noted, Teddy Roosevelt represented 'the pioneer in taking the cowboy seriously'. During his three-year stint in the Dakotas, Roosevelt had loaded cattle onto railcars bound for the hungry cities of the industrial East – now he broadcast the myth of the frontier to an equally ravenous public imagination. Tall tales of pioneer adventure sat alongside beef stew as hearty Western exports. On the lecture circuit, audiences betrayed a keen appetite for a cult of the West trading in paradigms of wildness, the strenuous life, agrarian simplicity and codified violence. As the *Bismarck Daily Tribune* reported: 'Since Theodore Roosevelt gave his lectures on ranch life, he has received about 100 applications for places on his ranch . . . the evident desire of each one was for an opportunity to lead an easy and carefree life away from the hard work of the city.' Meanwhile, in a digest of books and articles on the West including *Hunting Trips of a Ranchman* (1885), *Ranch Life and the Hunting Trail* (1888), *The Wilderness Hunter* (1893) and the multi-volume *Winning of the West* (1889–96), Roosevelt projected the region as a theatre of boisterous action, 'iron desolation' and 'bold, restless freedom'.[9]

In Roosevelt's narrative of sanctification, the realities of life on the cattle trail, as well as the ethnic composition of the cow-puncher himself, experienced wholesale reinvention. The grimy tedium of the trail, meagre wages, feeble rations and the Hispanics and

African-Americans who comprised one third of all range riders, failed to gain report in Teddy's frontier fictive. Where Joseph McCoy's *Sketches of the Cattle Trail* (1874) presented the cowboy as living 'a soulless, aimless life, dependent upon the turn of a card for a living; blear-eyed and dissipated', Roosevelt instead framed him as 'Brave, hospitable, hardy and adventurous, he is the grim pioneer of our race'. In Teddy's triumphal elegy to the winning of the West, the cowboy stood tall as a virile, Anglo-Saxon superman facing off against a wild frontier populated by savage Indians, rapacious wolves and dastardly outlaws. As *The Wilderness Hunter* articulated, 'In that land we led a free and hardy life . . . We knew toil and hardship and hunger and thirst; and we saw men die violent deaths as they worked among the horses and cattle, or fought evil feuds with one another.'[10]

Of course, Roosevelt did not effect the transformation of the cowboy single-handedly. Frederic Remington, who aptly provided the illustrations for *Ranch Life and the Hunting Trail*, advanced the cult of the cowboy hero in canvases and sculptures. In 1894, Winchester produced a limited edition rifle complete with commemorative plaque and complementary version of *Ranch Life and the Hunting Trail*. Linkage between the cowboy and the lore of the gun proved hard to dislodge. Complicit too in this process of myth-making and frontier fancy were Owen Wister, who dedicated *The Virginian* (1902) to Teddy, Prentiss Ingraham, author of the dime novel 'Buck Taylor: King of the Cowboys' (1887) and William F. Cody, whose Wild West show combined popular interest in the histrionics of frontier closure with the rise of the rodeo as a tourist attraction.[11]

The cowboy mystique which Teddy helped create also serviced his political aspirations. *Forum* magazine praised *The Winning of the West* for highlighting the 'heroic and noble deeds' of the pioneers and celebrated Roosevelt as 'a man and an American'. Regarded as an authentic speaker for the West, Teddy thus found himself graced with the attributes of his cowboy hero: a rugged man of action, self-reliant and reliable, a personification of Wister's *Virginian*. As rancher Lincoln Lang surmised: 'Had T. R. never been of the frontier – never known the Bad lands of the earlier days – the author does not think he would have been just the man he was.' Meanwhile, the cowboy brand readily adapted to the landscape of New York political culture, and emerged as central to Roosevelt's campaign persona. A cartoon during the gubernatorial campaign of 1886 depicted cowboy Teddy trying to lasso a runaway train called democracy. Cartoonist Thomas Nast portrayed him as a cowpoke on a bucking steer named 'civil service reform' before the cabin of 'Uncle Sam's ranch', while *Puck* had him riding the bucking bronco of the Republican Party with pistols blazing against 'wild talk'. Such images of a tough-talking cowboy mixing up the establishment ably suited Roosevelt's reformist, anti-corruption attitude and duty to serve.[12]

Further development of the 'cowboy-soldier' motif came courtesy of the Spanish–American War (1898). Within the broader contexts of manifest destiny, anxiety at the closure of the frontier and the flexing of American power, the conflict in the Caribbean betrayed remarkable resonances with narratives of westward conquest. Moreover, in the creation of the Rough Riders – a volunteer cavalry regiment comprised of expert horsemen, sharp shooters and all-round survivalists from New Mexico, Arizona, Oklahoma and Indian territories – the iconic cowboy looked set for a foreign frontier adventure. Boasting the motto 'Rough, tough, we're the stuff, we want to fight and we can't get enough', troops mustered for training at San Antonio, before navigating parades and cheering crowds en route to shipping out. Heading up the posse of Rough Riders was none other than Theodore Roosevelt, Undersecretary of the Navy, architect of the corps and cowboy-soldier incarnate. Before leaving for Cuba, Lieutenant Colonel Roosevelt posed for a photograph in full regalia, sporting broad brimmed hat, necktie and riding boots. The fact that Roosevelt had already gained his spurs in Dakota counted in his favour. As the *Daily Oklahoma State Capital* blustered: 'Secretary of Navy Roosevelt was himself a cowboy early in his life and is willing to take desperate chances. He does not know the meaning of fear.'[13]

Immortalised in picture by Frederic Remington and celebrated in word by embedded journalist Richard Harding Davis, the charge up San Juan Hill became the enduring image of the Rough Riders' escapades in Cuba. In Remington's canvas, the posse of all-American (and all White) cavalrymen raced up the hill for death or glory, led by a pistol-wielding Roosevelt on a galloping charger. In reality, the Rough Riders crawled up Kettle Hill (San Juan had already been captured) on their stomachs, African-American soldiers were part of their contingent, and ninety men lost their lives taking the position. As the newspaper editor famously said in the concluding scene of John Ford's *The Man Who Shot Liberty Valance* (1962), 'When the legend becomes fact, print the legend.' The American public wanted their Rough Riders as they wanted their cowboys – prodigious, plucky and triumphant. For the *Santa Fe New Mexican*, the corps appeared as exemplars of patriotism and steadfastness: 'America possesses a class

Figure 4.1 'The Charge of San Juan Hill: Wm. H. West Impersonating Col. Roosevelt, Leading the Famous "Rough Riders" to Victory, 1899.'

of men who, when . . . brought face to face with the enemy, never quit fighting until victory or death comes.' William F. Cody's West-themed show, always a functional barometer of popular tastes, ditched 'Custer's Last Stand' as the finale set piece for the 1899–1900 season in favour of re-enacting the charge up San Juan Hill. The show featured fourteen veterans of the Cuban campaign, and lionised Roosevelt as the ultimate cowboy hero abroad.

> Roosevelt of the Rough Riders, on horseback, presses to the foot of the death-swept hill and calling upon the men to follow him, rides straight up and at the fortressed foe. There is a frantic yell of admiration and approval as the soldiers – white, red and black – spring from their cowering positions of utter helplessness and follow him and the flag

thundered Cody's press release. Meanwhile, when the Rough Riders demobilised in September 1898, they presented a bronze statue, 'the bronco buster' (made by Remington) to their commanding officer, while Captain C. J. Stephens lobbied for Roosevelt to receive the Congressional Medal of Honor for his battle performance.[14]

With the mantle of the cowboy and the Rough Rider, Roosevelt gained the governorship of New York in autumn 1898. During the political campaign, Buffalo Bill spoke out for his friend and fellow conjurer of the Western brand by stating: 'They don't make any better men than Teddy Roosevelt'. Teddy also manufactured political capital by deploying veterans from the Rough Riders to ride point on his civic tours, the cowboy-soldier escorts introducing their commander with a bugle call and charge. Leaving for Dakota, Roosevelt wrote to Henry Cabot Lodge of exchanging his politician's hat for a cowpoke's Stetson – now the two seemed blissfully conjoined. Teddy successfully applied the cowpuncher motif to further his political career by projecting himself as a Western knight parading a strident masculinity and affectation for frontier justice. The crafting of a mythic cowboy (undertaken in no small part by Roosevelt himself) proved to be critical to this success, as did popular fascination surrounding the closure of the frontier. Even the Winchester gun company benefited from the cult of cowboy Teddy. Sales of the famous rifle boomed after Roosevelt confessed it to be his weapon of choice during the Spanish–American War.[15]

Roosevelt rode the cowboy brand to the vice presidency in 1900, and, following the assassination of President McKinley in 1901, found himself saddled up at the White House. Teddy credited the West as playing a critical part in his political success, noting that the time spent ranching in the Bad Lands of Dakota that made him President . . . there he met the cowboys who formed the nucleus of . . . the Rough Rider regiment; it was the regiment that made him Governor of New York . . . and it was the days and nights he lived in the open in God's country in the magnificent American solitudes which induced that love of native land that burned with brighter and brighter luster.

Throughout his presidential tenure (1901–9), the iconography of the cowboy hero prevailed, obscuring Roosevelt's competing identities of a Dutch immigrant and an Eastern aristocrat. As Roosevelt observed, 'the media invariably represented me in the rough rider uniform, or else riding a bucking broncho and roping a steer, or carrying a big stick and threatening foreign nations.' For critics and satirists, the cowboy moniker serviced accusations of reckless and trigger-happy behaviour that harked back to the myth of the lawless West. When Theodore Roosevelt assumed the presidency, Senator Mark Hanna of Ohio famously exclaimed 'Now Look! That damned cowboy is president!' Mark Twain quipped that Roosevelt was 'clearly insane . . . and insanest upon war and its supreme glories'. That said, the majority of depictions of the Rough Rider President were complimentary. The mythic cowboy spoke of all-American rugged individualism and an assertive morality backed by the six-shooter, an image well suited to the triumphal and expansionist political mores of the age. *Punch* cartoonist Bernard Partridge pictured Teddy as a saluting cowpuncher, surveying the landscape of his new presidency from atop a butte, astride a horse with a snazzy stars and stripes saddle, while artist Clifford Berryman offered Roosevelt as Rough Rider sparing the life of the 'Teddy bear' on a famous Mississippi hunt in 1902. The administration, too, touted its Western credentials with pride. Inauguration celebrations in 1905 featured actors portraying Rough Riders, and a defeated Geronimo paraded before the all-conquering cowboy commander-in-chief. Cowboys, meanwhile, proved frequent guests of the president – notably Jack 'Catch 'em alive' Abernathy, famed wolf-hunter, cowpuncher and deputy Marshall from Greer Country, Oklahoma, who wore his pistol in the White House.[16]

Theodore Roosevelt successfully played cowboy in the White House. As well as speaking *of* the West, he also managed to maintain a reputation as speaker *for* it. Charles Lummis explicated: 'T.R. by his own initiative, and furthermore by adoption, is a citizen of the great West'. During the 1904 election, Roosevelt carried all the Western states aside from Texas. Meanwhile, his tour of the region in 1903 issued a firm declaration of affinity. The sixty-five-day sojourn took in 14,000 miles and saw the President deliver 265 speeches. On several occasions, Roosevelt left the confines of the Union Pacific railcar for impromptu gatherings with Westerners. En route to California, he disembarked the train for a cowboy breakfast at the state line, while at Hugo, Colorado he spotted a grub wagon, shouted 'that's the real thing' and joshed with the cowboys. Journalist G. B. Luckey eagerly reported how Teddy talked their 'lingo' and 'just like any "cattle puncher", helped himself to meat and bread, and coffee and devoured his homely meal with a relish'. Meanwhile, residents greeted Teddy as a returning hero and prodigal son. On a visit to Wyoming, the presidential cavalcade left the Union Pacific at Laramie for a six-hour ride across the Black Hills to Cheyenne. The President, riding a horse named 'Teddy', received the following oration from Governor Chatteton: 'The President is in his West, where there are no gloved hands, where his welcome is as pure as the sunlit air, as broad as the plains and as steadfast as the mountains'. The Cheyenne *Tribune* reported the event with similar lyricism:

> Down a mountain valley he came in a whirl of dust . . . Superbly mounted, he rode with a plainsman's ease, forward in the saddle and with shoulders loose. The West was written in every line of his frame, and clothes and bearing: he might have been a ranchman leading a round-up gang for all the chance observer knew – yet there was something about him, an indescribable air of subdued authority, that marked him a greater leader of men.[17]

Roosevelt captured the allure of frontier days – yet proved to be well aware of the needs of the twentieth-century West. Charles Lummis noted 'his admiration and approval of the progress and ambitions of the West'. Conservation loomed large on his political agenda, expressed through landmark decisions on irrigation, resource sustainability, development and preservation. His administration presided over the Reclamation Act (1902) and Enlarged Homestead Act (1909), established the Forest Service (1905) and expanded national parks and nature reserves (including the Grand Canyon) to the tune of a staggering 194,000 acres. During the 1903 tour, Roosevelt camped with co-founder of the Sierra Club, John Muir, for three days at Yosemite and the Mariposa Grove. Carl Ackerman reported the recuperative effect of this sojourn in the wilds on the cowboy president, 'when he returned to his party, his mood had changed, his whole physical make-up, worn almost to the limit by the busy day at San Francisco, revived, and he was once more the unweary President'. Meanwhile, the net result of his activist presidency facilitated the growth of government bureaucracy in the West, what historian Carl Abbott labelled 'the federally sustained frontier'.[18]

When Roosevelt died in 1919, cartoonist J. N. Darling drew the President in cowboy garb headed over the hills to the Great Divide, looking back, smiling and waving his hat. Commenting on the depiction, Owen Wister mused: 'On his horse: the figure from other days; The Apparition, the crusader bidding us farewell.' For Jack Abernathy, Roosevelt represented the ideal American, while poet Edna Dean drew salient parallels between the cowboy hero and the stalwarts of medieval folklore: 'Knight of the lance that was never in rest . . . liberty's champion, Cid of the West.' Roosevelt duly earned his place on Mount Rushmore (though without any cowboy affectations), while *The Rough Riders* (1927) replayed the heroics of the Spanish–American War on the silver screen. Throughout the twentieth century, the image of Roosevelt as cowboy president continued to earn popular currency. Andy Warhol included Teddy alongside John Wayne and George Armstrong Custer, for his 'cowboys and Indians' (1968), a series of screen prints that juxtaposed the pantheon of White male American heroes of empire against marginalised 'others' including Geronimo and an Indian mother and child. In *A Night at the Museum* (2006), the statue of Teddy cut a familiar figure as a fearless Rough Rider, poised to charge his horse at assailants in the museum lobby of the New York Museum of Natural History. Every night, however, Roosevelt (Robin Williams) came to life to aid security guard Larry (Ben Stiller) in keeping the peace between miniature cowboys, Roman centurions, a hungry T-Rex and capuchin monkeys. Along the way, Teddy the great White hunter pitted his wits against nature red in tooth and claw, traded in exhortations to masculine vigour – 'some men are born to greatness while others have it thrust upon them' – while stealing admiring glances at Sacagawea in the Lewis and Clark diorama. Keen to inspire Larry to find his inner cowboy, Teddy quipped, 'I'm made of wax . . . What are you made of?'[19]

Ronald Reagan and the Hollywood Cowboy

A succession of American presidents after Theodore Roosevelt toyed with the myth of the West and the cowboy brand. President Calvin Coolidge rode an electronic horse in the White House to keep fit

Cowboy Presidents 101

(reputedly wearing only his underwear), and received a cowboy outfit as a gift from South Dakotans while holidaying in the state in 1927. Coolidge gained a modicum of gravitas in Teddy's old haunts by donning the garb of a Westerner, but many greeted his performance with amusement. As Basil Manley commented: 'This cowboy stunt will make 'em think that you're a regular second Teddy Roosevelt.' In 1953, security guards at the inauguration of President Eisenhower sat tight while cowboy star Montie Montana threw a lasso around the commander-in-chief. John F. Kennedy, meanwhile, articulated an uneasy relationship with the iconography of the West. Happy to use the metaphor of the frontier to launch his vision for the 1960s, JFK refused to wear a cowboy hat presented to him by the Fort Worth Chamber of Commerce on the morning of his assassination in Dallas. Lyndon Johnson likewise maintained a complex relationship with the cowpuncher label. In the contest for the 1960 Democratic nomination he sold himself as a Westerner. As president, he readily entertained dignitaries at his Texan ranch. However, the debacle in Vietnam saw Johnson recoil from the cowboy brand and its associations with violence and aggressive patriotism – especially pertinent given reports that GI's dubbed areas controlled by the Viet Cong as 'Indian country'.[20]

The election of Ronald Reagan in 1980 ventured the most substantive airing of the cowboy president since the days of Roosevelt. In his public guise, Reagan offered himself as a tough-talking cowboy with a code of honour, what biographer Cannon has called 'the wholesome citizen-hero who inhabits our democratic imaginations, an Everyman who was slow to anger but willing to fight for the right and correct wrongdoing when aroused'. In his political mandate, too, Reagan relied on the rhetoric of the Old West to sell his policies, combining references to the frontier past, a world of simplicity, homely values and patriotism, with aspirations of a new golden age based on American prowess, order, certainty and prosperity. As *Reagan, The Man, The President* (1980), articulated: 'his purpose is to stir the sleeping giant of America back to a sense of its manifest destiny, to oversee the restoration of an economically robust and militarily sturdy nation active in the world arena, and to rekindle the rawhide heroism and patriotic pride of John Wayne.' However, where Roosevelt had played cowboy in the Dakotas before following the trail to the White House, Reagan's training in the lore of the range came from a different source: Hollywood. In place of the cowboy from the Dakotas came the star of *Cowboy from Brooklyn* (1938).[21]

Reagan's formative years were spent in Tampico, Illinois. Born in 1911, he graduated from Eureka College in 1932, and took a job as a local sports announcer in Iowa. In 1937, Reagan migrated to California on the back of a movie contract with Warner Studios, and soon crafted a career as a B-movie actor. His inaugural film, *Love is on the Air* (1937), told the story of a radio announcer, Andy McLeod, fighting the good fight against corruption in city hall, while *Murder in the Air* (1940) featured Reagan as a have-a-go-hero defending America's super weapon – the 'inertia projector' – from enemy spies. In *Knute Rockne, All-American* (1940) Reagan highlighted his sporting prowess as Notre Dame football star George 'the Gipper' Gipp. By 1941, such appearances afforded Reagan a respectable slot at number 82 in Gallup's poll of the top 100 stars, his appeal summed up as 'Mr Average Guy on the bright side . . . the clear-eyed, clean-thinking young American in uniform. You can see a montage of American Background when you look at him.'[22]

Like Reagan, John Wayne also made the trip from the mid-West to California and found a career in the bright lights of Hollywood. After working as an extra for Fox, Wayne earned his first starring role in Raoul Walsh's *The Big Trail* (1930) and thereafter carved a name for himself as an all-action Western hero, playing cowboys, soldiers, cavalrymen and other exemplars of rugged masculinity. For Reagan, who confessed a particular attraction for the American frontier and labelled himself a 'cavalry-Indian buff', a lack of Western roles generated discontent. Reagan's first shot at reliving the days of the Old West on screen finally came courtesy of *The Santa Fe Trail* (1940), a rip-roaring tale of patriotism, progress and duty, viewed through the lens of the arrival of the railroad to Kansas and the fortunes of abolitionist John Brown. Reagan played Custer to Errol Flynn's Jeb Stuart – a role offered to John Wayne who had refused to play second fiddle to Flynn's lead. On the back of *The Santa Fe Trail*, Reagan starred in B-Westerns *The Bad Man* (1941), where he played a man saved from lynching, and *Stallion Road* (1947), as a vet who caught anthrax.[23]

Still nurturing disgruntlement with Warner, Reagan quit the studio. The commanding presence (and box office clout) of John Wayne, together with Reagan's cravings for a starring role as a celluloid cowboy, played an integral role in this decision. Biographer Cannon dubbed him a 'frustrated cowboy, who had repeatedly pleaded with Warner Bros for western roles'. Through the 1950s, his gamble paid off. Where Gallup had billed him as a solid fellow, a common man, patriotic, loyal but far from exceptional, new movie contracts developed his screen persona as a self-reliant and rugged outdoorsman, a man of the West (albeit in B-movie guise). In *The Last Outpost* (1951), Reagan played a confederate cavalryman, while *Cattle Queen of Montana* (1954) saw him offer a manly shoulder and pistol to Barbara Stanwyck's feisty rancher Sierra Nevada Jones. Publicity stills for the movie presented Reagan as an affable cowpoke wearing a broad-brimmed hat, check shirt and necktie. The tag-line read, 'the easy-going left-handed gun'. Further Western credentials came courtesy of *Law and Order* (1953), in which Reagan played lawman Marshall Johnson, a man who articulated his brand of frontier justice down a gun barrel. The movie poster promised a thrilling ride: 'The last of the great shooting marshals! He lived by the gun . . . killed by the law . . . and loved a woman even his bullets couldn't tame.' *Tennessee's Partner* (1955), in which Reagan played 'cowpoke', completed his roster of Western movies.[24]

While the 1940s and 1950s saw Reagan firming up a role as a big screen cowboy, he also forwarded a political agenda. As president of the Screen Actors Guild (1947–52, 1959), Reagan vociferated a strident conservative ideology. With a desire to root out the 'red peril' of Communism that rivalled his remonstrations against the 'red peril' of Indian menace in *Cattle Queen of Montana*, Reagan testified before the House Unamerican Committee in 1947. Meanwhile, as the host of *General Electric Theater* from 1954, a variety show that played on television every Sunday, Reagan gained a sizeable pay cheque and national exposure. As corporate spokesman, Reagan toured the company's 135 power plants, using his on-screen personality to champion the cause of American capital and berate the government for intervening in business (causes which would later define his presidency). In his speeches, Reagan touted General Electric as 'the cavalry' of the post-1945 world, rescuing the United States from 'the Dark Ages' with their new fangled appliances and cheap electricity.[25]

The early 1960s signified an important period in Reagan's political development. Previously a lifelong Democrat, the election of JFK convinced Reagan to switch teams, and in 1962 he allied himself with the Republican cause. In 1964–5, Reagan served as the 'old timer' host of the TV series *Death Valley Days* – not an obviously political act, but one which cemented his public visage as a cowboy. The casting also situated Reagan as an authentic narrator of the Old West, as well as connecting him to the romance of the frontier age. In that sense, *Death Valley Days* invited comparison with Roosevelt's *Ranch Life and Hunting Trail*.

After impressing audiences with his oratory in support of Barry Goldwater, Reagan decided to hit the political trail. Campaigning for the governorship of California in 1967, Reagan stressed an anti-welfare agenda and ventured sharp criticism of student protests playing out at campuses across the state. He spoke of a government abandoning its people by leaving White Americans as the victims of ethnic militancy and countercultural infestation. Such projections hit a chord with the disaffected mainstream. As Richard White reflected, 'For people who were the beneficiaries of conquest, white westerners have had a persistent knack for portraying themselves as victims – of Indians, of the federal government, of eastern corporations.' Reprising his role as Marshall Johnson from *Law and Order*, Reagan projected himself as a timely antidote for civil rights unrest, urban chaos and student disquiet. Presented as an outsider to the political establishment (he tended to refer to the government in a deprecatory tone as 'them'), Reagan cultivated the image of a straight-talking cowboy riding into the malaise to speak up for ordinary folk. This conjoining of rugged individualism and the victim motif proved a tricky product to sell – 'akin to having John Wayne whining that the Chinese laundryman in Tombstone was pilfering his shirts and the sheriff refused to do anything about it', as Richard White put it – but Reagan deployed the mystique of the West to capable effect. The simple appeal and ideological security attached to the cowboy brand saw Reagan installed as governor of California from 1967 until 1974.[26]

Gaining the American presidency in 1980 offered Reagan his biggest stage on which to perform as a cowboy. As a movie star, Reagan had appeared in more than fifty pictures, only six of which could be described as Westerns. Yet, Reagan managed to market himself in the political arena as the archetypal cowpoke. In the election of 1980, he carried forty-four states (and left the West with a distinct red hue), while in 1984 he won a staggering forty-nine (only Mondale's loyal Minnesotans voted otherwise). At the 1984 Republican Convention, Reagan played lead to old rival John Wayne (deceased), who appeared on a film reel introducing the cowboy president.

Reagan's political career allowed him to play gunslinger far more successfully than his celluloid career had done. Where Hollywood had offered him B-movie parts in the 1940s and 1950s, but in the 1960s and 1970s traded in 'westerns without heroes', on the political stage Reagan played the traditional cowboy saviour with aplomb, using the regenerative power of the frontier to ignite American pride and promise a future as golden as the Old West. The same year as Michael Cimino's $40 million revisionist epic *Heaven's Gate* (1980) flopped at the box office and sent the Western genre into a tailspin, Reagan asserted the lasting power of the Turnerian myth of unreconstructed American White male heroes and Manifest Destiny. Not afraid to utilise the frontier 'f-word', Reagan waxed lyrical about the pioneer spirit in his inaugural presidential address:

> I have always believed that this land was placed here between the two great oceans by some divine plan . . . It was placed here to be found by a special kind of people – people who had a special love for freedom and who had the courage to uproot themselves and leave hearth and home and come to what in the beginning was the most undeveloped wilderness possible.

Meanwhile, the ideology of a New Right marked by patriotism, freedom, individualism, distrust of government, old-fashioned morality and exceptionalism was effectively holstered by the cowboy president. Sheriff Reagan thereby served up ideology as well as idealism, using an imagined Old West as the model for a roseate American future.[27]

In terms of personality, Reagan played the cowboy president role with ease, grinning affably from beneath a Stetson, firing off anecdotes about the old days of the West and developing a penchant for snappy quips. According to journalist Don Santina:

> President Reagan could do the Aw-Shucks/Jimmie Stewart thing while being queried about attacking small countries like Libya and Grenada, and he could do the There-You-Go-Again/Gary Cooper thing over questions about Iran Contra or homelessness. For the many Americans, everything was OK; a nice old familiar cowboy was in charge.

When he played host to Gorbachev, Reagan reputedly asked the Soviet Premier which side he mounted a horse from. When Gorbachev replied 'the left', the American cowboy president ventured a joke and a wry smile. Meanwhile, Reagan could often be found at his Santa Barbara ranch chopping wood, riding horses and clearing brush (three of his favourite pastimes). He spent a total of 345 days of his presidency at Rancho del Cielo, a 'western White House' where security details referred to him by the code word 'rawhide'. Back East, Reagan furnished the White House with the iconography of the West in prints by Frederic Remington, Thomas Moran and George Catlin. It scarcely mattered that Reagan's cowboy credentials had come courtesy of the movies. For the moral majority, this cowboy president articulated a code of honour, air of masculine confidence and reputation for being 'daring, decent and fair' in the words of his second inaugural presidential address, exactly how an idealised cowpoke should behave. For the man himself, the difference between history and Hollywood often seemed blurred. One apocryphal tale related how Reagan actually thought he had been in the Second World War (rather than making war movies for the Department of Defense in Culver City, California), while Nancy reputedly yelled 'cut' at the end of each day. The American public seemed happy to read authenticity in the script of the 'reel' cowboy. As Richard Slotkin noted, 'the myths produced by mass culture have become credible substitutes for actual historical or political action in authenticating the character and ideological claims of political leaders'. In fact, the Hollywood lustre proved integral to Reagan's appeal. Hollywood taught him how to be media savvy, situated him in American celebrity culture and lent him a familiar and relaxed demeanour on camera. The campaign poster 'Reagan Country', that depicted a beaming figure in denim shirt and white cowboy hat, offered a salient visual example of this fusion of Hollywood screen-idol allure and Old West mystique.[28]

In the arena of domestic policy, the West also proved to be an important emblematic tool. For *Nation* magazine, Reagan's plan could be summed up in two words: 'cowboy capitalism'. The President utilised the mythology of the frontier as a realm of opportunity, bonanza and super-abundance to sell his New Right ideology of self-help and supply-side economics. The advertising of the 1980s as a 'boom time' for 'go-getting' entrepreneurial talent and productivity and the extolling of aggressive capitalism and the rugged individualism of the boardroom certainly bore a Turnerian hue. Meanwhile, Reagan's determination to roll back big government, slash taxes and welfare spending (notably axing a third of all American Indian programmes), articulated an anti-federal sentiment that had long been a feature of the Western mentality. *It's About Times* (a newspaper distributed by the Californian anti-nuclear group the Abalone Alliance) reported: 'As if he were still playing the hero in one of his old B-Westerns, Ronald Reagan is heading off government spending and slashing taxes.' Significantly, Reagan earned a particular constituency from the 'Sagebrush Rebellion', a cacophony of disaffected farmers and Western political interests mired in a regional crisis precipitated by low agricultural returns due to falling market prices, drought and grasshoppers, rising interest rates, energy costs and debt payments. For them, Reagan's rubric of opening up public land for exploitation, offering tax bonuses, and reducing user restrictions promised a lifeline of economic freedom of action.[29]

In common with Roosevelt, Reagan enlisted the cowboy moniker in the arena of foreign policy. The second Cold War, in all its bellicose polemics, resonated with references to American manifest destiny, moral certainty and redemptive violence. In this superpower duel between capitalism and communism, the rhetoric of the Old West emerged as a powerful metaphor. In his first term, Reagan projected himself as an upstanding lawman, defender of civilisation, facing off against the outlaw Soviet Union, 'the focus of evil in the modern world'. A satirical poster entitled 'Bedtime for Brezhnev' (1981) parodied Reagan's movie escapades in *Bedtime for Bonzo* (1951) – in which he played comic foil to a chimpanzee – with his East versus West standoff. The fictitious movie promised an Old West shoot-out between the cowboy Reagan and outlaw Brezhnev (easily distinguished as hero and villain by their black and white Stetsons), under the tag-line: 'From out of the West they dusted off their guns to protect the world they knew and the women they loved.' Meanwhile, the cowboy president emerged as a fervent advocate of the 'six-gun mystique'. Championing the law of the gun in the mythic West, Reagan asserted strength as the only language the enemy understood, and embarked on a determined mission to stockpile a nuclear arsenal in the rifle cupboard. As he quipped, 'I once played a sheriff who thought he could do the job without a gun. I was dead in twenty-seven minutes of a thirty minute show.' Significantly, Reagan's second term saw the 'evil empire' rhetoric toned down as the president recast himself as lawman-peacemaker.[30]

The cowboy swagger of Reagan's foreign policy earned him plaudits. At home, his projection of a polarised world of 'good versus evil', rhetorical flourishes and faith in atomic weapons won votes and stirred patriotic hearts. After all, the idea of the cowboy hero using the gun to bring peace to the West represented a trope of the Western played out in such movies as *High Noon* (1952) and *Shane* (1953). Further afield, the political party 'Solidarity' used an image of the Western sheriff, a rugged standard bearer for democracy, in posters imploring Polish citizens to exercise their right to vote in the elections of 1989. The cowboy brand was a global symbol, but with its leitmotifs recognised as quintessentially American. That said, the cowpuncher label did not win universal acclaim. Back in the 1950s, Stalin had viewed the American cowboy icon as so seditious that he ordered the KGB to assassinate John Wayne. Meanwhile, in the early 1980s,

Reagan's stance as a rooting tooting cowboy with his trigger finger on the nuclear button generated serious anxiety. The critical voice proved especially widespread in Europe, where concerned citizens and peace groups including Britain's Campaign for Nuclear Disarmament (CND) feared that their continent would be reduced to a radioactive wasteland in the superpower shoot-out between the United States and the Soviet Union. Critics castigated American foreign policy as unduly cavalier, and shuddered when they heard tales of Reagan firing off his pistol-fingers to staff after hearing that Libyan jets had been shot down by a US fighter in 1981. Such images of 'Ronnie le cowboy', as he was known in France, offered protesters a fecund symbol to use in their gesture politics – shocking and comedic in equal measure. In the 'Land of Confusion' video (1986) for rock band Genesis, Reagan played a blundering fool in a fantasy world, riding a triceratops in full cowboy regalia, while the Abalone Alliance featured a cowboy Ronnie riding an atomic missile on the front page of *It's About Times* in May–June 1982. Such propaganda devices ventured a keen sense of wit as well as a sophisticated understanding of movie genres and the mythology of the Old West. In 1982, the Polish fake movie poster 'The World and the American Way' featured an image of Reagan not as a smiling cowboy hero but a grimacing, sinister outlaw raising a gun. The mythic cowboy had become the 'fascist gun in the West' – the positive attributes associated with America's favourite hero now read in negative terms.[31]

The iconography of the cowboy proved resilient enough to stick to the Teflon president in perpetuity. In the videogame *Nuclear War* (1989), 'Ronnie Raygun' earned billing as one of several world leader opponents lined up to nuke the world. Once more the idea of Reagan as a gung-ho gunslinger playing out a movie role loomed large. In the words of the manual, 'he sometimes thinks that he is living in a Spaghetti Western . . . [this] makes Ronnie somewhat of a mindless warmonger. Ronnie is always a step away from his favorite, shiny toy, The Button.' None the less, the traditional veneer of the cowpuncher as a man of honour, action and patriotism continued to lend Reagan kudos. Action hero California Governor Arnold Schwarzenegger spent his very first weekend in the United States buying cowboy boots and a poster of Reagan as a Hollywood cowpoke for his Los Angeles apartment. In 2001, thirteen years after leaving office, Reagan topped the list of 'greatest US Presidents' in a Gallup poll, earning 18 per cent of the popular vote. Likewise, when Reagan died in 2004, President George W. Bush paid respect to him as an archetype of the cowboy-hero: 'when he saw evil camped across the horizon, he called that evil by name ... Our 40th president wore his title lightly, and it fit like a white Stetson.'[32]

George W. Bush and the Simulated Cowboy

The young George W. Bush liked to dress up and play cowboys and Indians. A photograph of 'Dubya' as a toddler in 1949 depicted him on a tricycle, with cowboy necktie, checked shirt and jeans, pointing a pistol at the camera. Unlike most kids, George W. earned the chance to reprise this role later in life on the world stage. Whereas his cowboy president predecessors, Theodore Roosevelt and Ronald Reagan, played cowboy in the Dakotas and on a Hollywood set, respectively, Dubya's cowboy heredity proved harder to discern. In place of the Rough Rider antics of Roosevelt, Bush's background lay in Texan oil ventures and ownership of the Dallas Rangers baseball team. A lack of horse-riding skills identified him as a 'windshield cowboy'. As Alexandra Keller has noted, unlike Ronald Reagan, Bush 'is (only) a real spectator of western film narratives'. The success of Bush as a cowboy president thus raised several questions. How could he become a cowpoke without any saddle-time? And, what did this say about the brand itself?[33]

Like Teddy Roosevelt, George W. Bush boasted an Eastern lineage. He was born in New Haven in 1946, educated at Philips Academy High School, Andover, and then Yale (where he gained a 'C' average and a reputation for drunken Fraternity hi-jinks with the 'Skull and Bones' society). In between, however, the young George W. spent time in Midland and Houston, where his father operated a successful oil business. After completing his MBA at Harvard, Bush junior worked in Texas, where he presided over several failing ventures, Arbusto, Spectrum Seven and Harken Energy, before moving back to Washington, DC to assist his father's presidential campaign. In 1989, Dubya became co-owner of the Dallas Rangers baseball team. In a sense, this 'boom and bust' existence and involvement in the Texas oil industry allied him with the modern West.

Dubya's first shot at politics proved to be somewhat of a false start. He failed to get elected to the House of Representatives in 1978, but in 1995, on the back of his oil and baseball money, he won the Texas gubernatorial race. Bush ran on a Republican ticket, opposing Democrat Ann Richards' veto of recent gun laws allowing Texans to carry concealed weapons and cultivating a reputation as a plain-talking political outsider. Once installed as Governor, Bush advocated a conservative philosophy by proposing tax cuts to aid business, supporting religious welfare groups and enacting reform of the prison system. Notably, he emerged as a stickler for law and order – a hard-line sheriff who signed execution warrants for 152 prisoners on death row during his tenure.

George W. Bush's campaign for the presidency lofted his ideology as a 'compassionate conservative', emphasised his evangelical Christian stance and stressed themes of honour (a deliberate reference to Bill Clinton's romantic escapades). The rolling back of federal programmes and gun control legislation comprised part of the campaign vernacular, but it was with the terrorist attacks of 9/11 that Bush really found his cowboy voice. Whereas his background in Texas could be construed as more J. R. Ewing than Wyatt Earp, Bush cultivated the image of the sheriff running villains out of a global Dodge City in the wake of 9/11. 'The axis of evil' framework in which Bush placed rogue states proved reminiscent of Reagan's 'evil empire' rhetoric, as did his predilection for sloganeering Old West style. Alongside his infamous 'Wanted Dead or Alive' address, Bush rallied the National Cattlemen's Beef Association in Denver with the polemical 'You are either with us or you are with the terrorists. This is civilization's fight' and offered a rousing 'bring 'em on' at a press call situated rather appropriately in front of a picture of Theodore Roosevelt on horseback. Bush admitted that the old Western talk might be 'a little informal in diplomatic terms', but it aptly fitted his style as an everyman politician. Moreover, recourse to the rhetorical flourishes of frontierism lent a morally just and heroic veneer to his foreign policy agenda. The Bush doctrine of pro-activity against so-called rogue states, of no compromise, certainty of belief and defence through offence fitted well in the traditional Western mythology of good versus evil, duty not to retreat and protection of the innocent.[34]

Public and media alike endorsed Bush's assumed identity as a cowboy. Cartoons and articles consistently defined the President in such terms. In February 2003, more than 800 references on Lexis-Nexis contained the Bush–cowboy analogy. The Seattle *Post Intelligencer* spoke of how the 'latest "cowboy president" shoots from hip' while *Mother Jones* used a cover image of Bush as a gunfighter president on horseback with pistol cocked. However, just as in the days of Roosevelt and Reagan, the cowboy label proved both a boon and a burden. Advocates championed Bush's cowboy code of standing up for justice, plain-talking moral certainty and staring confidently down the barrel of a loaded gun. The Dallas *Morning News* bristled:

'If America fully embraces this cowboy wisdom and courage, then the Islamic terrorists and the regimes that support them had better run for cover. They stand no chance in the resulting showdown.' Country star Claude King sang about how he 'liked having a cowboy in the White House' while Kathleen Parker responded to Iraqi Defence Minister Ali Ahamkhani's statement that 'Bush thinks he is still living in the age of cowboys, and that the world is like Texas with him as its sheriff' with 'Well yippie-yi-o-ki-yay to you, too'. However, where supporters perceived the 'cool, calculating courage' of Bush as an attribute, opponents instead read the cowboy's masculine confidence and penchant for violence as a sign of misplaced aggression and trigger-happy bloodlust. Protest T-shirts asserted a need to 'Stop Mad Cowboy Disease' and advertised fictional sports teams such as the 'Unilateral Cowboys', while writers parodied Bush's Old West styling with book titles such as *Cowboy Republic: Six Ways the Bush Gang has Defied the Law* (2007). Bush's showmanship (he took Saddam Hussein's pistol and mounted it in the Oval Office as a trophy) bespoke a triumphalism that liberals and Europeans read as inflammatory and ignorant. *Pravda* criticised Bush's 'cowboy magazine intellect', Al Gore bemoaned his Jesse James style politicking and the French hosted a play entitled 'Ou le Triste Cowboy de Dieu' (translated as 'God's sad cowboy'). As Piers Morgan noted in the British tabloid, the *Mirror*, 'I think people look at him and think John Wayne. We in Europe like John Wayne; we liked him in cowboy films; we don't like him running the world.'[35]

At an address for students at Oklahoma State University in 2006 (an institution with the nickname 'cowboys'), Bush vociferated with a smirk, 'If you read the papers, you know that when some want to criticize me they call me a cowboy ... This cowboy is proud to be standing amidst of a lot of other cowboys.' The crowd offered a resounding cheer. In the political arena, too, Bush curried favour with his cowpoke style, old-fashioned values and stress on military strength. In the presidential elections of 2000 and 2004, he carried the heartland of the West (although failed to win the Pacific states). Bush, had never been a real cowboy, but his assured performance seemed enough to earn credibility among Westerners and the broader American nation. Like the cowpokes of the early 1900s who cast off their working clothes to don the garb of the mythic cowboy in order to gain employment in Hollywood, Bush crafted himself according to a globally recognised brand with popular appeal. He talked the talk of an idealised cowboy, wore the white Stetson, belt buckle, boots, jeans, ventured a characteristic tough guy swagger, owned a ranch in Texas where he raised 200

Figure 4.2 'Playing the Last Card.'

longhorns (Ofelia even boasted her own web page), rode the range in his Ford pick-up and cleared brush. In the White House, Western art adorned the walls, including 'A Charge to Keep' by William Henry Dethlef Koerner and a Julian Onderdonk painting of the Alamo. The power of these signifiers, the iconic images of an invented tradition, carried sufficient currency to confer on Bush the mantle of cowboy president. Just because his cowpoke seemed almost entirely a simulation, an imitation to rival Yul Bryner's *Westworld* (1973) gunslinger robot, this scarcely mattered. The cowboy brand had always been an invention. It proved decidedly at home in a post-modern world of collapsed temporal and geographical boundaries where authenticity could be purchased by imagination and performance.[36]

On a wall in Glebe, Sydney, a graffiti artist immortalised George Bush as a grinning cowboy, pulling his pistol on unsuspecting pedestrians. The urban installation mimicked a style popularised by Banksy, and paid homage to Andy Warhol's screen print of a pistol-packing Elvis in similar stance (1963). The depiction of Bush on the wall of an Australian sidewalk indicated the global dissemination of the cowboy as a strident emblem of Americanism. Moreover, the collision of political and popular cultures expressed in the graffiti art provided comment on the adventures of the cowboy brand in the twentieth century. As the historical reality of the cowpuncher's life faded into the background, his mythic persona cut a new trail, aided by mass media, all the way to the White House. From Roosevelt to Bush, a succession of presidents exploited the mystique of the cowboy to present themselves as idealised figures of American masculinity, and to sanction (and indeed sanctify) American geopolitical dominance. The mythical cowboy proved a credible and adaptable figure, able to ride point on America's own creation story of the West, and, in so doing, facilitate the construction of an imagined community. As the *High Country News* mused:

> Cowboy imagery is particularly useful because it's so culturally loaded, and yet so flexible. The man in the hat could be the new sheriff – read 'tough.' He could be a rancher – read 'independent'. Or he could be an ordinary cowpoke – regular folk like you and me, whittling away at his problems with the unthreatening genius of common sense.

Significantly, the values that defined the mythical cowboy could be readily inverted. As Annie Proulx noted, 'The West has come to symbolize the policies and character of a country increasingly hated in the larger world, cutting fences and forcing its cows through.' Whether commended as hero or anti-hero, one thing remains certain, the iconic cowboy has earned a top billing in the political rodeo for more than 100 years. With this trail firmly blazed, the adventures of the cowboy brand looked set to ride confidently into the twenty-first century.[37]

Notes

1. 'Guard and Reserves "Define Spirit of America": Remarks by the President to Employees at the Pentagon', 17 September 2001. Transcript available at: http://www.whitehouse.gov/news/releases/2001/09/20010917-3.html; 'Comforter in Chief', *Newsweek*, 3 December 2001, p. 34.
2. Autry's 'Cowboy Code' available online at: http://www.geneautry.com/geneautry/geneautry_cowboycode.html; Richard Aquila (ed.), *Wanted Dead or Alive: The American West in Popular Culture* (Urbana: University of Illinois Press, 1996), p. 286; Michael Johnson, *New Westers: The West in Contemporary American Culture* (Lincoln: University of Nebraska Press, 1996), p. 45.
3. Kennedy combined visions of an illustrious pioneering past – 'I stand here tonight facing west on what was once the last frontier' – with those of an optimistic future – 'we stand today on the edge of a New Frontier – the frontier of the 1960s, the frontier of unknown opportunities and perils, the frontier of unfilled hopes and unfilled threats.' See Sarah Watts, *Rough Rider in the White House: Theodore Roosevelt and the Politics of Desire* (Chicago: University of Chicago Press, 2003); Richard Slotkin, *Gunfighter Nation: The Myth of the Frontier in Twentieth-Century America* (Norman: University of Oklahoma Press, 1998), p. 3; John F. Kennedy, '1960 Democratic National Convention Acceptance Address'. Transcript available at: http://www.americanrhetoric.com/speeches/jfk1960dnc.htm; Sheldon Alberts, 'What if John Wayne was U.S. President?', *Victoria Times Colonist*, 2 January 2008.
4. Richard White, *'Its Your Misfortune and None of My Own': A New History of the American West* (Oklahoma: Oklahoma University Press, 1991), p. 57; Patricia Nelson Limerick, *The Legacy of Conquest: The Unbroken Past of the American West* (New York: Norton, 1987), pp. 134–75; Robert Hine and John Mack Faragher, *The American West: A New Interpretive History* (New Haven: Yale University Press, 2000), p. 520; Clyde A. Milner II, Carol A. O'Connor and Martha Sandweiss (eds), *The Oxford History of the American West* (Oxford: Oxford University Press, 1994), p. 490.
5. G. Edward White, *The Eastern Establishment and the Western Experience* (Austin: University of Texas Press, 1989 [1968]), p. 83.
6. White, *Eastern Establishment and the Western Experience*, pp. 80, 79.
7. Pittsburgh *Dispatch*, April 1885; White, *Eastern Establishment and the Western Experience*, pp. 83–4; *Badlands Cowboy*, 19 June 1883.
8. Watts, *Rough Rider in the White House*, pp. 126, 127, 130; *Badlands Cowboy*, 11 December 1884; *Badlands Cowboy* quoted in: Ray H. Mattison, 'Roosevelt and the Stockmen's Association', Reprint of Report for Northern Dakota History, 17/2–3 (April–July 1950), p. 17. Held at the Autry Library (hereafter cited as Autry); White, *Eastern Establishment and the Western Experience*, p. 88. On

vigilantism and the code of the West, also see Richard Maxwell Brown, *Strain of Violence: Historical Studies of American Violence and Vigilantism* (Oxford: Oxford University Press, 1975) and *No Duty to Retreat: Violence and Values in American History and Society* (Oxford: Oxford University Press, 1991).

9. Owen Wister, *Roosevelt: The Story of a Friendship* (New York: Macmillan, 1930), p. 31; Mattison, 'Roosevelt and the Stockmen's Association', p. 31; Watts, *Rough Rider in the White House*, p. 158; Theodore Roosevelt, 'Ranch life in the far West', *Century*, 3/4 (February 1888), p. 510.
10. McCoy: quoted in Marshall Fishwick, 'The cowboy: America's contribution to world mythology', *Western Folklore*, 11/2 (April 1952), p. 82; Theodore Roosevelt, *Ranch Life and Hunting Trail* (New York: Century 1896 [1888]), p. 34; Roosevelt's *Wilderness Hunter*: quoted in White, *Eastern Establishment and the Western Experience*, p. 91.
11. Roosevelt: quoted in White, *Eastern Establishment and the Western Experience*, p. 91; Roosevelt, *Ranch Life and Hunting Trail*, p. 131; Prentiss Ingraham, 'Buck Taylor, King of the Cowboys; or, the raiders and the rangers. A story of the wild and thrilling life of William L. Taylor', *Beadle's Half Dime Library*, No. 497 (1887).
12. *Forum*: quoted in Watts, *Rough Rider in the White House*, p. 156; Lincoln A. Lang, *Ranching with Roosevelt by a Companion Rancher* (Philadelphia: J. B. Lippincott, 1926), p. 7; cartoons reproduced in Albert Shaw, *A Cartoon History of Roosevelt's Career* (New York: The Review of reviews Company, n.d), p. 65.
13. Quoted in White, *Eastern Establishment and the Western Experience*, p. 152.
14. Younger readers could indulge in the growing cult of Teddy through the *Young Rough Riders Weekly*, a magazine for boys that capitalised on the success of the dime novel with vibrant covers and action-packed tales of upstanding Deputy Marshall Ted Strong ridding the frontier wilderness of bad guys. C. J. Stephens framed his pitch with the words, 'Colonel Roosevelt was among the first to reach the crest, and his dashing example, his absolute fearlessness, and gallant leading rendered his conduct conspicuous and clearly distinguished above that of other men.' See White, *Eastern Establishment and the Western Experience*, p. 159; Watts, *Rough Rider in the White House*, p. 165; Paul Andrew Hutton, 'Col. Cody, the Rough Riders and the Spanish American War', *Points West*, Autumn 1998, pp. 8–11; John A Barsness, 'Theodore Roosevelt as cowboy: the Virginian as Jacksonian man', *American Quarterly*, 21/3 (Autumn 1969), p. 619.
15. Cody: quoted in Hutton, 'Col. Cody, the Rough Riders and the Spanish American War', pp. 8–11. Intriguingly, William Jennings Bryan received criticism during his 1896 presidential campaign as a provincial Nebraska cowboy rather than 'a broad-minded experienced statesman'. See B. Byron Price, 'Cowboys and presidents', *Convergence: Autry National Center Magazine* (Spring/Summer 2006), p. 9.
16. Roosevelt: quoted in Edward Cotton, *The Ideals of Theodore Roosevelt* (New York: Appleton, 1923), p. 184; Roosevelt: quoted in Watts, *Rough Rider in the White House*, p. 171, Hanna: quoted in Price, 'Cowboys and presidents', p. 9; Twain: quoted in Bernard DeVoto (ed.), *Mark Twain in Eruption* (New York: Harpers, 1940), p. 8.

17. Charles Lummis, 'Roosevelt: a western man', *Los Angeles Express*, 28 May 1903; Carl Ackerman, 'President Roosevelt in California', *Sunset*, XI/2 (June 1903), pp. 104–12; G. B. Luckey, 'President Roosevelt as a traveler', *Leslie's Weekly*, XCVII/2499 (30 July 1903); *Cheyenne Tribune*, 30 May 1903; William Chapin Deming, *Roosevelt in the Bunkhouse and other Sketches; Visits of the Rough Rider to Wyoming in 1900, 1903 and 1910* (Laramie: Laramie Printing Co., 1927), p. 21.
18. Lummis, 'Roosevelt: a western man'; Carl Ackerman, 'President Roosevelt in California', p. 112; Carl Abbott, 'The Federal presence', in Milner et. al. *Oxford History of the American West*, p. 471.
19. Wister, *Roosevelt*, p. 8; John Abernathy, *In Camp with Theodore Roosevelt, or, The Life of John R. (Jack) Abernathy* (Oklahoma City: Times Journal Publishing Co., 1933), held at the Autry; Charles Hanson Towne (ed.), *Roosevelt as the Poets Saw Him* (New York: Charles Scribner's Sons, 1923), p. 65; *Variety*, 16 March 1927; *The New York Times*, 16 March 1927; *A Night at the Museum* (2006, Twentieth Century Fox).
20. Price, 'Cowboys and presidents', p. 11.
21. Lou Cannon, *President Reagan: The Role of a Lifetime* (New York: Touchstone, 1991), p. 41; Hedrick Smith, Adam Clymer, Leonard Silk, Robert Lindsey and Richard Burt, *Reagan the Man, the President* (New York: Macmillan, 1980), p. 154.
22. Quoted in Stephen Vaughan, *Ronald Reagan in Hollywood: Movies and Politics* (Cambridge: Cambridge University Press, 1994), p. 37.
23. Garry Wills, *Reagan's America: Innocents at Home* (London: Heinemann, 1985), p. 87.
24. Cannon, *President Reagan*, p. 527; Paul Dellinger, 'From power to politics: the Western films of Ronald Reagan', *Under Western Skies*, 15 (July 1981), p. 7; Vaughan, *Ronald Reagan in Hollywood*, p. 233.
25. Cannon, *President Reagan*, p. 89.
26. White, *Its Your Misfortune and None of My Own*, pp. 603, 604.
27. Hine and Faragher, *The American West*, p. 531; Reagan's address: quoted in *The New York Times*, 22 September 1980.
28. Don Santina, 'Cowboy imagery and the American presidency', *Counterpunch*, 19 December 2005. In his second inaugural address Reagan spoke of 'The men of the Alamo call out encouragement to each other; a settler pushes west and sings his song, and the song echoes out forever and fills the unknowing air. It is the American sound. It is hopeful, bighearted, idealistic – daring, decent and fair', *The New York Times*, 22 January 1985; Slotkin, *Gunfighter Nation*, p. 644; 'Reagan Country' campaign poster, held at the Autry.
29. *The Nation*, 7 March 1981; *It's About Times*, March–April 1981, 5. 'Its High Noon, June 4 1989' (Solidarity, 1989) and 'The World and the American Way' (1982) held at the Autry. Also see Kevin Mulroy (ed.), *Western Amerykanski: Polish Poster Art and the Western* (Los Angeles/Seattle: Autry Museum and University of Washington Press, 1999), pp. 69, 71.
30. 'The Evil Empire' speech was delivered by Reagan to the Annual Convention of the National Association of Evangelicals, Orlando, Florida, 8 March 1983; 'Bedtime for Brezhnev', available online at: http://www.colorado.edu/AmStudies/lewis/west/bedtime.htm; John Cawelti, *The Six Gun Mystique* (Bowling Green:

Bowling Green University Popular Press, 1970); Michael Rogin, *Ronald Reagan, the Movie, and other Episodes in Political Demonology* (Berkeley: University of California Press, 1987), p. 38.

31. Genesis, 'Land of confusion' (1986) directed by John Lloyd and Jim Yukich, featured puppets from the popular U.K. satire show 'Spitting Image' and won a Grammy; *It's About Times*, May–June 1982, p. 1.
32. *Nuclear War* (1989, New World Computing); Bush quoted on CNN, 11 June 2004.
33. Alexandra Keller, 'Historical discourse and American identity in Westerns since the Reagan era', in John O'Connor and Peter Rollins (eds), *Hollywood's West: The American Frontier in Film, Television and History* (Lexington: Kentucky University Press, 2005), p. 256.
34. Bush's address to the Cattleman's Association, 8 February 2002, transcript available at: http://www.whitehouse.gov/news/releases/2002/02/20020208-1.html; CBS News, 3 July 2003; Bush quoted on BBC News, 5 May 2006.
35. Marvin Olasky, 'Bush the cowboy, take two', available online at: http://www.townhall.com, 26 February 2004; *Seattle Post Intelligencer*, 28 November 2002; *Mother Jones*, 28/1 (January–February 2003); Dallas *Morning News*, 26 February 2003; Kathleen Parker: quoted on http//:www.townhall.com, 3 June 2002; Wayne Lutz, 'The cowboy in us all', *The Tocquevillian*, 30 November 2002; Marjorie Cohn, *Six Ways the Bush Gang has Defied the Law* (Sausalito: Polipoint Press, 2007); *Pravda*, 15 December 2005; Al Gore commented, 'If you're going after Jesse James, you ought to organize the posse first, especially if you're in the middle of a gunfight with somebody who's out after you', See *Washington Post*, 23 September 2002; Piers Morgan: quoted in Karen Dodwell, 'From the center: the cowboy myth, George W. Bush and the war with Iraq', *Americana: The American Popular Culture Online Magazine*, March 2004, online at: http://www.americanpopularculture.com.
36. Bush's comments quoted in the *Boston Globe*, 7 May 2006.
37. 'Cowboy George W. Bush – Glebe Sydney', available online at: http://www.flickr.com; Mary Greenfield, 'There are perils in cowboy diplomacy', *High Country News*, 10 February 2003; Annie Proulx, 'How the West was spun', *The Guardian*, 25 June 2005.

Part Two
New West

Chapter 5

Women in the West: The Trailblazer and the Homesteader

The traditional narrative of the winning of the West lionised vigorous male heroes – cowboys, fur trappers, explorers and army officers – who collectively tore across the plains with gun-toting buckskin-clad assurance. According to the popular discourse, these all-American idols conquered the virgin land, first, in the name of civilisation and, second, in the name of masculinity. The West was won by self-reliant and spirited frontiersmen, exemplars of American manifest destiny and manhood in the outdoors style celebrated by Theodore Roosevelt's *The Winning of the West* (1889–96). As revisionist historian Susan Armitage has noted, this landscape of heroism and action is markedly gender specific: a 'Hisland' almost entirely bereft of female presence. A cursory glance at the work of Frederick Jackson Turner, Theodore Roosevelt and William F. Cody elucidates this point. In Turner's 'The Significance of the Frontier in American History' (1893), women played a meagre role in the waves of frontier settlement that saw wilderness transformed into civilisation. Roosevelt likewise devoted attention to the explorer, the fur trapper, the miner and the cowboy in his self-styled celebration of American progress and masculine vigour in the wilds. Buffalo Bill's contemporaneous take on Western history afforded more space to women, notably frontier novelties of pistol-packing ladies such as Annie Oakley. Bill reputedly told a reporter that he felt women were as qualified to vote as men. However, the show, together with the larger than life dime novel theatrics of Cody himself, placed the male hero firmly at centre stage. The vernacular of the Old West, both popular and academic, thereby situated women as window dressing, 'prairie beauties' and damsels in distress under threat from Indian braves and in need of rescue by White males.[1]

As the story of the West was told and retold over the twentieth century a pattern of gender conventions emerged. Women were either sidelined in the story of the frontier or cast in accustomed, primarily domestic roles. These included the 'gentle tamer', the pioneer mother or school teacher too delicate for the Plains, who brought a sense of gentility and morality to the rough world of the West; the (often reluctant) homesteader, who toiled away for the good of the family in a supporting role; and the bad girl, the fallen woman (saloon dancer, bar-keep or prostitute) and petticoat floozy who usually had a heart of gold under all the paint and taffeta. Only gradually has the integral role played by women in the process of westward movement come to light.

In 1920, Emerson Hough paid heed (albeit in somewhat patronising tone) to the dearth of women in writings on Western history when he noted:

> The chief figure of the American West, the figure of the ages, is not the long-haired, fringed-legging man riding a raw-boned pony, but the gaunt and sad-faced woman sitting on the front seat of the wagon, following her lord where he might lead her . . . Who has written her story?

In the 1950s, Dee Brown highlighted the role of the feminine 'gentle tamer' who worked with 'quiet force' to transform the frontier. But it was the tide of feminism in the 1970s that truly kick-started substantive discussion on the place of women in Western history: what roles they played and, significantly, to what extent the process of westward movement brought new opportunities, even liberation, for frontier women. In 1972, a year after its inception, the *Western Historical Quarterly* published its first article with 'women' in the title. In 1988, Glenda Riley touted the importance of the 'female frontier', that women emigrants possessed commonalities of experience in daily lives marshalled as much by extant gender codes as by the particular dictates of the western region. In the last few decades, a swathe of insightful revisionist historiography provided a rich and detailed survey of the important contributions of women to processes of westward conquest, to the extent that Patricia Nelson Limerick noted in *Legacy of Conquest* (1987) that to 'Exclude women from western history and unreality sets in'.[2]

This chapter considers the roles played by frontier women by exploring two case studies that incorporate the trail and the homesteading experience – settings common to many women. It points towards the diverse and adaptive roles that women assumed and reveals them as critical players in the drama of Western history. In some cases, the

West provided a theatre for liberation, as demonstrated by Wyoming in 1869 becoming the first state to embrace female suffrage. At the same time, however, gender conventions and codes of behaviour continued to impose limitations on many women. Constraints of class and race created special problems for poor women and ethnic minorities, whose story still remains a fragmentary one. Overwhelmingly, though, the experience of Western women speaks of resourcefulness, resolution and agency.

Women on the Trail: Carrie Call

The trail blazed west by the likes of explorers and mountain men in the early 1800s paved the way for a greater exodus in the mid-century. Lewis and Clark may not have found a navigable waterway to the Pacific, but, as Bernard DeVoto recalled, their expedition turned the nation's eyes westwards. Intrepid fur trappers found more expeditious routes over the Rockies, notably the South Pass in 1812. From the 1830s missionaries and farmers traversed the western trails to Oregon country. Mormons and Argonauts joined the procession in the 1840s, peeling off the Oregon Trail to Utah and California. In the 1840s, women comprised only 10 per cent of travellers, but by the 1850s gender ratios on the trail had reached parity. Land hunger, economic gain, the lure of a pleasant climate, all underscored the captivating promise of opportunity bound up in the Western dream. Between 1841 and 1867 350,000 people travelled to Pacific haunts.[3]

The promise of a new life in southern California inspired Carrie Call, her husband Jimmie and their two children to make the journey from Salt Lake City in 1886, swapping one western clime for another. Like many other emigrants, the Calls were enticed by presentations of California as an earthly paradise, a realm of free land and boundless opportunity. Projections of the region as a utopia seemed well entrenched in popular culture by this point, with the likes of San Francisco entrepreneur Samuel Brannan and the Santa Fe Railway selling the region (and making a tidy profit to boot) as a land of milk and honey or, more accurately, gold fields and citrus groves. In her journal, Carrie Call none the less confessed a degree of reluctance and uncertainty about the move to Los Angeles: 'we left the Call family looking rather blue'. Her thoughts proved representative of female emigrants, many of whom expressed unease about leaving friends and family behind and often agreed to go West out of obedience to their husbands or for the sake of keeping the family together. That said, the female pioneer rarely conformed to the submissive and reluctant sun-bonneted maiden of popular stereotype. In fact, many women exhibited hope and excitement for what the frontier might offer. Their imagined West elicited plenty, opportunity, excitement and promise. In 1845, Catherine E. Beecher, the sister of Harriet, recommended that the nation's schoolteachers embrace the frontier out of feminine obligation in *The Duty of American Women to their Country* – her cry 'go west, young woman' predating Horace Greeley's adage by six years. Meanwhile, in the opening pages of her journal, Carrie Call sketched her own aspirations for an idyllic Western future: a homely cabin, trees, fences, birds, all surrounded by a cascade of flowers.[4]

In common with many emigrant families, the Calls invested considerable time and money organising their trip. A sturdy wagon, oxen, rifles and supplies set the average family back $500–$1,000. Women played a key role in preparing supplies. They weaved cloth for the tarpaulin, made soap and blankets and collected provisions of salt, bacon, sugar, coffee and flour, all essential items for mobile domestic living. Emigrants gleaned information on what to expect and what to take from guidebooks, popular literature and word of mouth. Contemporary publications offered practical advice and indicated discreet gender conventions. In *The Emigrants Guide to Oregon and California* (1845), suggestions for salt and coffee rations per person sat alongside advice to female travellers on spousal diplomacy and how to placate men to 'lead and guide them' should the camp experience interpersonal strife. The *Godey's Ladies Book* story 'Beauty Out West: or How Three Fashionable Ladies Spent a Year in the Wilderness' (1856) cast women as genteel creatures clasping ladles, moral values and babies as the men brandished guns and testosterone against 'herds of wild beasts of prey, and danger and death'.[5]

Carrie Call began her journal the night before departure, 24 October 1886: 'Tomorrow morning we start on our journey to California. We have been making preparations for several weeks and now we are ready at last.' It was in the act of westward movement that she found an authorial voice. The fact that so many women chose to record the experiences of the trail in diary form suggested not only a dedicated writing culture, but also what Dee Brown called an 'awareness of being involved in events bigger than themselves'. For Call and many others, the trip West denoted a landmark event, the beginning of a grand and meaningful adventure. Female diarists may not have been palpably aware of Manifest Destiny in all its bluster and patriotism, but they did exhibit a sense of auspiciousness, of personal or genealogical destiny.

In many cases, diaries served a specific function as a family record, women thus serving a key role in documenting not only the practicalities of the trip and the landscapes travelled, but also life histories and deaths. As Lillian Schlissel noted, westering women represented 'the actuaries of the road, tallying the miles with the lives that were lost'. Moreover, the diary afforded a place of refuge amid the bustle of the trail, a place for empowerment and also for reflection and confession. Given the relative lack of opportunities for contact between women, the trail diary served as an important locus for social dialogue, a surrogate meeting place where the author could trade the thoughts of the day with those already recorded. Significantly, female diarists dealt in elaborative codes – sentimental and descriptive tones – while male writers tended to be more restrictive, focusing on the utilitarian and the specific. Images such as the iconic Madonna of the Prairie presented female travellers as silent, angelic creatures but writing at the end of the day provided a forum for many in need of emotional release and cogitation. These precious few minutes afforded the opportunity to mull over the day's events, gain control and closure. Women used their journals to let off steam, express fears, reinforce their social world and cultivate a sense of personal vantage over trail decisions and moments in which they served predominantly as spectators. As Mary Elizabeth Warner wrote of her travels in 1853, 'They talk about the times that tried men's souls but this was the time [that tried] both men and women's souls.'[6]

The trip for Carrie Call began with a sense of excitement and novelty. Family members vied to sit upfront, as Call exclaimed: 'we are what you would call emigrants'. Hitting the trail for the first time, the mobile life seemed fresh and full of vibrancy. Carrie mused: 'I expect we will get so accustomed to travelling that we will not stop when we get to the coast but will go right on to China.' For Virginia Reed, age thirteen, travelling across the Plains from Springfield, Illinois, life on the road proved equally exhilarating. She described her family's wagon as a 'pioneer palace car . . . so comfortable that mama could sit reading and chatting with the little ones and almost forget that she was really crossing the plains'. Needless to say, the realities of the wagon trip dented greenhorn enthusiasm pretty early on. At the end of day one, Carrie Call complained about travelling all day, with hungry children crying and the weather 'too cool for comfort this evening'. She retained a sense of humour nevertheless: 'Katie and I have a gay time as we travel along. We can either sit in the seat in the boiling hot sun or we can go to bed and have a good jolting up.' Meanwhile Virginia

Reed's experience of trail life became decidedly less comfortable when her family joined up with the ill-fated Donner Party to cross the Sierra Nevada Mountains.[7]

Life adhered to a daily rhythm for the emigrant family, dictated by the trail and also by gender conventions. Women performed domestic roles, including cooking, keeping provisions, darning, laundry, looking after the children and playing trail nurse, while men presided over the task of keeping wagons trundling westwards by driving the team, repairing equipment, tending to the animals and assuming guard duty. Both focused on keeping the family together, safe and on the move, but, in common with broader societal norms, the feminine sphere centred on the private (family well being and morality) while the masculine looked out into the public domain and played a leading role in decision-making. Many women sought security in their traditional roles. Routine tasks conferred a sense of order and regimen to the uncertainty of the trail. That said, maintaining a functional household economy proved no easy job. While men grappled with the dangers of floods, snakes, broken axles and the chimera of Indian attack, women faced equally challenging tasks. The rigours of trail life demanded stamina. Women rose first to cook breakfast, walked the trail to gather firewood and were the last to finish chores when the wagon had stopped for the night. Leisure time appeared in short supply. Call spoke of leaving her journal musings to read to husband Jimmie or keep him company in the evenings. Resourcefulness proved a requirement, too, and women were forced to learn quickly. Carrie Call started out on day one baulking at picking wild watercress to add to ham sandwiches because of the bugs, but wrote later in her diary of collecting snow to mix with condensed milk for ice cream and rolling dough as the wagons rolled west. Back home she washed potatoes before and after peeling, but on the trail, seemed 'very glad to get them without their being washed at all'. Meanwhile, as the miles went by, the wagon became more and more a surrogate home. It sustained the family's practical needs and served as a psychological hub around which they galvanised. A sketch in Call's diary of the wagon and its accoutrements offered an artistic display of domestic refuge: the mobile equivalent of the 'home sweet home' cross stitch. Women played an integral role in sustaining this economy and took great pride in keeping the house tidy and family spirits up. Holed up in a ranch house near Las Vegas, Call glowed: 'Mrs Stewart says we have the most comfortable outfit for travelling she has ever seen.'[8]

Although the sexual division of labour remained relatively consistent, sometimes the necessity of the trail mandated a blurring of roles. Men did not normally take on domestic duties but many women found themselves assuming traditionally masculine roles as the journey proceeded. If men fell ill or died, became tired, or if more hands were needed, women could be found driving the team, pitching tents, setting up camp and even hunting. Typical Sunday rituals also fell by the wayside as emigrants strove to complete their trip as quickly as possible. While some women clung to petticoats and bonnets as signifiers of their cultural and gender identity, many adapted feminine attire and custom to fit the demands of the terrain, especially as the trail miles clocked up. Gloves were cast off and long flowing skirts trimmed as women faced the realities of dirt and sunburn. One female emigrant advised her fellow travellers: 'Side-saddles should be discarded – women should wear hunting frocks, loose pantaloons, men's hats and shoes, and ride the same as men.' Such practices conferred a range of emotions upon the frontier woman, including elation, empowerment, adventurousness, but also guilt and unease. As young Mary Ellen Hixon took the reigns of the wagon team, her mother chided: 'I am afraid it isn't a very lady-like thing to do.' Later in her diary, Mary admitted, 'After this, while I felt a secret joy in being able to have a power that set things going, there was also a sense of shame over this new accomplishment.'[9]

Nature loomed large in the consciousness of female emigrants. Diary entries typically cast the environment as a principal actor in the great drama of westward movement. The landscape often inspired strong emotions, with commentary clustered around three points of reference. On some days, nature presented a tiresome dirge, a chore to pass through en route to the paradise at the end of the trail. Mary Ronan, travelling to Montana in the 1860s described 'monotonous miles of jolting, weariness, illness, heat, acrid dust, alkali water, mosquitoes, cactuses, rattlesnakes, perilous ascents and descents on scarcely broken roads'. Frequently the landscape assumed a malign countenance. In this frame, nature appeared instrumental in determining the fortunes of the travelling party, a dastardly enemy to the progress of the wagon and the survival of its precious inhabitants. In Ronan's case the presence of natural threat led her to feel 'forebodings that all this painful change to new surroundings might hold worse not better fortunes'. Sometimes, however, the terrain proved far more inspiring, with evocations to magnificent scenery gracing many journals. Such landscapes of plenty were drunk in for their aesthetic charms and whimsy. Moreover, they served as harbingers of a greater West of verdant utopian living and a suitably monumental backdrop to the gravitas of the family expedition. Ronan spoke gleefully of 'gorgeous sunsets gilding distant mountain peaks and flooding with magic light great valleys . . . the rhythm of going going going combine to make a backdrop and a theme-song for that long trek into the land of gold'.[10]

Early on in her journal Carrie Call wrote, 'We don't stay long in a place. We are anxious to get through as soon as possible,' suggesting that nature represented a trailside nuisance or irrelevant detail in the tunnel vision vantage of the westbound traveller. However, as the journey proceeded, nature assumed a prominent position in the acuity of the emigrant. Carrie's diary, in common with many others, offered vivid descriptions of the road travelled. Although the family's eight-week trip to California proved substantially shorter than the six months endured by emigrants headed west to Oregon, the landscape proved a recurrent theme in Call's narrative. She spoke often about nature 'red in tooth and claw' – a lurking threat, omnipotent, changeable and powerful. Call talked of searing heat on Saturday, 30 October, then a blizzard the next day that left her hands so cold she could hardly write. The family faced treacherous river crossings, rocky roads and wrong turnings. On several occasions, Carrie confessed private fears of succumbing to natural hazards and the family becoming lost in the wilderness with their fate never known. On the Black Ridge she wrote, 'It is altogether a dangerous road . . . Fortunately we have not met a team so far. If we should undertake to pass one I think we would all land in the stream below. Then who would telegraph the news to our friends? We expect to camp at Bellevue Fort tonight if we are alive.' Glad to strike camp after their perilous trek, the family holed up in a deserted house for five days while their lame horse recuperated. The break gave Carrie time to contemplate the trip ahead, across the Virgin River and 'the fatal desert':

> I don't know whether we will ever get to our destination or not – every one we meet tells us such frightful stories of the desert and Indians and especially on the Virgin River. They say the quicksand is so bad that if the wagon wheels should once drop, a hundred horses could not pull us out.[11]

Carrie none the less retained faith in Jimmie's strength as defender of the family and stalwart trailblazer. 'Our captain can give a cowboy whoop to frighten the horses so we will cross it a flying', she remonstrated. Such projections of female fearfulness alongside masculine heroism conveyed dominant gender codes. As Glenda Riley noted, even when women emigrants found themselves taking on more roles, they still employed 'traditional female values as their guides'. Meanwhile, the next part of the Call's trip highlighted the feminine resolve commonly displayed by emigrant women. The family crossed the Virgin River twenty-two times in four days, before tackling the forbidding Vegas range and desert. Locals had offered directions to a spring, but the wagon team found it dry. Facing another thirty miles in failing light, Call noted, in a matter of fact tone 'it was what I would call "a state of things"'. She sat upfront in the wagon with Jimmie until nine o'clock, when they spotted water and, with great relief, struck camp. Carrie confessed, 'I don't think I was ever so alarmed in my life.' Both two- and four-legged travellers learned a new appreciation for water: 'to use an expression of Jimmie's, the horses bit the spring in two – and each swallowed half'.[12]

Environmental dangers assumed many guises: fast rivers; quicksand; rocky paths; and thirsty deserts. Animals also figured in diary prose, including snakes, vultures and spiders. The mournful howls of a coyote led Carrie to think that, 'they would surely take us last night'. Significantly, the threat of wild nature maintained strong links with the idea of Indian attack. As Call and her family crossed into what she called 'wilderness' (lands without ranches and camps), the notion of lurking Indians took root. On the Virgin River, Call feared that 'the Indians will surround our wagon at night and bother us for something eat. I am afraid it will be for a lock of our hair to wear at their belts so I guess we are in for it.' Such anxieties drew on popular stereotypes of Indian aggression, kidnap and violence. As Glenda Riley noted, 'many women had already served childhood apprenticeships as potential victims before they took their places in the wagons'. Scalping loomed large in the canon of imagined atrocities – hence Call's comment about losing a lock of hair. However, an element of excitement adorned the Indian mystique, as though 'seeing one' denoted a necessary part of the trail experience. Camped in the desert, Call eagerly collected an arrow to remind her of the place. Thrill at the exotic gave way to socially constructed judgements when Call finally happened upon 'her first Indians' at a trading post. 'Parading around with their bows and arrows and painted faces. They are such dirty looking creatures, I hate the sight of them,' she remarked: her linking of hygiene with refinement an implicit assumption of moral vantage. In common with many emigrants, material interaction between Call and the Indians traded in the discourse of barter rather than combat. When they reached the Las Vegas ranch, the Call's realised that the bottom had fallen out of their mess chest. Vital provisions, including a bake oven, lay strewn across the desert. Jimmie bargained with a local Indian to collect their wares in return for payment in flour. Carrie duly recorded, 'Well the Indian returned with everything but the whiskey – he says he did not find that.'[13]

Sandwiched between calamities and moments of mortal danger, Call found time to comment on the beauty of western scenery. Her feminine compatriots proved equally likely to record pleasing landscapes, from grand and unusual landmarks rising from the prairie like Chimney Rock to the vibrant colours of trailside wildflowers. Even on the Black Ridge, Call observed a splendid vista in the midst of disaster. Writing that night, she mused, 'Well we are safely over our perilous road. The scenery was grand but I had more of it than I wanted.' Just the next day, she waxed lyrical about green grass, hills and warm weather, drawing an illustration, in detailed colour, of their camp by a mountain stream. At the Las Vegas spring, Call talked in gushing, romantic prose about the unusual feature: 'We all got out to look at it and it is a sight worth looking at I assure you . . . It is so odd to see the surface of the water perfectly smooth and the bottom a perfect turmoil of boiling water.' In the midst of the dreaded desert, Call crafted an intricate sketch of a mirage containing a large lake and island. The sight of attractive and unusual natural features brightened the monotony of trail chores as well as signalling popular interest in the West as an exceptional and intriguing landscape. Even the coyotes drew praise from Carrie, who wanted Jimmie to shoot one so she could keep its 'pretty' tail. Grandeur and desolation seemed equal parts of the wilderness experience.[14]

The wagon reached California in December 1886 to find citrus groves and temperate weather in 'civilized country'. Call's journal projected visions of California as a veritable paradise of 'green trees, singing birds, roses', worlds away from Christmas in Utah and the harsh environment of the trail. Carrie had enjoyed the journey but issued the following warning to her sister Kate: 'never . . . come this way if you value your life and cold water when you are thirsty'. Aridity proved the defining feature of the desert. Certainly the trip had proved a trying time for the family, but they had made it. Call's record, full of drama, fear, danger, action and excitement echoed the narratives of the Old West as told by Turner or by Hollywood, but with one critical difference – the female emigrant stood centre stage.[15]

Homesteader and Hunter: Evelyn Cameron

The traditional narrative of westward conquest cast the female homesteader in a harsh and alien landscape unbefitting of feminine wiles. Out of place in the wild, women appeared destined to become reluctant pioneers or 'gentle tamers'. Revisionist scholarship has questioned this narrative, instead positing that the privations of the frontier offered women an opportunity to redefine gender relations based on necessity, self-sufficiency and the relative absence of social strictures. More often than not, the Western woman found herself living a life of domestic purgatory in a remote shack, a reality far removed from the heady invocations to Western paradise many had entertained before they headed west. For Patricia Nelson Limerick, the 'long suffering white female seemed to be the closest thing to an authentic innocent victim'.[16]

Looking at the life of Evelyn Cameron, the vision of the female homesteader appears rather more complicated. Certainly, Cameron's experience contained resonances of traditional and revisionist narratives, but her identity was not encapsulated by any single one of them. She failed to fit within the moulds of reluctant pioneer, gentle tamer, proto-feminist, or hapless victim, although nuances of each could be found in her everyday activities. Significantly, Evelyn Cameron suggested the life of the Western woman to be a multi-layered one based on environmental conditions, extant codes of class and gender, daily routines, personalities, cultural values and a growing sense of regional identity. One aspect in particular set Cameron apart from both traditional and revisionist narratives – she appeared resolutely at home in the West.

Evelyn Cameron's route west began in the unlikely setting of aristocratic England. Born into a well-to-do family in 1868, Cameron grew up in the family country house at Furze Down, Streatham, her needs catered for by fifteen servants. She arrived in Montana in 1889 on honeymoon with husband Ewen, destined for the badlands on a hunting trip with one of General Custer's old guides. Images of striking Montanan scenery, abundant game and vast grazing ranges lodged firmly in the consciousness of Ewen and Evelyn, and, after a restless year in England they returned to settle in the West. Evelyn exchanged pastoral life and London soirees for an existence on the rolling prairie with entertainment courtesy of the small but rowdy cow town of Terry.

The Camerons rented the 4.4 Ranch on the Powder River, before settling at the Eve Ranch in 1893. Evelyn analogised the landscape to her Old World haunts, noting that the grass-covered hills and fruit trees offered 'littler bits of views that will equal a Kent or Sussex landscape'. That said, Evelyn in no way pined for the old country. She found the rugged landscape and the independence conferred by life on the frontier captivating. Not long after moving to the Eve Ranch, Evelyn came across a stack of old letters from her family. Her journal recorded, 'Shall have no more in the same strain ever, but I certainly (if possible) wouldn't change my lot for all their love.' Photographs of Evelyn depicted a woman entirely at ease in her surroundings. One snap shows her standing upright on the saddle of a horse, face suntanned, lips cracked, wearing simple attire. Another illustrates her sitting on a rock with a tame coyote on her lap, the picture of the American frontier woman (albeit with a tiny British flag pinned to her hat).[17]

Conditions at the Cameron homestead were spartan. The rough-hewn log cabin that she shared with Ewen featured three rooms, few home comforts and many bedbugs. The couple's plan to raise polo ponies on the free grass of the Montana plains and ship them to England ran into trouble early on. With debts mounting, Ewen suggested they cut their losses and return to England. Evelyn, however, dug in her heels. On 20 August 1893 she wrote, 'Out here there is some chance of money making even if we kept quiet, saved, bought and sold osses.' And the next day, 'I would rather stay here, I don't care about home now, feel as tho' I would like to never hear nor go near it.' The pair stayed on, making ends meet by renting a room to Ewen's brother Alec and other paying guests.[18]

Each day Evelyn's journal offered a record of activities undertaken, weather conditions, quantities of food produced and local news. With paper scarce, Evelyn wrote in tiny script, and at the end of the page, turned it sideways, picked up a new colour ink pen and started writing again. Her style favoured direct prose, painstaking detail and an efficient delivery. According to historian Donna Lucey, daily moments spent updating the journal allowed Cameron to give 'shape and meaning to her days' as well as offering a practical almanac of farm work for consultation in later seasons. Moreover, writing allowed Evelyn a rare moment of leisure and time for personal reflection in a day full of chores. A typical day entailed rising at dawn, starting the fire, cooking breakfast, then washing, needlework, cleaning, organising the animals and tending the garden during daylight hours, before cooking supper after dusk for Ewen and the boarders. On one occasion Evelyn wrote the following ditty, offering commentary both on her life of domestic drudgery and her resonant sense of humour: 'From repose arose, none the worse for my dose. In worn and tattered raiment sallied forth to do the chores, & then returned to cook for those everlasting bores.' Nevertheless, Evelyn spoke of her existence not with despond but tenacity. She relished the hard work and physicality of the pioneer environment – writing to her mother 'I rise at 5am & enjoy it. There is nothing like work to make one contented, is there?'[19]

Gender roles as dictated by popular culture translated into 'men's' jobs and 'women's' jobs on the homestead. In common with societal norms casting men as physically strong breadwinners, the heavier work tended to fall to them, including clearing land, ploughing and mending equipment. Women typically worked around the house and its hinterland, including gardening, raising chickens and milking. However, the dictates of the frontier economy frequently saw this system break down. For one thing, the 160-acre lots available under the Homestead Act (1862) could be claimed by any head of a household, male or female. According to historian Harriet Sigerman, single women comprised a sizeable number of claimants – independent types eager to embrace the opportunities conferred by a West of land and promise. Meanwhile, many married women assumed male roles when their husbands left the ranch on business, became indisposed or experienced illness, disability or death. The cult of true womanhood could not survive intact when faced with the rigours of life on the frontier. Survival demanded adaptation and straying into masculine controlled terrains. As writer Page Smith noted: 'When Eastern ladies were fainting at a coarse word or a vulgar sight, their Western sisters fought off Indians, ran cattle, made homes and raised children in the wilderness. It was in the West, in consequence, that women had the greatest status.'[20]

Evelyn Cameron's diary illuminated the pivotal role played by women in the homestead economy. Like many women, she worked tirelessly as a rural artisan, playing a key role in growing, processing and preparing food. Meanwhile, the prospect of building a new home from scratch demanded hard graft, resourcefulness and adaptability. Survival required innovation. When the polo pony business faltered, Evelyn raised vegetables and hauled them by wagon to sell at the cowboy roundup and the railroad station. She learned to cope with the Montana climate – sometimes fifty degrees below zero – in innovative ways. Yeast bread mix came to bed with Evelyn at night to prevent it from freezing, while a homemade concoction of horse manure and flour plaster plugged holes in the walls of the draughty animal shed.

Evelyn served as ad hoc prairie veterinarian and doctor by cutting up dead calves, sewing up gashes in her arm and removing grit from her eye with a needle. Suffering from toothache one day, Evelyn wound wire around the offending rotten molar, attached the line to a rafter and jumped off a trunk.

In August 1897, Ewen travelled to England on a trip to sell polo ponies, caught a chill and only returned the following February. For the intervening period, Evelyn managed the ailing ranch and dealt with restless creditors single-handedly. With so many responsibilities to discharge, three months elapsed before Evelyn found time to visit the local town, conferring upon her a 'residential isolation' with which many homesteading women could identify. When Ewen returned, he spent most days immersed in nature study, leaving his wife to manage the day-to-day running of the ranch. In this milieu, Evelyn Cameron undertook errands often perceived to be the domain of men such as branding cattle, hunting predators, collecting wood and breaking-in horses. She demonstrated vigour, resolve and independence – values commonly associated with the male heroes of the frontier rather than the cowering maidens of popular stereotype. The 25 March 1895 saw her 'Out to catch a coyote but instead fought prairie fire', giving substance to Donna Lucey's interpretation of life on the Cameron ranch as one of 'high drama, and monotony' as well as illuminating the myriad roles that Evelyn embraced. Heavy ranch work demanded a tough disposition and a willingness to challenge accustomed gender boundaries. Accordingly, Evelyn Cameron readily abandoned the side saddle and took to wearing trousers. She was one of the first women in Montana to wear a divided skirt. For Cameron, the vigorous life seemed equal parts appealing and empowering. As she wrote, 'manual labour . . . is about all I care about, and, after all, is what will really make a strong woman. I like to break colts. Brand calves, cut down trees, ride & work in a garden.'[21]

An interest in photography demonstrated Evelyn's capable nature. She purchased her first camera in 1894 and learned the rudiments of dry-plate glass photography from Mr Adams, a boarder at the ranch. The camera served multiple functions. It fostered connectivity with family back in England and allowed Evelyn to communicate a nascent frontier identity to her kin. Evelyn pictured pioneer life at the ranch and her neighbours at work and play, preserving a sense of time, place and her own sense of belonging. A voracious appetite for the close-up saw Evelyn scour cliffs and shimmy down ravines to get shots of nesting birds. On one occasion, a charging animal and a mishap with her skirt left Evelyn holding a camera tripod in one hand and an antelope horn in the other. Such audacious pursuits allowed Evelyn to indulge her spirited nature and also brought critical acclaim. In 1907, an article featuring Evelyn's tame wolves (which Ewen later sent to Coney Island because he felt his wife was too 'daring' with them) appeared in *Country Life* magazine to popular applause. Glowing with pride, Evelyn wrote of receiving a letter from famous Western photographer L. Huffman, who remarked of a recent trip to New York: 'seen many photos, professional and amateur, but none that pleased him better than mine.'[22]

Evelyn's aptitude with the camera provided the Camerons with a vital means of subsistence when the ranch ran into trouble. With a steady stream of pioneers jostling for the chance to immortalise their lives on film, Evelyn developed a tenable business as a roving chronicler of the plains. She photographed immigrant farmers, cowhands, railroad gangs and even regional celebrities like the all-action Buckley sisters, renowned for their horse riding, lassoing and cattle branding exploits. A fixture of the local carnival and celebration circuit, Evelyn attended weddings, parties and other gatherings to preserve moments for posterity and the family record. Writing to thank Evelyn for his album in 1904, J. H. Price motioned: 'I am charmed with it – & in my old age I shall be able to look through it and recall incidents of my Montana life.' Evelyn's business appeared well placed to capture the pioneer verve of the times. She secured a hearty trade from locals seeking to purchase visual signifiers of their own success, resolve and embryonic frontier identity. Ranchers posed in front of fattened cattle, children with scrubbed-clean faces and freshly starched Sunday best stood straight-backed for the camera, and homesteaders assembled around their rough-hewn log homes with favoured possessions and pets in tow: each saying this is us, this is our place. With her photographic skills gaining currency, Evelyn rented a room at a Terry hotel, took orders from the local Post Office (at 10 per cent commission), and toured local ranches to secure contracts. Success, however, meant a late dinner on a Wednesday night, much to Ewen's consternation.[23]

In her photography business, Evelyn Cameron offered a pertinent example of female entrepreneurship on the frontier. She identified a keen market, acquired new skills and worked hard to earn money. Evelyn counted distinct advantages in terms of her ethnicity and class. She boasted a privileged education, access to funds and useful contacts. That said, women from disadvantaged backgrounds also found ways to make money in the transient and embryonic settlements of the trans-Mississippi region. Mrs Ah Lum, or 'China Mary', an emigrant from the Chinese province of Zhongshan, earned a tidy nest egg peddling a range of rather less respectable, but highly sought after commodities in Tombstone. Arriving in the rowdy town on the back of the mining boom in 1879–80, she swiftly cultivated a reputation as a matriarch of the community, becoming, like Evelyn Cameron, a 'public woman'. While Cameron sold provisions and photographs, China Mary cornered the market in domestic services: prostitution; laundering; and a general store (complete with backroom gambling den). In an environment dominated by single men, selling a range of culturally sanctioned 'feminine' skills proved a canny business decision. Locals came to Mary to hire servants, maids, and cooks – rendering her as a powerbroker in the 500-strong Chinese community of 'Hoptown'. The experience of China Mary indicated that fortunes could be made by enterprising women in the rough and ready West, as well as pointing to the critical economic and social roles played by marginal groups. Mrs Ah Lum ended up with her own burial plot in the famed 'Boot Hill' cemetery when she died in 1906. However, a lurking culture of Orientalism also rendered the West a land of contest and prejudice for women of colour. In common with Mrs Ah Lum, most Chinese women earned the label 'Mary' – a reflection of cultural prejudice, linguistic laziness and subjection. White supremacist demagogues and Christian reformers alike assumed all Chinese women on the frontier to be morally bankrupt, unclean drudges who worked as prostitutes. Certainly, many working girls failed to earn the cash or the cachet of Mrs Ah Lum, but they scarcely conformed to the passive victim or bad woman archetypes. Prostitution in the West connoted exploitation, abuse, poverty and abandonment, but it also suggested female companionship, a decorous lifestyle, the promise of monetary gain and a modicum of female agency.

The independence of mind that Evelyn Cameron displayed as frontier photographer also manifested on the hunting trail. Every autumn until 1900, she and Ewen left their ranch to pursue game in the Badlands, typically for a few months at a time. Living in a tent through the Montana winter demanded a hardy disposition. In the first few days of the 1894 trip, Evelyn confessed that her bones ached with the cold, but noted that she would become used to it. In camp, as at home, it fell to Evelyn to perform domestic duties of housekeeping. She packed provisions, tended the fire, darned, did laundry and cooked. Holed up in an abandoned cabin on 12 November 1894, Evelyn noted her roster of activities: 'I washed 5 handtowels, 2 napkins, 1 dish cloth,

2 pillow cases. Did even graze my knuckles. I swept out the shack, under the bunks, full of green brush carried in by a skunk I think.' On this trip, the couple took an acquaintance with them, Mr Colley. On 1 January Evelyn recorded, 'Mr C shot a fawn. I toiled all day in camp.' When she did hit the trail, Evelyn often served in a support capacity – minding the horses and skinning bagged animals. She waited for hours while Ewen stalked game, spending the time nature spotting and reading *Titbits* magazine. Confiding in her diary, Evelyn expressed frustration at being confined to an essentially domestic faculty.[24]

The hunting trail did not always cultivate a culture of homespun servility. Although Evelyn played a supporting role in camp, her contribution proved integral to the functioning of the hunting outfit. Moreover, as an accomplished sportswoman, Evelyn seized every opportunity to participate in the hunt directly, proving at least as good a shot as her male compatriots when she had the chance. In winter 1894–5, Evelyn regularly chastised companions Mr C and cousin Alec for their weak disposition and poor marksmanship: 'Having these kind of young men to take out spoils all our pleasure. Mr C's terribly green and too fond of his ease to care about hunting much.' On successive trips, Evelyn showed little concern about wiling away time in the wilds unaccompanied. In November 1894, she described being surrounded by howling wolves as she looked after the horses, and in 1899, spent a couple of nights camping alone north of the Yellowstone River while Ewen restocked provisions. When Ewen returned, he reported that the residents of Terry thought he was 'dreadful' for leaving her alone in the wilderness. Meanwhile, during the 1898 season, Evelyn hit the hunting trail by herself – her bravado in the Badlands a stark contrast to female companion Effie, who demanded breakfast in a china cup, promptly lost her 'lucky stone' and spent most of the trip in camp, suffering from headaches and talking about her sister. Evelyn gained a name for herself among frontier folk for her flouting of gender conventions and fearless exploits in the name of sport. Returning from their 1895 hunt, the Cameron's paused at the MacQueen House hotel in Miles City, where the maid Molly lent Evelyn a skirt for the evening soiree. Evelyn's journal duly recorded: 'Mrs Malone introduced me in to sitting room and said "it was like talking to some character out of a book talking to me!" The hunting trip seems to make them think the woman who hunts a wonder.'[25]

In 'A Woman's Big Game Hunting' the *New York Sun* of 4 November 1900 looked back on Evelyn's distinguished sporting career. It revelled in her transformation from well-heeled aristocrat to mountain lion and grizzly hunter extraordinaire. The western wonderland of the Rockies conjured dramatic scenery, fierce animals and fearsome weather, through which strode Evelyn, a sharp shot and indefatigable explorer. Her larger than life stories of deliverance in the wilds rivalled those of legendary frontiersman folklore: 'I've spent January and February in a tiny Indian tent . . . with the mercury 40 degrees below zero, and our noses and chins were all blistered with the cold. And I've had my hair frizzled by lightning so that it made a cracking sound.' The imagined West of Evelyn Cameron certainly appeared as action packed and vigorous as anything Turner or Cody had to offer.[26]

In fact, in all her walks of life – at the ranch, behind the camera, and on the hunting trail – Evelyn Cameron revelled in the frontier condition. As she advised: 'For the woman with outdoor propensities and a taste for roughing it there is no life more congenial than that of the saddle and rifle, as it still may be lived in parts of the Western States.' She adapted to the terrain and tested the boundaries of women's work by kicking dust in the face of the stereotype of women as weak, inferior and reliant on men. Evelyn Cameron demonstrated the opportunities for women in the West, their willingness to take on new roles and the attendant distending of gender conventions. At the same time, she, in common with many women, remained subject to subtle restrictions and social strictures. On one occasion, Evelyn faced arrest in Miles City for her divided skirt, while her hunting exploits caused local tongues to wag. Moreover, she discharged her domestic duties as hostess at the hunting camp and ranch house without complaint and often with relish, and eventually reined in her photography business in the face of Ewen's grumblings. In a sense, Evelyn Cameron's life bespoke the frontier tensions experienced by many Western women – of domesticity versus liberation, the known versus the unfamiliar. For Cameron, however, there appeared little contradiction in these roles. Evelyn actually found power and poise, purpose and persistence in her daily routines. As Glenda Riley observed, 'a significant number of western women . . . kept going, finding ways to appear domestic while doing what they wanted to do.' In ranch work, hunting and photography, Evelyn Cameron embraced the country, found her voice and identity and even became a frontier legend of her own design. When authoress Marguerite Remington Charter visited Billings in the late 1800s she was advised to 'go to the Eve Ranch and see Mrs Cameron, she is one of the wonders of Montana'. A century later, speaking at the National

Cowgirl Museum in Forth Worth, Lynne Cheney hoisted Evelyn as a stalwart example of 'a spirit of equality' in the West.[27]

Notes

1. Theodore Roosevelt, *Winning of the West, selections*, H. Wish (ed.) (Gloucester: Peter Smith, 1976 [1889–96]); Susan Armitage and Elizabeth Jameson (eds), *The Women's West* (Norman: University of Oklahoma Press, 1987), p. 9; Frederick Jackson Turner, 'The Significance of the Frontier on American History' (1893), paper delivered to the American Historical Association, 12 July 1893; Frederick Jackson Turner, *The Frontier in American History* (New York: Henry Holt, 1921); Glenda Riley, *Confronting Race: Women and Indians on the Frontier. 1815–1915* (Albuquerque: University of New Mexico Press, 2004), p. 30.
2. Emerson Hough, *The Passing of the Frontier* (New Haven: n.p., 1920), pp. 93–4; Dee Brown, *The Gentle Tamers: Women of the Old West* (London: Barrie & Jenkins, 1958); T. A. Larson, 'Dolls, vassals, and drudges – pioneer women in the West', *Western Historical Quarterly* 3/1 (January 1972), pp. 4–16; Glenda Riley, *The Female Frontier: A Comparative View of Women on the Prairie and the Plains* (Lawrence, University Press of Kansas, 1988), p. 2; Patricia Nelson Limerick, *Legacy of Conquest: The Unbroken Past of the American West* (New York: Norton, 1987), p. 52.
3. Bernard DeVoto, *Journals of Lewis and Clark* (Boston: Houghton Mifflin, 1953), p. ii; Georgia Read, 'Women and children on the Oregon–California Trail in the gold-rush years', *Missouri Historical Review*, XXXIX (1944), p. 6; Julie Roy Jeffrey, *Frontier Women: The Trans-Mississippi West, 1840–1880* (New York: Hill & Wang, 1979), p. xi.
4. 'Diary of Carrie Call', Mss HM60317, Huntington Library, San Marino, CA (hereafter cited as Huntington); Jeffrey, *Frontier Women*, p. 3. See: Catherine Beecher, *The Duty of Young Women to their Country* (New York: Harper & Bros., 1845).
5. Quoted in Jeffrey, *Frontier Women*, pp. 15–16.
6. 'Diary of Carrie Call'; Brown, *Gentle Tamers*, p. 16; Lillian Schlissel, *Women's Diaries of the Westward Journey* (New York: Schoken Books, 2004 [1982]), p. 14; John Mack Faragher, *Women and Men on the Overland Trail* (New Haven: Yale University Press, 1979), p. 4.
7. 'Diary of Carrie Call; Brown, *Gentle Tamers*, pp. 94, 96.
8. 'Diary of Carrie Call'.
9. Quoted in Brown, *Gentle* Tamers, p. 17; Quoted in Paula Bartley and Cathy Loxton, *Plains Women: Women in the American West* (Cambridge: Cambridge University Press, 1991), p. 15.
10. Margaret Ronan, 'Memoirs of a frontiers woman: Mary C. Ronan', Masters thesis, Montana State University, 1932, p. 35. Held at the Montana Historical Society Library and Archives, Helena, Montana. Hereafter cited as MHS.
11. 'Diary of Carrie Call'.
12. 'Diary of Carrie Call'; Riley, *The Female Frontier*, p. 4.
13. 'Diary of Carrie Call'; Riley, *Confronting Race*, p. 97.
14. 'Diary of Carrie Call'.
15. 'Diary of Carrie Call'.

16. Brown, *Gentle Tamers*, p. 297; Limerick, *Legacy of Conquest*, p. 48.
17. Cameron: quoted in Donna M. Lucey, *Photographing Montana, 1894–1928: The Life and Work of Evelyn Cameron* (New York: Alfred Knopf, 1990), pp. 17, 13–14.
18. Evelyn Cameron, 'Diary 1893', box 1, folder 4: Diaries,-1893–4, MC226: Evelyn J. and Ewen S. Cameron Papers, MHS.
19. Lucey, *Photographing Montana*, pp. 77, 78.
20. Harriet Sigerman, *Land of Many Hands* (New York: Oxford University Press, 1997), p. 48; Page Smith, *Daughters of the Promised Land: Women in American History* (Boston: Little, Brown, 1970), p. 221.
21. Faragher, *Women and Men on the Overland Trail*, p. 112; Evelyn Cameron, 'Diary 1895', box 1, folder 5: Diaries,-1895–6, MC226: Evelyn J. and Ewen S. Cameron Papers, MHS; Lucey, *Photographing Montana*, pp. xv, xii.
22. Ewen Cameron, 'The wolf in Montana', unpublished manuscript, MC226: Evelyn J. and Ewen S. Cameron Papers, box 6, folder 15, MHS; Lucey, *Photographing Montana*, p. 184.
23. Lucey, *Photographing Montana*, p. 152.
24. Evelyn Cameron, 'Diary 1894', box 1, folder 4: Diaries,-1893–4, MC226: Evelyn J. and Ewen S. Cameron Papers, MHS.
25. Evelyn Cameron, 'Diary 1894'; Evelyn Cameron, 'Diary 1899', box 2, folder 1: 'Diaries 1899–1900', MC226, Evelyn J. and Ewen S. Cameron Papers, MHS; Evelyn Cameron, 'Diary 1898', box 1, folder 6: 'Diaries 1897–8', MC226, Evelyn J. and Ewen S. Cameron Papers, MHS; Evelyn Cameron, 'Diary 1895'.
26. 'A woman's big game hunting', New York *Sun*, 4 November 1900.
27. 'A woman's big game hunting'; Riley, *Confronting Race*, p. 28; Lucey, *Photographing Montana*, p. xvii

Chapter 6

Women in the West: The 'Indian Princess' and the 'Lady Wildcat'

The trail lifestyle experienced by Carrie Call represented the median for many female emigrants who found life in the West a mixture of rigour and routines, social and geographical isolation, daily domesticities and adaptive practices. Defiance of gender conventions was according to Glenda Riley 'random and intermittent'. Nevertheless, for those women who chose to venture a more public form of resistance, the West volunteered an intense and colourful theatre for female advancement. This chapter considers issues of gender liberation and empowerment by exploring the experiences of two women, Sarah Winnemucca and Calamity Jane, whose exploits led them into unusual scenarios. A bead-adorned Indian speaker and a cross-dressing 'lady wildcat', these two women gained eminence on the entertainment circuit. Here stood two female characters who highlighted the possibilities for women to speak in a public domain usually dominated by male voices. Yet, for all their vigour and oratorical power, both women struggled with prejudice and negative stereotyping.[1]

Cultural Mediator: Sarah Winnemucca

In 1980, Joan Jensen and Darlis Miller recommended a multicultural approach that considered 'the experiences of all ethnic groups of women within a historical framework incorporating women's history into western history'. Many heeded that call and sought to give voice to those marginalised in Western history by a potent triumvirate of race, class and gender oppression. Using post-colonial and feminist discourses, scholars extended debate beyond the confines of traditional history and the experiences of (predominantly) White emigrants to consider the involvement of women of colour in 'all contests for power taking place in a given place'. Narratives of diversity, cultural interaction, stereotype, deconstruction, resistance and agency emerged as *modus operandi*. The life of Sarah Winnemucca represents a germane example of the interplay between gender and race as functional modes of repression. Her life shows the West as a meeting point of different cultures and a locus of empire. Euro-American cultural codes cast Sarah in the role of native princess, yet advocates argued that she successfully manipulated this image to highlight the plight of her people. Significantly, Sarah Winnemucca emerged as a critical player in debates over Indian rights – a public political role scarcely occupied by women or indigenous peoples in general during the nineteenth century. Her West appeared as a contentious and convoluted one, a world of constraint and opportunity in which she served as both redeemer and pariah.[2]

Born around 1844 into the Northern Paiute tribe in western Nevada, Sarah Winnemucca or Thocmetony (shell flower) boasted a distinguished lineage as the daughter of chief Winnemucca and the granddaughter of chief Truckee, famed for guiding Captain John Fremont across the Great Basin. Her birth coincided with a period of great disruption for the Paiute due to Euro-American encroachment. As her autobiography recalled, 'I was a very small child when the first white people came into our country. They came like a lion, yes, like a roaring lion, and have continued so ever since, and I have never forgotten their first coming.' Wagon trains passed near tribal lands on the banks of the Humboldt River, bringing disease and the occasional rifle shot. At the age of six, Sarah apprehended White society as an exotic 'other', in equal parts frightening and captivating. She analogised the emigrants' pale skin to that of owls, raising the spectre of the 'Cannibal Owl' who gobbled up errant Paiute children. As a teenager, Sarah travelled to Genoa, Nevada to stay with William Ormsby (one of Truckee's contacts), and boarded at St Mary's Sisters of Charity convent school in San Jose. Such experiences left her with English and Spanish language skills and a particular vantage on cultural exchange.[3]

The silver rush and the coming of the railroad to Virginia City in the 1860s accelerated the marginalisation of the Paiutes. Following skirmishes with prospectors and the US Army, the Paiutes found themselves relocated to the Pyramid Lake Reservation (established in 1859). With corruption rife and the tribe lacking even basic supplies, Sarah Winnemucca emerged as a key negotiator between tribal elders and Indian agents. Following successful mediations, the Army allowed the Paiute to relocate to Fort McDermitt, 300 miles away on the Oregon border, where Sarah worked as interpreter for $65 a month (1868–71).

Her standing as a cultural intermediary mirrored that of female Indian icons Sacagawea and Pocahontas, not to mention the less famous indigenous women who served as arbiters between tribal and settler society at forts and fur trading posts across the West. Working in this capacity, Sarah cultivated a reputation as an eloquent diplomat (a strong woman far removed from contemporary stereotypes of the 'squaw drudge') and became a strident orator for Indian rights. This ability to communicate across Indian and Euro-American worlds generated respect. Major Henry Douglas, Indian superintendent for Nevada, endorsed Sarah's criticisms of the Pyramid Lake reservation as 'appropriate and just' and praised her (albeit in rather condescending tone) as 'passably good looking, with some education and . . . much natural shrewdness and intelligence. She converses well . . . [uses] civilised customs, and will as readily join in an Indian dance.' Paiute elders regarded Sarah with esteem for her abilities to decipher the written texts which Euro-Americans prized so greatly. That said, Sarah's role as a cultural arbiter left her with a bi-cultural identity that sometimes proved hard to resolve. As she confessed: 'I like this Indian life tolerably well; however . . . I would rather be with my people, but not to live with them as they live . . . My happiest life has been . . . living among the whites.'[4]

In 1872, Sarah lived with the Northern Paiutes and the Bannocks on the newly established Malheur Reservation, where she taught in school and served as an interpreter. Corruption under Agent William Rinehart and land seizures by settlers none the less caused disquiet, and by 1878 disgruntled Bannocks had co-opted (some say forced) members of the Paiute into raiding stores and settlements for food. Sarah played a critical role as a peacemaker during this insurgency, pleading with her father and other Paiutes to extricate themselves from the rebels. In her autobiography, Sarah noted the physical strain attached to her vocation as well as her atypical role as female heroine: 'This was the hardest work I ever did for the government in all my life . . . having been in the saddle night and day, distance about two hundred and thirty three miles . . . I only an Indian woman, went and saved my father and his people.' This display of feminine stamina and bravado so impressed General Oliver Howard that he employed Sarah as a scout and interpreter, a remit that afforded her further opportunities to communicate tribal sentiments. Alignment with the military drew criticism from some Paiute elders, especially when the tribe earned the designation of 'hostiles' by virtue of association with the Bannock and were forcibly marched 350 miles for internment at the Yakama Indian Reservation, Washington.[5]

Faced with flagrant examples of government mismanagement and heavy-handed behaviour toward the Paiute, Sarah Winnemucca adopted more of an activist mantle. When a group of religious revivalists visited Yakama, members of the tribe dressed in rags and picketed the home of the Indian Agent. In 1879–80, Sarah and her father conducted a lecture tour of California and Nevada to highlight the plight of the Paiutes, conditions on the reservation and the improper seizure of ancestral lands. The Winnemuccas had resorted to public oratory before, in 1864 parading in Virginia City to disclaim responsibility for the Pyramid Lake War and publicise their suffering. In the same year, they performed stage shows in Virginia City and San Francisco, offering theatrical displays of Indian atrocity such as 'the war council' and 'taking a scalp' to paying punters. A decade on, however, Sarah and her father prioritised the serious business of gesture politics. In 1883 they took the lecture tour nationwide, visiting 300 venues across the north-east.

Adorned with buckskin and eagle feathers, Sarah more than satisfied her 'Indian Princess' tour billing. She projected both the noble savage and a 'civilised' Indian, winning hearts and minds in the process. The *San Francisco Chronicle* reported, 'Sarah's lecture was unlike anything ever before heard in the civilized world – eloquent, pathetic, tragic at times; at others her quaint anecdotes, sarcasm's and wonderful mimicry surprised the audience again and again into bursts of laughter and rounds of applause.' The *San Francisco Illustrated Wasp* magazine featured her on its cover bedecked in fringed dress, moccasins, feathered headdress and a beaded bag. Designed for performative impact rather than historical authenticity, such apparel resembled that of the plains tribes rather than the Paiute (who wore skirts of fibre, bark or skin, adding European-style shirts after 1850). By adopting such techniques, Sarah effectively re-invented her indigenous identity for popular consumption, utilising Euro-American perceptions of Indianness to gain currency and legitimacy for her cause. Audience members purchased an autographed photograph of the 'Indian princess' for fifty cents.[6]

Sarah's command of English and familiarity with Euro-American social mores aided her acceptance. She 'played Indian', earnestly revealing the story of her life and the injustices wrought against the Paiute. Sarah betrayed a shrewd understanding of contemporary reformist impulses, and especially the role of women in such movements. On the tour circuit, Winnemucca adroitly conjoined the Indian princess motif with contemporary notions of female moral guardianship as articulated by the Victorian cult of true womanhood. She spoke of the beneficent child-rearing practices of the Paiute and the foresight of women in the tribal council, thereby breaking down prevailing assumptions of 'savage' Indians. Educator and supporter Elizabeth Peabody recalled that Sarah's lectures 'never failed to arouse the moral enthusiasm of every woman that heard it, and seal their confidence in her own purity of character and purpose', while fellow Bostonian reformer Mary Mann noted: 'It is of the first importance to hear what only an Indian and an Indian woman can tell.' Audiences warmed to Sarah's rhetoric as someone configured as an indigenous 'gentle tamer', a spokeswoman for co-existence and humanity on the frontier. As one attendee remembered, 'Speaking with zest, expressing herself perfectly in good English, able to translate quite naturally the most intimate feeling of her soul . . . She did it with such passion and conviction, she had such pathetic emotions that many people were moved to tears.'[7]

In January 1880, Sarah journeyed to Washington, DC, as part of a Paiute delegation to meet Secretary of the Interior Carl Schurz and President Rutherford Hayes. She performed customary roles as both advocate and translator, and earned plaudits from the *Washington Post*, who related how 'dashing Sarah . . . in deportment and appearance would compare favourably with most of her pale-faced sisters'. Schurz duly signed an executive order granting the Paiutes the right to leave Yakama and reclaim land in the Great Basin under severalty. Sarah dubbed this a 'beautiful letter' and eagerly carried it back West. However, Indian Agent James Wilbur refused to honour Schurz's directive on the grounds that relocation would incite violence among the Paiute. From esteemed cultural mediator, Sarah became pariah. Tribal elders read her ability to decode White wisdoms as a sign of treachery, while Wilbur banished her from the reservation.[8]

Undeterred, Sarah developed an interest in committing her cause to paper. Published in 1883, *Life Among the Piutes: Their Wrongs and Claims* combined history, autobiography and political treatise. Mary Mann editorialised the book, labelling it 'the first outbreak of the American Indian in human literature . . . [with] a single aim – *to tell the truth*'. Sarah's heartfelt rendition began with a recollection of her early life, followed by accounts of tribal customs, life at Pyramid Lake, the Bannock War and the forced relocation to Yakama. Her writing style stressed the personal and the sentimental, imploring the 'dear reader' to take note of the tragic fate of the Paiute. A savvy political operator, Sarah deployed the skills she had learned on stage to win over her audience. *Life Among the Piutes* thus combined emotionality and righteousness to create a powerful discourse of suffering. Sarah made repeated references to God, thereby cultivating empathy for the 'educated Indian' and tugging at the morality of the reformist reading public. The book also demonstrated a keen understanding of the power of American patriotism and the rhetoric of liberty and equality:

> Yes, you, who call yourselves the great civilization; you who have knelt upon Plymouth Rock, covenanting with God to make this land the home of the free and the brave. Ah, then you rise from your bended knees . . . and your so-called civilization sweeps inland from the ocean wave; but, oh, my God! Leaving its pathway marked by crimson lines of blood . . . I am crying out to you for justice.[9]

Life Among the Piutes ended with a petition to Congress for the return of tribal lands and a call to activism from Mary Mann: 'whoever shall be interested by this little book . . . will help to the end by copying the petition and getting signatures to it.' A twenty-page appendix contained references from leading figures in the US Army and Government attesting to Sarah's good character.[10]

In its deployment of Christianity, American political doctrine, romanticism and autobiographical forms, *Life Among the Piutes* reflected Sarah's familiarity with Euro-American literary conventions. Some scholars argued that the book's tacit acceptance of such tropes elucidated her acculturalisation into White society. Others emphasised the tactical nature of Sarah's language. While it utilised literary models from Euro-American culture, *Life Among the Piutes* subscribed to patterns of oral articulation familiar to native storytellers. Sarah situated her own past in the context of the tribe and elevated her achievements according to the vernacular of Paiute hero folklore. Her book used the garb of the Euro-American moral treatise to issue a potent call for Indian rights. Although aimed at a White audience, Sarah orated from an indigenous vantage. For A. LaVonne Ruoff, this rendered her 'the mightiest word warrior of her tribe', able to assimilate aspects of the dominant culture and use it for the purposes of survival and resistance, or 'survivance'. Significantly, *Life Among the Piutes* laid claim to several 'firsts'. It was the first book published by a Native American, the first by a Native American woman and the first to convey Paiute cultural traditions in written form.[11]

By the mid-1880s, Sarah Winnemucca faced a conundrum. She had secured the adoration of Eastern reformers who supported her calls to abandon the reservation system, and, in April 1884, received an audience before the House Subcommittee on Indian Affairs. Sarah's oratory as well as *Life Among the Piutes* had taken the Paiute cause to a national stage and elevated her to celebrity status. According to Richey, 'she was probably the best known Indian in the country', a considerable achievement given the constraints of race and gender stacked against her. On the lecture circuit in Carson City during September 1884, Sarah sported an entourage of fans, notably a group of women from the Washo tribe who waited eagerly outside her hotel. The Reese River *Reveille* reported: 'Just as the Princess emerged through the main entrance of the hotel, rigged out in good toggery, an exclamation of delight ran down the line of Washoe squaws.'[12]

At the same time, institutionalised ethnocentrism, cultural ignorance and bureaucratic politicking blunted her achievements. Support among the Paiute waned as some accused her of being 'the mouthpiece for so many lying promises'. The reformist constituency proved equally divided. As Elizabeth Peabody pointed out, 'already the organized sympathy for Indians in the East was pre-engaged' and Sarah's criticism of the missionary zeal of reservation officials did not go down well among religious revivalists. Sarah's nemesis from Malheur days, Agent Rinehart, proved a vocal critic, besmirching Sarah's reputation as a 'civilized princess' with charges of prostitution, fakery, drunkenness and fist-fighting.[13]

Frustrated by a lack of progress and aware of ebbing public interest in Indian affairs, Sarah returned to Nevada in 1884 to the 160-acre ranch near Lovelock that her brother Natches had purchased from railroad baron Leland Stanford. She began a new phase in her life as educator. Eager to teach Paiute children but denied the opportunity to work at the Pyramid Lake School, Sarah established an independent institution paid for by book royalties, school fees and donations. A year after its establishment, twenty-four children enrolled. Housed in a brush shelter, Sarah's 'Peabody Institute' offered instruction in English language, mathematics, reading and writing. The Nevada *Silver State* remarked: 'attendance is large, and little Indians may be seen on the streets every morning with their lunches, wending their way to school.' Newspaper editorials celebrated the school, presenting Sarah's work as part of a progressive and teleological journey towards civilisation. As the *Daily Alta California* elucidated:

> Out in Nevada is proceeding an experiment that deserves the respectful sympathy of the world. Princess Sarah opened a school for Indian

children . . . In this effort to reclaim her primitive people this Indian woman rises to a nobility that puts her in line with the best of the superior race.

Despite such paeans, the Peabody Institute scarcely represented a tool of assimilation or an exercise in 'killing' the Indian with regimentation, Christianity and the three Rs. Instead, Sarah promoted a more subversive agenda: education as a route to power, influence and land. Children received the skills necessary to prosper in Euro-American society, yet retained an indigenous identity through the speaking of Paiute. They returned to their families at night. Significantly, the school favoured the teaching of Indians by Indians, an ethos that not only put indigenous people in control but also contravened governing bureaucratic ethics of paternalism and Euro-American moral and cognitive superiority. As Elizabeth Peabody noted:

> instead of being . . . a passive reception of civilizing influences proffered by white men who look down upon the Indian as a spiritual, moral, and intellectual inferior, it is a spontaneous movement, made by the Indian himself, *from himself*, in full consciousness of free agency, for the education that is to civilize him.

The institute thus served as an institutional beacon broadcasting mediation and linguistic empowerment. It also illuminated Sarah's ongoing negotiation between two cultures and her fractious relationship with government. Dwindling financial resources, the passage of the Dawes Severalty Act (1887) and the intensification of Indian resistance courtesy of the Ghost Dance assured the closure of the Peabody Institute in 1889.[14]

Sarah Winnemucca died in October 1891 at Henry's Lake, Montana, the home of her sister Elma. The following year, the Paiute received land allotments at the Fort McDermitt Reservation (established 1889), although Sarah's efforts failed to gain mention from tribal elders or the Indian Bureau. A century on, the reputation of the Paiute princess continued to provoke mixed responses. In 1994, she earned induction into the National Women's Hall of Fame and became the first woman to receive a Nevada historic state marker. In the contemporary revisionist vernacular, Sarah symbolised frontier oppression, ethnicity and empowerment. She earned laurels as an activist, community builder and female heroine. In 2005, a statue of Sarah was erected in the Capitol building in DC. The bronze figure of a buckskin-clad woman holding a writing pad and a book lionised her as a diplomat, interpreter and educator: a figure emblematic of peaceful intercession in the West. Elsewhere, plans to commemorate the Winnemucca legacy spurred controversy. In 1994, the Washoe County School District announced plans to name a Reno elementary school after Sarah, provoking opposition both from Indian families, who continued to view her as a collaborator and white families, who favoured naming the institution after the local housing estate 'Suncrest'. Emotions ran high at a public meeting, where it fell to Alexandra Voorhees, an actor known for performing as the Paiute Princess, to delineate Sarah's significance in Western history. Voorhees ruminated on her forward-thinking educational philosophy and mantra of cultural mediation, tireless campaigning and literary success. To resounding cheers, the audience voted to bestow the name Sarah Winnemucca on the elementary school.[15]

Frontier novelty: Calamity Jane

Unlike Sarah Winnemucca, who had to wait a century before taking her place in the annals of female frontier heroes, Martha Jane Canary, or Calamity Jane, was always a staple of Western folklore. Her reputation as a pistol-packing, hard drinking, cross-dresser drew great attention, to the extent that the show-business image defined who she was. Calamity proved to be a fitting character in a West which, according to Richard Slotkin, seemed rapt in its own 'dilemma of authenticity... both an actual place with a real history and as a mythic space populated by projected fantasies'. This dialectic of invention began with Jane herself, who like Buffalo Bill, proved keen to participate in the manufacture of her own legend. Journalists, dime novelists, biographers and Hollywood directors abetted the process, transforming Calamity into one of the most illustrious personages in Western mythology. As the 'Westerners Corral of Chicago' heard as they gathered at their monthly 'Round Up' to hear a talk by Clarence Paine entitled 'Calamity Jane – Man, Woman or Both?' in September 1945: 'Anyone attempting to divine the facts in the life of Calamity Jane is soon impressed by the fact there is as much to be unlearned as to be learned.'[16]

How can we account for the enduring fascination with Calamity? Perhaps it relates to her role as a signifier of a wild and exceptional time (and landscape). Moreover, she cut an inimitable picture of female presence on the frontier. Unlike projections of 'gentle tamers' who civilised the West from the hearth and the schoolhouse, Calamity blazed

Figure 5.1 'Calamity Jane Carey [sic], Scout for Gen. Crook in Black Hills, 1880–1900.'

a trail into the masculine worlds of the army scout and the outlaw. Here stood a female agent in a patriarchal world, inverting gender norms and challenging codes of propriety. For some, the appeal of Calamity Jane bespoke that of frontier novelty. Voyeurism and prurience marked the public gaze. Calamity's atypical behaviour generated curiosity, reverie and titillation – marking her as a harmless whimsy in the history of the West along the lines of Belle Starr and Annie Oakley. Others read her exploits in more radical terms. A 'lady wildcat' who flouted convention and formulated her own identity, Calamity epitomised female empowerment on the frontier. Accordingly, she roamed the nineteenth-century West wearing the badge not of eccentric cross-dresser but feminist incarnate. But her life scarcely matched the romantic image of a gartered gunslinger or a gender liberationist. Instead, she inhabited a world in flux, with social and gender codes, geography and mythology under constant modification.

Born in Princeton, Missouri on 1 May 1852 as Martha Jane Canary, Calamity emigrated with her family to Iowa in 1862, and then to Montana in 1864. In her autobiography, *Life and Adventures of Calamity Jane, By Herself* (1896), Calamity depicted the journey West as dangerous and exhilarating, and paid heed to her childhood affectation for masculine pursuits: 'I was at all times with the men when there was excitement and adventure to be had . . . I was considered a remarkable good shot and a fearless rider for a girl of my age.' Arriving in Virginia City, Montana, the family eked out a precarious existence in the mining camps where mother did laundry and father gambled. After the death of her parents in 1866–7, Calamity wandered between forts and railroad camps, before striking up an association with the US Army (1870–6). During this time, Calamity described how she rejected 'the costume of my sex' in favour of military uniform. As she confessed: 'It was a bit awkward at first but I soon got to be perfectly at home in men's clothes.' *Life and Adventures* suggests Calamity scouted with Custer in Arizona (almost certainly erroneous) and saved Captain Egan from a Nez Perce ambush at Goose Creek, to which the officer uttered the immortal lines: 'I name you Calamity Jane, the heroine of the Plains.'[17]

In 1875 she travelled with the Jenney Expedition to the Black Hills and joined General George Crook's reconnoitre of Sioux territory the following year. During this period, Calamity Jane built a reputation as a resilient, charismatic and feisty character, perhaps unsurprisingly given that she was operating far beyond the usual parameters of women's culture. General Dodge described her as a 'regimental mascot' and 'a queer combination' of nursemaid, cook and thrill-seeker, while the earliest photograph of Calamity (1875) depicted a young woman attired in masculine clothes lounging on a rock near French Creek. According to journalist Thomas Macmillan, 'she had the reputation of being a better horse-back rider [and] mule and bull whacker [driver], and a more unctuous coiner of English, and not the Queen's pure, either, than any [other] man in the command.' An incipient cult of Calamity Jane took root among the ranks, evident in the poems of scout Jack Crawford and the naming of 'Calamity Peak' in honour of the enigmatic young drifter. Writers stoked the fires of celebrity. The first published illustration of Calamity Jane came courtesy of Horace Maguire's *The Coming Empire* (1878), in which she appeared galloping through a valley, adorned in manly apparel and fervently brandishing a pistol.[18]

Despite the colourful depictions of military service set out in *Life and Adventures of Calamity Jane* (such as the indefatigable female scout galloping ninety miles through Indian Territory in inclement weather and swimming the Platte River to deliver important news), Calamity Jane played a peripheral role in the Western US Army. She trudged the plains with the Army, and some eyewitnesses described her as a scout, yet it remained far more likely that she accompanied the freight teams or served as cook, laundress, nurse or prostitute. Citations of Calamity Jane in the historical record during the mid-1870s suggested not a boisterous pathfinder on the army payroll but a woman struggling to survive in the boom and bust melee of the West. In this world of transient mining settlements, railroad towns and military camps, Calamity lived hand to mouth. One traveller recalled meeting her at Coffee's Ranch on the Platte River in 1874, where she reputedly served as 'entertainer – dancing, drinking much bad whisky and in various ways relieving her victims of their coin, which she spent with a free and willing hand'. In May 1876, Calamity appeared in court in Cheyenne charged with stealing women's clothing, won an acquittal after a three-week jail term, hit the saloons and careened off in the direction of Fort Laramie in a rented wagon. A penchant for liquor and an oddball demeanour marked her out as a local celebrity. According to the Cheyenne *Daily Leader*, she partook of 'frequent and liberal potations completely befogging her not very clear mind'. The *Rocky Mountain News* described her as an 'eccentric female resident'.[19]

Deadwood offered the next setting for the augmentation of the Calamity Jane legend. In *Life and Adventures*, Calamity Jane recalled an auspicious hook up with Wild Bill Hickok at Fort Laramie in July

1876 before heading to Deadwood. Contemporary accounts corroborate that the Hickok party took on hitchers at the fort including prostitute Madame Moustache and Calamity Jane. According to Joseph 'White Eye' Anderson, Calamity was 'very drunk and near naked' at the fort, but proved her mettle during the two-week trek by driving mules, cooking and regaling the party with grand stories. When they rode into Deadwood, the *Black Hills Pioneer* reported '"Calamity Jane" has arrived', a headline suggestive of her growing status as regional luminary. According to Calamity, she spent the summer engaging in fearless exploits as a Pony Express courier, locating mining claims and striking up a romance with Wild Bill (at least before he was shot in the head). *Life and Adventures* boldly claimed that she apprehended Jack McCall, the desperado responsible for killing Wild Bill, and that Calamity also effected a daring rescue of the overland stage from Indian attack, where she 'removed all baggage from the coach except the mail . . . took the driver's seat and with all haste drove to Deadwood, carrying the six passengers and the dead driver'. In Calamity's autobiographical fictive, she played a feisty *deus ex machina* in a Deadwood full of violence and bravado.[20]

Period testimony provides another story. Accounts of the capture of Jack McCall and the Deadwood stagecoach fail to mention her role as a roving redeemer. Eyewitnesses instead presented Calamity as an audacious dance-hall girl with a weakness for hell-raising. However, people wanted to believe the folklore of the frontier. As a charismatic, larger than life figure, Calamity won local converts. As biographer J. Leonard Jennewein remarked, she combined 'flair, with exuberance, with a native sense of showmanship'. Newspapers reported her alcohol-fuelled high jinks and bullwhipping swagger with a mixture of voyeurism, rumour-mongering, moralising and delight. Writers embraced the Calamity Jane mystique as part of a Wild West redolent with volatility, vigour and valour. In Horatio Maguire's *The Black Hills and American Wonderland* (1877), Calamity appeared as a raven-haired buckskin-clad 'dare-devil boy . . . giving as good an imitation of a Sioux war-whoop as a feminine voice is capable of'. In Thomas Newson's *Drama of Life in the Black Hills* (1878), she earned a dual role as pathfinder and nursemaid, blessed with 'all the characteristics of the sterner sex, with her pistols, bowie-knives and other weapons of death' as well as a 'generous, forgiving, kind-hearted' nature.[21]

Images of the West as a locus of action-packed gunplay gained national circulation through the medium of the dime novel. From the 1860s until the turn of the century, 'penny dreadfuls' churned out stories of frontier melodrama for the eager digest of the American public. Readers readily consumed history as story with the West cast as a rough and tumble world of double-crossing villains, murderous ambushes and mistaken identities. The growing mythology of Calamity Jane proved worthy fodder for the genre. Edward Wheeler introduced Calamity as a main character in *Deadwood Dick: Prince of the Road* (1877) and featured her in around twenty novels thereafter. Depictions of Calamity as a dime novel heroine conformed to extant narratives. She cursed, smoked cigars, twirled her guns and saved Deadwood Dick from fixes. At the same time, traditional models of gender propriety remained intact. Wheeler's Calamity acted with integrity, honesty and a decidedly feminine morality. As *Deadwood Dick: Prince of the Road* intonated, the buckskin-clad pretender retained hallmarks of femininity beneath the masculine bluster: of a wayward beauty, flowing locks, refined countenance and alabaster complexion. Wheeler explained her masculine affectations as a form of (albeit novel and intriguing) deviance. In the dime novel narrative, Calamity's aberrant behaviour had been caused by the trauma of sexual assault, being 'ruined' by a ruffian who 'stole away her honor'.[22]

Following several supporting roles, Calamity Jane featured centre stage in *Deadwood Dick on Deck, or Calamity Jane the Heroine of Whoop Up* (1878). The frontispiece depicted her in romantic style with flowing dark hair underneath a broad brimmed hat, a face reflecting both grace and austerity and rifle slung nonchalantly over her shoulder. A visual encapsulation of the story within, the cover image spoke of a frontier hellcat who wore the breeches yet retained feminine wiles. The yarn opened with two prospectors, Joe and Sandy, listening to 'the song of the gay mountaineer' drifting across the valley. According to Joe, this 'nightingale' was no other than Calamity Jane, 'a dare-devil' and 'the most reckless buchario in ther Hills'. Having aroused the reader's adventurous spirit, Wheeler took a sentimental tack. Joe motioned, 'Janie's not as bad as the world would have her' before qualifying her brusque stance as a product of the go-it-alone West: 'ef a female ken't stand up an' fight fer her rights, et's durned little aid she'll git.' The mysterious Calamity Jane, 'the strange woman of the Hills', also earned star billing in *Deadwood Dick in Leadville; or, a Strange Stroke for Liberty* (1879). With pistols drawn, the cover featured Calamity apprehending bad guy Ralph Gardner (he had won the right to cut off a fellow gambler's head after winning it in a game). Meanwhile, in *Deadwood Dick's Doom* (1881), Calamity confronted her romantic feelings for Dick (and embraced her latent sexuality) by melting into the arms of her male lead and lauding him as 'the only man she ever worshipped'. Things none the less ended tragically for the pair in *Deadwood Dick's Dust; or, the Chained Hand* (1885), with Calamity hanged and Dick killed in a fight. They were buried side by side.[23]

According to Richard Etulain, 'Calamity's appearances in the widely circulated dime novel dramatically and irreversibly changed her identity'. The real life of Martha Canary faded into the background and the enigma of Calamity Jane took over. However, as biographer James McLaird noted, particular scenarios set out by Edward Wheeler in the 'Deadwood Dick' series failed to provide lasting grist for the Calamity Jane rumour mill: 'Legendary feats in the dime novels such as battling Cattymount Cass, being kidnapped by Tra-la-la Charlie, and resuscitating Deadwood Dick are not found in other popular accounts of Calamity Jane.' Instead, tales of the Deadwood stagecoach rescue, the killing of Wild Bill and the Army scouting days, retained lasting currency in popular mythology. These adventures appeared fleetingly (if at all) in the dime narrative. While the dime novel may not have contributed lasting tales to the Calamity Jane mythology, it still played a vital role in stoking the fires of her invented identity. Widely available and cheap to buy, these publications proved to be instrumental in catapulting the character of Calamity Jane from regional misfit to national icon. The details of Wheeler's stories may have held only passing fancy, but his constructions of a buck-skinned broad, brandishing pistols at the ready, stuck firmly in the public mind. The relationship between Calamity Jane the dime novel frontierswoman and Calamity Jane the self-proclaimed wildcat thus appeared symbiotic. They fed off each other for energy and vogue. In actuality, such stories were far removed from the experiences of an alcoholic itinerant woman who traipsed the forts and towns of Dakotas in the 1880s making a living from prostitution, laundry, nursing and saloon work.[24]

Calamity Jane: A Story of the Black Hills (1887) by Mrs George Spencer represented the first full length novel to tackle the Calamity Jane myth. It combined a frontier romance, focusing on the relationship between Calamity Jane and a female emigrant called Meg. The tale began with Meg following her husband West on the back of the mining boom. En route, Old Ned the stagehand asked, 'who could have been so cruel as to have brought you to this wild country?', while the rowdy milieu of Deadwood prompted 'shuddering fascination' and a fainting fit. Meg embodied two stereotypes of frontier women, the fragile doll unsuited for the wildness of the West, and the willing emigrant bride. Soon after her arrival, Meg attended a fete held by the belles of Deadwood where she encountered Calamity Jane for the first time. Meg spoke of a 'character of romance ... whose eccentricities were so numerous and daring, so remarkable, that she was suspected to be in every deviltry from robbing trains to playing faro'. Wearing a 'mannish jacket and powder horn slung over her shoulder', Calamity signified an outsider, a feral presence uncomfortable with the social graces and feminised domesticity of the Deadwood picnic. Demanding a lock of hair from each partygoer, she threatened 'If you do not agree, I'll ——.'[25]

As the novel unfolded, Spencer unveiled a Calamity Jane more complicated and tortured than her dime novel persona. Calamity embraced a life of masculine bluster, yet yearned for feminine companionship and resolution of her sexual identity. As she confessed to Meg at the picnic: 'what interest can they have for a woman, a vagabond like Calamity Jane. I who wander foot-sore, grow desperate, commit crimes. I have no fancy for *dolls.* But when a woman sweet and pure looks into my face, my soul cries.' Also an outsider in Deadwood society, Meg warmed to this lonely pariah. Playing the role of 'gentle tamer', she befriended Calamity, exchanged her mother's prayer beads for a gold nugget, begged her to repent and offered her lodgings. Their relationship spoke of empathy, sisterhood and an inference of romantic attachment. At the picnic, Calamity mused, 'Sweetest creature, I would give ten years of my life just to kiss you.' Meg replied 'You may, kiss me now' while 'still quivering with pity at this sister woman'. The ambiguities of this *tête-à-tête* appear manifold. Was Meg attracted to Calamity because of her masculine demeanour? Did Meg represent the femininity Calamity suppressed in herself? Spencer may simply have been making merry with the cross-dressing theme as a comic device and melodramatic form of masquerade. An alternative reading aired pertinent (and unanswered) questions about Calamity Jane's sexual orientation in terms of the butch/femme paradigm. As Clarence Paine noted (somewhat pejoratively) in his paper for the Westerners Corral in 1945, 'even in melodrama, those are hardly scenes between two normal women'.[26]

After years spent drifting through the Dakotas, Montana and Wyoming, Martha Jane Canary returned to Deadwood in October 1895. It had been sixteen years since she last graced the town, and in that time she had become a national celebrity. The Black Hills *Daily Times* announced her arrival as 'Calamity Jane! The fearless Indian fighter and rover of the western plains'. The hubbub surrounding her return reflected a community in the process of memorialising its own pioneer past. The reappearance of Deadwood's famous feral femme prompted talk of the lawless and lively days of yore. As the frontier passed into history (the Census Bureau declared it closed in 1890), many Western communities – on gaining stature and respectability – still exalted the wild abandon of their formative years in a process of historical myth-making and teleological back-slapping. Money could also be made from such promotions, especially given the stream of Easterners venturing west in search of the imagined landscape of the dime novel. The legend of Calamity Jane sat comfortably within this formulation of a riotous past juxtaposed with a civilised present. As the Rapid City *Journal* noted, Calamity served as 'the prickly cactus symbol of the pioneer days at the heart of their depravity'.[27]

For her part, Calamity was keen to capitalise on her marketability as a wild woman of the frontier. She posed for photographs in full buckskin attire at H. R. Locke's studio in 1895 and sold the prints to eager punters (she spent the cash living it up in Deadwood's saloons). The following year, she gained permission to sell postcards of herself in Yellowstone National Park. Intriguingly, the vast majority of period photographs depicted Calamity in female attire, scarcely distinguishable from any other pioneer woman, perhaps suggesting a performative aspect to her masculine dress code and affectations. In 1896, Calamity played frontier hellcat on stage as part of the Kohl and Middleton dime museum touring exhibition. She had previously dabbled in show business by working with Tom Hardwick's 'Great Rocky Mountain Show' (1884) alongside acts such as 'liver eating Johnson'. She now took her act to the urban East. Billing at the Palace Museum, Minneapolis advertised: 'The Famous Woman scout of the Wild West!' and 'The Comrade of Buffalo Bill and Wild Bill'. Complete with new boots and Winchester rifle, Calamity related tales of scouting, the Deadwood stagecoach and catching Wild Bill's killer. Launched at the Kohl and Middleton show in spring 1896, *Life and Adventures of Calamity Jane* offered audiences literary purchase of frontier fancy. Collectively, these photographs, stage shows and book offerings revealed Calamity as an entrepreneurial figure adept at selling an imagined West to herself and to others. Unfortunately, she drank most of the profits. Calamity took particular umbrage at any accusations of fakery. One night, she leapt into the crowd and bawled at a heckler: 'I'm the real Calamity Jane, General Crook's scout. I'm a howling coyote from Bitter Creek, the further up you go, the bitterer it gets, and I'm from the head end. Now apologize before I shoot the toes off your d—d feet.'[28]

The Calamity Jane legend gained export overseas courtesy of Samuel Franklin Cody's Wild West show. Cowboy, showman playwright (and no relation of Buffalo Bill), Cody had masterminded successful performances of his 'Wild West burlesque' show at London's Olympia in 1890. Eight years later, the flamboyant frontier melodrama 'the Klondyke nugget' opened to thrilled audiences. For his follow-up project, Cody focused on Calamity Jane. Pitched as a comedy drama in three acts, the play built on the success of the dime novel formula to conjure a tale of rowdy mining camps, double-crossing villains, murder and thwarted love between lead characters Clarence and Mabel. The character of Calamity Jane earned billing as 'a wild harum-scarum sort of girl, without a mother's influence', a quick-drawing resilient type so-called because if she was insulted then 'calamity occurs'. She first appeared on the scene to pistol-whip Drince, a villain making advances on the leading lady. Configured as a rough-hewn trickster, the actress threatened to ram a poker down Drince's throat to teach him how to treat a lady. Audiences were no doubt entertained by the irony of Calamity's outburst, especially when she screamed 'You imitation of a man! You ought to be hung . . . I ain't got any manners, but I know a lady when I see one.' The ridiculous plot reached denouement with Calamity Jane saving the day (disguised first as a miner and then as a sleeping Indian) and reuniting the two lovers.[29]

Back across the pond, the gap between image and reality became harder to square. In July 1901, Martha Canary holed up in a poor house in Livingston, Montana, destitute, in poor health and suffering from alcohol abuse. Then, later the same month, she travelled west with advocate Josephine Brake, appeared at a banquet in her honour at Niagara Falls, before joining the Colonel Fred Cummins Indian Congress show at the Pan-American Exposition. Calamity wowed audiences with horse riding, shooting and tall tales, ably fitting within the show's grand depiction of Western histrionics. However, once the curtains came down, Calamity struggled to maintain her composure, exhibited a typical restlessness and got into trouble drinking. Those who knew the Black Hills girl warned Calamity's legion of adoring fans that the real Martha Jane was in fact decidedly less glitzy and alluring than her legend suggested. As the editor of the Billings *Gazette* observed 'the picture of "Calamity" clad in Buckskin' owed much to the 'romancer and the writer of "yellow backs"' and proved scarcely comparable to the 'true stories of Martha'. Eventually, the contradiction between stage presence and private life overwhelmed Calamity, and she reputedly borrowed the train fare from Bill Cody to escape to the Black Hills in autumn 1901. Over the next two years, brief moments of settled life, domesticity and sobriety (with daughter Jesse and various partners including Clinton Burke) were punctuated by wanderings from town to town, drunken altercations and tall stories.[30]

Calamity Jane died in Terry, South Dakota on 1 August 1903. The Princeton *Press* called her 'one of the most picturesque and daring characters that has ever roamed the Western plains'. Old timers span yarns about the times they met Calamity, while further a field, a reporter from the London *Star* asked Bill Cody for a eulogy. Cody spoke of whisky drinking, Jane's role as US Army 'mascot' and her typical place 'on the firing line'. In the broader frontier vernacular, Calamity Jane served as a veritable celebrity, a symbol of wildness, gun-toting Western spirit, eccentricity and bristle. William Allen in *Adventures with Indians and Game* (1903) recalled meeting Calamity on a remote trail headed for Custer City. Allen remembered: 'We were surprised to see a white woman riding towards us at full gallop' and noted her 'daring intrepidity, her rapidity of movement and her deadly skill with firearms'. The Society of Black Hills Pioneers organised the funeral arrangements for the town's famous hell-raiser. Her body lay in state at Deadwood mortuary for a few days. Local papers reported that women came and cut locks of her hair. Presiding minister Dr Charles Clark noted Calamity's propensity for excess but also her 'kindness and charity'. She was buried next to Wild Bill Hickok in Mount Moriah cemetery – her last wish, and certainly one that lent itself to the designs of town promoters. As the Belle Fouche *Bee* commented 'Deadwood will have a double attraction to exhibit to visitors from the East'.[31]

As the twentieth century unfolded, writers and movie directors further embellished the legend that Calamity Jane, Deadwood boosters, dime novelists and Wild West showmen had nurtured. In November 1921, the Casper *Tribune Herald* pointed to her story as evidence of women playing 'important parts in the building of the great empire west of the Missouri'. Calamity symbolised the mystique of pioneer times past, of unconventionality, adaptability and vigour. Her wild antics fitted projections of the West as a venue of freedom and action. The legend of Calamity Jane was part of the patriotic drama of the winning of the West. At the same time, chroniclers of Calamity Jane seemed unsure as to how to present their subject in terms of contemporary modes of moral and model feminine comportment. Was she to be accepted as a frontier novelty, revered as a romantic outlaw, respected as a symbol of female resilience or castigated as a social misfit?[32]

In *The Black Hills Trails* by Jesse Brown and A. M. Willard (1924) Calamity took precedence as a historical figure. The authors insisted that they traded only in 'facts' and debunked the myth of romance between Calamity Jane and Wild Bill. Calamity proved nothing more than a 'common prostitute, drunken, disorderly and wholly devoid of any element or conception of morality'. Yet, *The Black Hills Trails* went on to depict Calamity as both outlaw and community carer, a personage in possession of both idealised male *and* female traits. In one moment, she appeared as a gung-ho sharp-shooting hero saving hapless hunter 'Antelope Frank' from Indian attack, the next, a nurturing Florence Nightingale of the frontier tending Deadwood's sick in the smallpox epidemic of 1878. As Brown and Willard related: 'In the hour of terror and death, there came to the front, a willing volunteer, the mule-skinning, bull-whacking, and rough, roving woman from the depths, Calamity Jane' to tend to the sick 'day and night'. The book thereby encouraged readers to revel in Calamity as a unique product of the wild frontier, yet maintained accustomed gender protocols. She elucidated the model of the 'bad woman' by engaging in prostitution and intemperance, but also redeemed herself by serving as ad hoc nursemaid, a vocation marked by its altruism and abiding sense of domesticity.[33]

In 1927, journalist Duncan Aikman published *Calamity Jane and the Lady Wildcats*, a sensationalised biography similar to Stuart Lake's contemporaneous *Wyatt Earp: Frontier Marshall* (1931). Aikman's narrative recalled the tales of Western belles including Cattle Kate, Pearl Hart, Madame Moustache and Belle Starr, with Calamity as the main attraction. The author insisted his remit lay in revealing the truth as opposed to the legend. As he noted, 'the closer one comes to the actual scene of Jane's heroic performances, the more they vanish.' That said, the author tendered his own fair share of tall tales. Calamity fought cowboys in bar rooms, drank hardened imbibers under the table and proved 'a man among men'. At the same time, the 'lady wildcat' retained a smidgeon of feminine wiles, a frontier floozy as keen to win men's hearts (notably Bill Hickok's) as to become one of the boys. Aikman's Calamity thus proved an ambiguous character. She appeared to be drawn 'instinctively' to a mythic West marked by its masculinity and violence, yet also played the 'bad girl' by her licentious and promiscuous antics. Pertinently, Aikman was keen to point out that the frontier condition which had allowed this addictive personality to excel in 'grotesque wildness as well as in feminine violence' had long since past. Calamity's 'macabre splendor' could thus be invoked, embroidered and treated as a harmless flight of the imagination.[34]

Notorious madam Dora Dufran's (or D. Dee) pamphlet 'Lowdown on Calamity Jane' (1932) represented one of the many treatments of Deadwood's famous hell-raiser by locals. 'Lowdown' centred on one of the brothels owned by Dufran, where she alleged Calamity Jane had worked in 1886. In common with Aikman, Dufran presented Deadwood as a rowdy town that adhered to all the stereotypes of the Old West. Famous for its dancing, drinking and dining, Dufran's establishment sported posters with the tag line 'a place where you can bring your mother', complete with comic disclaimer, 'I wouldn't want my mother to know I had been there'. Dufran's portrayal of Calamity Jane subscribed to convention by focusing on her wild nature, scouting exploits, hard drinking and equally robust pistol-packing. While critical of her insobriety and promiscuity ('Lowdown' labelled her a 'parody of womanhood, shorn of all decency'), Dufran fought to save Calamity's reputation for posterity. Musing how 'deeds, not morals, were needed in those days', she countered Aikman's 'camp trollop' billing with paeans to a 'rough diamond'. Dufran explained Calamity's foibles by reference to the privations of the frontier:

> It is easy for a woman to be good who has been brought up with every protection from the evils of the world with good associates. Calamity was a product of the wild and woolly West. She was not immoral, but unmoral. She took more on her shoulders than most women could.[35]

In October 1921, the *New York Tribune* pondered the absence of Calamity Jane offerings on the silver screen. Sporting the headline 'A Wild West heroine the movies overlook', the newspaper reflected on the sizeable cinematic potential of Deadwood's feral femme. In fact, Calamity had already made it to celluloid, albeit in a provincial romance from the Black Hills Feature Film Company called *Wild Bill and Calamity Jane in the Days of '75 and '76* (1915). Calamity gained her Hollywood debut in Paramount's 1923 motion picture *Wild Bill Hickok*, a movie that explained the leading lady's penchant for manly attire and mannerisms as a direct product of spurned affections for Wild Bill. In common with the dime novel 'Calamity', the celluloid heroine scarcely represented a role model of gender liberation, her reneging of female ways a product not of nascent feminist leanings but misery and unrequited love. The movie ended tragically. Calamity and Bill pledged to give love a chance, before boorish villain Jack McCall killed Hickok. The last shot showed an inconsolable (and re-feminised) Calamity crying at his grave.[36]

Calamity Jane's next major cinematic appearance came courtesy of Cecil B. DeMille's 1936 epic *The Plainsman*. The movie conformed to traditional mythology by focusing on masculine heroes securing the frontier for American civilisation. The heroes included Abraham Lincoln and General Custer (architects of making the frontier 'safe' from hostile Indians), a dashing Buffalo Bill Cody with new wife Lou playing his 'gentle tamer' and Wild Bill Hickok and Calamity Jane (representative of the gruff and self-sufficient Old West). Played by Jean Arthur, Calamity cut a striking presence in her first scene dressed in fringed buckskin and leaping from a stagecoach to admonish Gary Cooper's Wild Bill as a 'mangy coyote' before trying to smother him with kisses. She sported a frontier swagger and engaged in daring rides, the horse-whipping of Indians and all-round bravura to save Custer and Cody. Arthur reputedly accepted the role because she admired Calamity as one of the women who 'blazed the trail toward emancipation'.[37]

That said, DeMille's picture maintained traditional codes of womanhood. For one thing, Arthur's Calamity proved far removed from historic descriptions of Martha Canary as 'big boned and muscular', with skin 'brown and rough-looking'. Slight, attractive and feminine, this Calamity was wholesome and good-natured (if a little wayward), a leading lady in trousers rather than the eccentric outsider of Deadwood fame. *Variety* commended Arthur's depiction as 'particularly endowed with some punch lines and pungent expletives as the hardy daughter, but softening that historic character of the West, enough for the femme appeal'. As the movie progressed, Calamity's womanly attributes gradually came to the fore. She flirted with gentility in striking up a friendship with Lou, situated herself as an old-fashioned romantic by confessing her undying love for Bill and played the role of the kidnapped innocent and model of the 'weaker sex' by giving information to Yellow Hand in order to save Wild Bill from being burned alive. Significantly, each of the key characters in *The Plainsman* underwent a personal transformation that served as metaphor for the closure of the frontier and the onset of civilisation. For Buffalo Bill, that meant marriage and running a hotel after one last hurrah, for Calamity, it meant renouncing her feral ways and settling down with Hickok. Such promises of domestic bliss none the less proved short-lived. Much to the consternation of studio executives who clamoured for a happy ending, DeMille ended the movie with a tense poker game, Jack McCall shooting Hickok in the back in a vain attempt to acquire notoriety as a gunslinger, and a distraught Calamity Jane cradling her dying hero. *The Plainsman* reinvented Calamity Jane as screen idol, smoothing out the less desirable aspects of her reputation to focus on entertainment thrills and obscured femininity. This recipe of saccharine and adventure went down a treat. *The New York Times* had nothing but praise for the 'excellently contrived large-scale horse opera' in which Calamity 'doesn't chew tobacco anymore. She doesn't cuss. She doesn't run around with the boys. She just talks low and husky, is cute when she is being tomboyish, and she loves Wild Bill so much.'[38]

The 1940s saw Calamity Jane feature in several films including *Young Bill Hickok* (1940), *Badlands of Dakota* (1941), *The Paleface* (1948) and *Calamity Jane and Sam Bass* (1949). The decade also witnessed a new turn in the convoluted tale of Martha Jane Canary with the emergence of a new witness: Jean Hickok McCormick, a housewife in her sixties from Billings, Montana, who purported to be the child of Calamity and Wild Bill. McCormick claimed she had been born in September 1873 in Montana, but Calamity had left her in the care of a British sea captain, James O'Neil, who adopted her and raised her in England. To substantiate her story, McCormick produced an album dated 1877 to 1903, including letters supposedly from Calamity to her daughter 'Janey'. The collection of documents traded in the stuff of Western legend, of Calamity's liaison with Wild Bill, her days as an Indian fighter, treading the boards with Buffalo Bill and a friendship with Jesse James. It even presented Belle Starr (another lady wildcat of the West) as Calamity's long-lost sister. Supporting artefacts including Jane's handkerchief and Wild Bill's revolver. McCormick broadcast her revelation on CBS radio in May 1941, and spent the rest of the summer trucking her story around various rodeo venues. She appeared before crowds at the 'Wild Bill Frontier Celebration' in Abilene, laid flowers at the Deadwood cemetery and took to wearing vintage buckskin garb. Popular interest ran high, no doubt aided by the resonant mystique surrounding Calamity Jane, the lack of reliable evidence regarding her life, as well as public willingness to buy into an imagined West of gusto and adventure. However, serious doubts existed over the authenticity of McCormick's account. The letters to 'Janey' failed to mention scouting for the US Army or the Pony Express, and employed a language far more flowery than the stilted prose of

Life and Adventures of Calamity Jane. It seemed most plausible that McCormick forged the documents in an attempt to gain fame, fortune and satisfy her 'psychological need for an identity'.[39]

In 1953 the Hollywood musical *Calamity Jane* opened, a rooting-tooting extravaganza that popular culture has enshrined as the foremost cinematic jaunt for the Western heroine. Advertised by the tag line 'how the West was sung', the movie starred Doris Day as the fresh-faced tomboy Calamity and Howard Keel as the astonishingly deep-voiced crooner Wild Bill Hickok. The movie projected a raucous and vibrant Deadwood and Chicago as the setting for a comic and colourful tale of love rivals and mistaken identities. The movie set boasted designs from Harper Goff, who also worked on Disney's fantasy pioneer world 'Frontierland'. From the rousing opening lines of the 'Deadwood stage', the movie firmly situated 'Calam' as the star of the town, armed with a cracking whip, growling vocalisations, catchy tunes and playful dances. This Calamity Jane bespoke vivacity and pluckiness, and curried a certain amount of favour as the only woman in Deadwood. That said, the movie's treatment of its eponymous heroine sprayed a distinctly 1950s gloss over Western history. The lead character spent her time singing and dancing across the plains in the 'Deadwood Stage' and in the streets of Chicago, and drinking 'sasperillies' instead of hard liquor. Doris Day wore the familiar buckskin and carried a bullwhip, but her coarse language remained confined to such damning phrases as 'mangy coyote' and 'varmint'. In the words of Doris Day, the character represented 'a rambunctious, pistol-packing prairie girl' rather than a brusque alcoholic drifter. Beneath the trappings of the frontier cross-dresser stood a lip-glossed blonde idol who sat comfortably with 1950s conservative values and served as thrill-seeking female icon for the women making inroads into the world of men's work. Both upholding traditional values and presenting an empowered female, Doris Day's Calamity thus embodied the 'all-American persona'. For this 'Calam', playing macho meant striding around in a clumsy fashion, frowning, talking husky and sticking her tongue out to fire a pistol. Nobody could mistake her for a man or a frontier floozy. Moreover, as the film progressed, Calamity expressed her desires and wants in strikingly domestic terms. Wild Bill instructed her early on to adopt 'female fixings', and the arrival of actress Katie Brown in town proved a catalyst for Calamity to embrace her feminine side. Shocked at the rude cabin that Calamity inhabited, Katie promised to show her 'a woman's touch', which seemed to involve attending to appearance, posture and engaging in copious house-keeping duties. Together, the pair prettied the cabin with flowers, curtains and brightly painted walls in the style of the 1950s housewife advertising her funky new refrigerator and fitted kitchen. The film culminated in a heart-to-heart between Wild Bill and Calamity, where the leading lady confessed aspirations for marriage and 'young-uns' and her 'secret love' for Bill. This Calamity struck a more convincing pose as domestic kitten for the atomic age rather than disreputable frontier hellcat.[40]

Calamity Jane wowed audiences with its sanguine depictions of a Wild West where the good guys and gals won out, an heroic past far removed from the complexities of Cold War politicking and nuclear Armageddon. In glorious Technicolor, the movie traded in wholesome fun, old-fashioned romance, song and dance. *Variety* called it 'unimaginative hokum and colourful staging and good tunes to help provide fair business'. Reflective of the conservative gender codes of the age, *The New York Times* labelled Calamity as 'a frontier female whose indifference to the graces of her sex is both repulsive and ridiculous'. Noting that 'tomboyishness is not the lady's forte', the reviewer expressed a strong sense of relief once Doris Day's 'Calam' had renounced buckskin for a pretty dress. Meanwhile, in the Black Hills, locals seemed unsure of whether to embrace the movie as an opportunity to boost tourism or shy away from publicity due to the movie's inauthenticity. The same year the movie premiered, South Dakota historian J. Leonard Jennewein published *Calamity Jane of the Western Trails*, in which he painted Calamity as 'a disreputable old harridan, a disgrace to womankind'. Here stood a woman who 'dressed like a man, drank whiskey in saloons with men, before such practice was socially acceptable'. In the end, the whimsical nature of *Calamity Jane* the musical ensured that the public took Doris Day's character to heart. 'Calam' may have borne scarce resemblance to her historical namesake, but the punters appreciated the hearty depiction of a whip-cracking heroine. This easy-going depiction offered escapism for the atomic generation and a wholesome story that conformed to extant codes of female decorum. Baby boomers could even buy their kids 'Calamity Jane' branded rocking horses and pluck a sheriff's star with her image on it from the family's morning raisin bran.[41]

Past the 1960s, the mythology of Calamity Jane received further refinement on the basis of popular narratives surrounding the West and shifting expectations of the 'female hero' figure. Old stories certainly retained their allure, but were joined by alternative interpretations. In the consumer world, Calamity prospered as a Western brand connoting adventure and vibrancy. Tem Tex ran an advertising campaign for a new blouse called the 'Calamity Jane' in 1980 which depicted an attractive, hip young woman in chaps, jeans and cowboy hat. In 1981, the Muppet kids clothing line included a girls sportswear range called 'Calamity Jane', worn with aplomb by Miss Piggy (boys could buy the matching 'Billy the Kid' collection). In the 2000s, Deadwood's famed frontier wildcat earned billing as 'the Courtney Love of her age', a model of the rebellious female archetype, with the hoary image of the bad woman of the Old West updated as irreverent rock chick. A limited edition burger bearing her name graced the McDonalds menu in Italy in autumn 2007, homage to the international currency of the Calamity label and the spaghetti Western to boot. Meanwhile, the gender revolution and the rise of gay rights encouraged fresh and more reflective assessments of the Calamity Jane legend. Stella Foote, in *A History of Calamity Jane, America's First Liberated Woman* (1995) cast Calamity as a proto-feminist, striking out for women in a man's world, while the 1953 musical received a new interpretative veneer, courtesy of queer theory, that emphasised themes of empowerment, repression, homosexual subtext and multi-layered gender identities. In this reading, Calamity got her man and, more pertinently, her girl (by winning over Katie). The Academy award winning song 'Secret love' (covered by lesbian activist and country singer k d Lang) indicated a nascent single-sex relationship between Calamity and Katie, while playwright Carolyn Gage described Calamity as 'a butch woman who had the misfortune to be born into an era before lesbian culture'.[42]

Some New Western historians gave Calamity a wide berth. Glenda Riley derided traditional scholars for their 'Calamity Jane syndrome', neglecting the lives of typical frontier females in favour of focusing on exceptional, and thus unrepresentative, characters. That said, the inclinations of scholars to consider the West as 'a longer, grimmer but more interesting story' resulted in the construction of a more complex and graduated Calamity Jane. For Richard Etulain, Calamity represented 'a gritty pioneer endeavouring to hold onto her reputation as a woman who defined and lived in a sphere of her own making', complicit in her own glorified Western mythology and struggling to navigate the potentials and restrictions of women's lives in the West.[43]

More than a century after the publication of *Life and Adventures*, the Calamity Jane of popular culture reflected a melange of influences. Revisionism, realism, post-modernism and irony conspired to design an angst-ridden frontier femme inhabiting a West consciously referenced to frontier archetypes. Larry McMurtry's *Buffalo Girls* (1990) featured a forlorn and ageing Jane (friend to madam Dora Dufran and a possible hermaphrodite) writing letters to her daughter as a confessional device. In McMurtry's tale, Calamity and other stock legends including Annie Oakley and Bill Hickok tried to relive their glory days (and earn a dime or two) by riding the bronco of Buffalo Bill's Wild West show, only to be tossed into the dirt. Meanwhile, HBO Television series *Deadwood* (2004–6) featured Calamity Jane as a recurring character. Played by Robin Weigert, this 'lady wildcat' drank profusely, used the f-word (not Turner's, the other one) with regularity, and sported a shambolic appearance scarcely recognisable from the wholesome glamour of Doris Day's 'Calam'. Producer David Milch deployed Deadwood's renowned sot as a bumbling narrator in a late nineteenth-century West marked by chaos, materialism and violence, a 'Shakesperian fool, speaking truth to power, bearing witness to injustice, exposing what is normally kept well hidden in mythologizing westerns'. Milch's presentation of Calamity as a troubled 'ministering angel' bore some similarities with dime novel portrayals and early biographies. At the same time, Weigert's Calamity roamed an asinine, grubby and grasping world far removed from the heroic landscapes of traditional fiction and Hollywood cinema. Significantly, in both *Buffalo Girls* and *Deadwood*, Calamity Jane played raconteur and frontier storyteller: an identity long in the making.[44]

Notes

1. Glenda Riley, *The Female Frontier: A Comparative View of Women on the Prairie and the Plains* (Lawrence: University Press of Kansas, 1988), p. 4. The 'Lady Wildcat' phrase was used by Dunkan Aikman in his biography *Calamity Jane and the Lady Wildcats* (New York: Henry Holt, 1927). Held at the Gene Autry Museum of the American West, Los Angeles (hereafter cited as Autry).
2. Joan M. Jensen and Darlis A. Miller, 'The gentle tamers revisited: new approaches to the history of women in the American West', *Pacific Historical Review*, XLIX (1980), p. 174; Virginia Scharff, 'Else surely we shall all hang separately: The politics of western women's history', *Pacific Historical Review*, LXI (1992), p. 550.
3. Sarah Winnemucca Hopkins, *Life Among the Piutes: Their Wrongs and Claims* (Reno: University of Nevada Press, 1994 [1883]), p. 5. Story cited in Eleanor Richey, *Eminent Women of the West* (Berkeley: Howell-North Books, 1975), p. 128.
4. Quoted in Natalie Rosinsky, *Sarah Winnemucca: Scout, Activist, Teacher* (Minneapolis: Compass Point Books, 2006), pp. 58, 59.
5. Quoted in Cathy Luchetti, *Women of the West* (St George: Antelope Island Press, 1982), p. 110.

6. San Francisco *Chronicle* quoted in Mark McLaughlin, 'Sarah Winnemucca: Voice of the Northern Paiutes', *Sierra Sun*, 15 August 2006; San Francisco *Illustrated Wasp*, 13 December 1879.
7. Quoted in Malea Powell, 'Rhetorics of survivance: how American Indians *use* writing', *College Composition and Communication*, 53/3 (February 2002), p. 411; Elizabeth Peabody, 'Sarah Winnemucca's practical solution of the Indian problem' (Cambridge, MA: John Wilson & Son, 1886), p. 28; Sally Zanjani, *Sarah Winnemucca* (Lincoln: University of Nebraska Press, 2001), p. 239; Eleanor Richey, *Eminent Women of the West* (Berkeley: Howell-North Books, 1975), p. 145.
8. Quoted in Zanjani, *Sarah Winnemucca*, pp. 206, 214; Wilbur wrote: 'through whom they must pass, still smarting from the barbarities of the war two years previous, and that the Piutes, utterly destitute of everything, must subsist themselves on their route by pillage, I refused permission for them to depart.' See Report of Yakama Agent James H. Wilbur, 'Annual Report of the Commissioner of Indian Affairs for the Year 1881', pp. 174–5.
9. Sarah Winnemucca Hopkins, *Life Among the Piute*, p. 207.
10. Sarah Winnemucca Hopkins, *Life Among the Piutes*, p. 2; Powell, 'Rhetorics of survivance', p. 406; Sarah Winnemucca Hopkins, *Life Among the Piutes*, p. 247.
11. Gordon Bakken and Brenda Farrington, *Encyclopedia of Women in the American West* (Thousand Oaks: Sage, 2003), p. 296; Powell, 'Rhetorics of survivance', p. 400.
12. Quoted in Richey, *Eminent Women of the West*, p. 149.
13. Quoted in Zanjani, *Sarah Winnemucca*, pp. 259, 247, 249.
14. Peabody, 'Sarah Winnemucca's practical solution of the Indian problem', pp. 12, 11, 13, 3.
15. Glenda Riley and Richard Etulain (eds), *By Grit and Grace: Eleven Women who shaped the American West* (Golden: Fulcrum, 1997), p. xiii.
16. Richard Slotkin, *Gunfighter Nation: The Myth of the Frontier in Twentieth Century America* (New York: Harper, 1992), p. 234; Clarence Paine, 'Calamity Jane – man, woman or both', *The Westerners Brand Book*, 2/6 (September 1945), p. 5, held at the Autry.
17. Doubts none the less exist as to the efficacy of the Egan story, not least from Egan's wife who asserted 'no such incident ever happened'. The issue proved further complicated by the existence of other 'Calamity Jane's' across the West – courtesy of the moniker's usage as a generic marker for the unfortunate. The inaugural appearance of the 'Calamity Jane' name in print came courtesy of the Chicago *Tribune* on 19 June 1875. According to the report, a Jane Canary had become separated from Army Scouts she was travelling with on the Powder River in 1874. The men reputedly said 'it would be a great calamity if she should be captured or killed by the Indians.' Thereafter she was known as Calamity Jane. But if this was true why did the heroine herself neglect to mention it? See Martha Cannary Burk, *Life and Times of Calamity Jane, By Herself* (n.p., 1896); Gordon Bakken and Brenda Farrington, *Encyclopedia of Women in the American West* (Thousand Oaks: Sage, 2003), p. 92; Burk, *Life and Times of Calamity Jane*; M. L. Fox, 'A land of romance', Deadwood *Daily Pioneer-Times*, 5 September 1903; Chicago *Tribune*, 19 June 1875.
18. Crook: quoted in James McLaird, *Calamity Jane: The Woman and the Legend* (Norman: University of Oklahoma Press, 2005), p. 136; Macmillan: quoted in

Women in the West: The 'Indian Princess' and the 'Lady Wildcat' 169

Glenda Riley and Richard Etulain (eds), *By Grit and Grace: Eleven Women who shaped the American West* (Golden: Fulcrum, 1997), p. 80; Horace Maguire, *The Coming Empire: A Complete and Reliable Treatise on the Black Hills, Yellowstone and Big Horn Regions* (Sioux City: Watkins & Smead, 1878).

19. John Q. Ward to the Editor, *Western Story Magazine*, reprinted in McLaird, *Calamity Jane*, p. 30; Riley and Etulain, *By Grit and Grace*, p. 181; Denver *Rocky Mountain News*, 25 June 1876.
20. Anderson: quoted in McLaird, *Calamity Jane*, pp. 157–8; Black Hills *Pioneer*, 15 July 1879; Burk, *Life and Times of Calamity Jane*.
21. J. Leonard Jennewein, *Calamity Jane of the Western Trails* (Rapid City: Dakota West Books, 1953), p. 6; Horace Maguire, *The Black Hills and American Wonderland* (Chicago: Donnelly, Lloyd & Co., 1877), p. 304; Newson: quoted in McLaird, *Calamity Jane*, p. 103.
22. Wheeler, *Deadwood Dick, The Prince of the Road*, 15 October 1877. Also see Henry Nash Smith, *Virgin Land: The American West as Symbol and Myth* (Cambridge, MA: Harvard University Press, 1950), pp. 112–20.
23. Edward Wheeler, *Deadwood Dick on Deck, or Calamity Jane the Heroine of Whoop Up*, 17 December 1878; Edward Wheeler, *Deadwood Dick in Leadville; or a Strange Stroke for Liberty*, 24 June 1879; *Deadwood Dick's Doom, or, Calamity Jane's Last Adventure*, 28 June 1881; *Deadwood Dick's Dust, or, the Chained Hand*, 20 October 1885.
24. Glenda Riley and Richard Etulain, *Wild Women of the Old West* (Golden: Fulcrum, 2003), p. 184; McLaird, *Calamity Jane*, p. 99.
25. Mrs George Spencer, *Calamity Jane: A Story of the Black Hills* (New York, Cassell, 1887), pp. 35, 65, 74–80. Held at the Huntington Library, San Marino, CA.
26. Spencer, *Calamity Jane*, pp. 81–2; Paine, 'Calamity Jane – man, woman or both', p. 11; on queer theory see Tania Modleski, 'A Woman's gotta do . . . what a man's gotta do? Cross-dressing in the Western', *Signs*, 22/3 (Spring 1997), pp. 519–44.
27. *Black Hills Daily Times*, 5 October 1895; Dora Dufran, 'Lowdown on Calamity Jane' (Deadwood: Helen Rezatto, 1981), pp. 16–17.
28. Minneapolis *Journal*, 20 January 1896; D. Dee, 'Lowdown on Calamity Jane' (Rapid City, South Dakota: n p., 1932), p. 9.
29. Samuel Franklin Cody, 'Calamity Jane: A Comedy Drama in 3 Acts'. Manuscript held at the Autry.
30. Quoted in McLaird, *Calamity Jane*, p. 193.
31. Princeton *Press*, 12 August 1903; London *Star*, 7 August 1903; William Allen, *Adventures with Indians and Game, or Twenty Years in the Rocky Mountains* (Chicago: A. W. Bowen, 1903), pp. 32–4; McLaird, *Calamity Jane*, pp. 216, 220.
32. Casper *Tribune Herald*, 25 November 1921.
33. Jesse Brown and A. M. Willard, *The Black Hills Trails: A History of the Struggle of the Pioneers in the Winning of the Black Hills* (Rapid City: Rapid City Journal Co., 1924), pp. 411–18; Jennewein, *Calamity Jane of the Western Trails*, p. 31.
34. Aikman, *Calamity Jane and the Lady Wildcats*, pp. 59, 12, 3–8, 37, 47–53, 90, 68.
35. Dufran, 'Lowdown on Calamity Jane', p. 11; Edward Senn, *Deadwood Dick and Calamity Jane: A Thorough Sifting of Facts from Fiction* (Deadwood: n.p., 1939), p. 10; D. Dee, 'Lowdown on Calamity Jane', pp. 3–4, 11.

36. New York *Tribune*, 16 October 1921.
37. Arthur: quoted in McLaird, *Calamity Jane*, p. 231.
38. Jennewein, *Calamity Jane of the Western Trails*, p. 8; *Variety*, 20 January 1937; *The New York Times*, 14 January 1937.
39. See 'Calamity Jane's diary and letters, taken from an exhibit at the Wonderland Museum, Billings, MT' (c. 1951). Held at the Autry.
40. Day: quoted in McLaird, *Calamity Jane*, p. 235.
41. *Variety*, 21 October 1953; *The New York Times*, 5 November 1953; Jennewein, *Calamity Jane of the Western Trails*, p. 6.
42. Margot Mifflin, 'The real Calamity Jane', *Salon*, 6 December 2006. Available online at: http://dir.salon.com; Stella Foote, *A History of Calamity Jane: America's First Liberated Woman* (New York: Vantage Press, 1995); Emma Simmonds, 'Calamity Jane: creating a myth', London Lesbian and Gay Film Festival, Features Archive, 2006. Available online at: http://www.llgff.org.uk.
43. Glenda Riley, 'Images of the frontierswoman: Iowa as a case study', *Western Historical Quarterly*, 8 (April 1977), p. 191; Elliot West, 'A longer, grimmer, but more interesting story', *Montana: The Magazine of Western History*, 40/3 (Summer 1990), pp. 72–6; Etulain: quoted in McLaird, *Calamity Jane*, p. 273.
44. Larry McMurtry, *Buffalo Girls* (New York: Simon & Schuster, 1990); John Mack Faragher, 'HBO's *Deadwood*: not your typical Western', *Montana: The Magazine of Western History*, 57/3 (Autumn 2007), pp. 60–5.

Chapter 7

The Wild West Defiled: The American Indian, Genocide and the Sand Creek Massacre

Frontier imaginings of the dime novel and Hollywood showed the West as a land of conflict – the sheriff with pistols cocked, facing off against his outlaw nemesis across a dusty main street. This brand of High Noon-style violence – heroic, redemptive and honourable – offered an unproblematic narrative of the winning of the West: all glory and gun-play without gory details or moral qualms. In reality, violence in the nineteenth-century West proved to be far more inglorious, atavistic and disturbing. Ethnic, racial and religious issues fostered hatred, social conflict, community feuds and contests for resources; all promoting a brand of violence that was far less endearing to celluloid. As with the piles of bison bones left to rot on the prairie by sport and market hunters in the 1880s, the landscape was, on occasion, marked by bloodshed and brutalism. At Mountain Meadows (1857), a group of Mormon militiamen dressed as Paiute warriors massacred a wagon train of 120 non-believers, while in Rock Springs, Wyoming (1885) a mob of angry miners fuelled by anti-Oriental sentiment and labour strife went on the rampage in Chinatown, killing fifty-one people. The extremes of hatred meted out to the region's wolf population, with razor blades hidden in balls of fat, strychnine doused liberally across the plains and pups clubbed to death in their dens, suggested evidence of 'an American pogrom' to nature writer Barry Lopez.[1]

This history of a Wild West defiled is best personified by the mistreatment of the American Indian. In the 500 years between the arrival of Columbus and the closure of the frontier, indigenous communities lost over 90 per cent of their populations and ancestral lands to Euro-American conquest. Accordingly, in the vernacular of Ward Churchill, David Stannard and Russell Thornton 'one of the great American stories' was actually a narrative of final solutions, extermination and crimes against humanity. Unsurprisingly, the mention of words such as pogrom, holocaust and genocide in connection with the grand creation fable of the United States proved intensely controversial. Such analogies always court controversy. For example, Betty Friedan's critique of the housewife's 'comfortable concentration camp' in *The Feminine Mystique* (1963) or PETA's 'holocaust on your plate' animal rights exhibit (2003) led to heated accusations of impropriety and irreverence. Forget Frederick Jackson Turner's 'f-word', 'genocide' represents the new modish expletive in Western history.[2]

This chapter explores the Indian genocide debate by discussing the terminology at play, the arguments motioned by each side and offers a case study of the Sand Creek massacre, one of the most notorious flashpoints of Indian–White conflict in the West. While some detractors might question the felicity of applying a modern term (and value judgement) to a nineteenth-century context, it is argued here that historical subjectivity makes this inevitable. Moreover, given contemporary issues of tribal sovereignty, compensation and what Gerald Vizenor has called 'historical trauma' and 'survivance', how we choose to interpret (and, indeed, commemorate) the Western past remains of paramount importance.[3]

Terminology

Leo Kuper labelled 'genocide' as a 'new word' for an 'ancient' crime. Polish jurist Raphael Lemkin coined the phrase by conjoining the Greek *genos* (race) and the Latin *cide* (massacre). After writing in the 1930s on vandalism and barbarism, Lemkin's ideas on genocide gained articulation in *Axis Rule in Occupied Europe* (1944), a work framed specifically around the Nazi experience. Defined as the 'deliberate and systematic destruction of a racial, religious, political or ethnic group', Lemkin positioned genocide as a crime against international law that could be judged according to physical, biological and cultural markers. Mass killings, the curtailment of reproduction and the suppression of collective forms of expression all fell within his descriptive of a two-tier process based around the destruction of a national group and the corollary imposition of a 'national pattern of the oppressor'. For Lemkin, genocide denoted a

> co-ordinated plan of different actions aiming at the destruction of essential foundations of national groups, with the aim of annihilating the groups themselves . . . The objectives of such a plan would be a

disintegration of social and political institutions, of culture, of language, national feelings, religion, and the economic existence of national groups, and the destruction of personal security, liberty, health, dignity, and even the lives of individuals belonging to such groups.

Such a classification served commentary on the relationship between the practice of genocide and the mechanics of colonial conquest.[4]

Further codification of the term came courtesy of the United Nations *Convention on the Prevention and Punishment of the Crime of Genocide* (1948), that defined genocide as:

any of the following acts committed with intent to destroy, in whole or in part, a national, ethnical, racial, or religious group, as such: (a) killing members of the group; (b) causing serious bodily or mental harm to members of the group; (c) deliberately inflicting on the group conditions of life calculated to bring about its physical destruction in whole or in part; (d) imposing measures intended to prevent births within the group; (e) forcibly transferring children of the group to another group.

A product of realpolitik and compromise (the Soviet Union and the United States both vociferated concerns that the treaty might prevent the flexing of superpower muscles), the new taxonomy of genocide proved considerably more restrictive than Lemkin's precedent. Cultural assimilation, or ethnocide, no longer appeared in the criteria (although point (e) arguably implied it), while the UN stressed the necessity of proving intent to commit genocide as a key issue.

Following the ratification of the UN Convention, genocide, or the 'g-word', has prompted enormous debate and controversy. Just eleven months after the treaty passed into law, entertainer Paul Robeson charged the United States with genocide against African-Americans. In 1967, Jean-Paul Sartre provided a sharp indictment of American actions in Indo-China in his essay 'On Genocide', part of British philosopher Bertrand Russell's 'International War Crimes Tribunal against the Vietnam War'. One year later, the American Indian Movement began excavating the history of White–Indian encounter using the vocabulary of genocide as a figurative tool. Meanwhile, in the extrapolations of legal theorists, the neologism of genocide was comprehensively tested for applicability and veracity. Frank Chalk and Kurt Jonassohn argued that the term should be reclassified to denote the 'physical extermination of a group' alone, while Israel Charny favoured a more inclusive definition that included all mass killings of 'essentially defenseless and helpless' people. For Vahakn Dadrian, civilian bombings in war or the spread of diseases both counted as forms of 'latent genocide', while Tony Barta questioned the paradigm of genocide as necessarily state-directed by focusing on the importance of 'relations of destruction', especially in a colonial context. Surrounded by such interpretive fog, genocide emerged as a concept with its own complex trajectory of meanings.[5]

The American Indian in the West: A Victim of Genocide

Those who argue that the treatment of the American Indian in the West constituted an example of genocide stressed the severity, speed, brutalism and wholesale nature of the assault. As Alfred Crosby noted, the entire United States witnessed a comprehensive 'demographic takeover' from 1492 until 1900 that witnessed the devastation of indigenous peoples. From a pre-contact estimate of five million, the American Indian population of the United States in 1894 stood at a mere 237,000. Five hundred nations, all with discrete traditions, languages and practices, were comprehensively decimated. According to David Stannard, the scale of the conquest rendered the use of the genocide moniker as both appropriate and defensible. Accordingly, the destruction of American Indian cultures represented the 'worst human holocaust the world had ever witnessed, roaring across two continents non-stop for four centuries and consuming the lives of countless tens of millions of people'.[6]

Citing the universality of moral values, advocates of the 'g-word' perceived the application of twentieth-century terminology as both cogent and necessary. Issues of human rights and historical memory transcended chronological limitations. As Laura Turney pointed out, making comparisons with the Holocaust expressed neither a glib attempt at grand-standing nor a 'competition in atrocity'. Instead, confronting the more insalubrious aspects of westward expansionism, and applying appropriate epistemology, represented an exercise in responsible storytelling. As Turney elaborated, 'it's about providing an alternative account of the history of relations between colonising Europeans and the Native peoples/nations they encountered'. Moreover, the fact that contemporary commentators spoke out against extermination (in 1853 Thomas Fitzpatrick criticised Indian policy as 'the legalized murder of a whole nation') qualified the functionality of moral judgements and, in turn, the usage of genocide as a nomenclature. As Doug Sackman explained:

If that universe could not function in ways that would alter the course of action in order to stop the contagion and blood-letting . . . then we properly ask: did that culture, by wilfully not considering and pursuing alternative actions, create the conditions of genocide, and thus, in effect, pursue it as a policy.[7]

In the broader cultural milieu, the construction of the American Indian as doomed savage served as an actuator for genocide. In defining indigenous populations as useless and subhuman, journalists, missionary fathers, civic authorities and military commanders collectively advanced what David Svaldi called 'a rhetoric of extermination'. Sociological processes of ostracism and prejudice identified American Indians as a target group for abuse, and earned them associations with obsolescence, depravity and inferiority. Indians became 'hungry wolves' and 'the devils of the forest', a blend of extant religious, ethnic and environmental chauvinism filtered through the frontier experience. Such racialised codes inculcated among settlers the notion of Indians as bloodthirsty and primitive, aberrant in their social practices and uniformly warlike. This process of essentialisation encouraged the reading of indigenous tribes in homogeneous terms, hostile 'others' and enemies of the state deserving of eradication. In Humboldt County, California (1860) and Rogue River, Oregon (1855) residents fervently took up arms to massacre local Indians, while sport hunting of Apaches in the south-west became one occupation for settlers fuelled by gold-fever, racism and land-hunger. Meanwhile, the conjuring of the 'Vanishing Indian' motif bestowed further momentum by encouraging a sense of immutability to processes of conquest. After settlers wiped out the Yahi Yama of Sacramento Valley, California in the mid-nineteenth century, their last surviving member, 'Ishi', lived out his days as a novelty 'wildman' in the Museum of the University of California. The extermination of the American Indian had become acceptable, normalised and even laudable.[8]

On the issue of intentionality, Western history offered plenty of instances where individuals encouraged practices of ethnic cleansing. Major General Winfield Scott advised the Indians of the Plains to submit to his authority or face total extermination, while L. Frank Baum (of Wizard of Oz fame) commented after Wounded Knee: 'Why not annihilation? Their glory has fled, their spirit broken, their manhood effaced; better that they should die than live the miserable wretches that they are.' The policy of the US Army to 'go all out' in pursuit of certain tribes appeared to satisfy the terms of the UN

Convention, while the fact that twenty soldiers received the Medal of Honor for service at Wounded Knee (the highest number awarded in any one battle) suggested *de facto* support for ethnic cleansing. Moreover, tacit endorsement of Indian-haters on the frontier (either through encouragement or telling silence) implicated both state and federal authorities. Editorials from local papers and promulgations from politicians bristled with chatter about elimination, extermination and vigilante action. A British visitor in 1784 spoke of how 'white Americans have the most rancorous antipathy to the whole race of Indians; and nothing is more common than to hear them talk of extirpating them totally from the face of the earth, men, women, and children'. In Gold Rush California, Governor Peter Burnett proclaimed that 'a war of extermination will continue to be waged between the two races until the Indian becomes extinct', and gave mettle to his message by sponsoring private military forays against Indians to the tune of $1.5 million. The *San Francisco Bulletin* applauded the action, motioning 'extermination' as 'the quickest and cheapest remedy' to settle brooding conflicts between Argonauts and indigenous tribes.[9]

Situated in the context of continental conquest and westward expansion, genocide represented a tool of empire, an efficient medium to advance the Euro-American project in the West. Even without overt declarations of exterminatory intent, the imperative of 'winning the West' ventured a practical authorisation for genocide. The California Gold Rush offered a clear example of the way in which a scramble for resources precipitated state-sanctioned massacres of indigenous peoples. Likewise, the co-ordinated killing of bison herds (by sportsmen, market hunters and sharp shooters paid by the US Army) indicated a clever policy on the part of federal authorities to destroy indigenous means of subsistence. Anecdotal evidence even suggested that blankets infected with smallpox were deliberately passed to tribes on the Missouri in the 1830s, with 'biological warfare' perceived as an expedient and opportune route to facilitate subjection. According to the *Daily Alta California* (1853), the germane nature of the 'Indian Question' with regard to national progress warranted the use of knives, rifles and pathogens. Writ broadly as exploration, annexation and settlement, the mechanics of nation-building, capitalism and Christianity provided the material apparatus and theoretical justification for extermination. Indians were obstacles to progress. Modes of appropriation and dispossession invited comparison with Lemkin's musings on the 'destruction of the national pattern of the oppressed group'. Moreover, the conjoined ideologies of patriotism, God and the dollar imprinted honourable permit on the appropriation of territory. Read in this fashion, manifest destiny befitted all the tainted associations of 'lebensraum', a quasi-scientific, religiously ordained dogma of provident futures and racial superiority. According to M. Annette Jaimes, 'The Third Reich and the United States did what they did for virtually identical reasons.'[10]

Marked by warfare, treaty-making, relocation and assimilation, Indian policy in the nineteenth-century West carried forth the rubric of Manifest Destiny under the auspices of an expanding federal bureaucracy. In 1830, the Indian Removal Act mandated the relocation of the Cherokee, Choctaw, Chicksaw, Creek and Seminole to 'free land' beyond the Mississippi. Forced marches across unfamiliar lands in winter without adequate food or medical supplies left one in eight Cherokee dead from the 'Trail of Tears'. Thirty-four years later, the Navajo (Diné) endured a similar purgatory on 'the Long Walk', when Kit Carson marched them 300 miles to Bosque Redondo to live in poverty alongside the Apache, their historic enemies.

Reservation policy as a solution to the 'Indian problem' has invited comparisons with the creation of pariah communities and forced internment under the Nazi regime. According to David Stannard, the missions of Spanish California (1769–1833) signified not beacons of enlightenment but 'furnaces of death'. Incoming American Indians, or 'neophytes', faced corporal punishment, forced labour, a poor diet of starchy soup and religious doctrine, as well as virulent outbreaks of disease. Under the American reservation system, pioneered in the 1850s, indigenous tribes scarcely fared better. Curly Tso of the Navajo considered Bosque Redondo a place 'where they would be put to death eventually', while on the Apache reserve, Arizona, a visiting federal agent described the treatment of internees in the 1870s as tantamount to 'an extermination program'. Practices of cultural assimilation such as the subdivision of land under the Dawes Act (1887) together with a swathe of policies aimed at detribalisation, suggested a rubric of ethnocide at work. The prohibition of traditional religious practices encouraged the disintegration of Indian spiritual identity, while boarding schools removed children from their parents based on aspirations of 'killing the Indian and saving the man'. Clothed in 'civilised' garb, given English names and under religious instruction, amounted to, in the words of David Wallace Adams, 'education for extinction'. As Mark Twain noted in a letter to the Secretary of War: 'Soap and education are not as sudden as a massacre, but they are more deadly in the long run; because a half massacred Indian may recover, but if you educate and wash him, it is bound to finish him some time or other.'[11]

The issue of Indian genocide in the nineteenth century highlighted what Patricia Nelson Limerick called 'the meeting ground of past and present'. Users of the 'g-word' contended that conditions on reservations in the twenty-first century suggested the ongoing relevance of the terminology by pointing to social decay (unemployment, suicide, poverty and alcoholism); forced sterilisations of women in the 1970s; and environmental racism relating to the storage of nuclear waste. Meanwhile, the import of the genocide moniker reflected a conversation across time periods that reflected both the imprecision and power of historical memory. According to Leo Kuper, the reticence of the United States to ratify the UN Convention (it signed up, with conditions attached, in 1988) reflected 'fear that it might be held responsible, retrospectively, for the annihilation of Indians'. For Gerald Vizenor, the existence of a legal framework and epistemology of genocide afforded opportunities for empowerment, healing and justice. Proposing a system of criminal tribunals to try the perpetrators of human rights abuses in absentia, Vizenor found merit in exposing the 'deniers of genocide' while nurturing 'a reliable historical narrative of native survivance'.[12]

The American Indian in the West: War, Disease and Semantics

> They are all dead, who cares, you just have to alter the history a little bit.
>
> Gerald Vizenor

The reaction to accusations of genocide against the American Indian proved far less lackadaisical than Vizenor's quip suggested. In academic, political and public forums, the idea that the United States had participated in activities comparable to Nazi Germany prompted distaste, anger, defensiveness and explication. Critics railed against the 'g-word' and suggested that the use of such a portentous term smacked of shock tactics activism and the imprint of political correctness. Writing in the *New York Review of Books*, J. H. Elliott criticised the 'indiscriminate use' of the genocide moniker, and castigated those who used the term as opportunists who glibly touted the phrase because of its 'powerful contemporary freight'. Allegations of pogroms and holocaust 'downplayed' the exceptionality of the Holocaust and displayed flagrant disrespect to its victims. As Robert Utley vociferated, 'genocide' connoted visions of 'boxcars, the gaunt masses of victims, and the crematoria' not all-American processes of westward expansion. Critics cited the taxonomical mire surrounding the idiom as evidence of its misapplication. James Axtell advised that we 'stop flogging ourselves' about a 'largely imaginary' issue. As Elliott West contended, 'when we stretch those words, they lose just about all their power to describe'.[13]

Issues of intent and the absence of systematic mechanisms of destruction loomed large in arguments for the defence. For Elliott West, the history of territorial conquest offered many instances of arrogance, brutality, intolerance, duplicity and racism, but not genocide. Thinking in terms of the UN Convention, critics highlighted the lack of an over-arching, organised and consistent schematic to effect the extermination of the American Indian. For Stephen Katz, the disorderly, ad hoc, and often reactive policies enacted by the US government in the West bore little resemblance to the 'intentional principle and actualized policy' of the Third Reich. The methodical, state-directed and co-ordinated nature of Nazi atrocities rendered the Holocaust 'historically and phenomenologically unique'. In comparison, federal power in the West lacked the apparatus and the omnipotence to enact ethnic cleansing on a continental scale. The country hardly resembled 'one large concentration camp with Europeans firmly in control'. Moreover, government policy on the frontier at times offered articulations of friendship and mediation to Indian nations. The Treaty of Fort Laramie (1851), for instance, situated the Army as 'the Indian's best friend' poised to intervene to protect collaborating tribes from belligerents, White or indigenous.[14]

Instead, critics argued that the treatment of American Indians spoke of disparate cultures vying for territory and resources. For West, the decimation of the Indian told the story of 'small minorities overwhelmed and devastated by ... far larger, expansive cultures and economies'. Put simply, the treatment of the American Indian spoke of martial conditions, including military aggression, the implementation of total war tactics and resistance, rather than genocide. The US Census listed a total of forty 'Indian Wars' between indigenous tribes and the US Army in the years 1775–1854. In April 1863, Francis Lieber issued General Order No. 100, stipulating that Indian camps represented legitimate military targets by virtue of their designation as 'hostiles'. Thus, for Robert Utley, Wounded Knee signified 'a regrettable, tragic accident of war'. Meanwhile, both Indians and Whites proved guilty of committing acts of violence without provocation. They also fought side by side. The Crow battled with Custer's 7th Cavalry at the Little Bighorn against the Lakota and the Northern Cheyenne. In these terms, the simple nomenclature of genocide served only to mask the complexities of Western conflict, creating a 'victimology' of the Indian and presenting a 'history loaded with inevitability and stripped of moral complexity'.[15]

The demographic catastrophe that wracked the continent (some ninety-three pandemics between the early 1500s and 1900) situated disease as a critical agent in the demise of the American Indian. Accordingly, Katz couched 'nature, not malice' as 'the cause of the massive, incomprehensible devastation'. Pathogens such as smallpox, measles, bubonic plague, whooping cough, venereal disease and even the common cold obliterated indigenous communities that lacked natural immunity. Between 70 per cent and 90 per cent of indigenous mortalities occurred due to disease. Certainly, this 'virgin soil epidemic' advanced the project of European colonisation, and as such represented a form of 'biological imperialism', but its transmission proved inadvertent. Deaths from contagion in the Spanish missions, according to Guenter Lewy, 'bore no comparison with the fate of the Jews in the ghettos'. Moreover, that the United States government made overtures to Indian tribes in support of smallpox inoculation during the 1830s contested allegations of deliberate infection.[16]

In 1860, the report of the Special Joint Committee of the California legislature noted the following: 'History teaches us that the inevitable destiny of the red man is total extermination or isolation from the deadly and corrupting influences of civilization.' Such pronouncements, according to some scholars, indicated the United States reservation system as founded on the premise of 'refuge' rather than 'prison camp'. As Richard Perry explicated, 'reservations were a means of getting rid of people without having to kill them'. Official policy touted the rhetoric of Enlightenment paternalism in couching the segregationist project as one of improvement, civilisation, agrarianism and religious conversion. Relocating Indians to reservations isolated American Indians from settlers, afforded federal stewardship, encouraged progress towards modernity and, most pertinently, freed up territory for Euro-American control – all positive outcomes in the vernacular of the time. Meanwhile, with the terms of the UN Convention in mind, anarchist writer Bob Black drew a distinction between cultural assimilation and full-blown genocide. In somewhat derisory tone, he riposted: 'If non-Indian Americans are engaged in genocide, they're not very good at it. Although it outnumbers the vanquished by more than 100–1, the Master Race looks less like the S.S. than the Gang That Couldn't Shoot Straight.'[17]

The Sand Creek Massacre: A Landscape of Aberration or 'American Character'?

On 29 November 1864, Colonel John Chivington and his 700-strong 3rd Colorado Volunteer Regiment attacked a camp of Cheyenne and Arapahos at Sand Creek, Colorado. Surprising the sleeping Indians at dawn, Chivington and his men bombarded the lodges with Howitzer fire before charging in, all guns blazing. Believing his people to be under the protection of the US Army, Chief Black Kettle urged calm, and raised the Stars and Stripes aloft. Terrified villagers gathered around Kettle's lodge, only to see cavalrymen advancing into the camp firing indiscriminately. A young girl waved a white flag, and Arapaho Chief White Antelope approached the mounted soldiers pleading them to stop. Both were cut down by rifle fire. Some villagers sought sanctuary by digging out pits in the streambed, but Chivington's men followed them with a barrage of shot and shells. By mid-afternoon, a tonne of ammunition had been despatched and more than one hundred Cheyenne and Arapaho lay dead. Soldiers picked over the smoking battlefield, mutilating corpses and gathering scalps and souvenirs. Bivouacked on the site that evening, Chivington wrote to the *Rocky Mountain News* of 'one of the most bloody Indian battles ever fought on the plains'.[18]

The massacre at Sand Creek is a salient illustration of a West marked by atrocity. In Denver, residents fired up with frontier fury hailed the 'battle' (as it was first reported) as a worthy revenge for attacks on wagon trains and settler farms. Theodore Roosevelt characterised the event 'as righteous and beneficial a deed as ever took place on the frontier'. In later years, however, Sand Creek cast a deleterious shadow over the triumphal story of westward expansionism, and raised uncomfortable images of paranoia, sadism and psychosis. The event thus carries critical purchase on broader questions of Indian genocide in the West. Did Sand Creek portend actions elsewhere and provide an example of American exterminatory intent? Or was it instead an isolated case of a colonel poisoned by vitriol and ambition? Was this an aberration or a display of 'American character'?[19]

Competing claims to territory and resources laid material foundations for the Sand Creek Massacre. The Cheyenne proved recent migrants to the area, having engaged in their own westward meander from ancestral stomping grounds on the Upper Missouri courtesy of the advances of the Euro-American fur trade. By the 1830s, the Cheyenne had settled into two bands (the northern and southern) with a nomadic plains culture based on bison and horses. Conflicts over territory proved common on the prairie, showing indigenous groups as neither bereft of agency nor irrevocably peaceable. Through the early 1800s the 'fighting Cheyennes' routinely engaged in spats with their neighbours and enemies, the Crow and Lakota. In 1819, Cheyenne warriors attacked a Crow camp, engaging in mutilations and scalping (the latter a practice acquired from the British). By the early 1860s, the socio-political environment of the Plains, and competing claims for its resources had become yet more complicated. For more than a decade, Euro-American wagon trains had trundled through Indian Territory en route to the goldfields of California and the greensward of Oregon. An uneasy peace existed in the 'Great American Desert' under the terms of the Fort Laramie Treaty (1851). However, the discovery of gold in Pikes Peak (1858) brought thousands of prospectors and settlers to Colorado and this time they were not just passing through. During a single month in 1859, 100,000 fortune seekers descended on the area. They asserted mining, land and ranching claims on the Platte River. By 1860, Denver sported a population of 33,000 men and 1,600 women, and the following year saw the creation of Colorado Territory. With an influx of settlers, issues of land ownership and indigenous sovereignty gained prominence.[20]

Quarrels between settlers and indigenous tribes during the 1860s came under the mantle of 'the Indian problem'. The choice of phrase betrayed codes of ethnocentrism, manifest destiny and cultural primacy at play. In this 'dialectic of civilization', Euro-American authorities forwarded a policy of bi-partisanship with indigenous groups, but consistently lacked the capacity or the inclination to make good on their claims. Solving the issue of competing subsistence requirements invariably led to the shunting of Indians to smaller patches of ground. Accordingly, territorial authorities in Colorado sought the re-negotiation of the Fort Laramie Treaty (which gave extensive lands to the Cheyenne and Arapaho) in favour of a new Indian reservation on the South Arkansas River. Essentially, Coloradans wanted Indians 'out of the way' in order to advance the resource bonanza in the hills and on the plains, and while the 'absolute right' of incoming settlers to enact removal was never questioned, civic leaders put sizeable store by the importance of securing legal sovereignty. Hence, under the terms of the Fort Wise Treaty (1861), the Southern Cheyenne and the Arapaho relinquished land title to all of Colorado Territory in return for a new reservation, a $15,000 stipend, farming equipment and supplies. Only six out of forty-four Cheyenne chiefs signed the treaty, but the piece of paper provided enough sanction for the United States authority who classed those who failed to abide by its terms as 'hostiles'. At the official ceremony, Chiefs Black Kettle, White Antelope and Little Raven received medals, blankets, sugar and tobacco from Colonel Greenwood, the Commissioner of Indian Affairs. A veneer of peaceful co-existence and colonial pomp hid a process of land usurpation and the imposition of an 'ideological quarantine' to protect the nation-state. For the Cheyenne, the adoption of reservation life forwarded processes of social, economic and environmental disintegration that might usefully be seen in terms of Lemkin's 'cultural genocide' marker. Confined to a small reserve marked by its aridity and scarcity of game, the Cheyenne suffered epidemics and physical and ecological debilitation. As William Red Hat motioned, 'never stay in one place too long because if you do you become a civilization and destroy things. You have to move on and let the land replenish.' With the nearest bison herds 200 miles way, the tribe found themselves effectively cut off from a powerful source of sustenance and spirituality. In June 1861, Indian Agent Boone reported conditions of near starvation on the reservation.[21]

As well as contests for land, the idea of Colorado Territory as a frontier tinderbox ready to explode at any moment as well as a sense of Indian turpitude sufficiently serious to mandate a policy of proactive militarism led to Sand Creek. As Franz Fanon extrapolated in *The Wretched of the Earth* (1961), colonial projects of land appropriation gained propulsion from psychological formulas of dehumanisation. Certainly, tensions existed between Whites and indigenous groups that the Treaty of Fort Wise failed to temper. A contingent among the Cheyenne and the Arapaho (typically young males as well as the warrior Dog Soldiers) continued to roam the plains and engaged in skirmishes with Euro-American buffalo hunters, miners, settlers and military detachments. Both sides acted without provocation. Indians ambushed farms, rustled livestock, and burned stage stations, while military units opened fire on a Cheyenne party at Fremonts Orchard, April 1864 and killed Lean Bear (with Lincoln's peace medal pinned to his chest), a month later. Such engagements scarcely amounted to all-out plains war, but they did provide a framework around which civic and military leaders crafted visions of an apocalyptic frontier in which Indian extermination appeared an appropriate policy.[22]

John Evans became Governor of Colorado Territory in May 1862. Faced with 'the Indian problem', he recommended extinguishing indigenous land title and tribal resistance. Fort Wise had proved useful in making the Indian a pariah awaiting 'civilisation', but the lack of signatories to the treaty left a niggling issue of legal ownership. Through 1863 and 1864, Evans consistently spoke in threatening terms, warning of 'depredations' and imminent war. Such protestations fashioned a monolithic image of Indians as belligerent 'others' and asserted a concomitant imperative to armed action. Evans argued that additional troops from the War Department would settle the Indian issue. On 27 June 1864, Evans issued a proclamation advising 'friendly Indians' to surrender to the Army or face retribution: 'The great Father is angry and will certainly hunt them out and punish them, but he does not want to injure those who remain friendly to whites.' A few weeks later, on 11 August, Evans upped the ante by establishing a citizen militia to 'go in pursuit of all hostile Indians on the plains'. Conscripts received pay, ammunition and permission to keep their spoils. Two days later, the War Department authorised the creation of a 100-day volunteer regiment under the command of John Chivington. The remit of the 'hundred daysers' appeared clear from their recruiting poster: 'Attention! Indian fighters'.[23]

The conscription drive for the 'hundred daysers' equated the killing of Indians with the gaining of patriotic glory. Similar rhetorical mechanisms advanced on the pages of the *Rocky Mountain News* (founded in 1859), forged a connection between local settler identity and the Indian issue. Editor William Byers spoke of tribal atrocity and wanton behaviour, fostering a climate of fear, conspiracy and retribution among his readers. Certainly, some of the pieces smacked of cultural conceit – 'If this country was intended for civilized people, the savage must submit and adapt himself to the new order of things' – but on many occasions the *News* promulgated direct invitations to genocide. The March 1863 story 'Exterminate Them' portrayed Indians as 'a dissolute, vagabondish, brutal and ungrateful race and ought to be wiped from the face of the earth'. On 10 August 1864, Byers wrote: 'Self preservation demands decisive action, and the only way to secure it is to fight them in their own way. A few months of active extermination against the red devils will bring quiet and nothing else will.' The paper fostered a siege mentality and encouraged a pioneer identity founded on the construct of collective defence: us versus them. News of the massacre of Nathan

Hungate and his family by rebel Arapaho warriors in June 1864, just twenty miles from the city, inflamed the public mood. Reportage in the *Rocky Mountain News* commented on 'the barbarity of the red devils', while the decision to display the mutilated corpses in Denver provided a visual signifier of Indian savagery and gave macabre substantiation to the idea of a lurking red peril. Moreover, as Denverites reverently filed past the Hungates, they engaged in a ritualised process of community character-building that cast settlers as innocents and Indians as aggressors. In turn, this osmotic experience cultivated a sense of Indian eradication as justified and moral. As David Svaldi noted, the Hungate example 'could be appealed to without explanation to secure action'.[24]

When John Chivington mustered his troops on the edge of Sand Creek he stoked their fury with the refrain, 'Remember the Hungates'. For Chivington and his volunteer 'Indian-fighters', ethnic prejudice and rancour found articulation in acts of extreme aggression. Chivington had migrated to Denver in 1860, taking up a commission as 'fighting parson' rather than continue his Methodist ministry. In the years leading to Sand Creek, he proved a worthy foil to Governor Evans. In late August 1864, not long after declaring martial law, Chivington delivered a public address in which he uttered the infamous adage 'kill and scalp all, big and little; nits make lice'. The colonel's entomological analogy proved telling. By presenting Indians as lice he played on popular fears of infestation. This linguistic narrative of epidemic roused suspicions and also feted armed response as a logical step. Such an 'epistemology of justification' proved a feature of the 'war' against the plains wolf, as well as presaging comments made by Heinrich Himmler on the Holocaust as an exercise in 'de-lousing'.[25]

The collective rhetoric of extermination as advanced by Evans, Byers and Chivington situated the massacre at Sand Creek firmly in the flow of mainstream local sentiment. But what of broader government policy? Some would argue that Evans and Chivington stood as articulators (and perhaps actuators) of official doctrine by virtue of their appointments. According to Barta, determining intent, or sanction, in cases of genocide must account for 'intentions from action (and inaction) and from words as well'. In the context of Sand Creek, this question of culpability was a complex one. Chivington could not point to clear-cut instructions to exterminate from on high. However, the authorisation of the 'hundred daysers' and the pronouncements of General Curtis (in demanding the 'crushing' of Indians (June 1864) and mandating the killing of any Indian not at a fort (August 1864)) implied a degree of sanction from the chain of command. Meanwhile, in the immediate run-up to Sand Creek, voices of reason and rant both found voice in the martial establishment. Major Edward Wynkoop, commander of Fort Lyon, accompanied Black Kettle to Denver in September 1864 to convince Governor Evans that the Cheyenne warranted the designation of 'friendly Indians'. In his memoirs, Wynkoop identified a faction of 'exterminators' in the Army, as well as a broader culture of supposition predicated on the idea of the Indian as a 'savage'. Evans proved unmoved by Kettle's mediations, a sentiment that reflected his personal unease with peacemaking (not least because of the volte face he would have to perform given his own grandstanding on the Indian threat). Institutional momentum also offered a rationale for violence. Locals had begun to chide the Colorado Volunteers as 'the bloodless third', and with the end of service imminent, Evans wanted them to see (preferably glorious) service. As he pointed out, 'What shall I do with the third regiment, if I make peace?' After the meeting, Evans and Chivington continued to protest the rightful designation of the Cheyenne as 'hostiles', Black Kettle marched the tribe to Fort Lyon expecting Army protection and Major Wynkoop found himself relieved from duty for issuing supplies to 'hostile Indians in direct violation of orders' and undertaking an unauthorised peace delegation to Denver. His replacement, Major Scott Antony, refused to make peace with Black Kettle on the grounds of legitimate authority, and despatched a missive to his superiors – 'I shall try to keep the Indians quiet until such time as I receive reinforcements.' Such engagements suggested the US Army adhered to Philip Sheridan's famous lexicon 'the only good Indians I saw were dead'.[26]

As the 3rd Colorado Volunteer Regiment marched out of Denver on 14 November 1864, chatter among the officers included secret campaigns against the Indians, how they would arrange scalps and the whereabouts of Black Kettle's camp. Did such discussions imply a co-ordinated and premeditated campaign of genocide? Certainly Chivington had gained no official warrant from General Curtis to mount an attack, and the regiment's arrival at Fort Lyon proved unexpected. At the same time, orders advocated a strategy of fierce chastisement: 'pursue the offenders, force retribution, and "kill" those responsible'. When Chivington reached Fort Lyon, he forbade anyone from leaving (to preserve the element of surprise for his Indian ambush), and gained a warm reception from Major Antony. The commanding officer of the fort reputedly agreed that 'some of those Indians ought to be killed' and detailed 125 regulars from the

1st Colorado Regiment to join the campaign. Utterances of dissent from Captain Silas Soule and Lieutenant John Cramer received threats of court martial, as well as fearsome bluster from Chivington: 'Damn any man who sympathises with Indians! I have come to kill Indians, and I believe it is right and honourable to use any means under God's heaven to kill Indians.'[27]

On the evening of 28 November, Chivington and his force left Fort Lyon to march the forty miles to Sand Creek. Approaching the camp at dawn, cavalrymen rounded up Indian ponies grazing on the bluffs to prevent any possibility of escape. Believing his cause to be righteous, Chivington advised his men of the 'hostile' status of the Indians and added, 'Boys, I shall not tell you what you are to kill, but remember our slaughtered women and children.' Those refusing to heed the battle cry, including Captain Soule, earned charges of cowardice. As the carnage began, trader George Bent noted:

> All was confusion and noise, men, women and children rushing out of the lodges partly dressed; women and children screaming at the sight of the troops ... Black Kettle had a large American flag tied to the end of a long lodgepole and was standing in front of his lodge, holding the pole ... I heard him call to the people not to be afraid, that the soldiers would not hurt them; then the troops opened fire.

The indiscriminate killing lasted for several hours, during which soldiers cut out unborn foetuses and the genitals of dead Indian women and wore them as trophies on their saddles and hats. One officer spoke of his plan to fashion White Antelope's scrotum into a tobacco pouch. Soldiers sliced off the ears and fingers of the fallen to snatch their jewellery, and engaged in the summary execution of captives. Such an exhibition of atrocity reflected a martial force out of control and fired up on alcohol and frontier fury. But did the status of the Colorado 3rd as 'volunteers', as essentially untrained, undisciplined and prone to excess, exonerate or implicate the US military establishment? According to Robert Utley, such lack of restraint was scarcely found among regular Army units. Ward Churchill, on the other hand, regarded the engagement at Sand Creek as 'a symbol of the entire process by which this continent was "settled"'.[28]

Residents of Denver responded to news of the massacre in carnival spirit. Chivington's first (and largely erroneous) report spoke of how his noble force marched through the snow to slay 500 Indians, mostly warriors, and found White scalps interred in the camp. Hailed as the 'bloody thirdsters', the colonel and his detachment received a parade and public cheer, while the Apollo Theatre housed a grisly exhibit of Cheyenne and Arapaho scalps fresh from the battlefield. With characteristic bellicosity, the *Rocky Mountain News* rattled that 'the recent campaign of our Colorado volunteers will stand in history with few rivals, and none to exceed it in final results'. The headline for 8 December 1864 read: 'Great Battle with Indians! The Savages Dispersed!' Firm evidence of the heretical status of dissenters came in April 1865, when Captain Soule received a fatal gunshot to the head as he walked the streets of Denver.[29]

The Sand Creek massacre provoked a different response further afield. Humanitarian reformers baulked at the bloodbath and expressed anti-military sentiment. Federal authorities initiated three separate investigations, two under the auspices of the House and Senate and one from the War Department. In spring 1865, the Congressional Committee on the Conduct of the War travelled to Colorado, where it heard testimony and visited the Sand Creek site to find milk teeth peppered with bullets in the buffalo grass. At a public meeting at the Denver Opera House, remonstrations from the Committee met an unruly cacophony of 'Exterminate them! Exterminate them!'. In each investigation, federal officials condemned the slaughter as unwarranted and despicable. John Evans found himself relieved from the governorship, and Chivington (who had already mustered out of service) received sharp criticism for his role in planning and undertaking a 'foul and dastardly massacre'. The focus of the federal investigations on individual culpability deflected from the role of broader cultural forces and official directives in facilitating Sand Creek. After all, one of the testifiers against Chivington was none other than Kit Carson, a man who had left his own bloody trail across the south-west in subjugating the Navajo, but with the mantle of hero intact.[30]

The fallout from Sand Creek was significant on the Great Plains. With eight chiefs from the Council of Forty-Four lying dead on the smoking battlefield, the Cheyenne tribe experienced trauma, disarray and disintegration. Many survivors felt that the Whites could never be trusted, and sturdily rejected Black Kettle's policy of mediation in favour of all-out war. Gathered at a council on the Republican River, Cheyenne warrior Leg in the Water motioned, 'We have now raised the battle-axe until death.' For the next twelve years, Plains Indians and US forces engaged in a round of skirmishes that culminated in the Battle of the Little Bighorn (1876). Meanwhile, processes of treaty-making continued at Little Arkansas (1865) and New Medicine Lodge

The Wild West Defiled

Figure 7.1 In the White House Conservatory during the Civil War, Brady, New York. The photograph, taken 27 March 1863, depicted the Southern Plains Indian delegation. On the front row (left to right) are Cheyenne chiefs War Bonnet, Standing in the Water and Lean Bear, and Yellow Wolf of the Kiowas. All died within a year and a half of this meeting. Yellow Wolf succumbed to pneumonia, War Bonnet and Standing in the Water were killed at Sand Creek, and Lean Bear was shot as a 'hostile' by US troops in Colorado.

(1867). In autumn 1868, Philip Sheridan received permission for a total offensive against the Plains Indians that included attacks on vulnerable winter camps and scorched earth tactics – a policy that appeared to satisfy the terms of Jean-Paul Sartre's 'war by perpetual massacre'. On 27 November 1868, Black Kettle and the Cheyenne faced a repeat performance of Sand Creek as they camped at the Washita River, Oklahoma. Entering the camp from four directions, Custer and his 7th Cavalry fired at will, burned lodges and killed horses. By the end of the fight, ninety-two women and children had been killed, along with eleven men, including Black Kettle himself. Custer received praise from Sheridan for 'efficient and gallant services rendered' as he rode back to Fort Cobb carrying Black Kettle's scalp. The Washita attack destroyed any resolve possessed by the Cheyenne. The bison herds were no more, the tribe had been decimated and its members had become so hungry that they ate dogs. Surrender and relocation to a reservation in Oklahoma appeared the only option. On arrival at Fort Cobb, officiating personnel told Cheyenne leader Little Robe that his people could not make peace now and decide to declare war again in the spring: 'It is for you to say what we have to do,' he replied.[31]

In 2000, the National Park Service authorised the creation of the Sand Creek Massacre National Historic Site. Its enabling statement described the prairie locale as 'a reminder of the tragic extremes sometimes reached in the 500 years of conflict between Native Americans and people of European and other origins'. The designation represented an act of geographic and historical citation, remembrance and healing, as well as providing an important foil to the 'systematic forgetfulness' of dominant Euro-American culture. Those who failed to apprehend Western history as a ground of contest, complexity and moral ablutions were, according to Rebecca Solnit, little more than 'cultural Custers'. Elsewhere in Colorado, triumphal remnants of Sand Creek remained embedded in the landscape. A monument at the state capitol recorded the exploits of the 3rd Colorado Regiment in its roster of 'great Civil War battles'. The town of Chivington (founded in 1887, and razed courtesy of the Dust Bowl) offered homage to the Indian killer himself, while the Colorado Historical Society still held Cheyenne and Arapaho scalps in its collections. Navigations of this coded, and irrevocably historic, landscape required rigour, awareness of context as well as frank engagement with difficult issues of frontier ethnocentrism and bloodletting. Thus, the dedication of the Sand Creek Massacre site and, indeed, transfer of title to the Cheyenne and Arapaho under Park Service management, conveyed a potent message of authority and legitimacy. The woods that 'still ached from the spilling of innocent blood' became a sacred space and corroborated oral histories of native survivance. They also delineated a narrative of territoriality, identity formation and the power of rhetoric – for both indigenous and settler populations. Unsurprisingly, the dedication ceremony of 28 April 2007 steered well clear of the thorny semantics of the 'g-word', although Senator Sam Brownback offered a pertinent tender of official contrition: 'I acknowledge and admit wrongs were done by the federal government here and across the nation. I deeply apologize.'[32]

Notes

1. Barry Lopez, *Of Wolves and Men* (New York: Touchstone, 1978), p. 167.
2. Elliott West, *The Contested Plains: Indians, Goldseekers and the Rush to Colorado* (Lawrence: University Press of Kansas, 2000), p. 336; Ward Churchill, *A Little*

Matter of Genocide: Holocaust and Denial in the Americas, 1492 to the Present (San Francisco: City Lights Books, 1997); David Stannard, *American Holocaust* (New York: Oxford University Press, 1992); Russell Thornton, *American Indian Holocaust and Survival: A Population History Since 1492* (Norman: University of Oklahoma Press, 1987).

3. Gerald Vizenor, 'Genocide tribunals: Native human rights and survivance', Address to the Institute for Advanced Studies, University of Minnesota, 10 October 2006.
4. Leo Kuper, *Genocide* (New Haven: Yale University Press, 1981); p. 11; Raphael Lemkin, *Axis Rule in Occupied Europe* (Washington, DC: Carnegie Endowment for International Peace, 1944), p. xi.
5. Jean-Paul Sartre, *On Genocide, and a Summary of the Evidence and Judgements of the International War Crimes Tribunal* (Boston: Beacon Press, 1968); Frank Chalk and Kurt Jonassohn, *The History and Sociology of Genocide: Analysis and Case Studies* (New Haven: Yale University Press, 1990), pp. 8–11; Israel Charny, 'Toward a generic definition of genocide', in George J. Andreopolous (ed.), *Genocide: Conceptual and Historical Dimensions* (Philadelphia: University of Pennsylvania Press, 1994), p. 7; Dadrian: quoted in Chalk and Jonassohn, *History and Sociology of Genocide*, p. 14; Tony Barta, 'Relations of genocide: land and lives in the colonization of Australia', in I. Walliman and M. N. Dobkowski (eds), *Genocide and the Modern Age* (New York: Greenwood Press, 1987), pp. 238–9.
6. Estimates of pre-contact populations vary enormously – from George Catlin's 16,000,000 residents of North America to James Mooney's rather more conservative 1,148,000. Russell Thornton posits 5,000,000 as a plausible figure for the conterminous United States. However, the specifics of these figures cease to matter when faced with the final statistics. See Alfred Crosby, 'Ecological imperialism: the overseas migration of western Europeans as a biological phenomenon', in Donald Worster (ed.), *The Ends of the Earth: Perspectives on Modern Environmental History* (Cambridge: Cambridge University Press, 1988), pp. 103–17; Thornton, *American Indian Holocaust and Survival*, pp. 15–41; Stannard, *American Holocaust*, p. 146.
7. Laura Turney and Doug Sackman: quoted in 'Webforum: Native Americans and genocide', H-West Discussion log June 1999, available online at: http://h-net.org/~west; Fitzpatrick: quoted in John Killoren, *Black Robe: De Smet and the Indian Tragedy* (Norman: University of Oklahoma Press, 1994), p. 194.
8. David Svaldi, *Sand Creek and the Rhetoric of Extermination: A Case Study in Indian–White Relations* (Boston: University Press of America, 1989); Tomas Almaguer, *Racial Fault Lines: The Historical Origins of White Supremacy in California* (Los Angeles: University of California Press, 1994), pp. 108, 113.
9. Baum: quoted in the *Aberdeen Saturday Pioneer*, 20 December 1890; Guenter Lewy, 'Were American Indians the victims of genocide?', *History News Network Magazine*, George Mason University, p. 22, November 2004; Burnett: quoted in Vizenor, 'Genocide tribunals'; B. Madley, 'Patterns of frontier genocide, 1803–1910: the Aboriginal Tasmanians, the Yuki of California and the Herero of Namibia', *Journal of Genocide Research*, 6 (2004), pp. 167–92.
10. *Daily Alta California*, 16 March 1853; M. Annette Jaimes (ed.), *The State of Native America: Genocide, Colonization and Resistance* (Boston: South End Press, 1992), p. 3.

11. Stannard, *American Holocaust*, p. 137; Clyde Milner et al., *Oxford History of the American West* (Oxford: Oxford University Press, 1994), p. 181; Churchill, *A Little Matter of Genocide*, p. 145; David Wallace Adams, *Education for Extinction: American Indians and the Boarding School Experience* (Lawrence: University Press of Kansas, 1995); Mark Twain, *The Facts Concerning the Recent Resignation*, Washington, DC, December 1867.
12. Patricia Nelson Limerick, *The Legacy of Conquest: The Unbroken Past of the American West* (New York: Norton, 1987), pp. 134–75; Kuper: quoted in Chalk and Jonassohn, *History and Sociology of Genocide*, pp. 422–5; Vizenor, 'Genocide tribunals'.
13. Vizenor, 'Genocide tribunals'; J. H. Elliott, *New York Review of Books*, 24 June 1993; Utley and West: quoted in 'Webforum on Genocide'; James Axtell, *Beyond 1492: Encounters in Colonial America* (New York: Oxford University Press, 1992), p. 263.
14. See: 'Webforum on genocide'; S. Katz, 'The uniqueness of the Holocaust: the historical dimension', in A. S. Rosenbaum (ed.), *Is the Holocaust Unique? Perspectives on Comparative Genocide* (Boulder: Westview Press, 2001), p. 7.
15. 'Webforum on genocide'; Utley: quoted in Lewy, 'Were American Indians the victims of genocide?'
16. S. Katz, *The Holocaust in Historical Context* (New York: Oxford University Press, 1992), p. 20; Lewy, 'Were American Indians the victims of genocide?'
17. Almaguer, *Racial Fault Lines*, p. 126; Richard Perry, *From Time Immemorial: Indigenous Peoples and State Systems* (Austin: University of Texas Press, 1996), p. 106; Bob Black, 'Up Sand Creek without a paddle', November 2006. Available online at: http://www.discxoverthenetworks.org.
18. Quoted in Stan Hoig, *The Sand Creek Massacre* (Norman: University of Oklahoma Press, 1961), p. 154.
19. Roosevelt: quoted in Dan Stone, *The Historiography of Genocide* (Basingstoke: Palgrave, 2008), p. 286.
20. See: George Grinnell, *The Fighting Cheyennes* (Norman: University of Oklahoma Press, 1956 [1915]).
21. The term 'Dialectic of Civilization' was coined by Roy Harvey Pearce. See: Svaldi, *Sand Creek and the Rhetoric of Extermination*, p. 3; Kate Kane, 'Nits make lice: Drogheda, Sand Creek and the poetics of colonial extermination', *Cultural Critique*, 42 (spring 1999), p. 95; Elizabeth Michell, 'Sand Creek Massacre site: an environmental history' (Department of History, Colorado State University, January 2007), p. 31.
22. Franz Fanon, *The Wretched of the Earth* (New York: Grove Press, 1965 [1961]).
23. Brown's proclamations: quoted in Dee Brown, *Bury My Heart at Wounded Knee: An Indian History of the American West* (London: Vintage, 1991 [1970]), pp. 74–5.
24. *Rocky Mountain News*, 24 July 1865, 24 March 1865, 10 August 1865; Svaldi, *Sand Creek and the Rhetoric of Extermination*, p. 190.
25. Robert Perkin, *The First Hundred Years: An Informal History of Denver and the Rocky Mountain News* (Garden City: Doubleday, 1959), p. 271; Reginald Craig, *The Fighting Parson: The Biography of Colonel John M. Chivington* (Los Angeles: Westernlore Press, 1959); Richard Drinnon, *Facing West: The*

Metaphysics of Indian-hating and Empire-building (Norman: University of Oklahoma Press, 1997 [1980]), p. 502; Kane, 'Nits make lice', p. 98.
26. At the meeting, Chivington offered Black Kettle the ambiguous comment regarding Indian protection at the forts: 'I am not a big war chief, but all the soldiers in this country are at my command. My rule of fighting white men or Indians is to fight them until they lay down their arms and submit to military authority. They are nearer Major Wynkoop than any one else and they can go to him when they are ready to do that.' See: Svaldi, *Sand Creek and the Rhetoric of Extermination*, p. 257; Barta, 'Relations of genocide', pp. 238–9; Edward Wynkoop and Christopher Gerboth, *The Tall Chief: The Unfinished Autobiography of Edward W. Wynkoop, 1856–1866* (Denver: Colorado Historical Society, 1994), pp. 85–6; Svaldi, *Sand Creek and the Rhetoric of Extermination*, p. 253; Grinnell, *Fighting Cheyennes*, p. 166; Brown, *Bury My Heart at Wounded Knee*, pp. 84–6.
27. Svaldi, *Sand Creek and the Rhetoric of Extermination*, p. 283; Hoig, *Sand Creek Massacre*, pp. 137–44; James Wilson, *The Earth Shall Weep: A History of Native America* (London: Picador, 1998), p. 273.
28. Svaldi, *Sand Creek and the Rhetoric of Extermination*, p. 293; George Hyde, *Life of George Bent: Written from his Letters* (Norman: University of Oklahoma Press, 1968), p. 152; Robert Utley, *Frontiersmen in Blue: The United States Army and the American Indian, 1848–1865* (Lincoln: University of Nebraska Press, 1967), pp. xiii, 2, 294–7; Churchill: quoted in Jaimes, *State of Native America*, p. 5.
29. *Rocky Mountain News*, 17 December 1864, 8 December 1864.
30. Svaldi, *Sand Creek and the Rhetoric of Extermination*, p. 188; Hoig, *Sand Creek Massacre*, p. 168.
31. Utley, *Frontiersmen in Blue*, p. 301; Brown, *Bury My Heart at Wounded Knee*, pp. 169–70.
32. Rebecca Solnit, *Storming the Gates of Paradise: Landscapes for Politics* (Berkeley: University of California Press, 2007), p. 50; Simon Ortiz, *From Sand Creek* (Tucson: University of Arizona Press, 1981); *Denver Post*, 29 April 2007.

Chapter 8

The Thirsty West: Grand Canyon, Hoover Dam and Las Vegas

On Independence Day 1941, a family from Kelso, Washington embarked on a two-week excursion to the West. Their automobile tour took in the romance of the open road and striking landscapes. A scrapbook recorded the 'unforgettable miles' travelled, with a range of textual entries, photographs, clippings and postcards. Entitled 'See Your West' (an auto-fuelled homage to the 'See America First' campaign promoted by the National Park Service in the early twentieth century), the scrapbook lofted the West as a realm of patriotic vigour, monumental scenery and frontier spirit. After drive-by tours of Bryce Canyon and Zion national parks, the family arrived at the Grand Canyon on 19 July. An accompanying journal entry described the 'gorgeous spectacle' before them, a 'a bird's-eye view' and a geological instruction on 'the world in the making'. Day two at the Canyon lent the trip an Old West flavour with Eagle dances at the Hopi House and a stay at the Bright Angel Lodge. The car trundled on to the Hoover Dam, which 'See Your West' presented as 'a gigantic project' bounded by a vibrant, emerald-green Lake Mead. Compared with the Grand Canyon, the Hoover Dam screamed man-made, yet sat comfortably on the tour roster courtesy of its Boulder Canyon setting, national lustre and monumental scale. At the dam, the family took the guided tour, eagerly recorded its vital statistics – '1,835,000 horsepower of electricity, harnessing the flood water, and [making] possible the all-American canal' – and pasted the Bureau of Reclamation pamphlet in their scrapbook. After the heat and starkness of the desert, their arrival in Las Vegas with its casinos and creature comforts proved welcome. The family scrapbook registered particular praise to the Nevada town for its tourist facilities, notably the 'loveliest air-conditioned cabins we had yet found on our trip'. Arriving home on 18 July, the round-trip had taken in some 4,213 miles.[1]

As indicated by 'See your West', the Grand Canyon, the Hoover Dam and Las Vegas represented 'must see' sites for the Western tourist buff in the twentieth century. Each of the three cut a striking presence as super-sized spectacles that symbolised American matchlessness, Manifest Destiny and moral authority. These monuments to American giganticism celebrated the wonders of nature, engineering prowess, the spirit of the West and the almighty dollar (often in synchronicity), and stood tall (or deep as in the case of the Grand Canyon) as commanding places. Moreover, alongside their status as iconic, imagined spaces, the sites shared one resource in common. The Colorado River represented the long-standing architect of the region in its 1,400 mile wending from the Rockies to the Gulf of Mexico. Some ten million years ago it began perhaps its most famous project, cutting a mile-deep through the rocks of the Northern Arizona plateau to craft the Grand Canyon. Less than a hundred miles downstream, the Hoover Dam bespoke the issue of aridity which marked Western history in its pioneer and consolidation phases. As Philip Fradkin noted, 'it was not the six-gun or barbed wire that won this part of the West' but water irrigation and storage that marshalled agriculture beyond the 98th meridian. Las Vegas, meanwhile, became a decided beneficiary of the federally sponsored reclamation project to make the desert bloom, gaining residents, tourists and all-important water and power from the Hoover Dam to furnish its neon oasis in the Mojave.[2]

This chapter considers the Grand Canyon, the Hoover Dam and Las Vegas as landmarks of the American West, paying particular attention to issues of resource conservation, ideas of scenic monumentalism, the persistence of the frontier motif and the rise of a metropolitan region. It also situates these landscapes as prime examples of competing visions. Set against the idealism of the 'See your West' scrapbook, recent years have seen the blooming of an environmentalist vernacular that promulgated the Grand Canyon, the Hoover Dam and Las Vegas as dystopic spaces. No longer perfections of the American dream, these locales have been read as emblematic of what Earth First!er Dave Foreman called the 'industrial conquest of the wilderness'. Whereas Walter Prescott Webb argued in *The Great Plains* (1931) that the arid quality of western lands cultivated virtues of democracy and ingenuity – a kind of Frederick Jackson Turner meets the teleology of thirst – environmental historian Donald Worster posited the rise of a 'hydraulic society' based on bureaucratisation, capital accumulation, high-technology and the exploitation of nature. According to the 'See your West' scrapbook, the American spirit could be seen in the majestic canyons of the Colorado. For Marc Reisner, writing in *Cadillac Desert* (1990), that moniker applied to the muddy and deeply contested waters of 'the most legislated, most debated, and most litigated river in the entire world'.[3]

Grand Canyon: The National Park as Western Product

Speaking in 1912, British Ambassador Lord James Bryce applauded the national park as 'the *best idea America ever had*'. Seventy-one years later, acclaimed western writer Wallace Stegner ventured a similar assessment in his famous adage: 'National parks are the best idea we ever had. Absolutely American, absolutely democratic.' The international lineage of the park label notwithstanding, Bryce and Stegner had a point. Certainly in its modern incarnation, the national park, sported American values. It also served as a product specifically of the American West.[4]

The first person to articulate the concept of a national park did so as a direct result of the westering experience. During a trip to Fort Pierre in 1832, George Catlin, famed artist and chronicler of Indian customs, became aware of the destructive impact of westward expansion on the land, people and wildlife inhabiting the plains of present-day South Dakota. Having witnessed the destruction of bison herds and the disintegration of Indian culture, Catlin determined that the government should step in to create 'A *nation's Park*, containing man and beast, in all the wild and freshness of their nature's beauty!' Engagement with the frontier experience and the aesthetics of the prairie proved formative to Catlin's thinking. Certainly, his call for a 'nation's park' proved a radical one in its lauding of prairie ecology and indigenous hunting. Although Catlin's comments reeked of primitivism and traded on the cult of the noble savage, he at least saw American Indians as part of the landscape (something national park authorities shied from when conjuring wilderness as a realm bereft of human impact). For him, the national park idea signalled American preservationist spirit (both natural and anthropological) and cultural erudition: 'What a beautiful and thrilling specimen for America to preserve and hold up to the view of her refined citizens and the world in future ages!' The idea of a prairie park none the less counted few champions. Catlin may have judged the plains 'useless' for cultivation but the legions of homesteaders and ranchers that colonised the region with their spotted bison and grain fields thought otherwise. Meanwhile, appreciation of the undulating sea of grass remained a minority viewpoint until the rise of ecological science and attendant appreciation of representative habitat.[5]

The creation of America's first national parks came with the discovery of monumental scenery in the far West. Catlin's Dakota prairie may have excited little interest, but western giganticism in the shape of the Sierra redwoods and Yosemite Valley in California and the rugged peaks and thermal novelties of the Yellowstone plateau captured the public imagination. Attracting attention ever since its discovery by miners in 1851, Yosemite Valley was dedicated as a state park in 1864, its forty square miles of pastoral scenery and towering mountains protected 'for public resort and recreation'. Yellowstone, meanwhile, earned status as a 'public park' in 1872 (although the first superintendent, Nathaniel Langford, favoured the term 'national park' in his inaugural report), following government expeditions to the area under the direction of David Folsom (1869), Henry Washburn (1870) and Ferdinand Hayden (1871). The Yellowstone Act set aside 3,300 square miles of Rocky Mountain ruggedness and geothermal freakery under federal protection as 'a pleasuring ground for the benefit and enjoyment of the people'.

According to Wallace Stegner, the national park movement seemed inexorable 'as soon as Americans learned to confront the wild continent not with fear and cupidity but with delight, wonder, and awe'. Westward expansion proved integral to this process of reappraisal, of seeing mountains of awe rather than ore, nature's redwood cathedrals rather than timber stands. The grandeur of western scenery proffered unfamiliar, exotic terrain, a realm of dramatic landscapes and gigantic vistas set in sharp relief to the eastern United States. As Albert D. Richardson wrote in *Beyond the Mississippi* (1867), in the 'New West' nature had veered away from providing 'repetitions' in favour of compositions 'originally, freshly, uniquely, majestically'. The monumentalism of the western diorama drew meaning (and admirers) courtesy of Romanticism and its elevation of rugged nature as a realm for uplift and spiritual renewal. This notion of nature as a tonic – a remedy for good health and elixir to protect against urban malady – had prompted earlier precedents in nature protection at Hot Springs, Arkansas (1832) and Central Park, New York (1864). The West of towering peaks, dismal chasms and crashing waterfalls proved an ideal setting for the veneration of the sublime and picturesque, and gained visual broadcast in the East courtesy of artists such as Albert Bierstadt and Thomas Moran. Aside from the Romantic valuation, the splendid scale of the western panorama earned further plaudits as a patriotic canvas – a place where Americans nurtured pride in their past and which served to stoke the fires of cultural nationalism. Europe may have had its castles and cathedrals, but the United States discovered in the West vast rock monuments and ancient trees on which to found its sense of destiny and moral purpose. For journalist Samuel Bowles, the beauty of the Yosemite Valley compared with 'the whole of Switzerland', while Clarence King hailed the Sierra redwoods as 'living monuments of antiquity' vastly superior to any 'fragment of human work, broken pillar or sand-worn image half lifted over pathetic desert'.[6]

Romanticism and cultural nationalism provided philosophical underpinnings for the glorification of western scenery. However, the shift from appreciation to preservation gained its principal thrust from the process of westward expansion itself. In this sense, the national park movement signified a post-frontier phenomenon: a reaction to the breakneck speed of continental conquest. Where the pioneer economy had advanced an ethos of nature as an expendable, profitable and boundless resource, the late nineteenth-century conservationist vociferated a new mentality. Species once seen as countless now eked out a fragile existence as itinerant faunal refugees. Plains bison numbered only 800 by 1890. The last wild passenger pigeon died in 1899, while the one remaining bird in captivity, Martha, gazed forlornly from her cage in Cincinnati Zoo. Vast acreages of forest had been cut, the plains had been fenced and populated with ranches and homesteads, and extractive mining had scarred the slopes of the Sierra Nevada. Such harsh realities eroded the fervent mythologies of superabundance, capitalisation and redemptive zeal that had marked the pioneer encounter with untamed nature. In the process, a fresh valuation of the natural world founded on sustainability, aesthetics, recreation and cultural import emerged. From George Perkins Marsh and Francis Parkman to John Muir and George Grinnell, a number of commentators expressed regret at what had been lost courtesy of the onward march of industrialism. As Parkman noted in the 1892 edition of *The Oregon Trail*, 'the Wild West is tamed, and its savage charms have withered'. For such campaigners, national parks afforded the chance to save remnants of the West for posterity, to demonstrate cultural magnanimity and preserve delectable locales from the ravages of rampant commercialism. As of 1900, the United States sported five national parks – Yellowstone, Sequoia, Yosemite, General Grant and Mount Rainier – all in the West, and all predicated on the preservation of grand landscapes of rock and ice.[7]

The Grand Canyon sat well in this ensemble cast. A ten-million-year-old exercise in erosion, its 277-mile length attested to the relentless grinding of water on bedrock. According to the creation story of the Hopi, the mile-deep canyon served as a *Sipapu*, a place from whence people emerged. The first explorers to the Canyon too referenced its magnitude. When Spanish explorer Captain Garcia López de Cárdenas happened upon the rim in 1540 he dispatched two men to search for the Colorado River. The men returned to camp having found no watercourse, but talking of boulders 'taller than the great tower of Seville'. Two centuries later, Father Francisco Tomás Garcés wrote of his astonishment 'at the roughness of this country'. For such travellers, focused on the search for gold, the Canyon appeared a hazard, a wretched inconvenience. American James Pattie, who trapped in the south-west during the early 1800s, likewise apprehended the Canyon in less than salutary terms – describing 'horrid mountains' that confined the river and confounded his travels. The 1858 report of Lieutenant Joseph Christmas famously stated: 'Ours was the first, and doubtless will be the last, party of whites to visit this profitless locality.'[8]

'What a world of grandeur is spread before us!': when John Wesley Powell wrote these lines in his *Exploration of the Colorado River of the West* (1875) the Grand Canyon seemed caught in the throes of reinvention. Still identified by its craggy enormity, the Canyon now assumed a spiritual, beautiful quality: a wow factor that provoked delight rather than antipathy. With echoes of the 'delightful horror' of the sublime aesthetic as expounded by eighteenth-century philosopher Edmund Burke, Powell couched his journey in monumental terms: 'by a year's toil a concept of sublimity can be obtained never again to be equaled on the hither side of paradise'. The big ditch had become, in the words of naturalist John Burroughs, 'a divine abyss'. The transformation of the Grand Canyon from 'land into place and place into symbol' attested to the power of Romanticism, cultural nationalism, aesthetics and science. The exigencies of the frontier process meanwhile encouraged the protection of the region's timber and game resources. On the back of its growing symbolic stature, the Grand Canyon earned status as a forest reserve in 1893, game reserve in 1906, national monument in 1908 (courtesy of the 1906 Antiquities Act) and became a fully fledged national park in 1919.[9]

The Grand Canyon National Park exemplified the importance of the West as a catalytic and cathartic geography. Descriptions of the Canyon in early tourist brochures and guidebooks from the Department of the Interior, Fred Harvey hotels, the Kolb Brothers photographic studio and the Santa Fe Railroad, eagerly traded in a discourse of scenic monumentalism. The Canyon landscape bespoke inimitability, giganticism and profundity. For Charles Lummis, here stood a landscape without parallel, simply put: 'the Grand Canyon is just the Grand Canyon, and that is all you can say.' For others, an engagement with the Canyon fermented a lyrical tone and encouraged spiritual epiphany. The opening line of the Department of the Interior's *The Grand Canyon of the Colorado River in Arizona* (1916) read: 'More mysterious in its depth than the Himalayas at their height'. Combining the sentiments of Immanuel Kant on the tendency of sublime scenery to invoke feelings of mortality, humility and divinity, with a sharp satirical turn, the travelogue *Roughing it Deluxe* (1913) related, 'You stand there, stricken dumb, your whole being dwarfed yet transfigured; in the glory of that monument you can even forget the gabble of the lady tourist alongside you.' Issuing an invocation to 'See Your West', Edith Tupper adopted a patriotic slant for the Sante Fe Railroad's promotional brochure: 'it is the only scenery on the globe that does not disappoint ... I longed for a trumpet to send forth a clarion call over this vast country and to cry "Stop, stop, Americans! Do not go abroad. Look at your own country first. Come here and see what God has wrought." ' The immensity of the Canyon appeared to confound and mesmerise in equal measure. As George Wharton James, author of *The Grand Canyon of Arizona: How to See It* (1918), elucidated, it 'expresses ... more than any one human mind yet has been able to comprehend ... there everything is massive and dominating. The colors are vivid; the shadows are purple to blackness; the heights are towering; the depths are appalling.'[10]

Raw nature loomed large in the Grand Canyon experience for obvious reasons. America's primeval past laid bare, the 'divine abyss' offered a vast panorama of geological splendour. A sense of timelessness and immutability represented a core aspect of the Canyon's appeal, and celebrators proved eager for the sacrosanct temple of American nature to remain undefiled. As Theodore Roosevelt articulated, 'Let this great wonder of nature remain as it is now. Do nothing to mar its grandeur, sublimity and loveliness. You cannot improve on it.' That said, the fashioning of the Grand Canyon as a resort fit for the tourist trade demanded the playground as well as the pristine. Americans expected a paradise experience, a tour of nature's handiwork, but also adventure, entertainment, a modicum of luxury and good transport links. Boosters thus proclaimed the Grand Canyon as 'the Mecca of the traveling world', an exotic locale with spectacle on and off the trail. Reverend C. B. Spencer, writing in one Canyon guidebook, advertised the place with the style of a dime novelist, exclaiming: 'Horror! Tragedy! Silence! Death! Chaos! There is the awful canyon in five words.' At the El Tovar Hotel (built in 1905), visitors arrived to find a rustic lodge with 'an unassuming luxury'. Guests sipped pure water brought ninety miles for their comfort. *The Grand Canyon of Arizona: How to See It* (1918) promoted the park as a superlative resort complete with quality lodgings: 'a miniature city, with its life and sparkle, its fellowships and social converse'. Irvin Cobb adeptly summed up this blend of chasm and comfort in the title of his travelogue, *Roughing it Deluxe*.[11]

Visitors came to the Grand Canyon for nature, resort and a taste of frontier experience. Alongside the joys of rugged geology and hospitality, the playground of the south-west offered, in the words of one Santa Fe Railroad brochure, a place 'where much of the charm of the old frontier still lingers'. The *Grand Canyon Visitors Almanac* (n.d.) advised visitors thus, 'you will find the greatest enjoyment in this natural wonder if you approach it as a discoverer'. Guests watched Indian dances outside the Hopi House and attended 'cowboy music programs' in the evening. The more intrepid signed up for mule trips down the winding trail to see abandoned mines and prospecting ephemera. Some even tried their hand at panning for gold. Adventure loomed around every corner when playing in the Old West theme park at the Grand Canyon. As the Santa Fe brochure exclaimed:

> off the beaten path anything may happen. You see Indians on their ponies, racing home. You glimpse a solitary camp fire. You hear the far-away howl of a wolf ... A sandstorm engulfs you. For you yucca and cactus open their timid flowers. It is all so new and so old, unlike the ordinary ways.

Nostalgia for capturing the pioneer spirit merged seamlessly with the irrevocably western environment of Grand Canyon marked by its dusty trails and air of natural solitude. As Harriet Monroe noted of her trip in 1906:

> We were exploring the wilderness with the pioneers. We were unaware of the road, of the goal; we were pushing out into the unknown ... And we, we could not believe that the forest would not go on forever, even when vistas of purple began to open through the trees, even when the log-cabin hotel welcomed us to our goal.

The pioneer life exerted a powerful allure for sojourners.[12]

One hundred years on, the projection of the Grand Canyon as a paradise landscape of perfectly preserved nature has come under scrutiny. While John Muir may have doubted the capacity of humanity to defile its confines – 'Nature has a few big places beyond man's power to spoil – the ocean, the two icy ends of the globe, and the Grand Canyon' – a century of industrial growth, urbanisation, recreation and technological toxicity have tarnished the Canyon's pristine mantle. In support of Bill McKibben's contention of the 'end of nature' (that nowhere on the globe escapes the imprint of human action), the Grand Canyon seemed under threat from the predatory advances of a metropolitan West. In the 1960s, the Sierra Club under David Brower masterminded a high profile defence of the Grand Canyon from the Bureau of Reclamation. Utilising a loophole in the enabling park Act which allowed the Department of the Interior to undertake 'development and maintenance of government reclamation projects', plans were aired in the early 1960s for dams at Marble Canyon and Bridge Canyon, effectively making the Grand Canyon 'a dam sandwich' in the words of Marc Reisner. The Sierra Club leapt into action to prevent the damning of thirteen miles of parkland for the almighty dollar and ventured a high profile (and expensive campaign) which saw their tax-exempt status revoked. Full page adverts in *The New York Times* invited readers to write to the Secretary of the Interior, using emotive tag lines including: 'Now only you can save Grand Canyon from being flooded . . . for profit'; and 'SHOULD WE also flood the Sistine chapel so tourists can get nearer the ceiling?'. The campaign highlighted a buoyant environmental consciousness (Sierra membership climbed from 39,000 in 1966 to 135,000 five years later) and situated the environment in the West as a highly politicised issue. The fact that the Grand Canyon, America's foremost symbol of scenic monumentalism, appeared under threat aided the fight immensely. As David Brower orated, in typically compelling style, 'If we can't save the Grand Canyon, what the hell can we save?'[13]

The Sierra Club won that particular battle, but competing visions of the West as a storehouse of economic potential versus a wild nature park ensured further contests into the twenty-first century. Air pollution from the booming sun-belt cities of Los Angeles, Tucson and Phoenix as well as nitrates, sulphates and chemicals from coal-fired power stations (notably the Navajo Generating Station) caused a haze over the Grand Canyon to rival the smog of the City of Angels. Reducing visibility on some days to as low as fifty miles, the visual pollution of the 'divine abyss' served to weaken its reputation as a pristine wilderness stretching far into the horizon. The impact of industrialism on the Grand Canyon led to forty violations of the California benchmark ozone standard between 2002 and 2004, a statistic perhaps to be expected in the urban gridlock of sprawling SoCal, but not in America's premier natural wonderland. Meanwhile, the Grand Canyon seemed in danger of being 'loved to death' by its visitors. In John Muir's day, the principal issue for nature preservationists lay in raising the profile of the parks and encouraging tourists to 'come home' to the mountains. A century on, the Grand Canyon received five million visitors, a year – clogging roads with traffic jams on the South Rim, fostering an explosion of visitor services and damaging the Canyon environment. Back in 1906, Zane Grey had written, 'One feature of this ever-changing spectacle never changes: its eternal silence.' Such solitude proved less in evidence a century later with 15,142 river runners travelling the Colorado in 1980 (leaving so much debris and effluent on the banks that rafters reported thirteen outbreaks of dysentery in 1972 alone) and 274 air flights per day (small planes, helicopter rides and the like) buzzing above the rim in 1986. The automobile rendered the park accessible to thousands of vacationers, but Route 66 culture had also changed the nature of the experience, encouraging visitors to see the national park as a drive-by diorama. Windshield tourists walked only from the parking lot to the next must-see photo of scenic monumentalism. Edward Abbey in *Desert Solitaire* (1968) bemoaned the rise of 'industrial tourism' and the crafting of the park as an auto-dystopia. As he railed: 'No more cars in national parks. Let the people walk. Or ride horses, bicycles, mules, wild pigs – anything – but keep the automobiles and the motorcycles and all their motorized relatives out.'[14]

Hoover Dam: The Machine in the Garden

If the Grand Canyon bespoke the story of nature preservation (or aesthetic conservation) in the West, the Hoover Dam attested to its late-nineteenth-century twin: utilitarian conservation. Equally embedded in the Western experience, utilitarian conservation related strongly to the closure of the frontier and the end of the myth of superabundance as well as a governmental commitment to what historian Samuel Hays has called 'the gospel of efficiency', namely technocratic solutions and grand public works. Whereas the preservationists, most notably John Muir, touted nature protection for its visual, spiritual, cultural and intrinsic values, advocates of utilitarian conservation (including head of the Forest Service Gifford Pinchot and President Theodore Roosevelt) championed the proficient use of nature resources and sustainable management.[15]

The lack of precipitation in the south-west and Great Plains (less than two inches (<1 cm) of rainfall a year) lent water resources an immense significance. For thousands of years, settlements in the region had grappled with the scarcity of water. The Hohokam of Arizona cut 250 miles of canals to irrigate fields of beans and squash, using stones to dam the flow of water. The collapse of Hohokam civilisation in 1450 related in part to over-stretched resources and the salinisation of irrigation canals. European settlers faced a similar battle in the nineteenth century, finding their 'energetic and venturesome' attitude and faith in the old adage that 'rain followed the plow' severely tested by the harshness of western lands. As John Wesley Powell motioned, the Mormons pursued a successful farming operation in Utah based on collective irrigated farming, but elsewhere a culture of localism and free-for-all abounded. By the late nineteenth century, the future of western agriculture seemed mired in a rough and ready water wrangle. Farmers jockeyed for limited water resources and would 'shut down each other's headgates and frequently resort to shotguns', while states flaunted competing codes of user rights. Some advocated riparian rights, that is, anyone could take water as long as the stream flow remained unimpeded (the California Doctrine); others favoured a quintessentially western route of 'first comes first' (the Colorado Doctrine); while a third gave all water rights to the state (the Wyoming Doctrine). As demand for water increased, this suffusion of contesting doctrines rendered itself unworkable, and developmental interests began to call for federal intervention. California boosters were particularly vociferous, notably William Smythe, President of the California Constructive League and author of *The Conquest of Arid America* (1899). He urged, 'Irrigation, colonization, cooperation – these are the three great questions involved in the making of our twentieth-century West.'[16]

A series of irrigation conferences from 1891 projected the West as a waiting utopia in need of an activist government to foster regional economic growth, provide water and power for metropolitan areas and create a sustainable agricultural empire. Two localities loomed large in this regard, Los Angeles and Imperial Valley. The population of Los Angeles grew by 600 per cent between 1900 and 1920; eagerly consuming water from the Owens River Aqueduct (1913), and thirstily seeking new appropriations. Imperial Valley, the heartland of California agriculture courtesy of a canal from the Colorado (1896), seemed in danger of returning to its pre-irrigated 'valley of death' days, especially after flood water from the Colorado burst the banks of the canal in 1905–7, ruined millions of dollars worth of crops and turned the Salton Sink back into the Salton Sea.

The creation of the Bureau of Reclamation in 1902 highlighted the seriousness with which the government regarded the issue of aridity in the West, and promoted water as a key aspect of conservation strategy. According to the official rationale of utilitarianism, the West appeared an under-watered wasteland, a place crying out for irrigation and technological fixes to forward a productive agrarian paradise. Only the government possessed the money, infrastructural resources, bureaucratic means and mettle to preside over a comprehensive plan for watering the region. The mandate of the Bureau, to solve the issue of irrigation in the West by funding dams and other projects, resembled more an exercise in conversion than reclamation, but the label proved pertinent. A Western empire, 'making the desert bloom', was perceived as altogether natural, with a provident future ordained by science, religion and Manifest Destiny. The rhetoric of a vanished frontier figured in official thinking. As Franklin Roosevelt motioned in 1932, 'Our last frontier has long since been reached and there is practically no more free land ... There is no safety valve in the form of a Western prairie to which those thrown out of the eastern economic machines could go for a new start.' In these conditions, 'wise use' and efficient planning appeared paramount.[17]

The Colorado River was a critical agent in this evolving drama. Advocates of reclamation projects cast the 1,400-mile river in two diametrically opposed roles. In the first, the Colorado appeared as a petulant wastrel, its 'wasted waters' running 'hog wild' after the spring snow melt, bursting its banks and spoiling crops before assuming a more sedate (and useless) trickle by the time of the autumn planting season. In *The Colorado Conquest* (1941), David Woodbury admonished the river as 'two thousand miles of alkali and desolation – an empty wasteland dotted with greasewood and mesquite, shunned by every living thing except the occasional buzzard waiting for the traveler whose luck had failed'. Others embellished their riverine personifications with decidedly western motifs, couching the Colorado as a wild and loose outlaw, unpredictable, dangerous and outside the productive purview of civilised life. In his *Cartoon Guide of the Boulder Dam Country* (1938), Reg Manning related 'Man's attempt to reform that notorious outlaw of the Southwest, "Ol' Two Gun" Colorado River' who 'tore up' the Grand Canyon and terrorised California and Mexico. His prose was accompanied by sketches of 'Two Gun' riding the canyons of the Old West. Set against this dastardly vision was a forecast of the Colorado as a 'marvel of American progress' and a 'giver of life'. In this portent, the river represented a reformed character, the frontier outlaw tamed by the forces of might and right to become a provident gardener tending 'the richest garden spot on the continent'. Such images of the Colorado sat comfortably within broader competing visions of the West as 'Great American Desert' and a utopia of agrarian democracy.[18]

Into this landscape of rivuline contest stepped the Boulder (renamed Hoover in 1947) Dam, the machine that would bring the Colorado's garden vista to life. Reclamation engineers had eyed up the river since the formation of the Bureau in 1902, but determined surveys of the region only proceeded in earnest during the early 1920s. In February 1924, geologists and engineers submitted an eight-volume report to the Secretary of the Interior recommending a concrete gravity arch dam at Black Canyon. By the end of 1928, the Bounder Dam Project Act had passed both Houses, and the Bureau of Reclamation had reined in state quarrels over the Colorado River Compact (the 1922 ruling that split the river into upper and lower basins for the purposes of distribution rights and ownership) by declaring the Colorado an 'all American River'. With the $49 million contract for the dam awarded to the Six Companies conglomerate, construction began in May 1931. Workers cut four tunnels into Black Canyon to divert the river's flow, each one large enough to fit a jet plane inside. Temporary coffer dams barred the Colorado from its usual course and 'high-scalers' cleaned the walls of the canyon down to the bare rock, dynamiting the cliffs before being hauled to safety on ropes. Construction of the dam proper began in June 1933. The 325 million cubic yards (248.5 million metre^3) of concrete required a novel system of five-foot (1.5-metre) blocks and embedded coolant pipes to allow the material to set. Completed on budget and on schedule, the Hoover Dam hosted a dedication ceremony on 30 September 1935. Celebrating the dam as a harbinger of growth and abundance, Franklin Roosevelt turned a golden key to start up the generator. Less than a year later, turbines from the Hoover hydro-electric project produced their first kilowatts of electricity.

Standing 726 feet (221 metres) high and measuring 660 feet (201 metres) at its base, the Hoover Dam represented a paramount example of engineering monumentalism, a concrete companion to the rocky splendour of the Grand Canyon. Frank Waters dubbed it 'the Great Pyramid of the American Desert', while *Westways* magazine (1935) reported that 'All previous conceptions of big things done in a big way are thrown in the discard at boulder dam'. At the time of construction, Hoover signified the tallest dam in the world, the greatest producer of electrical power which held back the largest artificial lake. Adjectives of superlative and spectacle proved just as applicable to its smooth lines as the Grand Canyon's craggy depths. Contemporary pamphlets and brochures emphasised the size and scale of the dam, offering readers a boggling array of statistics. Presented as a grand and exceptional landmark reminiscent of the scenic rock and ice national parks of the far West, Hoover inspired the kind of musings that visitors proffered at the South Rim. In fact, the attraction boasted some 750,000 visitors in 1934–5, the same as the Grand Canyon. On weekends and holidays, 10,000 cars a month descended on Black Canyon to drive across the roadway, and traffic gridlock ensued. Observers regarded the structure as a wondrous monument to American strength and cultural prowess. As Richard Lillard noted, 'Boulder Dam is to Americans what Chartres Cathedral was to Europeans, what the Temple at Karnak was to ancient Egyptians. The clean, functional lines, the colossal beauty, and impersonal mass and strength of the dam itself are as symbolic as real.' Others ventured ethereal judgements: 'At first glance the enormity of the sight is such that few persons possess the ability to grasp its full significance.' In common with the Grand Canyon, the Hoover Dam appeared unfathomable, mesmerising, even transcendental. As journalist Theodore White articulated, 'It is a beautiful tantalizing thing. It is complex. It has a meaning, not to be grasped in weeks, or perhaps years. It is subtle, sometimes cruelly obvious? I stay on, fascinated.'[19]

Unlike the Grand Canyon, the Hoover Dam symbolised not the glories of rugged landscape but its conquest. As Franklin Roosevelt orated at the dedication of the dam, 'as an unregulated river, the Colorado added little of value to the region'. Now the Hoover Dam brought 'the conservation, the regulation, and the equitable division' of water and offered itself as 'an engineering victory of the first order'. A brochure for Electrical West celebrated how the Colorado had been 'diverted from wasteful and destructive liberty to useful and economic purposes', while Woodbury's *Colorado Conquest* asserted 'its mighty strength no longer consumes and destroys; it builds. It has turned a broad wasteland of sand and sage into a garden; it is lighting and watering a new civilization.' Presentations of the Colorado as an epic foe assisted in this glorification process. With the river imbued with agency and power (an example of Kant's 'dynamic sublime') and

Figure 8.1 Three construction workers putting a coat of paint on a slanted wall of riveted-steel plates on the Hoover Dam spillway.

a force that elucidated terror and overwhelming energy, the struggle to tame its waters earned special weight. The project offered, in Kantian terms, a salient occasion 'to measure ourselves against the omnipotence of nature'. As Reg Manning explicated 'Today Two Gun Colorado River is imprisoned behind the grim concrete wall of Boulder Dam... But ol' Two Gun wasn't subdued without a struggle. It took centuries to get him.'[20]

The engineering monumentalism at the Hoover Dam paid homage to the cult of the worker. At the Grand Canyon, kudos for architectural design extended to the Deity and to nature. At the dam, man-made qualities stood centre stage. The engineers of the Bureau of Reclamation and the construction workers paid by the Six Companies gained sanctification for their efforts in taming the river. *The New York Times* connected the myth of the frontier with that of the mechanic to hail the dam as an example of 'pioneering of the machine-age'. For Woodbury, *The Colorado Conquest* came courtesy of the 'modern

Canutes' with the power to freeze geological time and make the river productive. A commemorative plaque to those who died working on the project featured a montage of muscular worker-supermen under the banner: 'they labored that millions might see a brighter day'. Meanwhile, the cult of the worker fused seamlessly with the fetishisation of machinery. Woodbury recalled how:

> Up out of the canyon innumerable great power lines leap along the rocks and hurry off into the desert in all directions. The whine of many busy generators plays a pedal point to the song of the wind in the metal arteries which flash a million horsepower to faraway houses and factories. Everywhere there is the image of man cut on the face of beaten nature – white concrete against black rock smooth structural lines against chaotic crags.

The Colorado Conquest advanced a kind of techno-utopia at the dam, a place where 'men, machines and material were co-ordinated in one beautiful mechanism'.[21]

Where the Grand Canyon offered the elevation of the primitive, the Hoover Dam hailed the modern. Architecturally, its functional lines appeared in sharp relief to the rough contours of the Black Canyon. Here stood a monument to invention and giganticism as well as a building of utility. Visitors to the site commented on the sharp juxtaposition of the dam structure after miles of empty desert scenery, its art deco symmetry suggestive of a robust fortress keeping nature in check. Beneath the wall of the dam, the symmetry of the machine age continued with powerhouses each side of the Colorado, each designed with the transformers in full view to emphasise the beauty and power of the hydro-electric process. The dam thus signified a site of genius, of science and technology. As J. B. Priestley wrote in *Harper's Monthly* (1937): 'Here in this Western American wilderness, the new man, the man of the future has done something, and what he has done takes your breath away.' In this regard, the Hoover Dam represented a salient example of the 'technologically sublime', defined by David Nye as 'a religious feeling, aroused by the confrontation with impressive objects'. In common with experiences of the Grand Canyon, those who visited the dam spoke of bewilderment, power, humility, radiance and nonpareil. Reg Manning described the beauty of the place especially at night, its elevator towers glowing in the dark like otherworldly beacons, lit, of course, by its own turbines. Paeans to flowing water, luminescent spectacle and technological wizardry proved particularly pertinent in a West defined by its aridity. Moreover, the concept of the 'technological sublime', the elevation of the man-made as spectacular, sacrosanct and intrinsic to American identity, seemed particularly pertinent to a post-frontier West which promised no more 'free land' or lurking natural marvels. On the Nevada side of the dam stood two thirty-foot (nine-metre) high winged figures of the Republic on plinths of black diorite, designed by Oskar J. W. Hansen to convey universal aspirations of humanity as well as the settlement of the West. On the floor of the monument, Hansen embedded the United States seal and a zodiac star map situating the construction of the dam in a histrionic timeline that included the building of the Pyramids and the birth of Jesus. Such ornaments lofted a cosmic significance for the dam far beyond the simple provision of water and electricity.[22]

Reg Manning dedicated his *Cartoon History of the Boulder Country* (1938) to the National Park Service and the Bureau of Reclamation, the two government outfits deigned 'twins for the Boulder County'. Alongside all its other plaudits, the Hoover Dam served as a monument to federal power in the West. Advocates hailed the project as an example of beneficent government planning, efficiency and technocratic solutions, founded on the good for all. Other commentators envisioned a less salubrious portent in Black Canyon and the Bureau of Reclamation, setting aside ideas of engineering monumentalism to focus instead on the cabal of business and government elites who manipulated water for their own means, disenfranchised Indian and small homesteaders and locked the rural West into a colonial relationship with its metropolitan hinterlands. For Donald Worster, the damming of the West had been enacted by 'a coercive, monolithic, and hierarchical system, ruled by a power elite based on the ownership of capital and expertise'. At the Hoover Dam itself, the idealisation of the worker offered a comfortable mirage that masked a starker reality of labouring away in 128 °F with few rest breaks, no union rights and fervent racialism against oriental and African American workers. Back at the workers 'paradise' of Boulder City, the town built by the Six Companies in 1932 to house employees, projections of a garden city in the desert, with parks, stores, public spaces and 'every modern convenience' sat rather uneasily with contrasting descriptions of a company reservation with its guard house, identikit houses, oppressive desert heat and equally stifling federally-appointed bureaucrats. Boulder City, with its regimentation and liquor and gambling ban, appeared to be the antithesis of the 'Wild West' flavour of Vegas and its cacophony of vices.[23]

In recent years, the conservation credentials of the Hoover Dam and the broader hydro-electric vision have come under review. Rather than the harbinger of a land of perpetual harvest, environmental critics berated the transformation of the Colorado into dead water. In Edward Abbey's *The Monkeywrench Gang* (1975), a group of eco-activists fantasised about blowing up Glen Canyon dam, Arizona and letting the outlaw Colorado out of its concrete jail. In spring 1981, Dave Foreman and some of his Earth First! buddies actually visited Glen Canyon to unfurl a black plastic 'crack' down its expanse. To Abbey and his ilk, the hydro-electric West represented not the technological sublime but the ridiculous. From its halcyon days as a signal of promise and prosperity (in the Bureau's words 'home creating, wealth producing, self-sustaining'), the dam was reconfigured to stand as an equally striking symbol of power, but one that lofted the dollar over ecology. Critics pointed to alterations in native rivuline habitat from taming the Colorado (salinisation, sediment build up, the decline of native fish such as the humpback chub), as well as the introduction of exotic stocks to eat weeds and furnish the fishing fraternity. A trickle of its former rogue self, historian Roderick Nash castigated it as 'a push button river', not quite a water show to rival the fountains of the Las Vegas Bellagio, but a salient indication of the fusion of water and technology in the modern West.[24]

'The Diamond of the Desert': Las Vegas, Hydro-Fetishism and the Modern Frontier

According to Hal Rothman, Las Vegas represented a place 'where the 21st century begins, a center of the postindustrial world'. Such a comment cast Vegas as a fantasy landscape, a post-modern mélange of entertainment tourism constantly reinventing itself to the delight of its public. If the Grand Canyon signalled scenic monumentalism, and the Hoover Dam the engineering variety, the artificial playground of Vegas offered itself as an exemplar of neon monumentalism. In 1911, local booster and newspaperman Charles Squires dubbed Vegas 'the magic city', a telling phrase, given Walt Disney's similarly synthetic and equally grand 'magic kingdom' constructed later in Anaheim. As of 2000, Vegas boasted nine out of ten of the world's biggest hotels. Thirty-seven million tourists each year played its casinos, gawped at its light shows and basked in hedonistic fun. The four-mile long 'Strip', situated in the aptly named Paradise district of Clark County, Nevada, provided a twenty-four hour barrage of consumption and spectacle.

In 1999, the gaming Mecca of Vegas even overtook the real thing as the most visited place on Earth. However, for all its associations with simulation and ahistoricism, Las Vegas boasted a strident frontier identity. While Mike Davis dubbed it the 'terminus of western history' and Hal Rothman situated it as 'a city without any claim to a past', the story of Vegas, its invented traditions, relationship with water, culture of opportunism and lingering pioneering ideology, marked it as a distinctly Western space.[25]

Water exerted a fundamental influence over the ecology and economy of early Las Vegas. Named 'the meadows' by Spanish traders travelling between Santa Fe and Los Angeles in the late 1700s, Las Vegas earned repute right from the start as an oasis in the Mojave, its three springs distinguishing it from the surrounding desert ecology. Travellers referred to it as 'the diamond of the desert', an interesting reflection on the latter day construction of Vegas as a venue of card-play and fortune. In 1844, John Frémont camped in the region, noting that the water tasted good, albeit a little warm. Eleven years later, a group of thirty Mormon settlers established a fort, fields and irrigation system at the springs. Abandoning the settlement in 1858 to return to Utah, Mormon elder John Steele exclaimed, 'The country around here looks as if the Lord has forgotten it'. The first permanent settler on the site, Octavius Decatur Gass, a former miner and irrigation inspector, established the Las Vegas Ranch in 1865. He grew produce on his irrigated fields and peddled wares including figs, wine and shady orchard respite to travellers on the Mormon Trail. Meanwhile, the arrival of prospectors en route to the mineral strikes at Goodsprings and homesteaders taking advantage of the 1885 State Land Act lent Las Vegas a distinctively Western character. Still, in 1900, the future of the desert oasis with its nineteen residents appeared somewhat precarious.[26]

The arrival of the railroad in 1904 saved Vegas from fading into obscurity. Serving as a regional entrepôt on the San Pedro, Los Angeles and Salt Lake City line, and aided by the fervent boosterism of railroad interests, Las Vegas witnessed a period of growth. The Las Vegas Land and Water Company (owned by the railroad) sold 1,200 town-site lots in a single day, and the town was formally incorporated in May 1905. Adverts for Las Vegas traded in a typically Western narrative, projecting the region as a future agrarian paradise and democratic utopia. The brochure 'Southern Nevada and its Resources' (published by the Southern Nevada Land and Mining Bureau) projected the place as a 'Virgin Country of Great Promise'. Touting a heady triumvirate of opportunity, wellness and money for the taking in Las Vegas soil, the pamphlet asserted: 'Today there is no better place for a poor man to get a home, the sick to find health and the capitalists to make a good investment.' In 1911, the Southern Pacific lofted Vegas for its 'semi tropical' and 'dry and healthful' climate, artesian wells, mineral wealth and railroad links. Keen to assure potential settlers of a secure and thoroughly modern experience, the advertisement insisted that Nevada lay not on the frontier but appeared 'peaceful and orderly' with 'all of the outward and visible evidences of civilization': banks, hotels, schools, churches, telephones and electric lights. Hedging its bets, the pamphlet added, 'life is a little freer in these wider spaces, and a little less conventional than in the older states, but there is a healthy moral tone'.[27]

The railroad kept Las Vegas in business after the mining booms of Rhyolite and Goldfield faltered in the late 1910s, and by 1930 the desert town had a population of 5,165. Fifteen years later, Vegas boasted some 20,000 residents. Two factors explain this meteoric rise: gambling and the federal government.

The legalisation of gambling by the Nevada legislature in 1931 secured Vegas as a prime gambling venue. After all, a profitable relationship had already been established between Nevada and gaming. Between 1869 and 1910, the Territory had experimented with legalised gambling, finding financial gain and good sport in the relatively lawless, individualistic, transient and male dominated towns of the frontier West. In 1931, the Vegas legislature decided to chance its arm once more, seeing in the gambling fraternity a route to insulate their town from the throes of the Depression by attracting money and punters. Outfits such as the Apache, the Pair o' Dice and the Golden Camel entertained sojourners with betting entertainment. In 1933, half of the 25,000 visitors who stayed over in Vegas on their way to the Hoover Dam never arrived at the Colorado River. The blackjack tables proved more enticing than the delights of Black Canyon.

Gambling pursuits signalled a vital and lasting part of the Las Vegas economy and culture, but the federal government was actually the critical actor in ensuring a steady flow of patrons and dollars to the town. The creation of a gunnery school (later Nellis Air Force Base) and the paving of Highway 91 to Los Angeles brought federal infrastructure, finance and population growth to the region. Meanwhile, the massive Hoover Dam project thirty miles away proved to be decisive in putting Vegas on the map. As the local paper asserted, the dam represented a 'turning point in the history of Las Vegas . . . The mills of the Gods grind slowly, but they grind exceedingly fine.' Every month, the Hoover Dam project paid out some $500,000 to its 3,500 employees. This offered a vital injection of capital to the regional economy. Its water and power ensured the future of Vegas as a neon oasis. Tourists coming to the south-west to see the engineering monumentalism on the Colorado invariably stayed in Vegas, which cannily advertised itself as 'the best city in the United States "by a dam site"'.[28]

In 1922, journalist George Holt bemoaned the transformation of the post-frontier West into an every-day American setting. Lamenting the replacement of cactus and gunplay with a 'mild, unwoolly west' of cars, theatres, roads and streets he recommended: 'You who want "western" stuff, go to the flickering screen: it doesn't grow wild anymore.' Such enchantment with the West of yore did not go unnoticed by the Las Vegas Chamber of Commerce. Discussing how best to attract tourists to their city, boosters raised the prospect of selling Vegas as a glistening nugget of the 'Wild West'. Of course, the deployment of Las Vegas as a relic of the frontier did not require a massive imaginative leap. The place boasted a credible pioneer past and an authentic setting of desert sands and tumbleweed. Old-timers already subscribed to the mantra of pioneering and found pride and purpose in their Western identity. *Westways* magazine quoted residents as saying that Vegas represented 'the last refuge of personal liberty in the United States', while *The New York Times* in 1949 reported how this was still 'a frontier town'. Meanwhile, the mythology of the Old West had already proved its mettle as a marketable and malleable property. Civic leaders needed only to look to the movies to see the burgeoning popularity of the West in such celluloid blockbusters as *Cimarron* (1930) and *Stagecoach* (1939). Although the emerging resort city of Vegas, with its service economy and federal dollars, hardly bespoke an obvious frontier oeuvre, boosters predicted an easy transplant of the Old West from history to amenity. The alliance of an iconic Western geography, fertile regional identity, an abiding national fable and a dash of Hollywood seemed a safe bet.[29]

In 1935, Vegas hosted its first 'Helldorado' parade – a fusion of the spirit of the Old West as 'Hell on wheels' and a land of promise. Civic authorities deployed the parades and rodeo displays as a way of enticing Hoover Dam tourists on a stop-over in the city to spend their money. Meanwhile, the selling of Vegas as a remnant of the Old West began in earnest during the 1940s. In the downtown 'Glitter Gulch', a homage to the mining booms of the nineteenth century conjoined with the bright lights of Hollywood, the roster of casinos and hotels included the Pioneer (1942), the Golden Nugget (1946), the Westerner Bar (1947) and Binion's Horseshoe (1951). Above the Pioneer stood a thirty-foot (nine-metre) high cowboy, 'Vegas Vic', complete with a check shirt, Stetson, jeans and lighted cigarette, all illuminated in vibrant neon. In order to preserve the authenticity of the Western experience, and the completeness of the immersion, civic authorities passed an edict in 1944 mandating that all new buildings downtown conform to a frontier aesthetic. In a city renowned for its theming, the Old West represented the original template.[30]

Las Vegans recognised in the Old West brand an ideal formula to sell their product. Already a keen link existed between gaming and the frontier. As John Findlay noted, 'gambling and westering thrived on high expectations, risk taking, opportunism and movement'. The process of westward movement allowed for the rise of the professional gambler and the emergence of poker as a prominent game of choice. Meanwhile, the imagined West of permissiveness and personal liberty, high stakes entrepreneurialism and a culture of acquisition all aided in the selling of Las Vegas. According to *The New York Times*, neon signs conferred 'a garish effect and signal invitations to try one's luck'. Casino slot machines traded in the lore of the gun and the lure of the dollar with 'One Armed Bandits' facing off against patrons eager to let loose their own trigger fingers on the outlaw's mechanical arm. Even the language of gambling boasted a Western dialect. The 'dead man's hand' (two aces and eights) was named after Wild Bill Hickok's last set of cards. In 1855, the Annals of San Francisco related, 'Gambling was the amusement, the grand occupation of many classes, apparently the life and soul of the place' and, a century on, wannabe 49ers embraced their own version of frivolous frontier entertainment in Vegas. In casinos bedecked with appropriate architectural trimmings, tourists indulged in an invented past of adventure, freedom from stricture, speculation and carousal. Journeying back to a world of vanished frontier ideals, the Argonauts of suburban America seized their manifest destiny by panning for gold on the slots, card tables and roulette wheels. Sociologically, this temporal and geographic dislocation facilitated total submergence in the game, and proffered a more complete separation from dominant social codes. For the gamer, that meant a more exciting encounter, loosening of the purse strings without consideration of real-world consequences.[31]

Besides Highway 91, on land that later became the famous 'Strip', fresh ventures in the 1940s pointed to a New West of entertainment

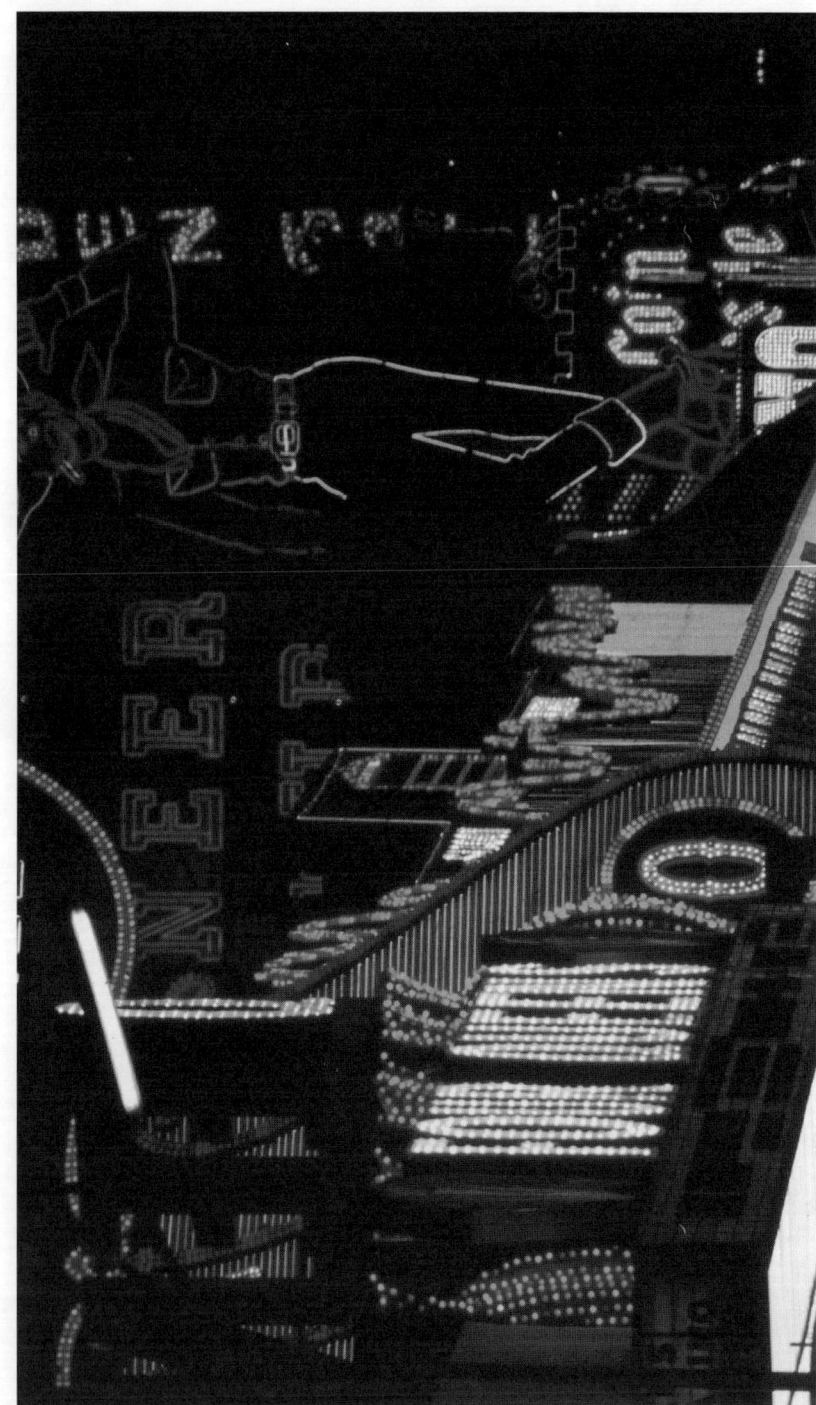

Figure 8.2 Night Lights, 05/1972.

tourism, auto-culture and resort-casinos. In 1940, the El Rancho Vegas motor hotel opened in resplendent mission architecture, with a swimming pool, showgirls and a fancy restaurant. March 1947 marked the opening of the Flamingo, Bugsy Siegel's famed hotel-resort sporting tropical theming, Miami–Hollywood influenced bright colours, exotic foliage and a modern, luxury allure. The brochure read 'Nature's handiwork and man's ingenuity have combined to create America's finest resort'. The Flamingo stood at odds with its arid Mojave setting *and* the pioneer adornments of downtown Vegas. Elsewhere, hotel-resorts fully embraced the Old West theme, seeing in the New West a fertile market for recycling the mythology of the frontier as a leisure product. The Last Frontier, which opened in October 1942, offered a motel and gambling resort based around the fantasy of the Old West. Staff dressed in vintage garb and ferried guests to the motel by stagecoach. Advertised as 'The Old West in modern splendour', the Last Frontier accomplished the reinvention of the westering experience from process to poolside attraction. Beyond the sun deck and palms, the low-rise building mimicked a main street from the 1800s. The hotel itself boasted the styling of an old fort, its lobby decked out with rough-hewn logs and murals of western scenes hanging on its walls. In the 'Gay 90's' bar, guests sat astride stools fashioned in the shape of saddles (complete with stirrups). The design of the Last Frontier harked back to the rustic architecture of the El Tovar in the Grand Canyon or Yellowstone's Old Faithful hotel – buildings designed to sit within their surroundings (whether geographic or imagined) and offer visitors a heady blend of action-packed primitivism and sumptuous modernity. As the resort brochure explained, 'Splashed in the sunshine of your desert dreams . . . Hotel Last Frontier recaptures the glories of the Golden West in the spirit of now. Located in the last frontier town where something is doing every minute.' The Old West flavour of the Last Frontier gained a boost with the addition of the Frontier Village, a rag-bag of pioneer ephemera owned by casino owner and gambler Robert Cauldhill, which went on permanent display as an adjunct of the hotel in 1947. Railroad cars, covered wagons, a jail, 'the Joss House' used by Chinese immigrants in Elko, an old trading post and a museum with rifles and Indian artefacts featured among the collection. Guests gambled in the authentic 'Silver Slipper Saloon', while *papier mâché* mannequins gave the place a populated 'village' look. The principal aim of the attraction was to bring punters into the hotel complex to gamble. It also presaged the lavish shows of latter-day

Vegas, while also tendering an Old West theme park a full four years before Disney's 'Frontierland' opened in Anaheim.[32]

Las Vegas sold itself on the Old West dream of prosperity and opportunity for all, assimilating Turner's frontier thesis of democratic virtue for the purposes of suburban consumption. Commentators broadcast Sin City as a place for all-comers: 'You see woodsman, sportsman, miner, rancher, movie star, divorcee, artist, writer, real cowboys and dude wrangler, pioneer, doctor, lawyer – the butcher, the baker, the candlestick-maker, all mingling at various night sports.' In *The New York Times*, Grady Johnson spoke of a 'Lively Vas Vegas' where 'dinner jackets, cowboy shirts, and jeans' mixed amicably together. Under this roseate veneer, however, extremes of inequality persisted. Las Vegas subscribed to a draconian policy of racial prejudice and segregation that earned it the dubious label of the 'Mississippi of the West'. African Americans were not permitted to own, work or gamble in the casinos. Even top billing stars found performing in Vegas a problematic experience. As Sammy Davis Jr recalled:

> In Vegas for twenty minutes, our skin had no color. Then the second we stepped off the stage, we were colored again . . . the other acts could gamble or sit in the lounge and have a drink, but we had to leave through the kitchen with the garbage.

The majority of African American residents (some 15,000 by 1955) lived in Westside, a downtrodden residential district physically separated from Fremont Street by a concrete barrier and without running water, paved roads or sewerage systems. May 1955 saw the opening of the first multi-racial casino in Las Vegas, the Moulin Rouge, a $3.5 million resort situated between Westside and the Strip. Betty Willis, designer of the famous 'Welcome to Las Vegas' sign, created the neon sign for the hotel and the Moulin Rouge graced the front page of *Life* magazine on 20 June 1955. The casino closed after only six months due to competition, financial problems and management brawls, yet exerted a substantial impact on the racial landscape of Vegas. Patrons of the hotel played a key role in planning a NAACP protest that threatened to shut down Vegas, and prompted city leaders and casino owners to end segregation under the famous 'Moulin Rouge Agreement' of 25 March 1960.[33]

In 1955, Vegas Vic gained a new trick: welcoming visitors with a friendly 'howdy partner' every fifteen minutes and waving a newly installed animatronic arm. Despite Vic's new lease of life courtesy of technological chicanery, elsewhere in Vegas the lure of the Old West receded. Glitter Gulch lost its lustre. The Last Frontier closed for remodelling, with the Frontier Village consigned to the same fate as the 'boom and bust' ghost towns which it emulated. When the hotel reopened on 4 April 1955 it sported a new name, 'The New Frontier', with a modish space theme. Reciting the slogan 'out of this world', the lobby murals featured astronauts not cowboys, while the Cloud Nine cocktail bar offered visitors a visual feast of celestial bodies. That year, the New Frontier took first prize for its flying saucer float in the Helldorado Parade. This marketing shift from the Old West to the space age bespoke broader cultural mores of the 1950s, such as modernity, consumption, paranoia and hi-technology fuelled progress, as well as the proximity of Las Vegas to the Nevada Test Site. With the nuclear age on its doorstep, Las Vegas cast off its elegiac frontier styling to play a new role as the 'up and atom city'. This moniker championed a value system in keeping with that of the frontier (adventure, patriotism, risk-taking, the idealisation of the masculine hero), but aligned itself with the Cold War military–industrial complex and the cult of modern science, not to mention a $176 million federal payroll. With more than a hundred nuclear tests in the decade after 1951, many clearly on view in the desert sky sixty miles away, Vegas sold itself on the back of atomic novelty. Sin City combined patriotism and frivolity with cocktails named after the A-Bomb, glamour shots of models posing in mushroom cloud dresses at Vegas hotels 'radiating loveliness instead of deadly atomic particles' and night-long testing parties that ended when the sky lit up. Mannequins from the J. C. Penney store in Fremont Street even took their place at the Atomic Energy Commission's 'Doom Town' on the missile range, before returning to the Vegas shop window bearing chilling placards that read: 'these could have been you'.[34]

In the years following the demise of the Last Frontier, Vegas cultivated itself as an exemplar of the post-modern, a place of simulation, consumption and image culture. Facing competition from Atlantic City and the proliferation of reservation casinos following the Indian Gaming Regulatory Act (1988), Vegas boosters shifted the focus of casino-resorts from gambling to the culture of gaming. By the 1990s, Vegas had become the home of entertainment tourism, a fantasy playground of giganticism, show-stopping spectacle and disposable novelty. Under the guiding mantra of neon monumentalism, Vegas played charlatan and chameleon, changing themes and styles to fit the times. The Strip had to be fresh, new and unfamiliar to retain its reputation as a bastion of technological bravura and high-stakes capitalism. The tradition of reinvention to which Las Vegas subscribed marked it as a fervent consumer of ideas and image across temporal and geographic boundaries. Casino designers looked to the past as a 'renewable resource', mining history and world cultures in order to conjure new, bigger and exciting attractions. In the 1950s, the Desert (1950), Sahara (1952), and Dunes (1955) resorts favoured a desert theme well suited to the arid landscape surrounding Vegas, and rendered exotic courtesy of Arabian and African motifs, not to mention lush green lawns and Middle-Eastern foliage. Caesars Palace (1966), the first mega-resort in the city, boasted Greco-Roman fountains and the Circus Maximus, while Steve Wynn's Mirage (1989) took Vegas' celebration of opulence and conspicuous consumption (of water and the dollar) to new heights. With a construction cost of $630 million, the Mirage offered an erupting volcano, rainforest atrium, Siegfried and Roy's Tiger show and the Cirque de Soleil. In the 1990s, the trend towards replication and super-sizing continued apace with the Luxor (1993), famed for its Egyptian pyramids, sphinx, robotic camels and 'Tut's hut'; the Venetian (1996) and its copy of St Mark's Square and the Grand Canal of Venice; and the Bellagio (1993), a replacement structure for the 1950s Dunes casino based around an eight-acre artificial lake reminiscent of Italy's Lake Como and adorned with fountains that erupted to light and music every fifteen minutes. Grand in scale and symbolic in stature, the 'Grand Slam Canyon' attraction (1993) at the Circus Circus resort (1966) offered a rollercoaster reappraisal of John Wesley Powell's famed thrill-ride down the Colorado: the natural spectacle of the Grand Canyon National Park replicated in plastic form. Collectively, these structures embraced a cult of the technologically sublime that bore similarities with the Hoover Dam in their fixation for push-button panoramas. On 14 November 2007, the local media paid heed to the ever-changing character of Vegas, as well as the city's penchant for pyrotechnics, when it reported on the implosion of the New Frontier resort. Even the blowing up of old casinos garnered an audience in this city of exhibitionism, noise and light.[35]

Press headlines that read 'the New Frontier is history' showed how the city had divorced itself from vestigial Western roots to confirm itself as a post-industrial space, a city on the edge of forever, without time or place. Within its four-mile confines, Vegas offered a global smorgasbord of non-stop entertainment, its jumble of world landmarks and lack of windows or sequential signatures (windows or clocks) a mark of geographic and temporal dislocation. The conspicuous use of water, what Mike Davis labelled 'hydro-fetishism', meanwhile suggested a city with a blatant disregard for its ecological context. In a region sporting only four inches (10 cm) of rainfall a year, Las Vegans used up to 400 gallons (1,818 litres) of water each, every day. And yet, for all its theme park pretences, Vegas still bore the hallmarks of a Western space, in both conceptual and geographic terms. The central premise of Vegas of imaginative design, suspension of belief and mythological journeys proved a comfortable fit with the adventures of the imagined West during the twentieth century. As David Nye noted, 'Built not on production but consumption, not on industry but play, not on the sacred but the profane, not on law but chance, Las Vegas is that rupture in economic and social life where fantasy and play reign supreme.' The status of the city as a monument to hedonism, a 'buccaneer economy' predicated on opportunism, libertarianism and the conquest of nature bore heed to decidedly Western values. Vegas offered a modern version of the nineteenth-century portent to 'go West' in search of fortune. To geographer Pauliina Raento, this rendered Vegas the 'ultimate frontier in the eyes of thrill-seeking post-industrial middle-class Americans'. As a city space too, Vegas lofted itself as an inimitable example of frontiering for the twenty-first century. A place where buildings went up and were duly torn down to be replaced by an ever more-dramatic skyline of artifice, Vegas situated itself as a new, vertical frontier. Such exercises in urban reclamation bespoke a post-industrial version of Turner's 'free land', a West of promise and progress where regeneration came from controlled explosions and could be endlessly reworked by technological chicanery.[36]

The desert hinterlands of Vegas, long considered irrelevant in discourse emphasising Vegas as a global resort that confounded conventional spatial relations, actually proved essential to its appeal. The Mojave, just like the moat surrounding Disney's Frontierland, allowed visitors to physically escape from prescriptive normalcy and embrace a more complete osmosis in Sin City. The desert buffer thus played a critical role in situating Vegas as a pariah landscape, a place of deviance and aberration sequestered away from suburban codes of propriety. From the flat emptiness of the Mojave, the lights of Vegas could be seen fifty miles distant, a luminescent symbol of a 'desert in bloom' that attested to the city's early days as an trailside oasis and also confirmed its status as an icon of gaudy neon monumentalism.

In the 1950s, a journalist wrote of Vegas: 'The visitor . . . finds himself whisked as if by rocket flight from the world of reality into a sun-baked neo-Klondike, as the Klondike might be depicted in a Hollywood musical with palm trees substituted for snow.' Such a definition proved apposite for the effervescent city in the Mojave. Vegas represented a fantasy landscape that conjoined the glamour of Golden State living with the glittering allure of the Old West. Riding a post-modern prospecting boom, casino owners encouraged tourists to suspend their understanding of temporal, geographical, moral and financial constraints to embrace a culture of risk and hedonistic play. Las Vegas thereby combined the myth of the frontier with a modern West of leisure tourism and Sunbelt suburbia. Meanwhile, as a salient example of the post-1945 metropolitan West, the city featured explosive population growth, urban sprawl, an economy centred on service and consumption and a mobile society fed by cheap air travel and the cult of the automobile. Some regarded its bright lights as an example of a twenty-first century techno-desert in bloom, while others were less complimentary. In common with the Grand Canyon and the Hoover Dam, the luminous monumentalism of Vegas faced off against a competing vision of a dystopian landscape where nature and technology ran amok. In *Hello America* (1982), J. G. Ballard utilised Vegas as the setting for a doomsday future in which a demigod called Charles Manson played laser shows of Marilyn Monroe, Mickey Mouse and the dollar bill before pressing the nuclear button. In the movie *Resident Evil: Extinction* (2007), the rag-tag survivors of the T-virus epidemic wandered a sand-ridden Strip populated by hungry zombies. Conceived in such fashion, Vegas manifested itself as a dazzling beacon of Edward Abbey's 'apocalyptic urbanism'. Between 1990 and 2000, the population of the metropolitan area grew 83 per cent, prompting concerns about territorial sprawl, overcrowding and environmental degradation. In common with Los Angeles, Vegas pointed to a metropolitan West of decentralised, privatised spaces, racial inequality, gated suburban communities and 'artificial deserts of concrete and asphalt'. According to its detractors, the mirage of economic prosperity floating over the place actually proved to be smog, earning it the dubious accolade of the fifth most polluted city in the United States. In sharp contradiction to the 'what happens in Vegas stays in Vegas' phrase coined by the Chamber of Commerce to sell their city as ultimate pleasure-dome, air pollution from the neon metropolis even drifted over the Grand Canyon. The traditional Western attitude of superabundance and technological salvation left Vegas in a fragile environmental position. With its desert springs dry by the 1960s, artesian wells heading that way and the city pumping millions of gallons from Lake Mead, the fantasy of Las Vegas extended far beyond its ecological limits. The future for the city may not be as bleak as that portrayed in *Resident Evil: Extinction* – a sharp lesson in the power of the desert to prevail over hydro-fetishism – but the issue of environmental sustainability remains prescient. A prosperous future for the gambling oasis in the desert depends not only on just staying in the black, but betting on green.[37]

Western Monumentalism Redux

At the dawn of the twenty-first century, the Grand Canyon, the Hoover Dam and Las Vegas collectively highlighted a West of fancy, enchantment and giganticism. For historian and ex-forest fire fighter Stephen Pyne, the Grand Canyon signified nothing short of a 'planetary monument'. The Hoover Dam recently found its way into the *Transformers* (2007) movie as a place colossal and robust enough (and with a certain Area 51 quality) to house dangerous alien technology, an interesting refrain to the cult of the machine, especially the publicly displayed transformers in the dam's turbine hall. Las Vegas seemed firmly installed as an 'American Versailles', a theme park extraordinaire devoted to consumption and escapism. Visitors navigated these landscapes according to the aesthetics of the sublime and the culture of spectacle, illuminating the West as a forum for grand imaginings and monumental sites. A full century on from its closure, the myth of the frontier remained salient. In its scenic, engineering and neon incarnations, the monumental West broadcast archetypal pioneering motifs of adventure, opportunism and risk-tasking bravado. Each landscape upheld the West as a heroic geography, a place of identity, illusion and fable. Yet, at the same time, the Grand Canyon, the Hoover Dam and Las Vegas boasted firm material connections. Each attested to an ongoing and contested relationship between man and the natural world, in particular the omnipresent issue of water in the West. The environment of the Grand Canyon confirmed water, and the Colorado River in particular, as a critical agent in the making of the Western landscape. At the Hoover Dam, the project to tame 'Ol' Two Gun' highlighted the pioneer *cause célèbre* of making the desert bloom combined with utilitarian conservation and federal oversight. Meanwhile, in the luminescent playground of Las Vegas, water from the Hoover Dam provided vital power and hydration, and even became an attraction in its own right. Significantly, at each of these landmarks, laudatory sentiment faced up against an equally exceptionalist rhetoric of doom-mongering. Environmental critics complained that the Grand Canyon was loved to death, the Hoover Dam sapped the life from the Colorado River and a predatory culture of consumption governed Las Vegas: writ large a 'bury your heads in the (desert) sand' mentality of ignored environmental context. As Marc Reisner warned in *Cadillac Desert*, 'If the Colorado River suddenly stopped flowing, you would have two years of carryover capacity in the reservoirs before you had to evacuate most of southern California and Arizona and a good portion of Colorado, New Mexico, Utah and Wyoming': a twenty-first century disaster scenario well suited to the West of redoubtable nature, boom and bust economics, monumental extrapolations and celluloid imaginings.[38]

Notes

1. 'Reclamation' pamphlet in 'See Your West', Scrapbook (c. 1941), held at the Autry Library (hereafter cited as Autry).
2. Philip Fradkin, *A River No More: The Colorado River and the West* (Berkeley: University of California Press, 1995), p. 17.
3. Foreman: quoted in B. J. Bergman, 'Wild at heart', *Sierra* (January/February 1998), p. 27; Walter Prescott Webb, *The Great Plains* (New York: Grosset & Dunlap, 1931); Donald Worster, *Rivers of Empire: Aridity and Growth of the American West* (New York: Oxford University Press, 1985); Marc Reisner, *Cadillac Desert: The American West and its Disappearing Water* (London: Secker & Warburg, 1990), p. 125.
4. James Bryce, 'National parks – the need of the future', in *Universal and Historical Addresses: Delivered During a Residence in the United States as Ambassador of Great Britain* (Freeport: Books for Libraries Press, 1968) [1913]), p. 406; Wallace Stegner, 'The best idea we ever had', in *Marking the Sparrow's Fall: The Making of the American West*, Page Stegner (ed.) (New York: Henry Holt, 1998), pp. 135–42.
5. George Catlin, *North American Indians*, I (Philadelphia: Leary, Stuart, 1913), pp. 294–5. Catlin's prairies finally gained protected status as Tallgrass Prairie National Preserve in 1996.
6. Stegner, 'The best idea we ever had', pp. 135–42; Alfred Runte, *National Parks: The American Experience* (Lincoln: University of Nebraska Press, 1979), pp. 13, 20, 21.
7. Francis Parkman, *The Oregon Trail* (Boston: Little, Brown, 1892), p. ix.
8. Stephen J. Pyne, *How The Canyon Became Grand* (London: Penguin, 1998), pp. 1, 18, 24; Ives: quote cited in 'The story of Boulder Dam', Conservation Bulletin No. 9 (Washington, DC: G.P.O., 1941), p. 9, held at the Autry.
9. Powell: quoted in Fradkin, *A River No More*, p. 182; See: Edmund Burke, 'A philosophical enquiry into the origin of our ideas of the sublime and the beautiful' (1757); Pyne, *How the Canyon Became Grand*, p. xiii; John Burroughs, 'The divine abyss', in *The Writings of John Burroughs*, vol. 14: Time and Change (Boston: Houghton Mifflin, 1912), p. 49.
10. Lummis: quoted in *The Grand Canyon of Arizona: Being a Book of Words from Many Pens, about the Grand Canyon of the Colorado River in Arizona* (Passenger Department of the Santa Fe Railroad, 1906), p. 36, held at the Autry; *The Grand*

Canyon of the Colorado River in Arizona (Department of the Interior, 1916), held at the Autry; Irvin S. Cobb, *Roughing It Deluxe* (New York: George Duran, 1913), pp. 37–8, held at the Autry; Tupper: quoted in *Grand Canyon of Arizona: Being a Book of Words*, p. 112; George Wharton James, *The Grand Canyon of Arizona: How to See It* (Boston: Little, Brown, 1918), pp. 3, 5.

11. Roosevelt: quoted in *Grand Canyon Outings* (Santa Fe Railroad, 1932), p. 57, held at the Autry; James, *The Grand Canyon of Arizona: How to See It*, p. 249; Spencer: quoted in *Grand Canyon of Arizona: Being a Book of Words*, p. 113.
12. See: *Grand Canyon Outings*, pp. 5–6, 59; *The Grand Canyon Visitor's Almanac* (produced for the Valley National Bank, AZ, n.d.), held at the Autry; Harriet Monroe, 'It's ineffable beauty', in *Grand Canyon of Arizona: Being a Book of Words*, pp. 54–5.
13. John Muir: quoted in *Grand Canyon of Arizona: Being a Book of Words*, p. 114; Bill McKibben, *The End of Nature* (New York: Random House, 1989); Roderick Nash, *Wilderness and the American Mind* (New Haven: Yale University Press, 1982 [1967]), p. 227; Reisner, *Cadillac Desert*, p. 283; *The New York Times*, 9 June 1966; *The New York Times*, 25 July 1966; Brower: quoted in Nash, *Wilderness and the American Mind*, p. 230.
14. Zane Grey: quoted in *High Country News*, 19 August 1996; Edward Abbey, 'Industrial tourism and the National Parks', in *Desert Solitaire: A Season in the Wilderness* (New York: Ballantine Books, 1968), pp. 57–61. Significantly, the National Park Service are now devoting substantial resources to tackle the car culture issue. See 'South Rim Transportation Plan' (2006).
15. See: Samuel P. Hays, *Conservation and the Gospel of Efficiency: The Progressive Conservation Movement, 1890–1920* (Pittsburgh: University of Pittsburgh Press, 1999 [1959]).
16. F. H. Newell, 'Progress in reclamation of arid lands in the western United States' (Washington, DC: G.P.O., 1911), p. 171, held at the Autry; William Smythe, 'The twentieth-century West', in *Out West* (formerly *The Land of Sunshine*), XVI/4 (April 1902), p. 426, held at the Autry; William Smythe, 'The twentieth-century West', in *The Land of Sunshine: The Magazine of California and the West*, XV/1 (July 1901), p. 63, held at the Autry.
17. Roosevelt: quoted in Robert Hine and John Mack Faragher, *The American West: A New Interpretive History* (New Haven: Yale University Press, 2000), p. 461.
18. 'The story of Boulder Dam', *Conservation Bulletin*, 9, p. 10; George Maxwell, 'The creation of an inland empire', Address to the Trans-Mississippi Commercial Congress, 1899. Reprinted in *The Homebuilder*, p. 2 (National Irrigation Association), held at the Autry; David O. Woodbury, *The Colorado Conquest: The Epic Story of Imperial Valley, Boulder Dam and the Taming of a Mad River* (New York: Dodd, Mead, 1941), pp. 30–1; Reg Manning, *Cartoon Guide of the Boulder Dam Country* (New York: J. J. Augustin, 1938), pp. 1, 4.
19. Waters: quoted in David Nye, *American Technological Sublime* (London: MIT Press, 1994), p. 137; 'Circling Death Valley and Boulder Dam', *Westways Magazine*, February 1935, p. 34, held at the Autry; Richard Gordon Lillard, *Desert Challenge* (Lincoln: University of Nebraska Press, 1942), p. 120; Quoted in Richard Guy Wilson, 'American modernism in the West: Hoover Dam', in Thomas Carter (ed.), *Images of American Land: Vernacular Architecture in the Western United States* (Albuquerque: University of New Mexico Press, 1997), p. 292.

20. Roosevelt: quoted in Andrew J. Dunar and Dennis McBride, *Building Hoover Dam: An Oral History of the Great Depression* (Reno: University of Nevada Press, 1993), pp. 312–15; Electrical West, 'Boulder Dam power: a pictorial history' (n.d.), held at the Autry; Woodbury, *Colorado Conquest*, p. 3; Kant: quoted in Nye, *American Technological Sublime*, p. 7; Manning, *Cartoon Guide of the Boulder Dam Country*, p. 2.
21. Quoted in Wilson, 'American modernism', p. 297; Woodbury, *Colorado Conquest*, pp. 3, 4, 347.
22. J. B. Priestley, 'Arizona desert', *Harper's Monthly*, March 1937, p. 365; Nye, *American Technological Sublime*, p. xiii.
23. Manning, *Cartoon Guide of the Boulder Dam Country*, p. i; Worster, *Rivers of Empire*, p. 7; Woodbury, *Colorado Conquest*, p. 347.
24. Edward Abbey, *The Monkeywrench Gang* (Philadelphia: Lippincott, 1975); 'Reclamation' pamphlet in 'See Your West', Scrapbook; Roderick Nash, 'Wilderness values and the Colorado River', in Gary D. Weatherford and F. Lee Brown (eds), *New Courses for the Colorado River*, (Albuquerque: University of New Mexico Press, 1986), p. 204.
25. Hal Rothman, *Neon Metropolis* (New York: Routledge, 2003), pp. xxvi, xxviii; Squires: quoted in *Las Vegas Age*, 29 July 1911; Mike Davis, *Dead Cities* (New York: The New Press, 2002), p. 86.
26. Quoted in John Findlay, *People of Chance: Gambling in American Society from Jamestown to Las Vegas* (New York: Oxford University Press, 1986), p. 111; Steele: quoted in W. Eugene Hollon, *The Great American Desert: Then and Now* (New York: Oxford University Press, 1966), p. 225.
27. 'Southern Nevada and its resources' (Southern Nevada Land and Mining Bureau, 1904), held at the Autry; A. J. Wells, 'Nevada, Southern Pacific' (Southern Pacific Passenger Department, 1911), held at the Autry.
28. Quoted in Michelle Ferrari and Stephen Ives, *Las Vegas: An Unconventional History* (New York: Bullfinch, 2005), p. 29; 'Circling Death Valley and Boulder Dam', p. 34.
29. George E. Holt, 'Where once was wild, woolly and wet', *World Traveller*, XIV/5 (May 1922), p. 36, held at the Autry; 'Circling Death Valley and Boulder Dam', p. 34; *The New York Times*, 24 March 1946.
30. 'Hell on Wheels' description offered by Herbert Asbury on the gambling town of Cheyenne, Wyoming. See Herbert Asbury, *Sucker's Progress: An Informal History of Gambling in America from the Colonies to Canfield* (New York: Dodd, Mead, 1938), p. 311, held at the Autry.
31. Findlay, *People of Chance*, p. 4; *The New York Times*, 26 March 1946; Annals of San Francisco quoted in Asbury, *Sucker's Progress*, p. 311.
32. Brochure cited in Ferrari and Ives, *Las Vegas*, p. 80; Last Frontier Brochure cited at 'Las Vegas Strip Historical Site'. Available online at: http://www.lvstriphistory.com.
33. See: 'Las Vegas Strip Historical Site'; *The New York Times*, 14 November 1948; Davis quoted in Ferrari and Ives, *Las Vegas*, p. 169.
34. *Life Magazine*, 12 November 1951; Mark Van de Walle, 'Blasts from the past', Las Vegas Travel and Leisure (October 2007). Available online at: http://www.travelandleisure.com.
35. Cornelius Holtorf, *From Stonehenge to Las Vegas: Archaeology as Popular*

Culture (Walnut Creek: Alta Mira Press, 2005), p. 130; *Associated Press*, 14 November 2007.
36. *Associated Press*, 14 November 2007; Davis, *Dead Cities*, p. 87; Nye, *American Technological Sublime*, p. 292; Wilbur S. Shepperson (ed.), *East of Eden, West of Zion: Essays on Nevada* (Reno: University of Nevada Press, 1989), p. 172; Raento: quoted in Gary Hausladen (ed.), *Western Places, American Myths* (Reno: University of Nevada Press, 2003), p. 245.
37. Journalist: quoted in Ferrari and Ives, *Las Vegas*, pp. 130–2; J. G. Ballard, *Hello America* (New York: Carroll, 1981), Davis, *Dead Cities*, pp. 91, 95.
38. Pyne, *How the Canyon Became Grand*, p. 157; Tom Wolfe, *The Kandy-Kolored Tangerine-Flake Streamline Baby* (New York: Farrar, Straus & Giroux, 1965), pp. xv–xvii; Reisner, *Cadillac Desert*, p. 125.

Part Three
Recreating The West

Chapter 9

The Western Renaissance: *Brokeback Mountain* and the Return of Jesse James

In 1903, audiences gathered in vaudeville and variety theatres across the United States to watch a movie. Some had never witnessed moving pictures before. They sat before *The Great Train Robbery*, a twelve-minute long film created by former projectionist Edwin S. Porter. It depicted a Wyoming railroad hijack. Audiences gasped at what happened before them as a billowing train was brought to a stop, a safe dynamited and several bandits fled on galloping horses. In the final scene of the movie, outlaw leader (played by Justus D. Barnes) moved towards the screen, pointed his gun directly at the audience and fired. Attendees left the theatre shocked and bemused.

A certain romance surrounded the very first Hollywood Western. Short films demonstrating the technology of moving images dated back to the 1890s. In April 1896, at Koster and Bial's Music Hall in New York City, Thomas Edison's Vitascope showed clips of moving water, people dancing and a boxing match. Fresh footage for the Vitascope (and Kinetoscope) included shots of Buffalo Bill's West-themed shows. However, Porter's work signified the first successful narrative picture, and was the first time a Western story was adapted for the silver screen. Influenced by dime novels and pulp fiction, *The Great Train Robbery* drew on the notion of the American West as a place of action and perpetual motion – of horses, guns and trains. This classic image of the West founded on movement suited the new medium of film perfectly. The familiar story of outlaws robbing rail locomotives needed little introduction or dialogue, ideal for a format that sported no sound at that time. The movie proved a huge success.

The Great Train Robbery established the conventions of the Hollywood Western. A total of fourteen scenes included a train hold-up, a robbery, a horseback chase, a Western music hall scene, a vigilante posse and a pistol showdown. What would later become

Western staples, the picture showed a gunshot-induced dance, a fist fight and the shooting of guns skyward. Right from the start, the authenticity of the Western seemed of great import. Edison advertised *The Great Train Robbery* as a 'faithful duplication of the genuine "Hold Ups" made famous by various outlaw bands in the far West' (despite the movie being shot in New York and New Jersey). Bold claims of facsimile and re-creation reflected a fascination with the potential of film technology to record and replicate real-life events. The story itself drew on a raid by the 'Hole in the Wall' gang on a Union Pacific train in Wyoming in August 1900, but could have been referring to any hijack between the 1860s and 1900s. The movie featured an authentic westerner, Bronco Billy Anderson, who, along with Bill Hart, went on to star in hundreds of short Westerns in the 1910s.[1]

In 1924, *The Iron Horse*, by John Ford, perfected the steam engine theme, and took more tickets than any other movie that year, grossing $4 million. During the Depression era of the 1930s, B-Westerns, marked by their cheap budgets and cheerful tunes, dominated the genre, until *Stagecoach* (1939), again directed by John Ford (and starring John Wayne), re-launched the big-budget oater. From the late 1920s through to the 1950s, the Western dominated Hollywood and movie theatres across the country. The number of oaters produced each year regularly exceeded one hundred. In 1940, 1948, 1952 and 1956, over 30 per cent of all features made were Westerns. Famous directors included John Ford, Howard Hawks and Anthony Mann, while actors such as Gene Autry, Roy Rogers, Gary Cooper, James Stewart and John Wayne enlivened the silver screen.

The wealth of movies refined and expanded the genre repertoire first set out in *The Great Train Robbery*. Early Westerns took advantage of the availability of 'real cowboy' actors, including Buffalo Bill and Wyatt Earp. With the frontier recently closed, movie directors exploited the opportunity to capture a moment in time and the passage of an historic period. The combination of authentic actors and fortuitous timing granted the first Westerns an almost documentary like quality. As contemporary pieces, they reflected the rush of sentimentality surrounding the Western frontier. Realism and nostalgia marked the genre. By the 1930s, B-Westerns incorporated musical qualities, as well as modern pieces of technology (radios, cars) in the Western diorama, making for a more fantastical ambience. Comedy also became important. Western characters were expected to volunteer dry quips and always answer back. In the movie *Arizona* (1940), in retort to shipper Lazarus Ward's (Porter Hall) announcement that 'There'll be no killing in my place', tough-talking woman Phoebe Totus (Jean Arthur) jokingly replied, 'Since when? Since this morning?'

While no two movies played the same, the sheer volume of Westerns established a credible formula for the genre. Stories typically focused on skirmishes between Cavalry and Indians, the movement of the railroad, stagecoach or cattle drive and problems of law, order and revenge. Stock Western characters included the cowboy, the drunken doctor, the weedy but overeager funeral casket-maker, the somber Indian and the female prostitute or bar-room entertainer. Cowboys regularly served as the heroes of such narratives. As Film Studies scholar Janet Walker identified, the cowpuncher amounted to 'the breakaway ride of Manifest Destiny' who provided a 'colonist's perspective' on the frontier experience. The cowboy tamed the wilderness, walked the line between savagery and civilisation, but could never fully settle in either landscape. In *Shane* (1953), Alan Ladd played a classic example of the Western hero: neat, tee-total, skilled with horse and gun, romantic, with a halo of freedom, but also unable to escape his past as a gunfighter, and ultimately resorting to violence to bring peace to a troubled township. By comparison, Native Americans in early Westerns (usually played by White actors) lacked any such character depth or honourable motivation. They often functioned as fancifully dressed but painfully bland villains. English Professor Jane Tompkins related how Indians simply 'functioned as props, bits of local color, textural effects. As people they had no existence.' Indian nations were identified by their generic sounds ('yips' and 'woos' and drumming) and costume (mostly based on the Apache or Sioux). As with classic presentations of the frontier in popular culture, the indigenous person represented the exotic other, the wilderness and an obstacle to colonial progress. Similarly women in Westerns seemed incapable of decision-making or independent initiative. Frontier females served as tokens of affection, symbols of domesticity and, as victims of wrongdoings, providing a potent reason for males to enact revenge. Occasionally, movies such as *The Cattle Queen of Montana* (1954), starring Barbara Stanwyck, bucked the trend by showing a tougher, more capable frontier female. Stanwyck was particularly good at playing courageous, strong-willed Westerners without compromising her femininity. Her first Western was appropriately about the female gunslinger *Annie Oakley* (1935). On the whole, however, the 'reel' frontier reeked of male bravado.[2]

Movies established a Western aesthetic that exaggerated some features of the real West (horses, cattle, sagebrush, dust, prairie expanse, aridity and remote townships), while sidelining others (temperate California, irrigation, mass settlement). The 'wild' nature of the 'reel' West provided heroes with ultimate freedom but also tested their survival skills. The harsh landscape, mostly desert, provided a pre-nuclear proving ground for Americans and their weapons (ironically, John Wayne's bout of cancer stemmed, in part, from filming Westerns on irradiated soil). That the land somehow made the hero granted a Turnerian logic to the Western (although, in contravention of Turner, Hollywood pictures celebrated cowboys rather than farmers as makers of the West). The prominence of Monument Valley in many movies (particularly John Ford's) attested to the monumental struggle between man and nature on the frontier.

In this struggle, the horse proved a useful ally to the cowboy. The equine served multiple purposes for its rider: friend, confidant, transport, mobile home, even lover. Roy Rogers sang to his loyal equine friend in *My Pal Trigger* (1946), a musical Western based around Trigger, 'The Smartest Horse in the Movies', while the masked *Lone Ranger*, radio and television hero from the 1930s to the 1950s, regularly relied on the stealth and loyalty of his gleaming white stallion Silver. Rescued from an angry buffalo, Silver provided animal transport for the Lone Ranger on his quest for justice. With a clarion call of 'Hi-Ho Silver, Away', the horse dutifully rushed the Lone Ranger from one crime scene to the next. Silver provided a contact point with not only the wild nature of the West but also the civilising aspect of it. The star horse, with its wild mane and habitual rearing, but tethered saddle, seemed itself caught up in the same paradox as its owner, forever shifting between domesticity and wildness.

The township meanwhile represented the emergence of society out of the wilderness, and served as the focal point for clashes between hero and villain, law and outlaw, rancher and farmer, pioneer and urbanite. Hollywood film sets re-assembled the classic frontier town into a collection of Western cultural signifiers: the dirt track on main street as an indicator of newness and rawness; the hitching posts as signs of mobility; the saloon as a reference to the rowdiness of cowboys; the jail the prominence (and problem) of justice. The town never seemed settled – there was always a struggle at play. Its survival appeared as flimsy as its Hollywood sub-frames.

Both the power and appeal of the oater rested on its dramatisation of the past. With most films set in the trans-Mississippi region between the 1860s and the 1890s, the Western chiefly operated as a historical genre. Naturally, the Western became strongly associated with popular understandings of American history. The widespread success of the Hollywood Western, its common imagery and motifs, meant that most audiences came to comprehend frontier history through the movie reel. More available, desirable and easier to digest than government reports or frontier diaries, Hollywood movies perfected a mainstream view of the frontier. A series of visual images became the common markers of Western history: wagon trails; Indian attack; and cowboy shootouts. Hayden White's concept of 'historiophoty' proved pertinent here: the shaping and presentation of the past by image, with audiences, consciously or not, processing 'westerns as histories on film'. Alongside conventional history texts, Hollywood oaters served as interpretive guides to the past. However, artistic licence meant that the 'reel' West rarely conformed to the real West. Like dime novelists before them, film directors homed in on conflict and action as markers of the frontier experience, in the process reiterating a populist understanding of the West as a simple tale of good over evil. The frontier was sanctified, nostalgised and patriotised in the movie-making process.[3]

The 'reel' West quickly came to embody American ideals, values and sentiments. As Frederick Elkin suggested, films showed 'the American West is beautiful and spacious and that the life of the frontier represents a free and admirable way of life'. Common filmic codes included the celebration of individualism (through the guise of the lone hero), the power of new democracy (through westerners being judged by merit and skills, not inheritance nor bloodline), the lure of freedom (through the open range) and the winning of justice (often through legitimised violence). The inevitability of progress resided in the backdrop to each Western. In *Shane*, the gunfighter hero departed from town because he recognised that he was no longer needed. The frontier was about to close and move on elsewhere, his shooter skills consigned to a past era. A better future lay ahead. This idyllic platform of Americana, both nostalgic for the past and optimistic in its portrayal of national direction, assured general confidence in the American experiment. For those suffering low incomes or local injustice, the Western offered temporary reprieve. The simple, well-ordered structure of the celluloid frontier appealed to those trapped in far more complex and morally ambiguous real worlds. The Hollywood oater offered comfort, satisfaction and audience identification with a hero who always knew best and won out in the end.[4]

However, as products of their own time, movies inescapably (and often intentionally) offered commentary on the present. Some of it could be subversive and critical. Directed by Fred Zimmermann and with a screenplay written by Carl Foreman, *High Noon* (1952) starred Gary Cooper as Will Kane, a marshal left to face a gang of thugs alone when his fellow townspeople refused to back him. The 'existential Western' operated as an allegory of contemporary McCarthy inspired witch-hunts and the silent response of Hollywood to its liberal members being blacklisted. John Wayne branded *High Noon* as 'un-American' because of its social criticism. However, the movie also offered subtle reassurance for Cold War anxieties. As seen by scholar Steven McVeigh, 'the model of gunfighter hero in *High Noon*, a hero who can to some extent determine his future, inaugurated in the Western a fundamental characteristic of the gunfighter as the Cold War accelerated'. That Cooper's character ultimately exercised control over his destiny proved a welcome notion to those perilised by thoughts of impending and unavoidable nuclear Armageddon. Movies such as *Little Big Man* (1970) starring Dustin Hoffman critiqued American involvement in the Vietnam War. Directed by Arthur Penn, the revisionist Western presented the Washita Indian Massacre of 1868 as an historic precursor to contemporary American military misadventures in Vietnam. Apparently, the Soviet newspaper *Pravda* loved it. Revisionist Westerns reflected growing liberal unease with adherence to triumphalist creation myths documenting the natural ascendancy of America over other countries and peoples. The intersection of the Hollywood oater with contemporary issues gradually moved it in new directions. The advent of the psychological Western (and the anti-hero) reflected in part new interests in psychology in the 1960s, as well as skepticism over simple American heroes. Increased roles for women and minorities reflected new pushes for equality in American society. Mirroring escalations in gun violence in domestic America, *The Wild Bunch* (1969), directed by Sam Peckinpah, detailed the final escapades of a ruthless gang led by Pike Bishop (William Holden), defined only by their brutish killing. Peckinpah explored issues of greed, immorality, treachery and nostalgia for the frontier in the nihilistic, ultra-violent movie. The Western no longer seemed simple in its politics or message.[5]

Arguably, the demise of the Western might be seen in the Italian Westerns of Sergio Leone, early vehicles for Clint Eastwood that excessively parodied the genre and stylised the violence. A genre once based on the celebration of American history and culture no longer seemed capable of providing deeper meaning, fundamental truths or patriotic rabble-rousing. The meta-narrative of the glorious frontier seemed out of touch with society. By the 1970s, the frontier West had exited living memory, and new generations identified more with cop thrillers and science-fiction movies (that themselves exploited Western conventions). Hollywood lost its confidence in the Western format as a successful money-spinner. After three-quarters of a century and more than 7,000 pictures, it seemed little more could be added to the franchise. The West no longer held sway. The death of the Hollywood Western was eulogistically linked to *The Shootist* (1976), the last movie starring John Wayne. In it, Wayne played John Bernard Brooks, a tired gunfighter close to the end. The character mirrored Wayne's own battle with terminal cancer. The tag line for the movie declared, 'He's got to face a gunfight once more to live up to his legend once more. To win just one more time.' Wayne related the classic appeal of the Hollywood Western, and pondered whether the format had a future:

> Every country in the world loved the folklore of the West – the music, the dress, the excitement, everything that was associated with the opening of a new territory. It took everybody out of their own little world. The cowboy lasted a hundred years, created more songs and prose and poetry than any other folk figure. The closest thing was the Japanese samurai. Now, I wonder who'll continue it.

The Western Renaissance

Few film companies backed Westerns over the next fifteen years. Following the success of *The Deer Hunter* (1978), United Artists financed its director, Michael Cimino, to make a Western based on the Johnson County War. Cimino delivered a project that cost $40 million (four times over budget), came in at over five hours in length and used up a total of 1.5 million feet (457,200 metres) of celluloid. During the filming, whole sets were rebuilt and Cimino employed a bodyguard to stop studio executives from hassling him. *Heaven's Gate* (1980) proved an artistic and commercial disaster. The gigantic flop contributed to the sale of United Artists to MGM, and ruined the career of Cimino. The Hollywood Western seemed a dead property, more buried at Boot Hill than unlatching Heaven's gate.

Two movies briefly reanimated the genre: a large-scale revisionist project by Kevin Costner and an inspired gunfighter tale directed by Western veteran Clint Eastwood. *Dances with Wolves* (1990) depicted sergeant John Dunbar's frontier outpost endeavour, his relations with the Apache and his ultimate 'going native' in defiance of a looming army threat. The movie posed a binary opposite to the celebration of frontier expansion archetypal to most Western pictures. Conquest was inverted, with Native Americans cast as the victims of White American military malice. Along with its revisionist roots, *Dances with Wolves* also served a valuable role as an ecological Western. Dunbar developed an emotive relationship with a wolf that he nicknamed Two Socks. He also partook in a bison hunt with the Sioux, a dramatic movie scene full of dust and stampeding animals. Documenting Dunbar's epiphany on the Great Plains, the picture posed the rhetorical question, 'what if whites had cared?'. The doomed narrative and sense of nostalgia for the pre-colonial West proved eminently seductive. The picture offered a perfect filmic companion to the rise of New Western history, with its own similar themes of conquest and ethnic sensitivity. *Dances* won seven Oscars, including best picture.

As a loyal backer of the traditional Western format, Clint Eastwood seemed an unlikely candidate to revolutionise the genre in any comparative sense to Costner. His tenth Western, *Unforgiven* (1992) documented the 'one last job' of retired gunfighter William Munny. The movie utilised a number of genre staples: revenge on behalf of mistreated women, the need for vigilante justice due to a corrupt sheriff (played by Gene Hackman), and the return of the veteran anti-hero. In tone, it resembled a classic psychological Western. William Munny's (Eastwood) ultimately fated attempt to leave behind violence, to escape his own past, provided an elderly and more jaded reprisal of Alan Ladd's gunfighter in *Shane*. Eastwood took a less openly revisionist path than Costner, but still offered fresh insight into the genre. Munny displayed serious doubts over his life accomplishments and the difficulties of being just average at pig farming (compared with past skills with a gun). *Unforgiven* impressed in its deconstruction of legend and myth, along with its recurring commentary on the merits of violence. The movie received four Oscars, including best picture.[6]

Shown alongside one another, the two movies imparted very different visions of the West. *Dances with Wolves* homed in on the mistreatment of indigenous peoples and animals to forge a political message. *Unforgiven* showed the trials of the White experience, although ultimately old-style frontier justice won out true to conventions. What they shared was a genuine nostalgia for the West along with a willingness to explore its problems and challenges. Significantly, both films offered something new for the viewer.

In response to the two blockbusters, the mass media anticipated a Western revival. '*Unforgiven* made westerns an acceptable genre again', commented one movie star agent. In the *Vogue* feature 'Shoot-out at the PC Corral', James Ryan enthused how, 'With westerns riding high again, Hollywood suddenly has dozens of multicultural, revisionist, and historically accurate variations in the works'. The *Vogue* contributor predicted a new Western bonanza thanks to the success of the Costner and Eastwood features. For Ryan, the new Clinton presidency also spurred interest in multicultural Westerns (several decades of social protest probably proved more decisive in opening the filmic West to colour). For a brief period, the return of the Hollywood Western seemed plausible. Costner followed up *Dances with Wolves* by starring in the bio-picture *Wyatt Earp* (1994). Also featuring the acclaimed Earp gunfighter, *Tombstone* (1993), directed by George Cosmatos and starring Kurt Russell and Val Kilmer, related the mythic shootout at the O.K. Corral. A remake of the 1950s television series, *Maverick* (1994) told the story of a humorous gambler (played by Mel Gibson) with a preference for playing his hand out of sticky scenarios. *Bad Girls* (1993) and *The Quick and the Dead* (1995) situated women at the forefront of the Western endeavour, usually with guns in hands. *Thunderheart* (1992) explored contemporary Sioux culture by way of an actual FBI case on an Indian reservation in the Badlands, South Dakota in the 1970s. Finally, *Posse* (1993) by Mario Von Peebles inserted African-Americans into the classic Western genre, updated with contemporary gang-type parlance. Serving as a remake of a classic frontier story or as a social-conscience picture, the early 1990s Western abided by one of two models. The choice was between two competing visions of the West: the glorious old frontier or a new frontier of ethnicity, gender and environment.[7]

The revival proved to be short-lived. Few studios showed consistent interest in the format. *Wyatt Earp* failed dismally at the box office. A remake of the 1960s television series, *The Wild Wild West* (1999) signalled that even a bankable actor (Will Smith) allied to an old franchise could falter. Warner Brothers invested a sizeable $150 million in the picture. The tag line promise of 'It's a whole new West' proved painfully true when a massive, steam-powered mechanical spider came on screen. However, the action comedy failed to impress. Will Smith joked, 'I think I pretty much killed the Western.' Although a commercial success, Kevin Costner's third Western, *Open Range* (2003), a classic cattle and cowboy picture, failed to inspire the critics. The *San Francisco Chronicle* savaged the Costner vehicle for its grand pretension, at the same time casting doubt over the genre in general.

'The script shows the strain of writing a Western after 90 years of Westerns. Can anyone really type the words "Let's rustle up some grub" and feel that it's coming from an honest place?' quizzed the *Chronicle*'s Mick LaSalle. *Rolling Stone* noted the similarities of *Open Range* with Eastwood's gunfighter picture, but lamented, 'Costner is quite a way from *Unforgiven*.' Costner meanwhile bemoaned, 'The general consensus is don't make Westerns. No one wants to see them.' In 2003, Warner Brothers dismantled a crumbling Laramie Street, classic Western studio set, replacing it with a suburban façade (Paramount's Western Street had been demolished in 1979, making way for a car park). Overplaying the hyperbole, NBC reported how, 'The Western once seemed as plentiful on the big screen as buffalo on the 19th century plains. Now the genre is as scarce as a tumbleweed on the Hollywood Walk of Fame.'[8]

The relevance of the cowboy hero in a twenty-first century America appeared to be seriously in doubt. What could the cowboy, a frontier outcast, offer a nation caught in post-9/11 terrorism anxieties and environmental maladies? Some suggested that the cowboy still had a few quips to offer. Like President George W. Bush, there seemed something safe and comfortable in a traditional, simple guy who knew what he wanted. The cowboy West offered a refuge from the ambiguities of the modern day. As Peter Rainer, from the National Society of Film Critics, pondered, 'Whenever the genre gets revived it generally means that there's some need in the culture to get back to basics. It's either used as a code for what's going on in America and the world or as a shield against it.' The Americanness of the cowboy appealed in a period of patriotic soul-searching. The *Boston Globe* related how 'The Western hero – whether wearing Davy Crockett's coonskin cap, the Cisco kid's sombrero, or the Ringo Kid's Stetson – is so essentially American that he can never die'. Chief Executive of Disney Michael Eisner hoped that a new studio version of John Wayne's *The Alamo* (1960) would capture the fresh sentimentality surrounding American identity. In London, *The Times* commented on the cynical exploitation of patristic fervour, noting how 'In the wake of the September 11 attacks, Disney put *The Alamo*, perhaps the most symbolic American myth of all, into production, to capitalise on the sacrifices that a nation under attack was expecting to make'. John Lee Hancock's remake none the less missed the mark. The Disneyfied Alamo, a plastic imitation of Wayne's heartfelt ode to American will, cost $107 million to produce, but took just $22 million in the American market.[9]

Brokeback Mountain

Into this uncertainty over the viability of the genre and the relevance of the cowboy to post-9/11 society entered *Brokeback Mountain* (2005). Based on the short story by Annie Proulx, first published in the *New Yorker* in October 1997, the Ang Lee movie related a twenty-year love affair between two ranch-hands, Jack Twist (Jake Gyllenhal) and Ennis del Mar (Heath Ledger) beginning in the 1960s on a Wyoming mountain. Attesting to studio wariness over financing Westerns, and in particular, concern over backing 'a story about gay cowboys', the film proved incredibly difficult to make. A script by Larry McMurtry and Diane Ossana (of *Lonesome Dove* (1989) fame) won over author Proulx, who felt her 'story was not mangled but enlarged into huge and gripping imagery that rattled minds and squeezed hearts'. Film companies proved less easily persuaded. Almost seven years passed before filming began in Alberta, Canada. Production cost $13 million. The movie proved a tremendous success, netting domestic takings of $75.4 million and winning four Golden Globes, three Oscars and the Golden Lion at the Venice Film Festival.[10]

Brokeback Mountain challenged the conventions of the classic Western genre. It lacked guns, villains, a nineteenth-century setting or a showdown where violence begot justice. It replaced heterosexual cowboys with gay sheepherders. The film broke from tradition in its realistic portrayal of on-screen sexual encounters. As literature scholar Chris Packard contended, 'In action-packed Westerns, discussions about sex, and sex acts themselves, appear far less frequently than sudden avalanches, surprising encounters with grizzlies, nighttime stampedes, sneaking Indians or thieving Mexicans.' Women were often worshiped from afar as the source of cowboy laments of lost or never-found sweethearts. Gay or otherwise, celluloid cowboys rarely got up close and personal with their partners. *Brokeback Mountain* showed a different side.[11]

Director Ang Lee insisted, 'The film is not a Western; it's a romantic love story,' and took particular offence to common descriptions of his movie as a 'gay western'. Lee claimed his ignorance of the Western genre made the movie more authentic, suggesting, 'Westerns are an invented movie genre about gunslingers, usually set somewhere in the back of the Grand Canyon. This is a more realistic portrayal of the West.' Producer Diane Ossana agreed, casting the movie as a eulogistic testimony to realism, a sort of visual companion to Richard Avedon's *In the American West* (1985) with its photographs of 'ordinary folk'.

Brokeback was a 'real' Western, mirroring true life and tragic events. It explored rural homophobia and social isolation. The death of Jack Twist in the movie, likely at the hands of homophobes, linked with the hate crime-led murder of Matthew Shepard, a gay resident of Laramie less than a year after the film's release. Ossana related how, 'It felt like an eerie mirroring of Annie's story and our screenplay'. For Proulx, the movie also captured 'the slow fade of cattle ranching in the west', and fitted within her broader work 'concerned with the Wyoming landscape and making a living in hard, isolated livestock-raising communities dominated by white masculine values, but also holding subliminal fantasies'. The movie presented an authentic regional identity (even with its trans-49th Parallel cinematography). As Proulx claimed, 'The film is intensely Wyoming. Lee included dead animals and good fights, both very western.' It presented the West as a real, functioning (albeit socially dysfunctional) landscape.[12]

Deliberate or not, the movie borrowed a number of filmic conventions from the Hollywood Western. McMurtry's and Ossana's script emphasised the Western aesthetic of the short story. The opening scene of 'a Cattle truck, running empty, tops a ridge on a lonely western highway', imparted classic themes of open range, isolation, movement and desolation. Similarly, the first description of Ennis del Mar played to several motifs of westerly attire and appearance in his 'outgrown faded cowboy shirt', simple belongings, and 'Tall, raw-boned, lanky [demeanour], possessed of a muscular, supple body made for the horse and for fighting'. Movie scenes borrowed custom Western locales, including the bar room (scene two), the trailhead (scene three), campfires, rodeo and the open range. As always, urban scenes proved claustrophobic, cage-like and inhibitive, while freedom (and true expressions of masculinity) came only from the 'wild' West, the true outdoors, from the mountain itself. Such a dichotomy reflected historic associations of the city with a stifling and unhealthy environment, and the pastoral with freedom and health.[13]

Minimal dialogue highlighted the difficulty of men coming to terms with their true emotions, but also adhered to the Western trope of silent, moody heroes. Ennis, in particular, resembled a typical screen cowboy in his disapproval of talk, detachment from feelings and proclivity for pained expressions. He struggled with self-loathing. Western heroes typically carried such crosses and burdens. As Jane Tompkins related, 'the price the western exacts from its heroes is written in the expression on Gary Cooper's face throughout *High Noon* . . . The expression is one of fear, distaste, determination and inward pain.' Cooper struggled with himself and with society around him. Exactly the same could be said of Heath Ledger. This also lent the character a certain charisma. As *The Independent* commented on *Brokeback Mountain*, 'there's a lot of Clint Eastwood style squinting, shuffling and staring into the distance'.[14]

Hollywood films frequently relied on a bond developing between two male leads, the formation of a 'buddy' relationship, as in the movie *Bonnie and Clyde* (1969) or the folktale of Doc Holliday and Wyatt Earp. Albeit on a deeper level of sexual commitment, the bond between Ennis and Jack replicated such male on male fascination. Ennis and Jack fought, herded, hunted and most controversially, 'fished' together. They started from a position of mutual distrust and ended up loyal to one another. Their relationship seceded all other human associations in terms of depth and feeling. This left their female partners, Alma (Michelle Williams) and Lureen (Anne Hathaway), out in the cold. Alma and Lureen never gained the same level of confidence or emotional display that Ennis and Jack offered each other. As with most Westerns, *Brokeback Mountain* asserted the subsidiary role of women to a homosocial relationship. Tompkins argued that women in Westerns ultimately provided an 'alibi function' for their male counterparts, presenting a façade of social orthodoxy, and 'masking the fact that what the men are really interested in is one another'.[15]

Brokeback was a cowboy movie. For both Ennis and Jack, the cowboy myth appealed to their instincts. As Proulx related, 'Both wanted to be cowboys, be part of the Great Western myth, but it didn't work out that way; Ennis never got to be more than a rough-cut ranch hand and Jack Twist chose rodeo as an expression of cowboy.' They walked, talked and acted like cowboys. The cowboy appellation was applied to everyday parlance, as when Alma asked Ennis of Jack Twist: 'Is he somebody you cowboy'd with?'. They also worked like cowpunchers. As Hiram Perez noted, 'Ennis's hard, itinerant work life arguably makes him a modern-day cowboy'. For Jack, his own sense of self became 'tied to both the authentic measures of the cowboy (roping and riding) and the performances necessary to maintain the illusion of Western, masculine ideals'. Like all movie cowboys, Ennis and Jack could never settle down and be content. They were social outcasts, not welcome in town, and having to drive off into the distance to be their true selves, treading in the footsteps of many celluloid heroes before them.[16]

Western historian Richard White labelled *Brokeback* 'conventionally, even reverentially, a Western', by its scenery, dialogue and hero bonding. In humorous style, White noted how, 'Beans have not played so large a role in a film since *Blazing Saddles*'. Rather than distinguish *Brokeback Mountain* from other Westerns, the realism of the picture, its sense of landscape and people close up, proved its true genre credentials. For Jane Tompkins, 'physical sensations are the bedrock of the experience Westerns afford', they 'satisfy a hunger to be in touch with something absolutely real'. *Brokeback* proved a visceral, physical and emotional experience for its viewers.[17]

Western or not, *Brokeback Mountain* generated a range of critical responses. One Salt Lake City movie theatre cancelled the movie. Dubiously headlining its article, 'Homo on the Range', the *Dallas Observer* commented, 'It's not hard to predict how Ang Lee's controversial *Brokeback Mountain* will play in John Wayne country'. The filmic 'queering' of the West led to protests by conservative Christian groups. Citing its Eastern publisher, Taiwanese director and Canadian film set, critics deemed the movie inauthentic and illegitimate. One letter writer railed against 'Hollywood propaganda to promote a liberal, homosexual life'. Promotional materials and some press reviews marginalised the gay romance. Rather than 'that gay cowboy movie', publicity for *Brokeback* emphasised a universal love story in the hope of more ticket receipts. The *Los Angeles Times* review stated that the lovers 'just happen to be men', while other reviewers focused on the 'universal appeal' of the movie. Gay communities thought otherwise, welcoming a film that debunked the assumed heterosexuality of the Western frontier. One website applauded the 'biggest budget gay love story ever'. When *Brokeback Mountain* lost the prize of best motion picture to *Crash* (2005) at the 2006 Oscars, it came as a shock. A multi-strand take on race relations set in contemporary Los Angeles, the 'hometown' status of *Crash* partially explained the choice, but some interpreted the rejection of *Brokeback* as a sign of lingering homophobia among older members of the Oscar Council. The *San Francisco Chronicle* described the decision as 'one of the most shocking upsets in Oscar history'.[18]

The biggest clash of opinion came over the Western image. What lay at stake was the presentation of the cowboy in twenty-first century America. Conservative types boycotted the movie, and firmly denied that real cowboys could be gay. One respondent to a *High Country News* article simply stated, 'No good, God-fearing Wyoming cowboy would engage in homosexual behavior.' Noting their sheep-herding work, some refuted the whole idea that Ennis and Jack had cowboy pretensions. *The New York Times* theorised that the reason *Brokeback* failed to earn best movie picture at the Oscars related to its take on 'a fairly sacred Hollywood icon, the cowboy', and that the last thing 'older members of the academy wanted to see [was] the image of the American cowboy diminished'. For traditional Hollywood frats, John Wayne's Sheriff John T. Chance from *Rio Bravo* (1959), not Heath Ledger's Ennis del Mar embodied the true cowboy hero. Wayne displayed all the ideal cowboy traits: tough but gentle; honourable; quiet; rugged; attractive; individualistic; and heterosexual. His characters proved their worth and their manhood by fighting for justice on the frontier. They kept their distance from women, from the home, from domesticity, and instead clung to classically heterosexual pursuits of the hunt, adventure and killing. The traditional Hollywood cowboy had provided a perfect (conformist) definition of masculinity and a role model of manhood for almost a century. The gay cowboy represented an affront to this heterosexual orthodoxy, a challenge to the cowboy icon.[19]

Historical evidence suggested that the gay cowboy was hardly the imagination of Annie Proulx. Given that the 'cattle kingdom was a masculine world', Western historian Robert Hine deduced that homosexuality likely existed 'given the nature of the situation' on the plains in the late nineteenth century. The McKinsey Report (1948) argued that the commonness of homosexuality in rural America related to the physical activity of professions such as ranching and farming, the exclusively male nature of the work and an element of pragmatism in the thinking of outdoorsmen. Accordingly, 'Older males in Western rural areas' had 'the attitude that sex is sex, irrespective of the nature of the partner with whom the relation is had'. That cowboys never looked 'that way' at each other seemed a fantasy, an invention. Gender scholar Eric Patterson attacked the reductive and inaccurate image of the American cowboy that critics of the movie held so dear. According to Patterson, the distinction between homosocial and homosexual had been artificially imposed by popular culture (and homophobia) in the twentieth century, and overlooked the reality of cowboy affairs on the frontier. He compared the retrogressive 'heteroizing' of the cowboy with the 'whitewashing' of the cowpuncher: 'The popular cultural mythology of the cowboy not only ignores the substantial participation of men of color in the cattle business, but also erases the presence of men who loved other men.' Patterson also questioned the idealisation of the traditional cowboy, a man who ultimately proved ambivalent over American society, law and ethics.[20]

For the gay community, the use of two homosexual cowboys in *Brokeback* helped debunk the stereotype of gay Americans as city-bound and discreet products of a modern, urban lifestyle. *Brokeback* proudly serviced as a gay Western, demonstrated by scenes such as Ennis opening his closet to touch his and Jack's shirts resting together, a euphemism for a repressed and hidden love. Even the movie's tag line, 'Love is a force of nature' implied that the gay cowboy relationship was something natural, and not to be maligned. At Brokeback Mountain, Ennis and Jack could be themselves, the wilderness providing a temporary reprieve from social intolerance. The Western genre itself revealed older gay subtexts. Many Westerns glorified, even fetishised, the cowboy aesthetic, such as the cowboy dandy. Homoeroticism could be found in classic movies such as *Red River* (1947), where young cowhand Matt Garth (Montgomery Clift) developed a deep relationship with his senior Tom Dunson (John Wayne), as well as comparing guns with compatriot Cherry (John Ireland). More obvious references to gay cowboys could be found in the ultra-violent Italian Western *Django Kill* (1967), including gang rape. Filmed in stretches of Arizona that Wayne had used as movie shoots, Andy Warhol's *Lonesome Cowboys* (1968) sported male models-cum-cowboys in a variety of homoerotic poses.

The strong reaction to *Brokeback Mountain* revealed not only a fundamental desire to defend the iconic West from attack, but also suggested just how much the myth depended on conservative and outdated concepts. Ossana herself feared a backlash from the same people who had backed her husband Larry McMurtry's Western TV series *Lonesome Dove* a decade earlier, that 'staunch *Lonesome Dove* fans' would turn 'against him for being involved with a film that subverts the myth of the American West and its iconic heroes'. *Brokeback* threatened the illusion of a West as an old and simple place, pre-modern and somehow better for it. As the *High Country News* elaborated:

> The truth is: Gays, lesbians, Democrats, Republicans, poverty, drug use, divorce, fundamentalists, homicidal teenagers and tree-huggers all coexist in the West, and always have. The cowboy West really only existed in Marlboro County ads and tourist brochures.[21]

The Return (Yet Again) of Jesse James

Two years on from *Brokeback Mountain*, Warner Brothers released *The Assassination of Jesse James by the Coward Robert Ford* (2007) starring Brad Pitt and directed by New Zealander Andrew Dominik. The psychological Western documented the last months of folk hero

Jesse James, including his final train robbery, the disintegration of his gang, the growing cult surrounding his criminality and his death at the hands of Robert Ford (played by Casey Affleck) on 5 September 1881. The slow-paced, cinematic Western received a range of plaudits, including a best actor award for Pitt at the Venice Film Festival and Oscar nominations for 2008. Its release coincided with several other Westerns, a remake of *3:10 to Yuma* (2007) starring Russell Crowe, a psychological neo-Western *No Country for Old Men* (2007) directed by the Coen brothers (sporting the same cinematographer, Roger Deakins) and *Seraphim Falls* (2006) starring Pierce Brosnan. The *Boston Globe* duly declared, 'The Western is back'. Filmed in Alberta, and based on the 1983 novel by Ron Hansen, *Assassination* bore some similarity to *Brokeback Mountain*. Both movies explored the jaded nature of Western characters with great attention to pace and landscape. In content, the two movies differed significantly, reprising the contrast between *Dances with Wolves* and *Unforgiven* in the early 1990s. With its challenging of Western stereotypes, *Brokeback Mountain* sported a similar revisionism to Kevin Costner's epic. *Assassination* offered a more traditional Western on par with Clint Eastwood's gunfighter picture. However, while *Unforgiven* had drawn on a fictitious near-retired gunfighter, *Assassination* took inspiration from a true-life bandit of the West, Jesse James.[22]

Born in the border state of Missouri on 5 September 1847, Jesse James grew up in a comfortable Southern-leaning family. Ardent supporters of slavery, the James family became embroiled in the American Civil War. Jesse's brother Frank served with the Confederate Army before joining a guerilla group led by William Clarke Quantrill. In June 1863, the Union Army ransacked the James home, hanging (but not killing) stepfather Dr Reuben Samuels. The Army also beat a 16-year-old Jesse. In the same week, his mother and sister were imprisoned. James later joined the Quantrill gang. By the end of the Civil War, a wounded and exiled James lived in Nebraska, then Kansas. His cousin Zee nursed James back to health (he married Zee in 1874). Around 1869, the James brothers joined the Cole/Younger gang, and began a career of banditry and crime. In December 1869, James appeared in newspaper headlines blamed for a raid on the Daviess County Savings Association in Gallatin, Missouri. In 1872, the gang famously robbed the ticket booth at the Kansas City fairground. Some revellers mistook the raid for a fair ground show. A range of bank, stagecoach and railroad hold-ups followed. The Adams Express Company hired the Pinkerton National Detective Agency to protect its freight interests,

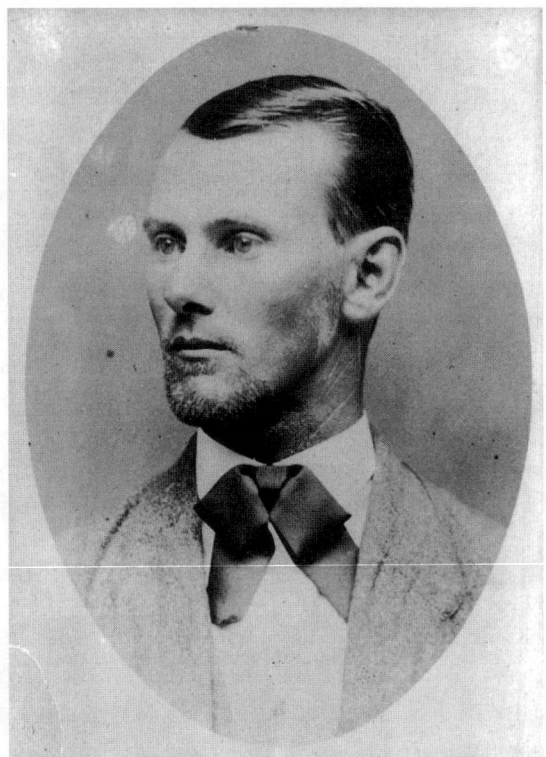

Figure 9.1 Jesse James.

but a bungled raid in January 1875 left James' relations injured but the criminals untouched.

On 7 September 1876, an attack on the First National Bank in Northfield, Minnesota, went disastrously wrong when several died, and only the James brothers escaped. The gang never fully recovered. New recruits included the Ford brothers from Missouri. Attracted by a $10,000 bounty and celebrity fame, Bob Ford arranged the capture of Jesse James with state Governor Thomas T. Crittenden. On 3 April 1882 Ford dispatched an unarmed James at his homestead. Ford went on to star in his own play, 'How I Killed Jesse James' that proved popular in the East, less so in the West, where sympathy for James undercut the drama. A relation of the Younger brothers later killed Ford.[23]

The notoriety of the James brothers grew in the 1870s. Local newspapers covered robberies, and, sometimes out of habit more than evidence, claimed the James/Younger gang as responsible for a wide range of criminal activities. Crime authors showed interest in the motivations and exploits of Western outlaws. Frank James's penchant for Shakespeare became a recurring citation. An entertainment angle seemed a natural part of the criminal performance. The *Kansas City Times* portrayed the County Fair raid as a dashing stunt, commenting on how for the James brothers, 'With them the booty is but the second thought; the wild drama of the adventure first.' Their actions turned into melodrama and folk story, outlaws quickly became heroes. Writers presented Jesse James as a romantic figure, handsomely polite to women (even during raids) and a mastermind of robbery. Excitement, danger and humour surrounded the outlaw.[24]

Journalist and author John N. Edwards helped give the Jesse James legend purpose. Serving in the Confederate Army as a major, Edwards nurtured lingering Southern sympathies. Although never having met James himself, Edwards became his most committed biographer. Edwards worked for the *Kansas City Times*. In 1877, Bryan, Brand and Company published his *Noted Guerillas, or the Warfare of the Border*, an indulgent biography of post-Civil War banditry. In it, Edwards presented James as a wild beast, an 'untameable and merciful creature', produced by the horrors and injustices of the American Civil War. The militia attack on the James farm served as the catalyst for Jesse joining his brother in the Quantrill camp and setting out on a life of crime. According to Edwards, James proved exceptional for his 'horsecraft', preparation, dialect, animal knowledge, daring and polite demeanour. James was a tall, blue-eyed Southern gentleman: 'On his lips there was always a smile, and for every comrade a pleasant word or compliment.' James was a man driven to action, or as Edwards reflected, 'What else could Jesse James have done?'. Edwards moulded James into a post-Civil War folk hero or Robin Hood of the South, an everyman figure who targeted the rich, but never the poor. Despite his comfortable upbringing, James became a symbol of hope for the destitute. He reflected the problems of a post-war Missouri, bankrupt, corrupt and struggling. True to Western tradition, vigilante justice seemed to be more capable than newly arrived law officials from the North. The unfolding James legend reflected a desire for protest against the new South.[25]

Other writers jumped on the James bandwagon. J. A. Dacus portrayed Jesse James as a scary but intriguing outlaw. His *Life and Adventures of Frank and Jesse James* (1879) began with a poem, 'Strange murmurs fill my tingling ears, Bristles my hair, my sinews quake, At this dread tale of reckless deeds.' Again, the attack of the

Union Army on the James family featured strongly. As if stagecoaches followed him looking for robbery, Jesse could not be left in peace. Dacus glorified James alongside other 'outlaws and highwaymen of the most remarkable character of any known in the annals of history'. He also included a range of letters by James himself. Three years later, and coinciding with the demise of James at the hands of Ford, St Louis author Frank Triplett published *The Life, Times and Treacherous Death of Jesse James* (1882). This work drew on testimony from James' mother and Zee (later disputed) and, in its criticism of Governor Crittenden sported great controversy.[26]

The sense of offering a truly authentic account of Jesse (as well as profit) spurred the family to act. In *Jesse James, My Father* (1899), Jesse James Junior attacked the book trade for turning his father into 'a veritable Frankenstein who slew mercilessly and robbed for the mere love of adventure'. His book set out to 'correct false impressions'. However, the James extravaganza continued. Lige Mitchell's *Daring Exploits of Jesse James and His Band of Border Train and Bank Robbers* (1912) sold James as a cavalier highwayman. According to Mitchell, Jesse James gave the cashier at the Kansas County Fair the simple choice, 'Leave that alone and keep quiet, or I'll blow your brains out.' So much for the gentlemanly conduct suggested by Edwards.[27]

By 1901, James had a whole series of Street & Smith dime novels dedicated to him. Entitled 'The Jesse James Stories: Original Narratives of the James Boys', episodes included W. B. Lawson's *Jesse James, The Outlaw* (1901). Lawson lionised James as 'a man of magnificent proportions, with close-clipped, reddish beard, handsome, stern features and a steely blue eye, whose penetrating glance might have pierced a three-inch plank'. James became the inspiration of plays, shows, ballads, novels and short stories. As each writer added something extra, the myth of the outlaw grew. James came to personify vigilantism, individualism, adventure and the frontier spirit. His less honourable actions went ignored. Caught between protest and criminality, James fitted perfectly within historian Eric Hobsbawm's theory of social banditry and popular resistance. The myth became so strong that some claimed the real Jesse James never died. Christopher Anderson saw in James, 'A first-generation, mass-media celebrity'. At the dawn of cinema, Jesse James had already been cast as a popular champion, a lady lover and the eternal action hero.[28]

Movies assured the progress of the Jesse James legend through the twentieth century. The Essanay Film Manufacturing Company produced the first James movie, *The James Boys in Missouri*, in 1908. Based on a play that travelled nationwide, Essanay covered a train robbery, the county fair hold-up and the killing of James, all in eighteen minutes of film. *Variety* applauded the short black and white movie as 'strongly drawn and the most sensational of its kind'. In 1921, Jesse James Junior starred in the next two productions that tackled the James legend. Merging fiction with authenticity in a similar way to Buffalo Bill's Wild West shows, *Jesse James as the Outlaw* and *Jesse James Under the Black Flag* depicted the hounding of James by federal officials. Early films carried a documentary style and simple filmic narrative.[29]

The shift away from authenticity and toward romanticism in James-related movies began with director Lloyd Ingraham's *Jesse James*, released in 1927. The movie served as a vehicle for Fred Thomson, a popular silent movie actor. In one scene using a sheep for a disguise, Thomson's James was presented as a loveable Robin Hood character. *Variety* noted the idealism at work in the picture, 'The James brothers terrorized their state (Missouri) for years, yet Paramount in "Jesse James" would present that life taker in a heroic frame.' The magazine recommended that the film was strictly 'not for the nice people; they will resent this picture and its idea if not scheme of cleansing Jesse James'. *The New York Times* derided the movie as typical mass-production, 'mills of Hollywood'. It none the less recorded an impressive $1.2 million in ticket sales.[30]

In 1939, Fox financed *Jesse James*, a big budget, Technicolor picture starring Tyrone Power. The movie related the rise of the outlaw, including the fated Northfield bank raid. A clean image of Jesse James proved crucial to the success of the feature. Handwritten comments on the script recommended the optimum lionising of the hero. Notes advised the movie-makers to 'show how he's framed for what he didn't do', and, in the classic Western tradition of the inescapable gunslinger, 'clear up his motivations – show more of this desire to quit, but can't'. The romantic interest between Zee and Jesse was also stressed, with recommendations to 'develop their love more'. Fox's Director of Public Relations Jason Joy wrote to the producer, enthusiastic about the project:

> Jesse James has about everything that adds up to top-notch entertainment – a famous character name, a period of dangerous adventure, thrilling action, a very human romance, natural comedy, and from the standpoint of the censors and reformers, almost perfectly balanced moral values.

Apart from creating more sympathy for James in the latter third of the movie, Joy recommended the picture move ahead. When it aired, Fox's rendition had perfected the romantic, moralistic outlaw. *The New York Times* applauded, 'an authentic American panorama, enriched with dialogue, characterization, and incidents imported directly from the Missouri hills'. The reviewer declared the movie, 'the best screen entertainment of the year (as of Friday, Jan 13)', something of a minor accolade. Again, *Variety* worried about the 'drastic bleaching' of the outlaw, noting, 'some circles may not like youngsters to get such an impression of an historical bad man'. But, more importantly, the movie intersected with the sentiments of the time. The Robin Hood qualities of Jesse James, his fight for the poor against the ogre of Northern business, appealed to the average punter in the midst of the Depression era. Jesse James had something to say to contemporary society. The movie proved a huge hit.[31]

By the 1950s, the romancing of James had digressed into outrageous fantasy. *Jesse James' Women* (1954) portrayed the outlaw as 'an irresistible ladies' man,' all snappy dressing and testosterone. The sexual allure of the outlaw seemed far more important than his personal history. The promotional poster showed two women fighting over Jesse, with the tag line reading, 'The battle of the sexes and sixes rages across the lusty West!' Allegedly, 'Women WANTED him . . . more than the law'. *The New York Times* responded in predictably nauseous wit, 'Perhaps this cheap caricature of a picture will become aware of its grubbiness and will quietly go away.' *The True Story of Jesse James* (1957) had more of a revisionist edge, but by the inappropriate casting of young actors ultimately played to a James Dean audience. The search for novelty reached its apogee in *Jesse James Meets Frankenstein's Daughter* (1966). The pitting of 'Roaring Guns Against Raging Monster' promised a certain inventiveness in the folklore tradition, but by collapsing geography and chronology in the process. The desperation of film-makers to make the outlaw relevant in 1950's McCarthyist America by reference to sex, youth and horror only partly succeeded.[32]

By the mid-1960s, Hollywood had produced over forty motion pictures tackling the Jesse James legend. Along with his brother Frank James, Billy the Kid, the Dalton Gang and lawmakers such as Wyatt Earp, Jesse James served as a stock character in Westerns. Creative impulses waned. In response to *The True Story of Jesse James*, *Variety* noted how, 'On celluloid Jesse James has had more lives than a cat', but that, 'just about every angle has been covered'. Hoping for the ghost

The Western Renaissance

NOTABLE MOVIE PRODUCTIONS BASED AROUND JESSE JAMES

The James Boys in Missouri (1908)
Jesse James Under the Black Flag (1921) star: Jesse James Jr.
Jesse James as the Outlaw (1921) star: Jesse James Jr.
Jesse James (1927) star: Fred Thomson
Jesse James (1939) star: Tyrone Power
Jesse James at Bay (1941) star: Roy Rogers
Jesse James Rides Again (1947) star: Clayton Moore
I Shot Jesse James (1949) star: Reed Hadley
Jesse James' Women (1954) star: Don 'Red' Barry
The True Story of Jesse James (1957) star: Robert Wagner
Hell's Crossroads (1957) star: Henry Brandon
Alias Jesse James (1959) star: Wendell Corey
Young Jesse James (1960) star: Ray Stricklyn
Jesse James Meets Frankenstein's Daughter (1966) star: John Lupton
The Great Northfield Minnesota Raid (1972) star: Robert Duvall
The Long Riders (1980) star: James Keach
Frank and Jesse (1995) star: Rob Lowe
American Outlaws (2001) star: Colin Farrell
The Assassination of Jesse James by the Coward Robert Ford (2007) star: Brad Pitt

♦ Notable Television Appearances of 'Jesse James' ♦

You Are There (1953): 'The Capture of Jesse James' (James played by James Dean)
Stories of the Century (1954): 'Frank and Jesse James' (James played by Lee Van Cleef)
Bronco (1960): 'Shadow of Jesse James' (James played by James Coburn)
The Legend of Jesse James (1965) TV series (James played by Christopher Jones)
The Last Days of Frank and Jesse James (1986) TV movie (James played by Kris Kristofferson)

Figure 9.2 Jesse James movies.

of James to disappear, *Variety* requested that film-makers 'let him roll over and play dead for real and reel'. Similarly, *The New York Times* bemoaned, 'About the last thing anybody might expect these days is a well-made film about that saddle-sore screen varmint Jesse James.' The reviewer posed the pertinent question, 'What in thunder can be said about old Jesse that hasn't been said before?'.[33]

Finally, in 2007, Andrew Dominik provided a new take on the James saga. Rather than document the various bank robberies of the James gang, or fantasise about Brad Pitt as a love interest, *The Assassination of Jesse James by the Coward Robert Ford* explored the motivations for Ford murdering his outlaw ally. Despite the dime novel quality of the movie title, *Assassination* was all about realism. As actor Brad Pitt divulged, 'I wasn't interested in doing a straightforward, shoot-em up western because that's been done really well before – this is different.' While usually presented as a desire for money, *Assassination* deviated from convention (and perhaps the historical record) by focusing on jealousy and obsession as the primary motivations for Ford's actions.[34]

The craving of Bob Ford to be as famous as Jesse James gave the film a welcome contemporary relevance. James served as the celebrity, Ford assumed the role of the stalker. In this light, Brad Pitt seemed perfectly cast as the star caught by his fame, and hijacked by his fans. Expert on all things Hollywood, *Entertainment Weekly* applauded this approach, noting: 'Stories about the loneliness of celebrity and the danger of firearms rarely get starker or more mesmerizing than that.' The relationship between James and Ford proved pivotal to the film. Like *Brokeback Mountain*, the movie explored the close bonds between men. The attraction verged on homosexuality, with Ford looking on at James in the bathtub, and James pondering the source of the attraction. James uttered aloud, 'I can't figure out: do you want to be like me, or do you want to be me?' For some, the relationship had religious connotations. Jesse James represented a (wildly unconventional) Jesus, with Ford cast as Judas. The *Times Literary Supplement* recognised in the movie, 'a study of a false messiah, and his doting but treacherous apostle'. The powers of myth seemed to reach even spiritual quarters.[35]

Rather than a classic Western, Pitt saw the movie as 'more a psychological drama, a psychotic breakdown than anything'. The musing on death certainly gave the piece an existential quality. The sense of tragedy won comparisons with classical, rather than Western, examples. *Variety* declared *Assassination*, 'A ravishing, magisterial, poetic epic that moves its characters toward their tragic destinies with all the implacability of a Greek drama.' *The New York Times* summarised, 'It's the beautiful bad man, knowing and doomed, awaiting his fate like some Greco-Hollywood hero, rather than the psychotic racist of historical record.' *Entertainment Weekly* applauded the 'elegiacally fatalistic tone' of the movie. Certainly, something new had been achieved in the filmic James legacy. According to *The Times*, *Assassination* differed greatly from past incarnations: it was 'like none of them'.[36]

The Assassination of Jesse James by the Coward Robert Ford was none the less a Western by convention. It sported wide, open spaces, freedom, death and tumbleweed. In pondering the fascination of Ford with James, Dominik had made a psychological Western likened to 1970's pictures such as Robert Altman's *McCabe and Mrs. Miller* (1971) and Sam Peckinpah's *Pat Garrett and Billy the Kid* (1973) by movie reviewers.

The movie also drew on the old folklore of James. *Assassination* focused on an already deeply mythologised scene in the canon: the death of the outlaw hero. One hundred years earlier, John Newman Edwards, the Hon. J. A. Dacus, Lige Mitchell and Jesse James Jr had all covered the event in detail. James' leaving of his pistols on the bed, his dusting of a picture, the shot from behind, the fleeing of the Ford brothers and Zee comforting her husband in her arms, were all well documented. Dacus provided a map of the crime scene in his book. James Junior described the crowds gathered to say goodbye to a folk hero. Edwards, in particular, took the killing of his Southern saviour personally, writing in the Sedalia *Democrat*, 'There never was a more cowardly and unnecessary murder committed in all America than this murder of Jesse James.' Edwards continued, 'if a single one of the miserable assassins had either manhood, conscience, or courage, he would go, as another Judas, and hang himself.' *Assassination* exploited this scene, adding new psychological depth to the so-called 'cowardly act'. The sense of inevitable doom and death in the movie also made it a classic Western. As Jane Tompkins related, from the arid landscape to the skulls and bullets, 'Death is everywhere in this genre.'[37]

Compared with past pictures, *The Assassination of Jesse James by the Coward Robert Ford* represented a return to realism for the James phenomena. Other than Robert Ford, there were no Frankensteins in the picture. CNN warmed to the 'reflective and self-conscious piece of mythic revisionism'. On some level, Dominik realised that in order for the Jesse James legend to remain alive, the myth had to seem convincing. It also had to fit the desires of a twenty-first century audience. *Assassination* took the James story in fashionable directions by its exploration of celebrity culture, religious iconography, social/psychological realism and crime interest. One review praised how such an enviable 'mélange of show-business, religion and crime is what makes both book and movie uniquely American'. Other neo-Westerns ventured similar engagements with contemporary social and political issues. *No Country for Old Men* captured a bleak view of criminality, violence and drug trafficking on the borders. The remake of *3:10 to Yuma* added a scene of torture, quickly taken by film critics as a reference to Abu Ghraib. *Brokeback Mountain* spoke to the debate over gay rights and same-sex marriage in America. The filmic cowboy had become an unexpected avatar for celebrity stalking, the narcotics trade, human rights and homophobia. Or was it that unexpected? Looking back on the Hollywood Western, *The New York Times* granted the format a quasi-historic mission in its continual soul-searching: 'They were part of the messy, improvisational process by which Americans define – and revise, and define again – a national self-image, and one of the many reasons to regret the demise of westerns is that without them it's just a little tougher for us to figure out who we are.' Apparently, the cowboy did have something to say in twenty-first century America.[38]

Notes

1. Edison Films Catalog, No. 200, January 1904 (Library of Congress).
2. Janet Walker (ed.), *Westerns: Films Through History* (New York: Routledge, 2001), pp. 9, 10; Jane Tompkins, *West of Everything: The Inner Life of Westerns* (New York: Oxford University Press, 1992), p. 8. Also see: John Cawelti, *The Six-Gun Mystique Sequel* (Bowling Green: Bowling Green University Popular Press, 1999).
3. Richard Slotkin, *Gunfighter Nation: The Myth of the Frontier in Twentieth Century America* (New York: Atheneum, 1992), p. 278; Hayden White: discussed in Walker, p. 8; Walker p. 13.
4. Frederick Elkin, 'The psychological appeal of the Hollywood Western', *Journal of Educational Sociology*, vol. 24, No. 2 (October, 1950), pp. 72–86.
5. Michael Coyne, *The Crowded Prairie: American National Identity in the Hollywood Western* (London: I. B. Tauris, 1997), pp. 68–9; Stephen McVeigh, *The American Western* (Edinburgh: Edinburgh University Press, 2007), p. 87; Coyne, p. 162; *Wild Bunch*: see Coyne, pp. 147–62.
6. Carl Platinga, 'Spectacles of death: Clint Eastwood and violence in "Unforgiven",' *Cinema Journal*, vol. 37, No. 2 (Winter, 1998), pp. 65–83; McVeigh (2007), pp. 202–12; John Saunders, *The Western Genre: From Lordsburg to Big Whiskey* (London: Wallflower, 2001), pp. 115–24.
7. Robert Bookman (Creative Artists Agency): Bernard Weinraub, 'The talk of Hollywood; Hollywood recycles the Western to offer new heroes: women', *The*

New York Times, 3 May 1993; James Ryan, 'Shoot-out at the P.C. corral', *Vogue* (July 1993), pp. 68–70.
8. Wyatt Earp (1994) cost approximately $63 million, but only accumulated $25 million at the US box office; Smith: 'In Hollywood, venerable Western rides again', MSNBC, 6 September 2007; Mick LaSalle, 'Costner rustles up some clichés in new Western', *San Francisco Chronicle*, 15 August 2003; Peter Travers, 'Open Range Review', *Rolling Stone*, 14 August 2003; Costner: Ryan Dilley, 'Is it High Noon for the western?', *BBC News*, 25 September 2003; 'In Hollywood', MSNBC.
9. Rainer: Ben Hoyle, 'Western revival looks back to simpler life', *The Times* (online), 30 July 2007; Paul Andrew Hutton, 'Western promises: once again, Hollywood straps on its six-shooters and saddles up', *The Boston Globe*, 30 September 2007; Christopher Goodwin, 'The Wilder bunch', *The Sunday Times*, 29 July 2007.
10. Diana Ossana, 'Climbing Brokeback Mountain', in Annie Proulx, Larry McMurtry, and Diana Ossana, *Brokeback Mountain: Story to Screenplay* (London: Harper, 2005), p. 147; Annie Proulx, 'Getting movied', in *Brokeback Mountain* (2005), p. 137.
11. Chris Packard, *Queer Cowboys: And Other Erotic Male Friendships in Nineteenth-Century American Literature* (London: Macmillan, 2005), p. 7.
12. Lee: Lee (2): Kirsty Lang, 'It's not a gay movie', *The Independent*, 16 December 2005; Ossana (2005), p. 146; Proulx (2005), pp. 129, 137.
13. Larry McMurtry and Diana Ossana, 'Brokeback Mountain: a screenplay', in *Brokeback Mountain: Story to Screenplay* (2005), p. 1.
14. Tompkins (1992), p. 19; Lang (2005).
15. Tompkins (1992), p. 40.
16. Proulx (2005), p. 130; Hiram Perez, 'Gay cowboys close to home: Ennis Del Mar on the Q.T.', in Jim Stacy (ed.), *Reading Brokeback Mountain: Essays on the Story and the Film* (Jefferson: McFarland, 2007), p. 77; Jen Boyle, '"When this thing grabs hold of us . . .": spatial myth, rhetoric, and conceptual blending', in *Brokeback Mountain*', (2007), p. 97.
17. Richard White, 'Brokeback Mountain: A Western', *Montana: The Magazine of Western History* 56/2 (Summer 2006), pp. 65–6; Tompkins (1992), p. 3.
18. Bill Gallo, 'Homo on the range', *Dallas Observer*, 15 December 2005; David Stalling, 'Yes, some hunters are gay', *High Country News*, 20 February 2006. On press reactions, see Daniel Mendelsohn, 'An affair to remember', *The New York Review of Books*, 53/3 (23 February 2006); Robert Ordona, 'Brokeback Mountain: as gay as it gets: an interview with Ang Lee', Gay.com, 29 March 2006; Peter Hartlaub and Carolyne Zinko, 'Theories abound on why "Crash" beat "Brokeback",' *San Francisco Chronicle*, 7 March 2006. See also: Charles Eliot Mehler, '*Brokeback Mountain* at the Oscars', in *Brokeback Mountain* (2007), pp. 135–51.
19. Stalling (2006); David Carr, 'Los Angeles retains custody of Oscar', *The New York Times*, 7 March 2006. On masculinity in the West more broadly, see Matthew Basso, Laura McCall and Dee Garceau, (eds), *Across the Great Divide: Cultures of Manhood in the American West* (New York: Routledge, 2001).
20. Robert Hine, *The American West: An Interpretive History* (Boston: Little, Brown, 1973), p. 136; Alfred Kinsey et al., *Sexual Behavior in the Human Male* (Philadelphia: Saunders, 1948), p. 457; Eric Patterson, *On Brokeback Mountain: Meditations About Masculinity, Fear, and Love in the Story and the Film*

(Lanham: Lexington Books, 2008), p. 109. For a classic view of the cowboy on the range, see Philip Ashton Rollins, *The Cowboy: An Unconventional History of Civilization on the Old-Time Cattle Range* (Albuquerque: University of New Mexico Press, 1936 [1922]).
21. Ossana (2005), p. 145; Dennis Hinkamp, 'Is Brokeback Mountain about the West? Sort of', *High Country News*, 6 February 2006.
22. Hutton (2007).
23. Recent biographical histories of Jesse James include: Robert Dyer, *Jesse James and the Civil War in Missouri* (Columbia: University of Missouri Press, 1994) and T. J. Stiles, *Jesse James: Last Rebel of the Civil War* (London: Jonathan Cape, 2003). Also useful: Harold Dellinger, *Jesse James: The Best Writings on the Notorious Outlaw and His Gang* (Guilford: Globe Pequot press, 2007).
24. Edwards, *Kansas City Times*, in Clive Sinclair, 'After Blue Cut', *Times Literary Supplement*, 21/28 (December 2007).
25. John N. Edwards, *Noted Guerillas, or the Warfare of the Border* (St Louis: Bryan, Brand, 1877), pp. 19, 15, 167–8, 450.
26. Hon. J. A. Dacus, *Life and Adventures of Frank and Jesse James: The Noted Western Outlaws* (Indianapolis: Fred Horton, 1880), pp. 1, 107; Frank Triplett, *The Life, Times and Treacherous Death of Jesse James* (Stamford: Longmeadow, 1992 [1882]).
27. Jesse James Jr, *Jesse James, My Father* (Independence: Sentinel, 1899), pp. 3, 4; Lige Mitchell, *Daring Exploits of Jesse James and His Band of Border Train and Bank Robbers* (Baltimore: Ottenheimer, 1912), p. 34; Also see Robertus Love, *The Rise and Fall of Jesse James* (New York: Putnams, 1926).
28. W. B. Lawson, *Jesse James, The Outlaw: A Narrative of the James Boys*, 1 (New York: Street & Smith, 1901), p. 3; James fits the 'outlaw hero' type as described by Graham Seal in *The Outlaw Legend: A Cultural Tradition in Britain, America and Australia* (Cambridge: Cambridge University Press, 1996), p. 11; Christopher Anderson, 'Jesse James, the bourgeois bandit: the transformation of a popular hero', *Cinema Journal*, 26/1 (Autumn, 1986), p. 44.
29. Frank Wiesberg, *Variety*, 23 April 1908.
30. *Variety*, 19 October 1927; *The New York Times*, Film Reviews, 17 October 1927, 20/2.
31. Film script, *Jesse James*, 'Revised Treatment', dated 28 March 1938 (20th Century Fox) [held by Braun Research Library]; Jason Joy to Darryl F. Zanuck, 'Jesse James', Twentieth-Century-Fox Film Corporation correspondence, dated 29 March 1938 [held by Braun Research Library]; *The New York Times*, Film Reviews, 14 January 1939, 13/1; *Variety*, 10 January 1939.
32. *Los Angeles Times* review quoted in Buck Rainey, *Western Gunslingers in Fact and on Film: Hollywood's Famous Lawmen and Outlaws* (Jefferson: McFarland, 1998), p. 93; Bruce Hershenson, *Cowboy Movie Posters* (West Plains, 1995); *The New York Times*, Film Reviews, 29 September 1954, 23/4.
33. *Variety*, 20 February 1957; *The New York Times*, Film Reviews, 23 March 1957, 17/2.
34. John Hiscock, 'Brad Pitt: what I share with Jesse James', *Telegraph*, 24 October 2007.
35. Lisa Schwarzbaum, 'The assassination of Jesse James', *Entertainment Weekly*, 19 September 2007; Sinclair (2007).

The Western Renaissance

36. 'In Hollywood', MSNBC; *Variety*, 31 August 2007; Manohla Dargis, 'Good, bad or ugly: a legend shrouded in gunsmoke remains hazy', *The New York Times*, 21 September 2007; Schwarzbaum (2007); Sinclair (2007).
37. John N. Edwards, 'The killing of Jesse James', Sedalia *Democrat*, April 1881, reprinted in John N. Edwards, *Biography, Memoirs, Reminiscences and Recollections* (Kansas City: Jennie Edwards, 1889), pp. 163–5; Tompkins (1992), p. 24.
38. Tom Charity, 'Jesse James different, terrific', CNN, 21 September 2007; Sinclair (2007); Terrence Rafferty, 'Jesse James, an outlaw for all seasons', *The New York Times*, 16 September 2007.

Chapter 10

The Arcade Western

In 1982, US brand Atari had its most successful year in the videogame business. Recalling Atari 2600 home consoles selling in droves, programmer Chris Crawford remarked, 'It's difficult to convey the wild gold rush feeling that pervaded the industry that year.' Every family seemed to want a 2600 at Christmas. Then, all of a sudden, the bubble burst. The software market collapsed due to an unexpected fall in consumer interest. Atari personnel buried unsold cartridges in a landfill in New Mexico, close to Alamogordo and Trinity nuclear test site. A myth fostered by computer geeks told of a 'Great Mass Burial' out in the desert. That personnel buried *ET: The Extra-Terrestrial* (1982) cartridges (based on the Steven Spielberg movie) within driving distance of the UFO mecca of Roswell gave added license to the story. The desert West – in the popular imagination, a realm of dried bison bones, Indian reservations, ghost towns and nuclear testing – seemed a dumping ground, a wasteland once again: this time for the silicon age.[1]

Although Atari never fully recovered from the crash of 1983, the computer chip itself weathered the storms of consumer demand and technological revolution. In the American West, the chip has made life more liveable and more entertaining. Tiny microprocessors control air conditioning in Phoenix, switch on neon lights in Las Vegas and monitor seismic tremors along the San Andreas Fault. Where nineteenth-century pioneers built homes and kindled fires using dried buffalo chips, twenty-first-century Westerners design solar cells and virtual cities with computer hardware. The microprocessor has revolutionised the West Coast entertainment industry. Wandering the glitzy spectacle of the Electronic Entertainment Exposition (E3) computer show in Los Angeles in 1999, *Mother Jones* contributor Paul Keegan reached the startling conclusion that Silicon Valley had begun to compete with Tinseltown. In terms of financial backing and cultural cachet, the computer (or video) game now vies with the modern Hollywood movie.[2]

Since the production of the first commercial arcade machine *Computer Space* by Nutting Associates in 1971, thousands of videogames have been released, each featuring a wide spectrum of backdrops and themes. Ranked in terms of total sales, the contribution of the 'arcade Western' to the videogame market is marginal. Around one hundred known titles venture a distinctly Western theme. However, a significant number emerged at the outset of the videogame era – and, thus, pioneered new play mediums (for example, the gun-shooting, or Western shooter genre), new technology (released in 1975, *Gun Fight* featured the first microprocessor in an arcade machine), and introduced Americans to videogames for the first time. Some have proved very successful, such as *Desperados*, released for the PC by Infogrames in 2001. Western games equally courted public controversy, with Mystique's adult videogame *Custer's Revenge* (1983) a common entry on lists of both the worst and most offensive games of all time.[3]

This chapter explores the cultural significance of videogames that employ the American West as their setting. It looks at their simulation of the Old West, fixation with frontier violence, aesthetic presentation of the region, and lastly, recent forays into New West realms with driving and sports titles. The chapter thus interweaves a basic history of Western videogames with commentary on four key elements of the digital West: simulation; violence; landscape; and tourism. Of central interest here is the idea of a new digital genre, the arcade Western that draws on established tropes of entertainment and myth-making in the West, as well as how competing visions of the West play out in the medium.[4]

Simulating the West

Videogames are about simulation. The majority of titles recreate everyday experiences from walking and talking to driving automobiles and playing sports. Some titles offer historic markers so that players can negotiate new virtual worlds more easily. Along with the Second World War, the nineteenth-century American West proved a popular 'past' for players to visit.

In the 1970s, the early days of videogame history, a number of key titles employed popular motifs of the Old American West to rouse consumer interest in the new gaming medium. Rather than provide digital takes on modern technological society, pioneer arcade machines such as *Boot Hill* (Midway, 1977) offered ephemeral escapes to a 'simpler' world of six-shooters, wagon convoys, and iron horses. The glorious 'frontier West' – as presented by Western artists such as Frederic Remington, fiction writers such as Zane Grey and Hollywood directors such as John Ford – was fed into the modern computer and spat out in pixel form. The videogame (and therefore the digital West) thus replicated past canvas, paper and celluloid dramas. Game titles regurgitated 'old West' myths and cheap novella fiction. In essence, the digital West started out as simulacra of simulacra.

Central to the recreation of frontier life in a digital domain has been the re-animation of classic heroes and villains. Setting out to capture a deeply mythological West via the computer chip, videogame designers in the 1970s and 1980s re-animated non pareil figures of Western folklore as game characters. The shooting game *Cheyenne* (Exidy, 1984) featured a roster of jocular pretend villains and legendary Wild West heroes with which to engage. The fictitious, burlesque 'Petticoat Floozies' of Lotta Love and Elvira rubbed shoulders with the Dalton Gang, while tomahawk-throwing 'Apache Braves' included Geronimo and Sitting Bull alongside Running Nose and Buffalo Breath. Characters abided by cultural stereotypes popularised in nineteenth-century Western art, dime novels and twentieth-century Hollywood celluloid. Digital women behaved as sultry lovers, gartered prostitutes, or sassy gun-fighters in the image of Calamity Jane. Overwhelmingly, the dominant male protagonists were White cowboys, with Mexicans relegated to the role of corrupt banditos and African-Americans notable only by their absence. Buffalo Bill appeared as an adept gun-slinging nemesis of Sheriff Quickdraw in the computer game *Gun Fright* (Ultimate, 1986), the two men battling for patriarchal control over the imaginary frontier town of Black Rock. It mattered little that one character in *Gun Fright* was purely fictional, the other based (at least in name) on an historic figure. As long as the gaming environment resembled public expectations of the old 'Wild West' and, thus, included its fair share of cowboys, outlaws and Indians, the authenticity of the simulation could be overlooked. After all, nobody had deserted Western-themed Frontierland in Disneyland, California due to its historical inaccuracy.

The presence of Buffalo Bill as a character in a digital Western fantasy seemed eminently just. The 'real' William Frederick Cody had, after all, sponsored a merger of fact and fiction in his celebrated Wild West live shows at the end of the nineteenth century. One hundred years

The Arcade Western

later the videogame excelled in a similar enterprise. Cody recognised in the West a raw excitement absent from 'civilised' Eastern states and European countries. Blending explosive action with frontier and imperialist nostalgia, Cody recreated, with consummate artistic licence, mail-coach ambushes, train rides through unfriendly Indian country and historic events such as the Battle of the Little Big Horn. His theatrical productions travelled the world, underlining the American West as an experience readily consumed by a global audience. The shows were spectacular, varied and, above all, action-packed. As Thomas Altherr noted, 'Most customers must have left the arena seats satisfied, having witnessed a full variety of western Americana.' Despite his own involvement in various frontier enterprises and a benevolent attitude toward Native Americans behind the scenes, Cody's interpretation of Western history betrayed remarkable flaws. Cody presented the bullet as the maker of the West, sidelining the contribution of the plough and the dollar to Euro-American progress. As noted by historian Richard White, Cody popularised a highly questionable narrative of inverted frontier conquest in his shows. Always the victims of Indian aggression, Cody's Anglo-Saxon cowboys suffered few pangs of guilt as they blasted their way out of trouble.[5]

This conscience-free conception of frontier life filtered into Western-themed videogames. Titles such as *Blood Bros.* (Tad, 1990) encouraged players to casually massacre digital Indians without rebuke or consequence. With his feather bonnet, war dance and tepee, the pixel Native resembled the classic Plains Indian stereotype captured in Cody's show-business extravaganza. The videogame simulation of the West readily mimicked Cody's simulated 'Wild West' bonanza. Game machines in arcades across London, New York and San Francisco staged elaborate and familiar fights between 'whooping Injuns' and all-conquering cowboys, cities where once 'real-life' Wild West shows had entertained. Like Cody, game designers recognised the global marketability of gunfighter glory, presenting the American West as an exciting and exotic mélange of six-shooters, wild horses, cowboys and Indians. Both entertainment genres offered viewers the opportunity to experience high noon shenanigans and feel part of the West. On several counts, the arcade machine emerged as the late twentieth-century 'pardner' to Buffalo Bill's Wild West.

Arcade Westerns further realised a dime novel presentation of the West rich in adventure but bereft of realism. Mass-produced 25-cent arcade machines served as the interactive dime novels of the 1970s and 1980s by bestowing affordable and accessible figments of Western reverie to all classes. Both the videogame and the cheap novella provided simplistic, sensational stories of loveable outlaws and Indian peril, heavily steeped in caricature but light in originality. Shrewdly identified by Henry Nash Smith, the 'objectified mass dream' of Western adventure offered within every dime novel had an audience. Such a dream transferred easily onto the computer screen.[6]

As a predominantly visual medium, the videogame also took its cue from the Hollywood movie. Intriguingly, the Western videogame arrived during a lull in the Western movie franchise. Marking the end of the Western filmic period, John Wayne's *The Shootist* (1976) and Clint Eastwood's *The Outlaw Josey Wales* (1976) coincided with the debut of Midway's shooting game *Gun Fight*. The videogame West began where those movies left off. Gun fights and sagebrush simply shifted mediums from one screen to the next, heroes and anti-heroes moving from one stage to the other. A global cognition of cowboys and Indians allowed Japanese and American game companies to produce an array of Western titles that could be easily digested by players. The familiar format of the celluloid Western enabled the new digital West to be realised.[7]

Videogame designers exploited a populist, international understanding of American history and iconography based around Hollywood. They simulated an already simulated West that was comprehended by all. The arcade Western built on the reputation of its luminary forebears in the entertainment industry. Game worlds imitated film sets, with computer characters walking into 'camera' view before delivering pre-coded scripts and actions. Game designers followed filmic conventions laid down by Westerns such as *Stagecoach* (1939) and *High Noon* (1952) by presenting familiar scenes of ambushes, chases and grand finale shoot-outs. The 'Western shooter', in the guise of *Gun Fight* and *Blood Bros.*, brought tangible involvement in 'winning the West' on a scale long desired by cinema audiences. While theatre attendees thrilled at an outlaw firing in their direction in *The Great Train Robbery* (1903), arcade devotees relished the ability to not only dodge the bullet, but also shoot back in *Cheyenne*. The audience finally had a role to play – victory over the West was theirs to be had. Games borrowed heavily from cinematic Old West nostalgia and Hollywood's partisan exploration of 'How the West was won'. The good and evil dichotomy rife in John Wayne movies re-emerged in game lore. Like the motion picture, the computer game rarely explored the middle ground between victory and loss. The simulation was simple in its politics.

What the Wild West show, dime novel and Hollywood Western had portrayed, the videogame reproduced. Games followed the rules laid down by prior simulations of the 'Old West', drawing on the same character types and good versus evil narratives. Nineteenth-century dime novels portrayed the frontier as a romantic realm of action, while movie directors derived from the Western experience musicals such as *Paint Your Wagon* (1969) and comedies including *Blazing Saddles* (1973). The game equally cast the West as entertainment. The core purpose of simulation emerged as amusement, not realism. A natural extension of the imagined world formulated in Hollywood and in fiction writers' lobbies, the videogame West deviated little from an established script. Players followed the rules on screen, participating in an old and familiar drama.[8]

Violence on the Electronic Frontier

Given the restrictions in computer technology through the 1970s and 1980s, games designers always had to choose which parts of Western folklore to assert. Meager computer memory and poor graphical capabilities compromised their vision. Many early titles reproduced movie scenes of wagon train hi-jinx and downtown duels in the simplest of forms. Plot details, overarching stories and character depth were all sacrificed in order to limit computer memory expenditure. Narrative was compromised in preference to action. This programming choice reflected the 'pick up and play' notion of gaming – after all, few wanted to spend hours in a dimly lit arcade reading text. Action also served as the prime rationale of the game itself. Titles encouraged quick response times with early videogames fostering trigger (or joystick) itch among their clientele.

Action also meant that the digital West *differed* in one crucial way from previous canvas, paper and celluloid Wests. Unlike dime novels and Hollywood Westerns, where immersion derived mostly from imagination and observation, the digital West demanded physical interaction from its guests. While Western movies may have inspired children to play 'cowboys and Indians' in school playgrounds, with the videogame the audience had no choice but to be active participants in the great Western drama. Immersion came through direct play rather than through observation. In this way, the videogame paralleled the theme park more than the movie house. However, in contrast to Disney's family-friendly take on the West, where innocent settlers and happy endings predominated, the arcade Western highlighted confrontation as the *modus operandi* of the frontier endeavour. The digital West (arguably mimicking the development of the mythic West) emerged as a place structured and given meaning by violence. Action in the game almost always meant hostile exchange.

In 1975, American manufacturer Midway released the first Western-themed arcade machine, *Gun Fight*. Sporting a dark wood grain appropriate to old saloon furniture, *Gun Fight* hid its technological roots and seemed out of place in neon-lit arcades. Its closest rival, and influence, was the Western-themed shooting gallery, where players queued up to take pot shots at ducks and other targets, sometimes for token prizes. The shooting gallery had proved a staple of seaside resorts, fairgrounds and amusement parks. An accompanying game poster for *Gun Fight*, with two hand-drawn cowboys in the midst of a shootout, resembled a dime novel front cover in its lurid promotion of live action and deadly confrontation. Following somewhat superfluous machine instructions to 'Kill your opponent before he kills you', arcade attendees faced off against each other on a monochrome screen. Thereupon, White cowboys, several thorny cacti and fast-moving wagon trains gathered on screen. Rather than memorising complex instructions or game mechanics, players drew on ingrained notions of cowboy action, knowing instinctively how to act on-screen. Two pistol handles rather than joysticks delivered an authentic feel of weaponry, as well as pioneering the use of replica guns in videogames (a controversial staple of the shooter genre in recent years). The West of *Gun Fight* existed as realm of violence without explanation, without context, almost without meaning. Players shot each other for points. Cody's showmanship and Clint Eastwood's deadly accuracy re-materialised in Western shooters such as *Gun Fight*. This reductive yet purist vision of the 'old West' was embraced by gamers and *Gun Fight* (as well as its successor *Boot Hill*) became bona fide collectors' items. *Gun Fight* also established a template for one of the oldest genres of videogame entertainment, the 'Western shooter', and with it, the shooter videogame in general.[9]

In 1977, *Boot Hill* emerged as a direct successor to *Gun Fight*. Named after the first cemetery at Dodge City in the 1870s, *Boot Hill* encouraged players to imagine themselves as gunslingers entering the most violent town on the frontier. The game drew on the mythology of the place and its core identity based on violence and bloodshed. A computer-controlled cowboy, capable of outgunning most arcade newcomers, patrolled the screen, reminiscent of Yul Brynner's ruthless android gunslinger in Michael Crichton's movie *Westworld* (1973).

The Arcade Western

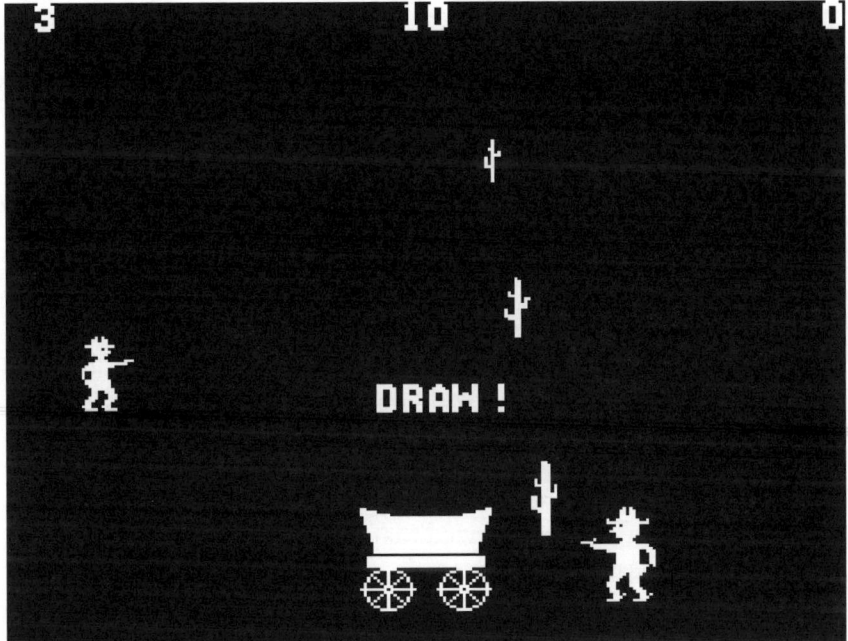

Figure 10.1 *Boot Hill*, 1977.

Boot Hill paralleled robots running amok in the frontier theme park of *Westworld* by employing a computer character similarly disposed to impersonating and killing its human counterparts. Pixel cowboys, identical to those featured in *Gun Fight*, uttered 'Bam. Shot Me' when hit in *Boot Hill*, their bodies rising up to the heavens (or the top of the screen), before turning into pure white tombstones. In keeping with the folklore of Dodge City's quick-draw duels, 'dead' game characters kept their boots on en route to the cemetery. A somber computer recital of the *Death March* tune accompanied each trip to the Hill. With only a wagon and a cactus between two trigger-happy contestants, on-screen encounters proved notoriously short-lived. Arcade players competed for the highest kill tally, their anonymous victims identified as simple numbers at the top of the screen. Not surprisingly, five-minute sessions on *Boot Hill* exceeded the total body count for Dodge City over its entire history.[10]

While representing only a small percentage of the arcade titles on offer at the time, the 1970s Arcade Western cemented an expectation of violence in electronic games. Reflecting its popular literary and filmic roots, the videogame relied on the palpable myth of the 'lone gunfighter' as its pivotal narrative. Recognising their target audience as adolescent and twenty-something males, electronics companies recreated the classic outlaw with attitude on screen, providing digital imitations of John Wayne in *Stagecoach* (1939) and Clint Eastwood in *A Fistful of Dollars* (1964). With a few dimes in their pockets, gamers indulged their Western fantasies, playing renegade cowboys inside city arcades in palatable, five-minute doses. Videogames transformed the stereotypical computer geek into the archetypal rugged individualist, the young player into Billy the Kid. Prolonged game play fostered a 'go it alone' mentality pertinent to the myth of the solo gunfighter, and conducive to an entertainment medium focused on the performance of the individual player. By inserting a coin into the Western shooter, players purchased the opportunity to see themselves as the last good cowboy or remaining soldier in a whirlwind on-screen adventure. The draw of being the last of an honourable breed of masculine heroes showed that the West retained currency as a redemptive crusade.[11]

Customary paperback and celluloid themes of law and order, frontier justice and the combating of violence with violence rose to dominance in the arcade Western. Prior to the advent of the electronic shooting game, dime novels, Wild West shows and celluloid Westerns (such as *The Wild Bunch*, 1969) had cast the American frontier as a mythic landscape marked by confrontation and killing. As Richard Slotkin explained, tied up with regeneration, nationhood and individualism, violence had always played its part in 'frontier psychology'. Conditioned into thinking of cowboys as gunmen and Indians as warmongers, arcade clientele expected videogames set in the West to offer their fair share of confrontation. Most companies responded with raucous action-based titles that presented the frontier as one continual showdown. Success in *Wanted* (Sigma, 1984) rested on the quickest possible annihilation of every human protagonist, the length of each game 'level' determined by a pre-set kill tally. *Gunsmoke* (Capcom, 1985) provided an overhead view of an unfriendly frontier town, with the player controlling a stocky outlaw on his stroll through dusty streets, dispatching all and sundry with his trusty Winchester rifle. *Express Raider* (Data East, 1986) transposed frontier violence to the roof of a moving train, with players sparring with (rather than shooting) a motley crew of bandits, while punching inquisitive coyotes for extra points. Mimicking gun-blazing Wild West shootouts, game scenarios typically granted players little time to think, relying instead on automatic, instinctive bouts of trigger-itch.[12]

Two of the most violent titles were *Blood Bros.* and *Sunset Riders* (Konami, 1991). The inaugural boomtown level of *Blood Bros.* featured tin can targets, wooden saloons and well-dressed ladies, who responded to gunfire by lifting their petticoats. Reminiscent of false-front Hollywood movie sets, building façades collapsed to reveal monumental desert landscapes. With no hint of public outcry, one level consisted of massacring an Indian village, while another resembled Leatherstocking's clash with the Hurons at Glens Falls in James Fenimore Cooper's *The Last of the Mohicans* (1826). Hogs and horses, when shot, rewarded players with dynamite, guns and bonus points, unconsciously endorsing Richard White's theory of real-life Western fauna as 'animals of enterprise', or simple 'biological dollars'. From runaway trains to kamikaze cavalry squads, everything and everybody represented a legitimate target in *Blood Bros.* The Old West appeared decidedly self-destructive and amoral. The scrolling action game *Sunset Riders* continued in a similar vein. Players moved from left to right, jumping to avoid cattle stampedes (with the screen 'shaking' under their combined weight), retrieving liquor and damsels from saloons and challenging 'wanted' criminals who delivered digitised speeches. *Riders* relied on the Italian Western for inspiration, introducing its major game characters, Steve, Billy, Bob and Cormano, by way of a movie reel. The four gunmen rode off into the sunset in a poignant closing scene. As in the case of the Spaghetti Western, few were left alive in their wake.[13]

The most violent (and controversial) Western videogame, however, dealt with violence of a personal dimension, rather than mass killing. It dealt not with guns, but with sexual licence. A puerile attempt at titillation, *Custer's Revenge* (Mystique, 1983) released on the Atari 2600 console reincarnated George Armstrong Custer as a computer game character seeking retribution against the Sioux nation for his defeat at the Battle of the Little Big Horn. Assuming the role of Lieutenant Colonel Custer, players manoeuvred a large man, dressed only in a blue cavalry hat, scarf and boots, across the screen, avoiding falling arrows, before raping a naked squaw, tethered to a pole outside her smoking tepee. Rhythmic Native American drum pounding preceded a climatic cavalry bugle ditty. Women's groups (especially Women Against Pornography) and Native American organisations protested the game's release, and many stores refused to stock the title. However, the ensuing controversy boosted sales figures to some 80,000 units, roughly double that of other Mystique adult-targeted titles. *Custer's Revenge* shocked Americans by its graphic depictions of violent rape, as well as its divergence from traditional portraits of the formative westerly experience, in particular its perversion of the Last Stand mythology. While slaughtering Native Americans served as a legitimate reprisal trope in dime novels, Hollywood Westerns and computer games, Indian rape went beyond the boundaries of frontier envisioning. *Custer's Revenge* indicated that frontier violence had its own strict parameters of public acceptability. Massacres of bad guys and angry Indians proved welcome, yet violence in the form of rape was not of the traditional Western canon, and thus off-limits to game players. Custer, as war hero and national sacrifice, could not be seen with his boots on, but pants down. While the overwhelmingly negative response to *Custer's Revenge* could be seen to replicate broader public attitudes toward on-screen violence, the Western dimension was pronounced in the familiar treatment of the Native American as adversary and the enduring fascination with Custer as hero.[14]

Custer's Revenge underlined an industry focused on fleshing out only the idealised violence of the West and unwilling to engage responsibly with frontier history. However, not all Western titles were about unrestrained violence. A few titles resisted the temptation to exploit a 'shoot-first-and-ask-questions-later' model by forcing players at the very least to differentiate between friendly bystanders and quick-draw villains. Concepts of vigilante justice infused the game of *Cheyenne*. While tracking down 'Wanted' gangs such as the Daltons and the Petticoat Floozies, players discovered their duty to protect innocent bystanders from stray bullets. At the Last Dance Saloon, responsibilities stretched to defending drinkers from falling masonry and from a wild bar-busting bison that, once shot, transformed into a convenient bar snack. Meanwhile, *Bank Panic* (Sega, 1984) invited players to assume the duties of a sheriff named Hero, guarding a capacious bank from a never-ending queue of robbers. A dozen entry doors opened in quick succession to reveal a mixture of earnest male and female customers carrying dollar-filled bags and gun-slinging bandits eager to make cash withdrawals. Although the Dixie soundtrack and frontier costumes evoked an earlier historical period, *Bank Panic* resembled a modern-day target range with its pop-up two-dimensional figures. True to Western dictum, only by the hero outgunning his foe could law and order prevail over anarchy.

Midway's first Western shooter *Gun Fight* highlighted the attraction of videogame violence in the late 1970s, fifteen years prior to the advent of the controversial fighting game *Mortal Kombat* (Midway, 1992) and killing marathon *Doom* (Id, 1993). The Western videogame thus anticipated a greater craze of violence in gaming quarters. By the 1990s, the shooter genre borne from games such as *Cheyenne* had mutated into sophisticated three-dimensional titles based on massacring miscreants and zombies. In April 1999, Eric Harris and Dylan Klebold, both obsessive players of the three-dimensional shooter *Doom*, killed fifteen people at Columbine High School, Littleton, Colorado. In response, Senator Joseph Lieberman charged that computer entertainment glamourised killing. The videogame arguably abetted a cancerous culture of violence in American society. In a roundtable discussion in *The Western Historical Quarterly*, historians pondered the influence of the nineteenth-century West on breeding violent behaviour such as that shown at Columbine. Stewart Udall, Robert Dykstra, Michael Bellesiles, Paula Marks and Gregory Nobles all agreed that salient, romanticised images of frontier violence rarely derived from real events, heralding instead from media, politics and popular folklore. Videogames represented the latest in a series of entertainment forms to tap the mythic West, yet few noticed the abiding links between Western imagery, computer software titles and the promotion of gun culture. While arcade machines never relied on Wild West backdrops, a cowboys and Indians narrative contributed to a genre of interactivity predisposed towards shooting and killing. The imaginary Old West thus remained significant not only for its questionable presentation of nineteenth-century society, but also for its impact on contemporary values. Immersing players in a digitally-rendered Western story, *Gun Fight* overcame the limitations of its black and white game world by blurring the distinction between fiction and reality. Players were invited to take part in the violence on screen, to participate in killing rather than watch others at work. Hence, videogame shooters took the myth of a violent West one stage further than the dime novel and the Hollywood Western. Western shooters made on-screen killing in arcades an acceptable activity. Whether digital frontier violence can be blamed for anything more is contentious – however, the role of the Western shooter should be included in debates over the contribution of the mythic frontier to the promotion of violence.[15]

A Moving Image: Rendering the Digital West

As we already know, the Western shooter fused late twentieth-century technology with classic frontier visions. As primarily a visual medium, images on screen proved to be crucial to successfully melding new machinery with old ideas. Significantly, rendering the digital West rested on the construction of a recognisably Western landscape where the violence played out. Rugged cowboys, desert vistas and frontier town showdowns – all potent signifiers of the Old West – were swiftly created in digital facsimile and transferred to the modern arcade.

On both technological and mythological levels, the Old West provided ideal terrain for early videogame programmers. As Michael Johnson notes, the mythic, popular West has been forged not by historians, but by the 'real tailors . . . artists in visual media: painters, sculptors, filmmakers, and the like'. Definitive Technicolor images of 'the West' were in place prior to the advent of computer technology. Widely recognised Western iconography suited machines with limited graphical capabilities and game play options. With the image of the cowboy familiar to all, a simple pixel version generated few problems in terms of identification. Likewise, few could mistake a cactus. Moreover, the fame attached to the West aided its translation to the computer screen. With a lone pixel cactus signifying nature west of the Mississippi, *Gun Fight*'s terminally empty landscape exploited a common misconception of the American West as stark and desolate. Its monochrome screen suited the black and white morality of old Western movies, of do or die politics and right or wrong decision-making.[16]

New arcade technology in the early 1980s expanded the gaze of the Western shooter. Colour graphics brought an aesthetic richness to games. In contrast to the minimalist monochrome landscapes of *Gun Fight* and *Boot Hill*, Sigma's *Wanted* boasted tiered panoramic views of green bushes and distant sand-coloured mountains. Bursting with vibrant colours in an almost abstract composition, Sigma's Western portrait loosely resembled Georgia O'Keeffe's emotive paintings of New Mexico. The West in *Wanted* appeared alive, natural and fertile rather than sullied, inconsequential and dead. The virtual world resembled the literary landscape of Mary Austin's *The Land of Little Rain* (1903).

Colour videogames thereby captured a region in transition, boasting prelapsarian beauty alongside signs of human progress. Reprising its recurring role as a movie backdrop, Monument Valley dutifully served as a staple background for successive arcade titles. Titles such as *Wanted* were marked by an epic sense of scale and monumentalism. On-screen drama, full of colour and action, resembled Alfred R. Waud's explosive (albeit monochrome) engraving of *Custer's Last Fight* (1876) or Remington's defiant, survivalist painting of *The Last Stand* (1890). Players looked out on to a scene of great spectacle. As if translating diary entries by Lewis and Clark on inestimable, incredible numbers of deer, wolves and antelope, the computer West of the 1980s featured fauna in abundance. Cattle thundered across the screen, vultures hovered in the air, wild mustangs snorted and bleached bison bones littered the prairie. A signature of painter Charles Russell's romantic, eulogistic Montanan canvases, the buffalo skull attested to the harsh, testing qualities of the Western environment and the sorrowful, untimely passing of the frontier. Computer graphics likewise captured a bygone era of Euro-American discovery, reinventing a vanished West on screen, as well as tapping profligate cultural interest in wilderness. While early titles used relatively static images, by the mid-1980s, the digital West was marked by an immersive and dynamic landscape. Videogames projected the human West as a kaleidoscope of fast-moving frontier snapshots. In brief arcade bursts, gamers experienced an unbridled medley of boomtowns, pioneer industries and Old West paraphernalia.[17]

The gun replica game *Cheyenne* offered tangible encounters with classic frontier locales through the scope of a large black rifle. By firing at representative pictures hung in a gallery, players chose to visit the Last Dance Saloon, a dingy gold mine and even hitch a ride on a stagecoach. A stirring, bugle-led cavalry charge marked the onset of each stage. Last Dance Saloon featured glass-filling bartenders, animal trophies hanging on the wall and piano music in the background. The claustrophobic mine included rolling stock, shadowy villains and dimming lights that gradually led to a blackout broken only by gunfire. The stagecoach ride appropriately sped by with all manner of projectiles whizzing through the air (including bird droppings), while Apache Braves shouted 'paleface' when dispatched with pixel lead. With its lively sounds, detailed settings and great atmosphere, *Cheyenne* perfected the dramaturgy of the Old West.

The speed at which players tackled (and conquered) the Western frontier put even the fast moving emigrants of the California Gold Rush to shame. One image was replaced quickly with another, one frontier replaced with another. Predicated on motion and change, videogames with scrolling action scenes suited popular conceptions of frontier progress, and endorsed the centrality of the overland journey in American consciousness. Along with train-based titles *Wild Western* (Taito, 1982) and *Express Raider* (1986), *Iron Horse* (Konami, 1986) related the breakneck speed of geographical annexation. With desert scenery whizzing past in the background, players moved through successive carriages while engaging bandits in combat, hoping to thwart a hold-up of the US Pacific Railway in an allegorical battle for unfettered Western progress. Authentic sounds of steel wheels clanking on rail tracks promoted sensations of forward motion. Whistling tunes conjured images of steam rising up from vintage locomotives and melodic showdowns in celluloid Westerns. Reminiscent of John Ford's seminal movie *The Iron Horse* (1924), Konami's title highlighted the role of the railroad in Western development.[18]

While Frederick Jackson Turner had declared the frontier closed in 1893, games such as *Iron Horse* re-opened the nineteenth-century West in a binary format. A new, electronic frontier serviced old frontier nostalgia. In arcades across the globe, the videogame presented a simplified version of the frontier to all nations, races and classes, promoting the American West, in its digital guise, as an experience lacking any tangible borders. All could travel to the frontier West and take part in its exploration and conquering. As Marguerite Shaffer observed wilderness travelogues in the 1910s and 1920s that 'encouraged tourists to reenact the nation's frontier past by camping and hiking', so too did videogames of the 1970s and 1980s furnish fake frontier experiences of killing and maiming. In essence, the arcade Western afforded the opportunity of both witnessing and taming the frontier without any of the associated costs. Exodus from the East cost less than a dollar, game machines providing fleeting chances to cross the Wild West by surmounting a series of pre-determined challenges. Players moved the line of discovery constantly forward by conquering successive territories (or game levels), moving speedily towards the end of the frontier, the title's grand finale. Everything was linear in the game, and every title worked perfectly in accordance with Turner's one-directional frontier story. Significantly, alternative images of the frontier and the West had made few inroads into the digital West during the 1970s and 1980s despite the emergence of more critical takes on Western history. Videogame designers stuck with a tried-and-tested formula of violent gunfights and pixel cowboys.[19]

Games of the New West: Recreation and Tourism

Despite the significance of the Western shooter as a gaming genre, and the success of individual titles such as *Boot Hill*, only a relatively small number of arcade Westerns were produced over the period 1975 to 1991. By the 1990s, the notable absence of new commentary in the videogame Western, allied to a lack of technical innovation, sealed its commercial demise.

As the computer Wild West failed to move on, videogames increasingly explored modern-day law enforcement showdowns, alien takeovers and the occasional zombie infestation. Such genres sometimes drew on Wild West conventions of 'duels and showdowns', 'ambushes', 'lone and silent heroes' and 'vigilante justice' – but cast them in new scenarios. In the same way that the movie *Star Wars* (1977), with its frontier locales and gunslinger heroes, was dubbed a space Western, *Outland* (1981) nicknamed 'High Moon' for its regurgitation of *High Noon* (1952), and *Mad Max* (1979) judged a post-apocalyptic Western with cars, a wide range of videogames featured Western staples. The hugely successful stealth game *Metal Gear Solid* (Konami, 1998), set in the contemporary period, featured a mysterious, silent hero (Solid Snake) sent in to dangerous situations and facing off a variety of foes in one-on-one showdowns, including a clash with Russian-born gunslinger Revolver Ocelot, complete with duster, spurs and Colt single-action firearms. With its desert backdrop and array of auto conflict and rival gangs, racing title *Vigilante 8* (Luxoflux/Activision, 1998) resembled a neo-Wild West. Fighting, shooting and science-fiction games in particular drew on Hollywood Western notions of honour, lonesome heroes and the law of the gun.[20]

The scenery of the American West survived in games, but gone were the days of tin cans, buffalo hide and stage coaches. Instead the West emerged as a modern entertainment landscape providing the backdrop to contemporary (and sometimes future-set) driving games, hunting games and God-games. Appended to a variety of titles, the West no longer serviced as a stand-alone gaming narrative or shooter genre. Videogames such as *18 Wheeler* (Sega, 2000) sported a new Western iconography, a rich visual tapestry, marked by automobiles, shopping malls and wilderness areas, but rarely delved deeper into the trans-Mississippi experience. Titles thus reflected a growing cultural perception of the West as a realm of recreation and pleasure, or, to borrow Marguerite Shaffer's phrase, 'a landscape of leisure'.[21]

SNK's *Turf Masters* (1996) digitised the monumental scenery of both the American East and West for a leisurely game of golf. The West became, in videogame vernacular, simple 'eye candy'. Tourists commonly treated the West as a landscape of spectacle, as did game designers. Earlier titles, such as *Blood Bros.*, employed sublime Western vistas as backdrops to gunfighter action. *Turf Masters* applied the same principle to tee shots. Alongside Japanese and European venues, *Turf Masters* hosted an American championship at the fictitious 'Grand Canyon Golf Course'. An instruction booklet declared the region 'nature's greatest creation'. However, just as the scale of the Grand Canyon had challenged painter Thomas Moran's artistry in *The Chasm of the Colorado* (1873–4), the majesty of a 277-mile long ravine proved to be impossible to capture on an arcade screen. Apart from its sandy façade, the digital Grand Canyon shared little in common with its organic counterpart. In post-modern fashion, the virtual golf course included views of the Niagara Falls and Monument Valley, presenting a globalised amalgam of tourist sites and recreating them for customer ease like a Disney theme park. While SNK professed that 'Golfers with long drives will be at home' at its digital Grand Canyon, those familiar with the material landscape probably felt disoriented.[22]

Games based around the automobile employed the monumental scenery of the West to better effect. Driving games resembled classic American road movies such as *Easy Rider* (1969) and *Vanishing Point* (1971), players travelling along deserted highways with rugged peaks flashing by in their rear view mirrors. *18 Wheeler* provided a *Convoy*-styled (1978) juggernaut ride from New York to San Francisco. As the 'Asphalt Cowboy', players powered past swirling prairie twisters, dawdling Winnebagos and Grand Canyon billboards. A paean to American freeway culture, *18 Wheeler* authentically replicated the buzz of westerly travel along Route 66. Unfortunately, the ability to complete the arcade game by recreating a 3,000-mile journey in less than thirty minutes defied logic as well as state speed limits.

Another product of the Japanese software giant Sega, *Crazy Taxi* highlighted the urban West as an avenue worth exploring by virtual transportation. Arcade players assumed control of a San Franciscan cab driver collecting fares from city-bred Westerners and foreign tourists, taking them to unique destinations such as Candlestick Park and the Transamerica Pyramid, as well as local branches of Kentucky Fried Chicken and Pizza Hut. By ferrying passengers to scattered locations, players steadily expanded their knowledge of virtual San Francisco, graduating from bewildered tourist to urbane docent. Tourists no doubt went through the same process in real taxi rides, just at a much slower speed. *Crazy Taxi* proved a highly successful title both in the arcades and in homes.[23]

Based on the concept of extended play, PC games embodied a different experience to that found at the arcade, and helped flesh out a more complex view of the modern West. Pioneering the cerebral management game, Will Wright's *SimCity* (Maxis, 1987) encouraged players to create their own virtual cities, as well as triumph over a number of ready-made urban challenges. Tasks set on the West Coast included rebuilding San Francisco following the Loma Prieta earthquake, halting a wild fire threatening Oakland and circumventing a volcanic eruption off Portland, together presenting a hazardous West along the lines of *Ecology of Fear* (1998) by Mike Davis. Players even tried their hand at eliminating crime in Las Vegas and beating back B-movie monsters ravaging Hollywood. The plethora of natural disaster scenarios set in the West reflected salient concerns over the demise of vast metropolises such as Los Angeles before a vaguely defined environmental backlash.[24]

Hardly any videogames in the 1990s returned exclusively to the Old West. In March 2001, a journalist for *CgOnline* puzzled, 'While the mythical American West – the land of John Wayne, Clint Eastwood, of train robberies and noontime gunfights – is firmly ensconced in our popular culture, it's never quite taken hold in Silicon Valley.' The journalist overlooked the contributions of early arcade Westerns. However, games designers seemed far more attached to composite virtual landscapes by the late 1990s, forging digital worlds that collapsed traditional notions of time and geography. Reflecting the marginalisation of cowboy showdowns, shooting game *Duke Nukem* (Eurocom/GT Interactive, 1999) employed the nineteenth-century frontier as just one of several digital realms to visit. Players travelled back in time to fight alien invaders, rather than cowboys or Indians, with Duke's mutterings of 'Remember the Alamo' hardly of relevance to extra-terrestrials. *Duke Nukem* showed the digital Old West as little different from any other virtual landscape of violence (be it jungle, urban downtown or war zone). History and authenticity mattered little in the focus on gaming progress and quick kills. Lost among countless imaginary worlds, the mythic old West no longer seemed exceptional.[25]

Giving the player directorial control over classic Wild West vignettes, Infogrames' *Desperados: Wanted Dead or Alive* (2001) and *Desperados 2: Cooper's Revenge* (2006), two real-time strategy games, nevertheless marked a return to the old frontier, but with a New Western tinge to the narrative. *Desperados* engaged with frontier storytelling by collecting together twenty-four mission-based 'best western adventures' for gamers to navigate. The official press release by Infogrames exploited plenty of cowboy clichés, requesting players to 'Dig out your poncho and dust down your stetson' and 'Saddle up for the wildest adventure this side of the Alamo!' However, the roster of six playable characters was remarkably revisionist by including an ex-slave, a Mexican, an Asian-American and an empowered female poker player by the name of Kate O'Hara. *Desperados* also allowed players significant freedom to create their own historic West as postmodernist digital authors.[26]

Reading the Digital West

From *Gun Fight* to *Crazy Taxi*, the computer entertainment industry has perennially engaged with the West, deeming it both a worthwhile game format and a marketable commercial property. In large part, computer games have followed an established set of conceptions governing the imaginary West that date back to the Great Migration. Since overlanders left their Eastern homes with dreams of Western fortune and prosperity, successive generations of newcomers have moulded the West into a land of adventure, individualism, entertainment and opportunity. The Western wish list has included everything from old gold to new age remedies. Within the digital West can be found the influences of dime novels, Western art, live shows and Hollywood. In their international origins and global marketing ploys, videogames have merely made this 'old West' experience more interactive and accessible. The videogame has thus provided fresh technology to preserve an old chimera.[27]

In part, the standardisation of the digital West reflects the continual dominance of the Old West vision in global popular culture. Back in 1996, Michael Johnson commented on the supreme fashionability of the West, how it continued to be 'mythologized, fetishized, stereotyped, commodified' on television screens, on magazine covers and in clothing stores. The mythic Wild West, of cowboys and Indians, wagon trains and showdowns, remains a story of interest to all. Given the potential of computer technology to revolutionise ways of conceiving the world, it is surprising how few games challenged us to think of the West any differently. After all, the arcade Western amounts to a fresh annex to what Richard Aquila labelled the 'pop culture West' of action stories and caricatured rogues.[28]

Does this virtual world add anything new to Western visions? First, it shows the survivability of the 'simpler' West. American, European and Japanese game designers in the 1970s and 1980s recognised that the traditional cowboy fantasy could still appeal despite Hollywood's desertion of it. They ignored the growing social criticism and complexity of movie Westerns (reflecting a crisis of national confidence in the 1970s), providing instead a simplified pop culture slice of 'cowboys and Indians'. Being able to actually play 'the cowboy' was deemed enough of a novelty and a new direction to attract an audience. The straightforwardness of the arcade Western helped with its appeal. While Western movies had become either passé or too caught in contemporary commentary, the videogame supplied the most pure and reductive take on the Western myth for some decades. As an entertaining toy, the videogame needed no intellectual justification, nor did the audience want one. Notable success followed. The arcade Western kept the 'old West' vision alive.

The action-packed mythic West also suited the mandate of the videogame to entertain in brief five-minute doses – suggestive of a dialogue between the dictates of new technology and more established cultural mores. Early computer hardware limited what stories could be told. However, audiences knew how to behave in the Wild West – they simply required a platform for their actions. The mythology of the frontier, in Slotkin's parlance 'progress through violence', fitted the linear, competitive path of game play. Players moved successively forward, fighting Indians, claiming digital territory. Redemption and renewal of spirit promised by frontier conquest came in the form of points on screen in the digital domain. In such a process, the linguistic and literal mythology of the frontier was often marginalised, and the visual mythology of the West strengthened more than ever before. Such a route was predictable given the success of the Hollywood Western and the dominance of the image in the late twentieth century. However, on entering digital space, the visual mythology of West became compressed into a series of stages, stereotypes and not much else.[29]

Finally, games furthered the conception of the West as a violent domain. Videogames such as *Boot Hill*, *Blood Bros.*, and even to some degree *Desperados*, presented the region as a series of continuous and gloriously iconic gunfights: propagating the singular, most important myth of the West as violence par excellence. Associating the firearm with the West was central to the success of titles such as *Gun Fight*, not just in attracting audiences, but also in familiarising them with a new medium of interaction and popularising a now staple gaming peripheral. Populist Western history as viewed through a gun barrel established game play conventions based on targeting and trigger-itch. Games thus extended the popular myth of frontier violence, and coupled that myth with new technology and a young audience.

Yet there is some hope in the digital West. Modern titles have proved to be far more open to represent the 'New West': in videogame tone, a diverse, albeit still clichéd, landscape of Hollywood signs, freeways, burger bars, fun rides and wilderness parks. The West has become a post-modern mélange of landmarks, with the videogame operating as a digital tour package for the twenty-first century armchair tourist. The evolution of the arcade Western from simple shootout to multi-faceted entertainment vehicle illustrates the widening popular interpretation of the West. Critical reaction to *Custer's Revenge* suggests some readiness to move beyond the inherent tyrannies in old frontier stories. *Desperados* indicates a safer potential trajectory for the frontier tale by setting the player up as story architect, akin to a Hollywood director, and presenting a revisionist take on Western history. Further frontier re-envisioning seems eminently plausible in this ever-reconstructing digital domain.

Notes

1. Pertinent popular histories of videogames include Leonard Herman, *Phoenix: The Fall and Rise of Videogames* (Union: New Jersey, 1994), Jessie Cameron Herz, *Joystick Nation: How Videogames Ate Our Quarters, Won Our Hearts, and Rewired Our Minds* (New York: Little, Brown, 1997) and Stephen Poole, *Trigger Happy: The Inner Life of Videogames* (London: Arcade, 2000); document available online at: http://www.erasmatazz.com/library/JCGD_Volume_5/The_Atari_Years.html. Widely acknowledged but rarely substantiated with documentation, the 'great mass burial' of Atari cartridges in the West signifies one of the first legends of the videogame era. 'Atari's mass burials and other tales', posted by the Atari Historical Society, dedicated to the preservation of Atari memories and memorabilia. See: online at: http://www.atari-history.com/burials.html.
2. In 1998, Hasbro Interactive purchased Atari from the JDS Corporation, and released many old Atari titles on modern console formats; Paul Keegan, 'Culture quake', *Mother Jones* (November–December 1999), available online at: www.motherjones.com/mother_jones/ND99/quake.html.
3. No wholly reliable chart exists for total sales of videogames. However, one useful indicator of the American market is the 'platinum' (one-million selling) chart for games released post-1995. Other than *Crazy Taxi*, no Western-themed game made the list of 262 titles. See: online at: http://www.the-magicbox.com/Chart-USPlatinum.shtml. For example, *Custer's Revenge* charted position three in PC World's Emru Townsend's 'The Worst Games of All Time', for *MSN Tech & Gadgets*, undated, http://tech.msn.com/products/article.aspx?cp-documentid=1225420&page=1 and position one in William Cassidy's 'Top Ten Shameful Games', for *Gamespy* magazine (31 December 2002): http://archive.gamespy.com/top10/december02/shame/index.shtml.
4. These are not the only themes open to discussion: it would equally prove worthwhile to analyse the digital West with reference to such issues as gender and ethnicity.
5. Journalists and historians of the time judged Buffalo Bill's Wild West to be a realistic (and thus educational) recreation of Western history. See Richard

Slotkin, *Gunfighter Nation: The Myth of the Frontier in Twentieth-Century America* (New York: HarperCollins 1992), pp. 68–9; Thomas L. Altherr, 'Let'er rip: popular culture images of the American West in Wild West shows, rodeos, and rendezvous', in Richard Aquila (ed.), *Wanted Dead or Alive: The American West in Popular Culture* (Urbana: University of Illinois Press 1996), p. 85; James R. Grossman (ed.), essays by Richard White and Patricia Nelson Limerick, *The Frontier in American Culture: An Exhibition at the Newberry Library, August 26, 1994–January 7, 1995* (Berkeley, 1994), p. 27. Works that tackle the eminent showmanship of William F. Cody include: L. G. Moses, *Wild West Shows and the Images of American Indians, 1883–1933* (Albuquerque: University of New Mexico Press, 1999); Robert A. Carter, *Buffalo Bill Cody: The Man Behind the Legend* (New York: Wiley 2000); Robert W. Rydell and Rob Kroes, *Buffalo Bill in Bologna: The Americanization of the World, 1869–1922* (Chicago: University of Chicago Press, 2005); Louis S. Warren, *Buffalo Bill's America: William Cody and the Wild West Show* (New York: Random House, 2005); and Paul Hedren, 'The contradictory legacies of Buffalo Bill Cody's first scalp for Custer', *Montana: The Magazine of Western History*, 55/1 (Spring 2005), pp. 16–35.
6. Henry Nash Smith, *Virgin Land: The American West as Symbol and Myth* (Cambridge, MA: Harvard University Press, 1950), p. 90.
7. Film footage of Cody dates back to 1898, when Thomas Edison recorded Cody firing a rifle. See Carter, *Buffalo Bill Cody*, pp. 424–5.
8. For further study of the West as an entertainment landscape, see: Richard Aquila, *Wanted Dead or Alive*; Michael L. Johnson, *New Westers: The West in Contemporary American Culture* (Lincoln: University of Nebraska Press, 1996); Hal Rothman, *Devil's Bargains: Tourism in the Twentieth-Century American West* (Lawrence: University Press of Kansas, 2000); and Lisa Nicholas, Elaine Bapis and Thomas Harvey (eds), *Imagining the Big Open: Nature, Identity and Play in the New West* (Salt Lake City: University of Utah Press, 2003).
9. The game mechanics of *Gun Fight* resembled Atari's coin-op tennis game *Pong*, with players manoeuvering their characters at opposite ends of the screen while watching bullet-shaped pixels ricochet off screen 'walls'.
10. For insight into the myths surrounding Dodge City and Boot Hill, see: Robert R. Dykstra, *The Cattle Towns* (Lincoln: University of Nebraska Press, 1983 [1968]); and Robert R. Dykstra, 'Imaginary Dodge City: a political statement', part of a roundtable discussion, introduced by Stewart L. Udall, entitled 'How the West Got Wild: American Media and Frontier Violence', *The Western Historical Quarterly*, 31/3 (Autumn 2000), pp. 278–84.
11. It is important to note that not all monochrome Westerns focused on the high noon showdown. Midway's *Desert Gun* (1977) brought Western hunting culture to the city arcade, whereby players amassed high scores by shooting various species that appeared fleetingly on screen. Meanwhile, *Dog Patch* (Midway, 1977) presented a shooting competition between two kneeling marksmen, with tin cans sporadically released into the digital sky above. *Dead Eye* (Meadows, 1978) tested the ability of players to keep a coin from falling to the ground by consistently shooting it in the air; lone hero or last gunfighter/last stand myth, see: John G. Cawelti, *The Six-Gun Mystique Sequel* (Bowling Green: Bowling Green University Popular Press, 1999), pp. 36–45; Richard Slotkin, *The Fatal Environment: The Myth of the Frontier in the Age of Industrialization, 1800–1890*

(Middletown: Wesleyan University Press, 1985), pp. 435–76. For several decades, videogames were marketed at, and played by, a predominantly male audience (especially teen and young adult males). However, over a third of gamers in the United States are now female, and the core age demographic has shifted upwards, towards the late twenties. See: Gloria Gondale, 'The games women play', *Christian Science Monitor* (11 June 2004). This idea draws on the work of Michael Coyne on masculinity in Westerns, *The Crowded Prairie* (New York: Tauris, 1997), pp. 84–104.

12. Richard Slotkin, *Regeneration Through Violence: The Mythology of the American Frontier, 1600–1860* (Middletown: Wesleyan University Press, 1973), p. 5. On the mythology of violence, see: Slotkin, *The Fatal Environment*, pp. 62–3.
13. In game mechanics, *Blood Bros.* closely resembled *NAM – 1975* (SNK 1990), a title loosely based on the Vietnam War. The name *Blood Bros.* likely derived from the ability of two players (as blood brothers) to collaborate in the destruction of the enemy, one taking the part of a cowboy, the other assuming the role of a Native American; Richard White, 'Animals and enterprise', *The Oxford History of the American West* (Oxford: Oxford University Press, 1996), pp. 273, 258.
14. See: Herz, *Joystick Nation*, pp. 68–9; Eugene F. Provenzo, *Video Kids: Making Sense of Nintendo* (Cambridge, MA: Harvard University Press, 1991), p. 52 On the myth of Custer's Last Stand, see, for example, Slotkin, *Fatal Environment*, pp. 7–32, 435–76.
15. See Udall et al., 'How the West got Wild: American media and frontier violence', pp. 277–95.
16. Johnson, *New Westers*, p. 200.
17. Witness Captain William Clark's difficulty in estimating vast numbers of 'Buffalow, Elk, Antelopes and Wolves' near present-day Billings, Montana. See Clark's entry for 24 July 1806, in Reuben G. Thwaites, *Original Journals of the Lewis and Clark Expedition, 1804–1806*, 8 vols (New York: Dodd, Mead & Co., 1904), 5: 206.
18. In 1998, English Professor Henry Jenkins compared scrolling videogames to boyhood 'frontier' adventures such as Mark Twain's *Adventures of Tom Sawyer* (1876). See: Henry Jenkins, '"Complete freedom of movement": video games as gendered play spaces', in Henry Jenkins and Justine Cassell (eds), *From Barbie to Mortal Kombat: Gender and Computer Games* (Cambridge, MA: MIT Press, 1998). Also, Mary Fuller and Henry Jenkins, 'Nintendo and New World travel writing: a dialogue', in Steven G. Jones (ed.), *Cybersociety: Computer-Mediated Communication and Community* (Thousand Oaks: Sage, 1995), pp. 57–72. For a valuable insight into parallels between the 'Wild frontier' and the internet, see Helen McLure, 'The wild, wild web: the mythic American West and the electronic frontier', *The Western Historical Quarterly*, 31/4 (Winter 2000), pp. 457–76.
19. Marguerite Shaffer, '"The West plays West": Western tourism and the landscape of leisure', in William Deverell (ed.), *A Companion to the American West* (Oxford: Blackwell, 2004), p. 376. Discussions of the appeal of the untamed West and the wilderness frontier can be found in Roderick Nash, *Wilderness and the American Mind*, 4th edn (Yale: Yale University Press, 2001) and Michael L. Johnson, *Hunger for the Wild: America's Obsession with the Untamed West* (Lawrence: University Press of Kansas, 2007).

The Arcade Western

20. While videogames drew on elements of the West, none went so far as Joss Whedon's television series *Firefly* (2002) in fusing the nineteenth-century frontier with action and futurism. Whedon forwarded the myth of the West to 2517, complete with pioneer towns, Old West dialect, vigilantism, old rifles and classic bar brawls (amongst space ships).
21. Shaffer, 'The West plays West', p. 385.
22. Instruction manual, *Neo Turf Masters* (SNK, 1999), published for the Neo Geo Pocket, a hand-held console released in American, European and Japanese markets during 1999. See also the original *Turf Masters* (SNK, 1996) arcade machine.
23. Released in January 2000 (USA), the game proved the first blockbuster title for Sega's troubled Dreamcast console, amassing total US sales of 1.11 million units (the fourth biggest selling title for the Dreamcast), while later incarnations for PS2 and Gamecube sold well. *Metropolis Street Racer* (Bizarre Creations, 2000) also featured sections of San Francisco to race across.
24. Videogames also altered human perceptions of reality. Prolonged exposure to *SimCity* led computer writer Stephen Poole to visualise the freeway-jammed confusion of real-life Los Angeles as 'sim city played by a maniac'. Poole, *Trigger Happy*, p. 103.
25. David Ryan Hunt, 'Desperados – wanted dead or alive: a tale of gunplay and deceit in the Wild West', 14 March 2001, available Online at: http://www.cgonline.com/previews/desperados-01-p1.html.
26. Infogrames Press Release, 'Desperados', 2 July 2001 (UK version), available online at: http://corporate.infogrames.com/IESA/pressreleases_archive.html.
27. Instructive here is Patricia Nelson Limerick, 'The shadows of heaven itself', William E. Riebsame (ed.), *Atlas of the New West: Portrait of a Changing Region* (New York: Norton, 1997), pp. 151–79.
28. Riebsame, *Atlas of the New West*, p. 16; Richard Aquila, 'Introduction: the pop culture West', Aquila, *Wanted Dead or Alive*, p. 1.
29. On frontier process, Slotkin, *Gunfighter Nation*, pp. 11–12; on mythic language, Slotkin, *Fatal Environment*, pp. 18–19.

This chapter is a version of an article that appeared in the *Pacific Historical Review*. Courtesy of the University of California Press.

Chapter 11

Turn here for 'The Sunny Side of the Atom': Tourism, the Bomb and Popular Culture in the Nuclear West

By backing an escalation in the nuclear arms race in the early 1980s, Hollywood cowboy turned President, Ronald Reagan, invited the wrath of veteran nuclear protesters. One cartoon drawn by California activists depicted Reagan in full cowboy regalia, riding an atomic missile as his surrogate pony. In defending the capitalist West from the 'red peril' of Communism, Reagan appeared to be confusing his presidential role with his movie star repertoire, expertly superimposing the mythic dramaturgy of the Old West on Cold War politics.[1]

In recent years, historians have begun to ponder what may prove to be a special relationship between the Cold War and the American West. The ties between the two run far deeper than popular rhetoric. Three hundred military bases and installations were located in the region. The conflict cast sizeable swathes of western territories as virtuoso military playgrounds, with thousands of square miles of Nevada set aside for training. Inside experimentation zones of the military–industrial complex, G.I. Joes were sent in to secure ground zero while atomic mushroom clouds hovered above them, becoming test subjects (or 'guinea pigs') in the battle for information in the Cold War. Outside the official boundaries of Cold War enterprise, Western settlers remained party to the transformations taking place. In southern Utah, 'Downwinders' of nuclear tests held in the adjoining state of Nevada fell victim to radiation sickness. In 'Landscapes of the Cold War West', María Montoya related her experiences growing up as a child in Colorado, looking out on the 'orange glow' of Rocky Flats, a Cold War city where plutonium triggers were assembled for bombs and where her father gained employment. As Kevin Fernlund pointed out, 'Perhaps nowhere in the country was the effect of decades of cold war felt more intensely than in the lands west of the Mississippi River.'[2]

Tourism, the Bomb and Popular Culture in the Nuclear West

As suggested by the examples above, scholars have been most interested in delineating how the nuclear component of Cold War technologies transformed the West. Early work on what might be labelled the 'Nuclear West' bears at least some of the hallmarks of New Western history. Fitting with the approach pioneered by Patricia Nelson Limerick and Richard White, scholars have highlighted the unfettered conquest of Native American peoples and lands, the strong exercise of federal and military authority and the despoliation of the natural environment. Likewise, the atomic frontier arguably resembles the greater Western experience in microcosm. Any discussion of 'the sunny side of the atom' seems amiss in a narrative dominated by Cold War drama, military exigencies and ecological destruction; yet, ideas of leisure and entertainment comprise important elements in the story of atomic development.[3]

This chapter explores concepts of recreation and pleasure in the Nuclear West. It shows how Western culture mixed with nuclear culture to produce Country and Western songs about atomic power and talk of a 'second gold rush' based on uranium mining. Images of the mythic Old West combined with utopian visions of a 'Future West' to produce a new atomic frontier: part science, part technology and part pioneer mentality. As Hal Rothman remarked, 'To a nation whose people had no way to fathom the remarkable impact of this new technology and had little personal experience with the devastation of war, the bomb was difficult to fathom.' By attending bomb blasts or visiting reactors, Westerners deciphered and decoded the meanings of the nuclear age. Even tourism acted as a valuable conduit for personal understanding. The influence of the atom over popular culture and leisure pastimes in the West relied on both the efficacy of nuclear industry advertising and the willingness of people to engage with Cold War histrionics. Although promotions of the 'sunny side' of the atom floundered in the late 1970s, Americans take tours of nuclear sites to this day. Nuclear symbols are presently found on outdoor leisure garments and in computer games offering cyber journeys through secret military bases. Nuclear history and culture continue to mark the Western experience, the atomic age adding to the heady iconography surrounding the trans-Mississippi expanse.[4]

Welcoming the Atom to the West

It would be presumptive to claim that in the late 1940s, the atomic bomb was the proverbial toast of every town, but many Westerners welcomed the advent of nuclear energy for its curtailment of a costly and drawn out war. As if to acknowledge its roots in local territory, Country and Western singers celebrated their new atomic friend in hearty ballads such as 'Atomic Power', a 1945 hit for Fred Kirby. Hollywood promoted bikini-clad, 'anatomic bombshells' as stars of a new atomic era, and urbane Westerners indulged in 'atomic cocktails' at fashionable parties. Nuclear energy boasted considerable novelty value. At movie theatres, science-fiction blockbusters entertained attendees with tales of atomic monsters hailing from bomb craters, the aridity and isolation of the western landscape well suited to tall stories of insidious alien invasion. In *Them!* (1954), mutant ants emerged from atomic bomb sites in New Mexico to wreak havoc on surrounding communities. From inspiring alcoholic drinks to furthering the success of show-business starlets, atomic power had gained a foothold in popular culture. By engaging with Hollywood movies and musical renditions, citizens worked out their relationship with the nuclear age. In the process, the atomic enterprise became thoroughly westernised.

For a number of Westerners, seeing the atom in action proved too good an opportunity to miss. The tourist industry in Las Vegas initially balked at the idea of bombs going off at nearby military lands. However, when the first explosions commenced at the Nevada Test Site in January 1951, people rushed to Vegas out of sheer curiosity. 'Atomic-Age Sight-Seeing Way Out West' declared *The New York Times*, in a headline that advertised the West as a wacky tourist haven, a potent mixture of historic and futuristic realms. The newspaper related how 'motels throughout Las Vegas ... filled up nightly with tourists curious enough to spend half the night huddled in blankets outside their lodgings in order not to miss the dawn concatenations'. Temporarily lured from their gambling halls, slot machine veterans sought out atomic entertainment in the desert. Parents loaded up station-wagons with picnic baskets, the atomic blast providing the excuse for a family day out. Like Yellowstone National Park visitors gathered attentively around Old Faithful geyser waiting for an elemental explosion, nuclear tourists in the Mojave checked their watches in anticipation of a man-made plume shooting into the sky.[5]

The mushroom cloud rising over a vast expanse of 'nothingness' transfixed a captive audience. Where once Civil War battles attracted their share of voyeurs, and singular gunfights in frontier towns garnered plenty of attention, now the atomic explosion invited the response of everyday Americans. Its dark magnificence enthralled

Figure 11.1 Atomic mushroom cloud from Operation Buster-Jangle, as witnessed from Las Vegas downtown, November 1951.

and horrified in equal measure. Yosemite and Yellowstone offered monumental natural wonders, but a nuclear explosion in the western desert had its own unique appeal. The picture of the atomic cloud soon became ubiquitous, with the Atomic Energy Commission (AEC) keen to publish lavish photographs of the iconic 'mushroom' rising above sagebrush and sand. Invocations to the technological sublime meanwhile seemed appropriate given its proximity to a city built on hydropower and basking in electrical light. Atomic fireworks at dawn complemented the neon radiance of Vegas at night. In recognition of the boom in nuclear tourism, at several local hotels and casinos AEC officials kindly announced nearby 'events'.

Reflecting a surge of interest in atomic matters, New Mexico witnessed a boost in tourism at a similar time to Nevada. The State Tourist Bureau reported being 'deluged with travel inquiries' in 1951. Noting how 'New Mexico's climate, scenery, natural wonders and historic sites are the same as they have been for years', *The New York Times* attributed 'much of the new interest... to the extensive current publicity regarding such recent additions to the scene as the Atomic Energy Commission's Los Alamos base and the rocket testing grounds at White Sands'. By making tracks for nuclear destinations, tourists intonated their 'favor of sights of today and tomorrow'. Atomic attractions followed on from hugely popular trips to the Hoover Dam, tapping popular interest in large-scale technological mastery and engineered landscapes. Nuclear energy represented America's future just around the corner, with western sites trailblazing the way ahead. Tourists valued their journeys into futurism as if party to a great pioneering experiment.[6]

However, given the official cloud of secrecy hanging over the atom, opportunities for nuclear tourism on the whole proved rare in the West. Los Alamos lab opened its doors to the families and friends of employees, as well as interested visitors, just once a year. Although prior to the public stampede, all the interesting stuff was hidden away, the open days proved immensely popular. 'Continuous bus tours' transported tourists around the sprawling site. Comprehensive tour booklets helped guests navigate the unfamiliar atomic scenery. Attractions in 1965 included 'big computers... programmed to sing [after a fashion] and to print souvenir sheets faster than the eye can follow'. Another computer could 'instantly print the name and address of any Los Alamos resident who tells it his telephone number'. Such innocuous, even banal, technological feats served to demythologise the nuclear landscape. Those visitors who entered Los Alamos with fears of finding a clandestine hub of atomic experiments, left only with contented smiles and printouts of their home addresses to return to.[7]

For most Westerners, trips to distant and remote nuclear facilities seemed impractical, even inconceivable. Auditoriums broadcasting promotional films such as *Understanding the Atom* (1952 onwards) provided far more accessible routes towards scientific knowledge. For home entertainment enthusiasts, a double long-player, featuring the voices of William L. Lawrence (official reporter of the Manhattan Project) and Bob Hope, recounted the story of the atom. One newspaper critic interpreted the choice of Bob Hope as 'presumably on the theory that even if he didn't grasp everything he would be thoroughly cheerful about it'. The upbeat musings of Hope, the entertainer, complemented the more serious tone of Lawrence, the expert witness. Entertainment married with nuclear history. The set sported an outlandish, and suitably 'Wild West' title – 'The Quick and the Dead' – that gave the story of the atomic bomb the appealing patina of gunfights at the OK Corral. Simplified, and westernised, for a popular audience, the coming of the atomic age became a classic tale of pioneer bravado.[8]

Launched with a speech by President Eisenhower to the United Nations in 1953, the 'peaceful atom' served to generate fantasies of nuclear-fuelled leisure at homes in the West. Eisenhower considered atomic energy 'a power for good which dwarfs that of any prior achievement of science'. Intertwining technological and social advancement, America's nuclear programme metamorphosed into a virtuous quest for a better way of life. Leaving behind its chequered destructive past, the atom plugged into the American dream of freedom, prosperity and progress. Such amorphous ideals had, of course, already found fertile soil west of the Mississippi.[9]

In the 1950s, the American nuclear industry promoted a consumer-oriented American dream of infinite prosperity and abundant leisure time complementary to wider motifs in society. Nuclear production was shrewdly linked with the attainment of an affluent lifestyle predicated on consumption, recreation and travel. AEC chairman Lewis Strauss prophesised that 'atomic electrical power surging through transmission lines to towns and villages, farms and factories' would 'make life easier, healthier, and more abundant'. Nuclear plants promised to fuel healthy and wholesome living, supplying electricity to new suburbs as well as encouraging new forms of consumption. Embedded into promotions of the peaceful atom were references to the 'nuclear family' and its path towards domestic bliss. Early industry propaganda highlighted atomic-style home improvements. Nuclear electricity, purportedly 'too cheap to meter', would meet consumer demands for modern kitchens with all the latest appliances. The atom promised to be a housewife's friend, the 'nuclear toaster' heating bread to perfection, ready to serve with eggs 'sunny side up'. After breakfast, family members could clean their teeth with atomic toothpaste, even travel to work (or the local park) by nuclear-fuelled car or bus. Atomic futurism fed off contemporary fascinations with suburban, high-tech homes and comfortable living. Modern homestead dreams domesticated the atom.[10]

Underlining the peaceful atom as fun and family-friendly, in 1950 the A. C. Gilbert Corporation announced plans for a child's toy allowing 'children to play with atomic energy at home'. Packaged 'complete with Geiger Counter and other professional-type gadgets guaranteed to appeal to youngsters from 9 to 90', the kit came with radioactive samples, although promotions manager Beanning Repplier insisted it was 'completely safe and harmless'. At summer camp in the 1950s, boy scouts built miniature reactors using straws and cardboard, earning 'atomic energy' badges for their engineering prowess. The ability to understand atomic energy hardly befitted the scouting themes of wilderness survival sported by Western heroes such as Daniel Boone and Davy Crockett. Instead, the 'atomic energy' badge related to a modern West of technological progress and urbanity.[11]

A transport priority influenced early atomic research programmes. In 1955, the AEC signed a study agreement with Baldwin-Lima-Hamiliton and the Denver and Rio Grande Western Railroad Corporations to pioneer an atomic locomotive capable of crossing the country many times without refuelling. Benson Ford, a grandson of Henry Ford, expected that atomic energy, rather than petrol, would fuel the country's automobiles in the future. Atomic developments promised revolutions in travel not only from East to West, but also across oceans and into space. One industrial spokesman, hopeful over ongoing research into nuclear airplanes, expected to 'see atomic-powered aircraft cross the Atlantic in thirty minutes'. In 1947, a professor at Yale University fully anticipated trips to Mars by atomic rocket 'during our lifetime'. Revolutions in transport promised the exploration, and settlement, of new frontiers, repeating what the railroad had done for the nineteenth-century West. Meanwhile, a few miles from ground zero at the Nevada Test Site, the American military sacrificed petrol-driven Buicks, Chevrolets and Oldsmobiles in order to judge the effectiveness of conventional cars and trucks as ad hoc nuclear shelters. 'Operation Hot Rod' produced a scrap yard of radioactive wrecks in the hot, open desert – a modern day rendition of abandoned wagons on the Oregon Trail.[12]

The first true 'atomic cities' in the American West began life as remote and secret places – townships off the beaten track, hidden in the vast expanses west of the Mississippi. The ramshackle nature of Hanford in the 1940s betrayed its wartime expediencies, a hastily constructed, utilitarian settlement vaguely reminiscent of mining towns in the gold rush era. However, in the 1950s nearby Richland heralded a new kind of post-war atomic city. Richland swiftly emerged as a concrete experiment in what a nuclear community could offer. By providing ample parking spaces in commercial and residential districts, town planners recognised the growing importance of the automobile to Westerners. They also created a non-central retail area similar in style to the modern shopping mall. At the same time as pointing the way toward a fresh suburban style of living, Richland staunchly defended White, conservative and monocultural values, with conventional church and civic organisations proliferating. Commenting on this tendency, Carl Abbott noted how atomic 'model towns' of the 1950s represented 'prototypical "suburban" environments erected in physical isolation but deeply embedded within middle-class American culture'. Their appeal lay in combining old traditions with novel forms of technology and planning. They also celebrated the coming together of nuclear energy and Western culture. Places such as Richland and Los Alamos represented boomtowns of the atomic frontier. As Richard White elaborated, just like nineteenth-century homesteaders and ranchers, inhabitants of new atomic towns 'thought of themselves as people on the frontier – the frontiers of knowledge'. Manhattan employees 'were pioneering in the desert'. Rather than expressing unease over their complicity in atomic development, townspeople took pride in their work on behalf of the security of the United States and applauded the fusion of Western spirit and atomic energy. Those who lived close to nuclear sites in the 1950s embraced the atom as part of their civic culture and quest for regional stature. Richland's town symbol poignantly depicted the atom and a covered wagon.[13]

In 1918, Lenin had claimed electrification as the necessary course towards communism in Soviet Russia. In post-1945 America, nuclear aficionados looked to the atom as a means by which to build a prosperous and productive society. The West frequently provided the great open spaces and frontier-like vistas on which to play out such grandiose schemes. The reputation of the region as a landscape of opportunity made it an obvious target for atomic experiments. In the late 1950s, the AEC investigated the possibility of using the atom to reconfigure natural geography. Nuclear scientists entertained notions of carving mountain passes and redirecting rivers with controlled explosions. Backers of Project Chariot anticipated a lucrative new harbour in Alaska using atomic detonations. As an executer of ecological transformation, the atom appeared capable of making barren parts of the West habitable. Just like the plough, the irrigation ditch and the wind pump, nuclear energy promised to make the Western environment more hospitable to our management. Lewis Strauss quoted biblical verse on the promises of atomic schemes, that 'They shall beat their swords into plowshares, and their spears into pruning hooks'. While Strauss referred to the bomb being put to good use, his comment was couched in farming imagery. Nuclear power harboured agricultural properties for application throughout the West. Research included the use of 'atomic rays' to preserve milk and the 'turning of sawdust into cattle feed'. Plans went far beyond the placement of Minutemen Missiles in 'the seemingly empty world' of the mid-Western farmer, silo next to silo. Jefferson's idea of a virtuous agrarian West resided in the backdrop to atomic visions. Nuclear tools promised technological solutions to ecological conundrums. Atomic scientist Edward Teller enthused how atomic projects would 'make deserts bloom'. Similar to the Western aphorism that 'the rain followed the plow', atomic planners fully expected green pastures to hail from nuclear bombs and electrical fields. Technological innovations spelled a landscape of promise.[14]

Advertisements promoting peaceful nuclear projects resounded with a frontier vernacular of 'Old West' romance. Once a gang of 'rough-and-ready pioneer gas and electric companies', Pacific Gas and Electric (PG&E) dominated energy provision in California in the twentieth century. The corporation built its first ('pioneer') nuclear plant, Vallecitos, near Livermore in 1957. In the mid-1960s, PG&E invited speculators to 'Join the Second Gold Rush' by investing in nuclear energy production. Although European scientists such as Wilhelm Roentgen and Marie Curie experimented with radioactivity in their laboratories during the late 1890s, atomic energy had been considered 'fool's gold' (Sir Ernest Rutherford called it 'moonshine') until hit upon in the American West in the 1940s. Now one Western electrical utility willingly speculated on a 'second gold rush' unfolding. Corporate advertising strategy presented uranium as the new ore of optimism for developers, with a return to the halcyon mineral days of 1849 beckoning. Nuclear industrialists, like mineral barons of the Gold Rush era, thought of the land primarily in terms of resource extraction. The rubric of Western advertising brought glory to such utilitarian endeavours by associating nuclear progress in the 1960s with the heroic stories of a lost frontier age.[15]

Nuclear dreams in the urban far West tapped into the perennial search for new frontiers and technological innovations. At the Seattle World's Fair in 1962, a Century 21 exposition foresaw a 'World of Tomorrow' where Westerners worked a twenty-four hour week, with plenty of leisure time to spend in their high-tech homes fuelled by solar and nuclear energy. 'Tomorrowland' at Disneyland, Anaheim, California was similarly impregnated with atomic utopianism. Nuclear energy appeared in several guises across Tomorrowland. 'Adventures through Inner Space' promoted an understanding of atomic particles as part of an exploration of scientific progress. Monsanto's 'House of the Future' included an 'Atoms for Living Kitchen' for the next-generation nuclear family. Meanwhile, General Electric's 'Carousel of Progress' boasted a 240-seat rotating theatre that travelled 'through time', with an audio-animatronic family accompanying Disney tourists through four 'acts'. The Carousel ended with a visit to 'Progress City' where 'Mother' and 'Father' apotheosised futuristic urban facilities:[16]

Mother: 'Today our whole downtown is completely enclosed. Whatever the weather is outside, it's always dry and comfortable inside.'
Father: 'General Electric calls it a climate-controlled environment. But Mother calls it . . .'
Mother: 'A sparkling jewel. Now far off to your right, we have a welcome neighbor . . .'
Father: 'Our General Electric nuclear power plant, dear.'[17]

The energy from the nuclear plant could be used to power a perfectly artificial lifestyle. General Electric promised to make any western location eminently liveable.

Shifting Fortunes

In the 1970s, escalating fears over reactor accidents, evidence of military personnel being used as atomic guinea pigs in the 1950s, along with growing discomfort over the effects of radiation on human life rendered atomic facilities unwelcome neighbours. While desperate to divert the anti-nuclear cloud descending on parts of the West, the American nuclear industry failed to innovate in terms of advertising. Themes of nuclear families and futuristic kitchens continued unabated, with the atom still promising healthy suburban living. At a power plant nuclear information centre in central California, exhibits proffered 'excitement, education and entertainment for the whole family'. A pulsating and strangely nihilistic 'future clock' anticipated a life of '3D television, home computers and electrical cars', with nuclear power in the backdrop. Rather than forwarding plans for first strikes on the Soviet Union, an unfortunately titled 'nuclear theater' relayed the story of atomic energy on film. One advertisement published in 1973 illustrated the difference between two potatoes stored for eighteen months, one full of maggots, the other perfectly preserved thanks to a process of irradiation. Radiation dosage from living near a nuclear plant (estimated at 1 mrem) was favourably compared against levels of natural radiation found in Western cities such as Las Vegas (48 mrem), Salt Lake City (72 mrem), and, worst of all, Denver (81 mrem). Loyal employees of Diablo Canyon nuclear plant in California wore T-shirts declaring 'a little nukey never hurt any one' as they faced crowds of protesters in the late 1970s. Nuclear energy seemed consistent with the attainment of a healthy way of life in the West.[18]

Nuclear tourism wooed those Westerners still undecided over the merits of atomic energy. However, during the late 1970s the atom faded out of fashion. Atomic optimism seemed stale and '1950s'. Modern anti-nuclear discourse, billing its own anti-consumer, anti-corporate values, poked fun at passé notions of atomic-fuelled consumption. In California, protesters designed their own pastiches of atomic advertisements. Kitchen pans made from recycled radioactive waste allowed you to 'Cook in the dark without lighting your stove', a 'Nu Clear' 'strontium-enriched' hair shampoo removed 'head and shoulders', while an MX 'export' beer advised, 'Before thirst strikes reach for the first strike!'. Western film studios also explored black comedy in nuclear scenarios. An *Airplane!*-style spoof of nuclear tourism, *The Big Bus* (Paramount, 1976) detailed the bizarre journey of an atomic-powered coach, 'Cyclops', from New York to Denver. Unveiled to the music of *Thus Sprach Zarathustra* by Richard Strauss (of *2001: A Space Odyssey* fame) and *America the Beautiful*, Coyote Company's Cyclops boasted a lounge, a bar, a bowling alley and a swimming pool. Once packed with tourists, the bus reached the West in record time thanks to its atomic fuel and hero driver, although it nearly crashed on tight corners in the southern Rockies. It seemed only natural that the bus travelled from East to West. As Henry David Thoreau mused in *Walking* (1862), 'we go westward as into the future, with a spirit of enterprise and adventure.'[19]

Hollywood producers also used nuclear war as a convenient backdrop for post-apocalyptic Western survival stories. Giving the Wild West an atomic makeover resulted in tales of vigilantism, lone heroes and ruthless bandits set in dusty, radioactive climes. *A Boy and His Dog* (LQJ, 1974) recounted the journey of Vic (Don Johnson) and his canine friend Blood across a post-nuclear Western landscape, including a doomed visit to a dark (both literally and figuratively), subterranean 'Topeka', full of bizarre post-holocaust Christian 'farmers'. The Western dream had become a nuclear nightmare. The stereotypical god-loving, small-town agriculturalist of the West had apparently regressed (or mutated) into an antediluvian eccentric. There seemed little hope for the classic Western farming community on first strike.

A far more mainstream movie, *Red Dawn* (United Artists, 1984) posited the loss of the American West to Soviet and Cuban invasion following limited atomic exchange. After the capture of their Colorado town, a band of young boys honed their frontier survival skills in local hills. They soon retook small-town America from the hapless Reds, demonstrating how Western woodcraft could bring national salvation. Meanwhile, in the *Mad Max* trilogy (1979, 1981, 1985), the classic gun toting, hardy Western hero was re-invented in a post-apocalyptic landscape (albeit of Australian origin). Along with themes of radioactive decay and deprivation, the celluloid atom encouraged cinema devotees to regain their westernness, to rediscover a frontier zeitgeist. Even if the worst fears came true, and atomic bombs reigned down on the United States, it seemed plausible that remote westerly regions would still survive and that frontiersmen would emerge victorious from the wilderness.

Commemorating the Atomic Frontier

With the 'ending' of the nuclear frontier in the 1990s came subtle shifts in how Americans related to the atom. As the threat of nuclear war receded, issues of decontamination and clean-up became more significant. Local communities puzzled 'what next' with the closing of nearby nuclear sites, and wondered how leaking barrels of radioactive by-products could be removed effectively from military facilities. Nuclear fear transmuted into reservations over where to dump the waste accumulated over a fifty-year period of experimentation. Atomic hotspots epitomised 'the Ugly West', a region made legendary by its toxic and impoverished places. 'These extraordinary landscapes put to rest the myth of the West as the final uncontaminated frontier', commented the late Alexander Wilson. Westerners reflected on the degree to which nuclear developments had changed their lives, and altered their landscapes.[20]

Nuclear tourism survived in the 1990s due to its rich heritage, off-the-wall status and the atom's firm associations with Western identity. As if its secrets had never been fully unravelled, the atom continued to intrigue the American psyche. For those interested in nuclear technology, a visit to the National Atomic Museum on Kirtland Air Force Base in Albuquerque, New Mexico represented a must. Museum staff invited tourists (with their cameras) into a time capsule of atomic culture, aboard a journey to an old atomic frontier. Enthusiasts gazed with wonder at the world's smallest nuclear device, 'Davy Crockett', as if a hero of the mythic Old West. At just 76 lb (approx 35.5 kilos), Crockett represented a one-man arsenal in the nuclear age, the missile equivalent of the deadly last bullet in a Colt six-shooter. The museum organised summer science camps and travelling exhibits. A gift shop sold a cornucopia of atomic-themed gifts, from 'Fat Man' and 'Little Boy' shot glasses to silk ties with atomic symbols, 'used' Geiger counters to the latest in DVD documentaries. Officials recognised that each visitor wanted a piece of the atom to take home with them. The nuclear age denoted something to commemorate and buy into. Whether at the National Atomic Museum, the Grand Canyon National Park or Disneyland, tourists proved eminently willing to part with their dollars.

Within driving range of the National Atomic Museum, Trinity Site, a national historic landmark since 1975, attracted tourists who desired a more tangible encounter with the nuclear era. Opened once in April and once in October, Trinity offered a unique Western experience to around 4,000 guests each year. A few tourists travelled by themselves along a prescribed route through White Sands Missile Range to reach the site, while others followed a military police caravan, an atomic convoy, from Alamogordo to Trinity. Visitors spent their day relaxing, eating hamburgers, sipping cola and taking snapshots of ground zero. 'Whatsgoingon.com' internet guide described Trinity as 'a Great Big Trip', sarcastically noting how any voyage into White Sands Missile Range automatically qualified as 'fun for the whole family'. Wandering tourists studied tiny pieces of Trinitite (also known as Trinite) lying on the ground, sand turned into radioactive green-coloured glass by the heat of the first atomic explosion. A visit to Trinity provided a rare opportunity to explore the mythic, regional and natural attributes of the Nuclear West, to engage in a post-atomic epiphany. The success of Trinity as a tourist site indicated a growing recognition of atomic facilities as valuable cultural and historic landmarks, part of the Western heritage to be preserved alongside military battlefields, national parks and Spanish missions.[21]

Although still under military jurisdiction, the Nevada Test Site entertained tourists daring enough to travel through a bombed and blasted domain. Opened to the public once every quarter, the test site was visited by up to 10,000 people each year. Leaving from Las Vegas, vacationers forwent their casino pleasures for a sojourn through atomic history. As if joining a theme ride at Disneyland, nuclear sightseers boarded a bus that transported them to a mythical landscape. Department of Energy guides provided commentary on the atomic attractions. Highlights included Shot Smoky Crater and 'Doom Town', a miniature suburbia (once replete with mannequins) hastily constructed in the 1950s to estimate the effects of a nuclear blast on the residential landscape. A consortium of ruined shacks covered with dust and cobwebs, Doom Town in the 1990s resembled an archetypal ghost town of the Old West. Like Cripple Creek, Colorado and Tombstone, Arizona, its name served as a storyboard of troubled human endeavours. A brief flirtation with 'atomic progress' had left the area desuetude and decrepit.[22]

Touring nuclear sites in Nevada and New Mexico, itinerant Americans experienced the palpable westernness of the atomic age: the dusty atomic cities, the barbed wire fences in desolate lands, the radiation warning signs trampled by cattle. At Trinity Site, the George McDonald Ranch House, restored by the National Park Service in 1984, testified to a fusion of Western and atomic culture. A German immigrant rancher constructed the house in 1913. In 1945, atomic scientists used the master bedroom for assembling the plutonium core of the world's first atomic bomb. Visiting the adobe in the 1990s, tourists were reminded of the romance of 'pioneering in the desert' and the allure of mixing hard work with natural tranquillity. In order to succeed, cattle ranchers and nuclear pioneers overcame their fears of physical and psychological isolation, triumphing over an arid, unfriendly trans-Mississippi climate. A poignant example of the placement of atomic structures on Western foundations, the McDonald Ranch somehow survived fiery radioactive blasts and the ravages of a desert environment. Rather than an abstract theme in history, the nuclear age was manifest in material form and assumed a cogent regional identity. Mushroom clouds reaching up to the heavens literally heralded from western soil and sand.

In contrast to AEC pictures of atomic tests in the 1950s – which usually focused on the ball of dust and debris thrown up by military excellence – tourist snaps of atomic enterprise in the 1990s showed mostly sky and desert. Nature loomed large in amateur photographs of nuclear schema, reiterating that atomic experiments occurred in real and distinctive Western environments. Big open spaces rendered atomic facilities small and insignificant, anthills against mountains. The unexpected presence of fauna and flora at bombed-out craters meanwhile suggested the transitory nature of the nuclear age. Icons of the naturally Wild West, bald eagles were spotted hunting in former atomic territories. Tour guides at Nevada Test Site 'sold' local wildlife as patrons of the atomic era, who, in their silence, had no opportunity to argue otherwise. Dedicated in June 2000, Hanford National Monument safeguarded the natural and nuclear assets of Hanford Nuclear Reservation, including an old town site, a reactor building, prehistoric remains of the sloth and mastodon and habitat used by a number of rare and endangered species. National Monument status guaranteed the preservation of the region's eclectic, distinguished past. New species were also discovered at Hanford in the late 1990s, and not of the mutated, three-eyed fish variety popularly documented in *The Simpsons* cartoon series. The latest arrivals included four species of leafhopper and three types of bee. Albeit on a near-microscopic level, natural forces appeared to be retaking the Nuclear West, and reshaping its identity towards a wilderness haven.[23]

With the re-naturalisation process likely to take some time, atomic landscapes none the less retained an aura of Machiavellian danger and Cold War expediency. Military presence remained high at the Nevada Test Site and White Sands Missile Range. 'Keep out' signs, giant unnatural craters and strange lights confirmed atomic places as pariah, even alien, landscapes. In the 1990s, a surge in public interest in alien life forms linked with traditional conceptions of the nuclear archipelago. Mysteries of unidentified flying objects over Nevada partially replaced, as well as built on, mainstream fears aroused by atomic testing. The *X-Files* television series propagated an elaborate tale of government lies, human experimentation and extraterrestrial invasion. Clandestine military activity at Western nuclear sites gave credence to notions of secret government projects. The atom seemed party to a greater story of deception. Those Westerners who sought out atomic spaces did so for excitement, danger and sometimes revelation. Trips to Trinity or the Nevada Test Site tapped into a broader cultural fixation with the curious and off-limits. People wanted to know what the government and military had been hiding in the desert since Roswell. The Nuclear West seemed to hold part of the answer.

During the late 1990s, Westerners debated potential uses of land once used for atomic purposes. The *Detroit News* published a feature on Topeka schoolteacher Ed Peden and his 'Home on the [missile] range'. Peden declared nuclear missile silos 'the castles of this 20th Century' due to their ability to survive nuclear attack. Peden had converted a fast-decaying atomic silo into a prototype enclave of 'civilized living', transforming 'what once housed an 82-foot Atlas-E rocket and a command center where two officers sat ready to push launch buttons that would bring about nuclear doomsday' into a multi-storey residence complete with an antique piano. Converted nuclear silos tapped into the Westerner's legendary longing for individualism and independence. Silos could serve as bastions of the rugged loner or the anti-federal agent. The nuclear age had promised brightly lit, clean and friendly American suburbs, but instead delivered concrete fantasies for isolationists. Peden's 'home on the range' was an eccentric paean to the joys of westerly independence. Portland General Electric meanwhile offered the land surrounding its decommissioned Trojan nuclear plant for use as a state park. One Western newspaper commented on the competition for uncontaminated sections of Hanford Nuclear Reservation in early 1996. Native Americans, farmers, ranchers and conservationists all laid claim to slices of the post-atomic pie. As if there was no land left in the West to buy up, soiled nuclear property spelled a land rush vaguely reminiscent of frontier times. According to the *High Country News*, 'the real estate' was 'hot' with interest.[24]

With plans to turn atomic sites into quirky homes and nature parks, and government officials preparing chambers below Yucca Mountain, Nevada, for radioactive waste storage, the material Nuclear West neared dinosaur-like status at the beginning of the twenty-first century. Trinity Site and the National Atomic Museum denoted rare monuments to a past age, preserving a Nuclear West of the Cold War era. Visitors entered such places to re-create the excitement and fear surrounding the atomic frontier, to rediscover a time when the atomic age seemed omnipotent.

For many Americans, the Nuclear West had become something encountered in movies rather than an objective reality. Recognising the entertainment value in atomic sketches, *The Simpsons* series frequently explored nuclear issues. In one 1995 episode, Sideshow Bob threatened to blow up Springfield with a nuclear bomb unless town residents gave up their insalubrious television addiction. Rather than fretting over atomic Armageddon, citizens obsessed about a world without the cathode ray tube. Bob detonated the ten-megaton bomb, but, as an antique of Cold War America, it failed to explode.[25]

The recreational side of the Nuclear West had clearly moved on from its rude awakenings, providing more than just anatomic babes and atomic cocktails. Austin, Texas featured an Atomic Cafe Night Club, while San Francisco boasted the rock group 'Nukes'. Nuclear proliferation literally translated into an atomic symbol harmlessly penetrating the shopping mall, local bar and television screen. Only at the beginning of the twenty-first century, after the nuclear coterie had long given up its quest to sell the atom as a recreational product, had Western culture re-branded the nuke as a leisure trademark.

Conclusion

In summer 1979, conservation journal *Cry California* considered the future of the Nuclear West past decommissioning and waste burial. One illustration featured a busy freeway next to a defunct reactor. Road signs invited drivers to stop and 'See the Historic Radioactive Ruins, Vistapoint – Mi.', to take a break at the 'Retired Reactor Restaurant', and purchase atomic 'postcards, souvenirs, contaminated soil and curios'. Gaudy promotions of fast food and atomic mementos had successfully transformed an aged reactor into a prime tourist attraction. The cartoon picture was not meant to impart serious comment, and yet, we may soon commemorate the nuclear age in a similar vein. Today, off tourist-boulevard Route 66, the town of Grants, New Mexico, features a sophisticated uranium-mining museum that recreates an underground mine for visitors to safely explore. Opposite the museum, a run-down Uranium Café competes with traditional Route 66 diners for custom. Tourists have always been drawn to the West for its collection of unusual monuments and curiosities. Vacationers travelled to Yellowstone in the late nineteenth century to witness the bizarre mud pots and geysers. The cities of Los Angeles and Las Vegas, by their sheer excess and opulence, attract thousands of migrants and holiday spectators. Nuclear monuments fit within this broader Western tradition of visiting the extraordinary, of seeking out the unnatural and the exotic. Atomic craters may yet rival the giant meteor crater near Flagstaff, Arizona, for sheer entertainment value.

Yet, for all its kitsch associations and Route 66 connections, the Nuclear West remains a 'place' of solemnity, solitude, conquest and sacrifice. Westerners attend atomic sites for personal contemplation and to deepen their understanding of times past. Visiting a nuclear site is a personal journey into memory as well as history – images of mushroom clouds, duck and cover drills, the Cuban missile crisis – grouped together under the category of Armageddon. Nuclear sites represent war memorials of the Cold War, places of silence and invisible power stretching across vast expanses of Western territory.

Rendered, at different points in time, as a fantastical cornucopia and an unredeemable wasteland, the Nuclear West can be found at opposite ends of a spectrum charting human imaginings. Visions of the Nuclear West draw on both the old, Turnerian frontier of glorious progress and the New Western narrative of environmental and human destruction. Irregardless of whether atomic energy generated social or economic improvements, the American West served as a place of hope as well as despair during the nuclear age. While the greater, more important, story of the Nuclear West indubitably remains one of sacrifice and loss, impressions of the Western landscape based loosely on the 'sunny side of the atom' remain important. Both 'good' and 'bad' atoms have altered how both residents and visitors to the American West engaged (and still engage) with the landscape. Pondering some of the social fallout of the nuclear age, María Montoya recognised that 'the Cold War has influenced how Americans, particularly westerners, think about the landscape around them, and their relationship with it'.[26]

Notes

1. 'Reagan's arms control plan is a bomb', Abalone Alliance newspaper *It's About Times* (May–June 1982), p. 1, Resource Center for Non-Violence, Santa Cruz. During the late 1970s and early 1980s, the Abalone Alliance served as a coalition forum for anti-nuclear activists across California.
2. María Montoya, 'Landscapes of the Cold War West', in Kevin Fernlund (ed.), *The Cold War American West* (Albuquerque: New Mexico University Press, 1998), p. 9. While conventionally seen as a global battle between two superpowers, Kevin Fernlund shrewdly points out that in reality 'The U.S. government *waged* this non-war as much within its borders as abroad', with the military–industrial complex littered across the American West: Fernlund (1998), p. 1.
3. Fernlund ponders if the most accurate phrase is transformed or deformed (p. 2). It should also be noted that the military transformation of the West was significant during the Second World War: see Gerald D. Nash, *The American*

West Transformed: The Impact of the Second World War (Bloomington: Indiana University Press, 1985) and *World War II and the West: Reshaping the Economy* (Lincoln: University of Nebraska Press, 1990). See: for example, Valerie L. Kuletz, *The Tainted Desert: Environmental and Social Ruin in the American West* (New York: Routledge, 1998); Rebecca Solnit, *Savage Dreams: A Journey into the Landscape Wars of the American West* (Berkeley: University of California Press, 1994); and Mike Davis, 'Dead West: ecocide in Marlboro Country', in Valerie Matsumoto and Blake Allmendinger (eds), *Over the Edge: Remapping the American West* (Berkeley: University of California Press, 1999). An educational radio broadcast by CBS during 1947 entitled 'The Sunny Side of the Atom' helped to popularise references to a 'brighter tomorrow' through nuclear technology.
4. Hal Rothman, *The Greening of a Nation?: Environmentalism in the United States Since 1945* (Orlando: Harcourt Brace, 1998), p. 137.
5. 'Atomic-Age Sight-Seeing Way Out West', *The New York Times*, 15 April 1951; Terrence R. Fehner and F. G. Gosling, 'Origins of the Nevada Test Site' (Department of Energy, MA-0518, December, 2000), p. 78; Scott Kirsch, 'Watching the bombs go off: photography, nuclear landscapes, and spectacular democracy', *Antipode*, 29/3 (1997), p. 239.
6. 'Atomic-Age Sight-Seeing', *The New York Times*, 15 April 1951.
7. 'Where the atom was born', *The New York Times*, 4 July 1965.
8. 'Records: the atom', *The New York Times*, 15 April 1951.
9. Message from President Eisenhower, read at 'Atoms for Peace' exhibit in London, England, June 1955.
10. 1955 speech, extracts featured in 'Commercial Electric Power from Atomic Energy', *Science* (29 July 1966), p. 192; Lewis Strauss referred to 'electrical energy too cheap to meter' during a speech to the National Association of Science Writers in September 1954; PG&E advertisement 'The nuclear powered toaster' reprinted in Mark Evanoff, 'The 18-year war against the truth', *Not Man Apart*, (11 September 1981). AEC promotional films of the 1950s anticipated atomic toothpaste, suitcases and cars: *Pandora's Box: A is for Atom* (BBC, 16 July 1992).
11. '"Play with atom at home" selling point of new toy', *The New York Times*, 28 February 1950. The marketing of official 'atomic' toys appeared preferable to teenagers freely experimenting with cocktails of chemicals. In December 1945, four children were hurt while attempting to 'construct' an atomic bomb in a Brooklyn apartment (NY); Michael Smith, 'Advertising the atom', in Michael J. Lacey (ed.), *Government and Environmental Politics: Essays on Historical Developments Since World War Two* (Washington, DC: Woodrow Wilson Center Press, 1989), p. 244.
12. 'AEC approves study for atomic locomotive', *The New York Times*, 25 March 1955; 'Benson Ford sees atom Fueling autos of future', *The New York Times*, 2 October 1951; '30-minute flight over ocean seen', *The New York Times*, 4 May 1955; Dr Lyman Spitzer, Jr, Associate Professor in Astrophysics. 'Travel by atomic rocket to Mars forecast at Yale', *The New York Times*, 23 June 1947; Fehner and Gosling, 'Origins of the Nevada Test Site', p. 66.
13. Carl Abbott, 'Building the atomic cities: Richland, Los Alamos, and the American planning language', in Bruce Hevly and John M. Findlay (eds), *The*

Atomic West (Seattle: University of Washington Press, 1998), p. 108; Richard White, 'Hanford: boomtown of the atomic frontier', *High Country News*, 28/1 (22 January 1996).
14. V. I. Lenin, 'Draft plan of scientific and technical work', written in 1918, published in *Pravda*, 4 March 1924. See: Peter Coates, 'Project Chariot: Alaskan roots of environmentalism', *Alaska History*, 4/2 (Fall 1989), pp. 1–31, and Dan O'Neill, *The Firecracker Boys* (New York: St. Martin's Press, 1994); Strauss quoted Micah 4:3 during his swearing-in ceremony as Chairman of the AEC in July 1953; 'Atoms on the farm', *The New York Times*, 29 August 1951; Montaya, p. 12. See: Edward Teller with Allen Brown, *The Legacy of Hiroshima* (New York: Doubleday, 1962), pp. 81–91.
15. 'The PG&E Story', www.pge.com, taken from Charles Coleman, *P.G.&E. of California: The Centennial Story of Pacific Gas and Electric Company, 1852–1952* (New York: McGraw-Hill, 1952); 'Special Report on Diablo Canyon', *PG&E Life*, x/6 (June 1967), p. 12, Sierra Club Collection, 71/103c, box 113, file 40, Bancroft Library, University of California, Berkeley. PG&E's claims noted in Martin Litton and Frederick Eissler, 'John Muir would have voted YES', *Sierra Club Bulletin*, 54/2 (February 1969), p. 7, Sierra Club Collection, 71/103c, box 117, file 33.
16. John M. Findlay, *Magic Lands: Western Cityscapes and American Culture After 1940* (Berkeley: University of California Press, 1992), p. 252.
17. Details of the nuclear exhibits can be found at Werner W. Weiss's unofficial 'virtual theme park' of disbanded Disneyland attractions at: www.yesterland.com.
18. PG&E, 'PG&E Diablo Canyon Nuclear Information Center', booklet (1976); Portland General Electric advertisement reprinted in *It's About Times* (February–March, 1984), p. 10; PG&E, 'Diablo Canyon Power Plant', brochure (undated). A Westinghouse Electric Corporation 'Radiation' (1979) booklet followed a similar tactic of highlighting cosmic radiation levels at cities above sea level.
19. Cookware, *It's About Times* (June–July, 1981), p. 2; Shampoo, *It's About Times* (December–January, 1984), p. 15; Beer, *It's About Times* (October–November, 1983), p. 13.
20. William Reibsame (ed.), *Atlas of the New West: Portrait of a Changing Region* (New York: Norton 1997), p. 132; Alexander Wilson, *The Culture of Nature: North American Landscape from Disney to the Exxon Valdez* (Cambridge: Blackwell, 1992), p. 279.
21. Attendance figures provided by the Public Affairs Office, White Sands Missile Range; 'The Great Big Trip: The Trinity Site Tour at Ground Zero', at: www.whatsgoingon.com. Trinity open days date back to the late 1950s.
22. '50 Years from Trinity: Part II, Nevada Test Site', *The Seattle Times* internet article, at: www.seattletimes.nwsource.com/trinity.
23. John Stang, 'Hanford habitat key to survival', *Hanford News* (online), reprinted from 'A matter of habitat' series in the *Tri-City Herald*, 25–8 February 1996; Solnit, *Savage Dreams*, pp. 204–11.
24. John Hanna, 'Home on the (missile) range: Silo living', *The Detroit News*, 11 November 1995, at: www.missilebases.com/20th_Century_Castles. For silo renovation ideas, see K. Turner's 'Home improvement for missile bases' website at: www.members.tripod.com/~kturnerga/silo.htm; 'From nuclear plant to state

park?', *Hanford News*, 15 August 1999; Ken Olsen, 'At Hanford, the real estate is hot', *High Country News*, 28/1 (22 January 1996).
25. 'Sideshow Bob's Last Gleaming', *The Simpsons* (26 November 1995).
26. Montaya, p. 11.

Chapter 12

Re-creation and the Theme Park West

Tourism is pivotal to the economic survival of the West. In 2003, the state of California alone amassed $12 billion in tax revenue from travel and tourism, the highest figure in the country. Around one-third of Nevada's workforce is employed in the sector. Each year, around seven million people visit Wyoming for its national parks, cowboy ranches and the Oregon Trail. The self-advertised 'Forever West' state retains a population of less than 500,000, with 10 per cent working in the tourist industry (the second largest sector employer). But the tourist industry is hardly a new phenomenon in the trans-Mississippi region. In the nineteenth-century West, railroad companies fervently encouraged Easterners to 'go West' as part of their travel plans. National parks depended on railroad travel for their early survival. Tourism often incorporated a colonial aspect with European hunting parties amassing huge kill tallies on trips to the Rockies and the Great Plains. The romance of the open range attracted people to dude ranches and rodeo shows. If the essential meaning of tourism is taken as travel to novel and unfamiliar environments, then arguably, many historic visitors to the West could be classified as tourists, including Meriwether Lewis and William Clark.

During the twentieth century, the tourist industry gradually came to dominate sectors of the Western economy. Early twentieth-century travelling shows exploited nostalgia for a newly lost frontier. Wild West shows provided circus-like frivolities celebrating Euro-American conquest. Akin to a 'staged history lesson', Buffalo Bill's Congress of Rough Riders combined popular education with entertainment up to 1915. Some Westerners recognised the potential in selling the West as a distinctive experience. In Las Vegas, city boosters conspired to forge a lucrative gambling Mecca in the desert. The city (and state) economy came to thrive on visitor dollars. Sometimes technological change boosted the recreational economy. Railroad excursions to national parks merged seamlessly into automobile rides through the wilderness – quite literally, in the case of the Wawona Tunnel Tree in Yosemite National Park, a sequoia 'drive-thru' experience until the tree, unsurprisingly, collapsed in 1969. As automobile use exploded in the 1950s, so too did mechanised tours of national parks. Few visitors wandered off the beaten track, preferring instead a 'windshield wilderness' experience. Park docents stopped at the concessionary outlets and restaurants. The sale of cheap mementos of the great outdoors in Fred Harvey park stores reflected the growing connection between heritage and consumption in the West. The tourist industry also kept towns alive. The demise of many extractive industries, including logging, mines and agriculture, left significant economic vacuums in the region. At some of these locations, tourism plugged the holes. Former railroad town and 'Carrot Capital', Grants in Cibola County, New Mexico, welcomed Route 66 tourism that outlasted even its significant uranium rush (1950 to 1982). Moab in south-eastern Utah similarly went through booms in agriculture and uranium mining before becoming a popular tourist destination thanks to its proximity to Arches National Monument, Canyonlands National Park and prime mountain-biking country. As historian Michael A. Amundson described it, Moab went from 'Yellowcake to Singletrack'.[1]

The tourist industry transforms places. While superficially about the preservation of an 'historic' West, fundamentally tourism remains about the 'marketing of images, of information, of spectacle' for money. As Hal Rothman observed, 'Regions, communities, and locales welcome tourism as an economic boom, only to find that it irrevocably changes them in unanticipated and uncontrollable ways.' Residents have to 'sell' their city to capture the public imagination and put on a pretence to fit visitor expectations, even assuming 'traditional' cowboy or Indian attire to ensure business. Marketing reaffirms outdated stories and stereotypes. It also contributes to the re-imagining of place, furnishing new myths of the West to maintain visitor interest. Corporations move in to erect generic motels at the gateways to the unique natural monuments of the far West, including the Grand Canyon, Yellowstone and Yosemite. Power seeps from the centre outwards. For Rothman, the process of tourism in the West represented 'a contest for the soul of a place', and those who took the contest remained in the grip of a 'devil's bargain'. That 'bargain' sometimes has payoffs. Places such as Moab, Santa Fe, Las Vegas and Los Angeles all thrive on their recreational and service industries. The success of national parks, with millions of Americans visiting them each year, has created an extensive public lobby for their protection. Yet that same lobby is also responsible for environmental degradation through overuse. Balancing recreation with preservation remains an unresolved issue in the contemporary West. As David Wrobel noted, 'The toured upon' remain an important but often neglected constituency in the tourist industry. Human and non-human residents alike need to be taken into account. For the tourist, too, the popularity of some locations can lead to frustration when the 'trip of a lifetime', becomes one shared in a traffic queue.[2]

Tourism in the West can be divided into two makeshift categories: the 'nostalgic retrograde'; and the 'neo-frontier'. The 'nostalgic retrograde' refers to a range of recreational activities based around frontier staples and a classic popular vision of the nineteenth-century West. It revolves around heritage in the form of museums, historic downtowns and ghost towns, parks and wildernesses. The 'old' necessitates a degree of realism or perceived authenticity. It often features actual relics from the period in question. Fundamentally, the 'nostalgic retrograde' seeks to simulate the past in a form of retroactive imagination, but always with a veneer of glorification. Ghost town haunts such as Calico, California, capture a market for mineral-boon excitement; ranching holidays in Montana recreate the buzz of riding in open space and big sky country; Spanish missions capture the puritan dedication of Franciscan monks. The 'old' is nostalgised, rendered an essentially romantic experience. It also serves as a fleeting reminder of a simpler and more 'savage' time. The 'back to basics' theme is part of the tourist appeal. People travel backward in time in such simulated experiences – modern technology, politics and problems all momentarily disappear. Tourists are encouraged to imagine themselves in the Old West, to take part in the familiar narrative of discovery and conquest. Photographs capture the 'frontier experience', their own standing witness at America's creation myth on the frontier. Such journeys allow the ready consumption of an 'historical experience'. However, the witnessing is always tempered by the tourist view. Spectator impulses for enjoyment and safety reel in the 'nostalgic retrograde' so that the 'frontier experience' replicates the positive elements of frontierism only – unsurprising given that tourists want, first and foremost, an enjoyable holiday.

In terms of the American West, visitors have specific expectations of what they want from a 'frontier experience'. This creates pressures to conform to (an often invented) image. The Monument Valley of rocks and sand is expected to resemble the Monument Valley of John

Ford Westerns. Native American communities are expected to fit the Hollywood Indian or noble savage prescriptive, to prostitute themselves by traditional dances and costume. The 'nostalgic retrograde' also seeks continuance with the Old West. The survival of entertainment forms such as rodeo, hunting and hiking demonstrates a powerful conservation element. However, processes of preservation rely on the gauging of popular whims and wants. Until the 1930s, national park stewards eliminated predators such as the wolf and coyote in part to boost the numbers of deer that could be seen by visitors. Bears were tied to posts to entertain and fed sugary treats. Recreation is squarely founded on the principle of re-creation – the return of the frontier. However, that frontier is always imagined.

Pulling in a different direction is 'New West' tourism, or the 'neo-frontier'. It uses historic frontier markers, the promise of a return to the nineteenth century, but only in the most superficial of forms. It rarely engages in total re-creation or the difficult task of revisionism. The West is presented as a fundamentally modern and user-friendly recreational and consumer landscape, but with a 'frontier tinge' or pioneer façade. Art boutiques in Santa Fe, Indian casinos, Route 66 tourist diners, the indulgent Madonna Inn at San Luis Obispo all retain a certain frontier 'dress code', but invite all-comers (not just middle-class Whites) to indulge in their creature comforts and spending opportunities. 'Neo-frontier' tourism exploits and amplifies a historic image of the West as a vast, open and wild space to escape to, but puts it in a contemporary vernacular of leisure tourism. Sports fans head for skiing at Aspen, mountain-biking at Moab and surfing at Malibu. Tourists drive convertibles along California's coastal-hugging Highway One, looking south to the movies of Hollywood and the scripture of the movie greats. Generic consumer fascination with mementos, shopping and leisure pursuits are packaged in fake pueblo architectural forms at out-of-town malls. The West thus preserves an historic, cultural and social distinctiveness in its manufacture of a neo-frontier identity.

'Neo-frontier' tourism simultaneously encapsulates modernity and post-modernity in the West. It draws on the new symbols of the Western economy. Computer chips, neon lights and café latte replace gold nuggets and cowboy boots. In contrast to the 'Old West', the neo-frontier welcomes ethnic diversity and multiple directions (not just travel westwards). Cheap motels employ a largely Hispanic workforce. All types of visitors are catered for. Occasionally, the new vision really does look forward in time. The fantasy architecture of Las Vegas, the skyscraper landscapes of Denver and Phoenix, point

Re-creation and the Theme Park West

to vertical progression. Dazzling lights and digital movie billboards enthral and captivate. Technology plays a key role in this neo-frontier recreational smorgasbord. At the Museum of Jurassic Technology in Los Angeles, the neo-frontier of technology is celebrated in quintessential LA bizarreness. The museum promotes scientific discovery and imagination in its assemblage of 'relics'. In gothic homage to P. T. Barnum's American Museum in New York that featured the fantastical (and fake) 'Feejee Mermaid', curators at the Museum of Jurassic Technology deliberately challenge their audience to ponder the authenticity and purpose of an array of technological and scientific curiosities such as 'stink ants' (allegedly from Cameroon), models of LA trailer park mobile homes and a 'microminiature' on a needle of Disney's Pluto. Temporal cracks outside the museum puzzle even more. Near to Knott's Berry Farm in Buena Park, the Medieval Times 'dinner and tournament', the apogee of post-modern tourism in the West, attracts punters eager to combine chicken basket meals and jousting knights. The International UFO Museum and Research Center in downtown Roswell utilises the frontier of space travel, crash landings and conspiracy culture to lure its guests. This clash of old and new visions – the retrograde versus the neo-frontier – provide different meanings of the West. Both 'new' and 'old' compete for tourist attention and hustle for revenue.

Frontierland and Frontier Village

Caught in the competition between old and new visions of the West are American theme parks. As of 2005, the West featured over 100 parks in operation, with a further 100 defunct. As three-dimensional fantasy lands of entertainment tourism, theme parks fit squarely within the template of the (post) modern, recreational West. Their emphasis on technology, the pushing of engineering boundaries in the manufacture of rollercoaster rides, situates them firmly on the neo-frontier. Drawing on science-fiction and space exploration, such parks point toward future directions for American society. Equally, most theme parks look backwards for inspiration, sometimes to medieval times, but most often (and most fittingly) to the halcyon days of pioneering. Disneyland in California provides the perfect example of 'Old West' meets 'New West.' Inside the park, two miniature worlds, Frontierland and Tomorrowland, directly face other as though engaged in a duel. The two worlds correspond with the competing visions of the West outside the park berms – of the 'old frontier' and 'new frontier'.

Disneyland opened in Anaheim, California, on 17 July 1955. Cowboy actor and later president Ronald Reagan was one of the hosts for the event. Walt Disney announced before his guests, 'Disneyland is your land'. With a gas leak and automobile gridlock, the fantasy 'land' seemed a little too similar to life in the real West. Critics showed their disdain for the new cartoon empire raised on 160 acres of orange grove, berating Disney for the rampant commercialism and anodyne nature of the exhibits. *Nation* magazine contributor Julian Halevy exclaimed how 'the whole world . . . has been reduced to a sickening blend of cheap formulas packaged to sell'. In fact, Disneyland sported five distinct 'worlds': Main Street USA; Adventureland; Fantasyland; Tomorrowland; and Frontierland. Complete with a working Mark Twain steamship, Yellowstone-styled bubbling mud pots, desert and stagecoach, Frontierland provided a fully interactive re-creation of the mid-nineteenth-century West. On opening day, Fess Parker, star of the *Davy Crockett* TV series that secured ABC the best ratings of the 1950s, patrolled Frontierland in his character. He greeted guests with a friendly Old West smile, as well as wet clothes from a miscreant park sprinkler.[3]

Although presented as something wholly new, the fabric of Disneyland drew very much on the old. Disney imagineers responded to technology fairs and park innovation. World Expositions, such as Chicago in 1893, fermented the interface of nostalgia, pride, high-technology and frontierism. Disney himself visited the 1939 Golden Gate International Exposition in San Francisco. European parks such as Tivoli Gardens in Copenhagen inspired the American cartoonist, who situated his own park, and its clean, family values, as a riposte to the sleaziness and degeneration found at Coney Island, New York.

Frontierland itself was hardly exceptional. The themed world borrowed heavily from older Western entertainment formats, including pulp fiction, Wild West shows and Hollywood Westerns. Owen Wister fittingly described his fictive West as a 'playground of young men' in *The Virginian* (1902). Following on from singing cowboys such as Gene Autry and showmen such as Buffalo Bill, Disney cemented the cowboy figure (and his home, the range) as a cultural signifier of play. Hollywood also infiltrated the Disney world. Park designer Sam McKim drew on his own experience as a bit actor in Hollywood. Harper Goff revisited his set designs for the movie *Calamity Jane* (1953), creating the Golden Horseshoe Saloon as a Disneyfied copy. The experience of Frontierland resembled that of 'living' in a movie. Tourists walked through 'scenes' of downtown duels, stagecoach hi-jinx and visits to exotic Indian villages. Frontierland provided a cartoon-like 'amalgam of many mythic Wests constructed to unfold like a movie'.[4]

Frontierland also borrowed from the amusement business. In 1940, Knott's Berry Farm, a home produce and 'chicken dinner' experience in Buena Park, California, expanded its business into park entertainment. Owners Cordelia and Walter Knott relocated extant structures from a range of ghost towns including Calico and Prescott to manufacture their own 'old frontier' experience. By the 1960s, the farm boasted an 'authentic' Wild West area sporting several amusement rides. Disney fashioned a similar project within his park, but had little interest in the preservation of historic buildings.

Despite Walt Disney's enmity toward Coney Island, the two entertainment landscapes shared some things in common. Coney proved that re-creation of the West did not need to entail museum pieces (or even be located in the West). At the peak of Coney's popularity (the 1890s to 1910s), each of its parks featured some Wild West themed entertainments. Owned by George Tilyou, Steeplechase Park (1897–1964), true to its equine theme, sported a mechanical jackass from 1908 onwards, a simulation of Western rodeo. A five-dollar prize was offered to anyone who could hang on for the full five minutes. In 1912, a man died falling off the jackass. Captain Paul Boyton found room for an American frontier wilderness motif in his marine themed Sea Lion Park (1895–1902). A cage of wild wolves sat alongside water toboggans and a curious 'water circus'. These two older parks were the least effectual in linking history with entertainment. A far more ambitious undertaking, Fred Thompson and Elmer 'Skip' Bundy's Luna Park (1903–44) orchestrated a fantastical themed world. Alongside the successful cyclorama, 'A Trip to the Moon', resided the scenic railroad 'Dragon's Gorge' (1905) that provided a compressed tour of the North Pole, Africa, the Grand Canyon, River Styx and Hades. A range of West-themed entertainments included the 'Great Train Robbery' (1906, just three years after the film), a live performance held on a platform measuring 760 feet by 170 feet (231.65 m by 51.82 m) and at that time the world's largest stage. The following year, Days of '49 (1907) exchanged the railroad robbery with a stagecoach hijack, the railcars traded in for seventy-five men on horseback. In 1912, Luna introduced a burro ride for tourists on a quarter-mile circuit. Pawnee Bill's Wild West Show, affiliated with Buffalo Bill's Rough Riders, also performed at the park. In 1914, the Oklahoma Wild West Show involved a fake 'Deadwood' town of three buildings, inhabited by thirty cowboys, girls and Indian riders. The final park, Dreamland (1904–11) indulged in even greater Western fantasies. Senator William H. Reynolds invested $3,500,000 in Dreamland, and it showed: one million lights made sure of it. Visitors witnessed a village of Moqui Indians, a group of snake dancers (with live rattlesnakes in their mouths), a re-creation of the San Francisco earthquake, a scenic railway 'through Yellowstone', and a Rocky Mountain hold-up. Along with Atlantis, Venice and Pompeii, the frontier West served as one of several 'places' in the Coney kaleidoscope. During the summer of 1909 alone, over twenty million people visited the fantasy worlds of Coney Island.[5]

Disney refined the exotic array of themed rides found at Coney and other amusement parks. Skills in animating a two-dimensional cartoon world for television were reapplied to a three-dimensional plastic/park canvas. Frontierland offered a participation dynamic beyond that of film and television Westerns. Visitors navigated a fully interactive environment that featured actors, moving scenery and rides. Disney heightened the sense of immersion by great attention to detail and the perfection of an internally logical and convincing world. In an article for *True West* magazine in 1958, Disney offered examples of his quest for authenticity. Built at shipyards in Long Beach, California, the Mark Twain steamboat was a perfect small-scale version of a frontier steamboat. A log stockade inside the park was made from wood from Lake Arrowhead, California, worked on by carpenters with cabin and shipbuilding experience; Walt took pride in stating, 'Those logs are the real thing'. Pine posts heralded from Jackson Hole, Wyoming, chosen by the cartoonist himself for their 'unusual burls'. The level of personal investment in Frontierland reflected Disney's love for the Old West, his boyhood fixations with riverboats, railroads and frontier heroes such as Davy Crockett and Daniel Boone. Walking around the park, Disney remarked how 'Frontierland evokes a special response because it reminds me of my youthful days on the Missouri'. It reminded him of home.[6]

The historical geography of the Disney West captured the sense of discovery, motion and adventure on the fictive frontier. The Mark Twain riverboat, the Yesterland & Santa Fe Freight Train, burro rides and stagecoaches all signified westward movement. Turning West off Main Street was akin to leaving St Louis for California, or trading civilisation for the wild. As Richard Francaviglia contended, 'In Frontierland, Disney encouraged visitors to vicariously experience the unknown, turning the theme park visitors into latter-day explorers far removed from the original time and place of exploration.' They entered a world of pioneer spirit. Visitors became tamers of the wild by their excursions on mine trains and Indian canoes: they felt the frontier; they partook in the American creation myth.[7]

Each ride offered its own miniature narrative, or cartoon snapshot, of westward progress. On boarding the Yesterland & Santa Fe Freight Train, the train narrator warned the newly embarked, 'Now, we're heading into the true backwoods. Watch for Indians and wild animals near the water's edge.' The journey took on both geographical and temporal dimensions. Passing through a compressed version of the frontier, Disney docents were encouraged to believe that history passed before them at railroad speed: 'This is the American West as it was a century ago,' continued the narrator. 'Our forefathers who tamed this great wilderness faced constant danger. And there, across the river, is proof – a settler's cabin afire!' Indeed, built on 'unfriendly' Indian Territory (as demarcated on the Disney map) resided the Burning Settler's Cabin. The narrator noted how, 'The old pioneer lies nearby – the victim of an Indian arrow'. Meanwhile, located on Tom Sawyer Island, Fort Wilderness replicated an army outpost on the frontier, complete with canteen and trading post to visit and a range of fake rifles to aim outside with. A park brochure from 1956 related, 'From the parapets and block houses can be seen the vast untamed American wilderness . . . the deer, moose, bear and wildlife of the primitive forest', while 'Beyond the stockade are tepees . . . hostile Indians are on the warpath.' The colonial aspect of the tourist mission was never openly identified, but Disney tour guides none the less participated in a virtual conquest of Native peoples and wildlife.[8]

Suffice it to say, the Disneyfied West diverged dramatically from true frontier experience. Indians were either 'good' or 'bad' – the good entertained with dances, the bad played war. Elements of the frontier story were simply missed out, with little room in the fantasy world for ethnic minorities or stories of atrocity. According to Michael Steiner, the Disney Corporation was guilty of 'Valorizing the European conquest of America, they muffle memories of plundering the land and killing its inhabitants, and they postpone the realization that the frontier is dead, that the real trip is over and there's nowhere to go but back'. Arguably, the Disney West functioned as a neo-Turnerian landscape in its glorification of White movement, in the winning of the West as the making of America. However, the Disney version of Turner put the family, rather than the farmer, first. Disney imagineers crafted the frontier into a family-friendly experience, with none of the threat of hard labour or danger that the Turner incarnation offered. None of the true hardships of westward conquest made their way into the park. Frontierland provided a perfectly safe environment to adventure through. The river rapids and 'unfriendly' Indians posed superficial dangers to travellers. Freedom on the Disney frontier was meanwhile simulated and tightly controlled. People navigated the park by signs and visual attractions, or Disney 'wienies', that directed their movement. Far from being lost in the wilderness, the flow of human traffic was highly orchestrated. The theme park operated like a videogame 'on rails'. While the Disney West was all about amusement and entertainment, it sported its own kind of frontier didacticism of linearity, whimsy and ethnocentrism.[9]

Frontierland succeeded because it captured and realised the West of popular fictive. Walt Disney rendered an already well-formed vision of the 'frontier West' within his parkland. With a supreme ability to both reflect and shape public opinion, the cartoonist forged a plastic West with which every tourist felt comfortable. All the stock items of Hollywood Westerns, dime novels and Wild West shows were in place. Cowboys, Indians, animals and technology all behaved as in the movies. Thanks to earlier fictions, visitors knew how to behave, where to look and what to laugh at in the Disney West. No additional education or preparation was necessary for full enjoyment of the experience. Hence, the 'discovery' of Frontierland by each intrepid visitor was more a case of gazing at Disneyfied sculptures of the known rather than the unknown. Familiarity and predictability ensured customer satisfaction. In realising all common stereotypes of the West, this Disneyfied version of the frontier offered the most reductive myth yet. It appealed to the lowest common denominator in popular culture.

Disneyland also prospered because it captured the aspirations of the 1950s inside its confines, while filtering out the concerns. The 1950s West was a time of affluence, recreation, automobile travel, new technologies and military expansion. It was equally a place of anxiety, conformity, sexism, racism, McCarthyism and Cold War realities (especially given the use of the region for military training). White middle-class families flocked to the 'magic kingdom'. The park pandered to the coveted nuclear family of the period, offering a psychological bomb shelter to escape the atom. Suburban family sedans pulled up in the car park, children and parents alike disbanding to enter a fun and protective environment. Americans could play happy families in Disneyland, irrelevant of any chaos outside. Disneyland offered an escape to the perfect 1950s. The park offered all the right messages and was full of instant rewards in the form of trinkets and wholesale thrills. For Disney, the best example of a perfectly functioning American society was firmly located within park berms. Walt professed that, 'the fantasy is – out there, outside the gates of Disneyland'. The park served more as a miniature society than a model village. Disney's statement of belief also reflected just how much the great cartoonist had retreated into his own personal fantasy.[10]

Frontierland in particular offered sound refuge during the 1950s. The 'old West' narrative appealed to the conservative sentiments of both the reclusive cartoonist and his fans. Like its historic namesake, Disney's cartoon frontier offered an escape for those who needed it. An 'architecture of reassurance' moulded the American West into a safe house for the American family. Carefully executed frontier nostalgia reminded visitors of the values of American exceptionalism, self-confidence, patriotism and the ultimate victory of the righteous over the barbarous. The success of Disney's own *Davy Crockett* television show highlighted the mass appeal of a story where the White American hero fought for his freedom against clearly identified enemies. The Wild West was a playground of analogy in the Cold War and Americans welcomed the comparison. For Francaviglia, Frontierland stood 'as a Cold War statement about the irrepressible spirit of America in overcoming the hostile frontier of that part of the world behind the Iron Curtain where individual aspirations were crushed'. Fantasies played out both within and outside the park.[11]

Disney's Frontierland spawned a number of imitations. In the same period, frontier theme parks opened across the country, including Frontier City at Oklahoma State Fair grounds in 1958 and Frontier Land at Cherokee, North Carolina in 1962. In 1960, Silver Dollar City opened as a twin attraction with Marvel Cave, a deep cavern with a marble-like appearance discovered by the Osage in the 1500s, and first opened as a tourist attraction in 1894. On 21 October 1961, Frontier Village opened in San Jose, California. Located on a thirty-three-acre site within Congressman Everis Anson Hayes' (1855–1942) old estate, Frontier Village promised a smaller, more intimate experience than Disneyland. Local businessman Joe Zukin financed the project, aided by Laurie Hollings, a creative designer with experience of working on film studio sets (including Westerns). Both men took inspiration from Disney. Families queued to pass through the entrance gates of a large wooden fort. The Western-themed environment included a main street, a wilderness, river rides and a museum. The main street resembled a film set with its thin line of buildings. A showdown took

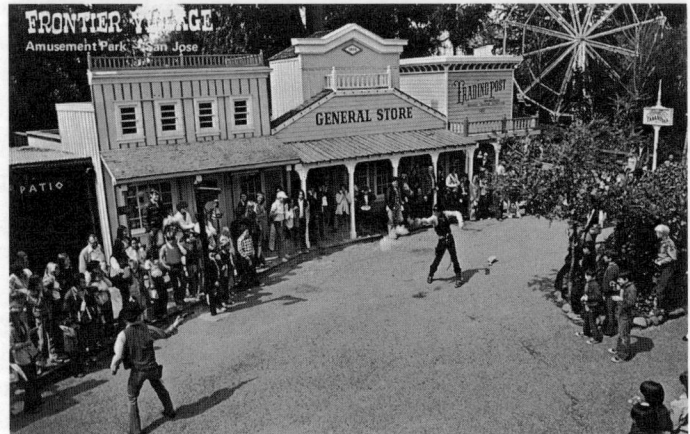

Figure 12.1 Frontier Village postcards, c. 1970s.

place every hour, like clockwork, with the local marshal providing Buffalo Bill-type shows. As with Disney, modes of transport dominated the theme park West. Visitors embarked on burro rides, a mine train (originally destined for the 'Last Frontier'), a railroad, a stagecoach and even canoes (courtesy of 'Indian Jim'). The Southern Pacific Railroad skirted the park, taking passengers past the majority of rides and amusements. The train engineer narrated the journey as part of the entertainment, threatening to send 'pickpockets, card sharks, gun slingers, carpet baggers, or any other polecat', back to town 'barefoot', and advising travellers to be on the best guard on entering 'the heart of Indian Territory, and the Indians out here aren't very friendly'. The possibility of engagement with material nature was higher than at Disney's Frontierland. The park boasted a fishing spot and a zoo, along with a sole buffalo named Cimmeron. However, 'Friendly Theodore Bear' was definitely a person dressed up, as was the later park mascot, Kactus Kong, a bright green gorilla wearing a cowboy hat. The Frontier Village cast Native Americans as pure entertainers. They danced, drummed and postured. Indian Island suggested some historic claim to the region, a sense of place, but was instead nothing more than imitation. Promoted as a 'full blooded Yosemite Indian', Princess Tenaya greeted visitors, including, in the 1970s, Tonto from the Lone Ranger television series. Frontier Village differed from Disney by incorporating a number of generic amusement rides, including a Ferris wheel, merry go round, car ride and puppet show all within the park. This upset the chronological authenticity of the frontier experience. The presence of 'antique autos' against a Wild West backdrop predated Pioneertown's coupling of the old and the new. Like Disney, the Village gained a reputation as a safe and fun family destination. Again, the frontier emerged as a risk free location or family picnic spot.[12]

The post-1945 'wild west' theme parks shared a number of things in common. They all presented the West as a realm of history-fuelled recreation. Stock amusement rides included the mine train, the miniature railroad, the log flume, the Wild West stage show and the shooting gallery. Such entertainments amounted to 'codes' of meaning: signifiers of a frontier based on motion and gun fights. Some parks boasted heritage value, as in the case of Knott's Berry and its preservation of old ghost cabins. But the real mixed with the fake in a periously fluid fashion.

The ability of the theme park to offer a fully immersive Wild West experience situated it as a step-up in simulation from the dime novel and the Hollywood Western. Theme park Wests offered 'Buffalo Bill' style shows that onlookers could finally participate in, even if firearms were disallowed. While the theme park West prospered, the classic 'cowboys and Indians' vision of the West survived, wrapped up in a new recreational and technological band-aid. Even twenty-first century 'virtual Wests' offered less satisfaction than the theme park West due to their lack of tactile functionality. Theme parks realised the popular myth of the West in plastic form, making it as close to a real experience as possible. Arguably, the perfect matching of the simulation to the myth enabled the victory of the 'fake' over the 'real', suggesting that simulated worlds provided a better tourist experience than any 'real' places on the tourist map. On visiting Disneyland's re-creation of New Orleans, Umberto Eco pondered on any need to tour the actual city when the fake version offered so much more and met his desires to ride a steamboat and see alligators. The timbre of the point gained even more significance in a post-Katrina gaze. The fake also had a purpose. French philosopher Jean Baudrillard understood the chief lure of Disney not in terms of its cartoon fantasy but in its genuine celebration of America, 'what draws the crowds is undoubtedly much more the social microcosm, the miniaturised and *religious* revelling in real America'. Rather than situated 'outside' American society, it was, to Baudrillard and Disney alike, the perfection of 'the "real" country, all of "real" America'.[13]

According to this logic, the theme park West left the real West in potential crisis. While the fake matched popular expectations of the American West, the material version inevitably disappointed by its sheer variety, fallibility and failure to match the myth. The facsimile assumed primacy. The authentic or real became not only tarnished but it verged on redundancy. The material landscape fell out of kilter with over-optimistic visitor expectations. As the themed fantasy became more dramatic, more perfected, the division between real and simulated grew, to the point where potentially people no longer needed the real. At that point, if ever reached, the tourist adventure would predominate. The 'West' would be read as one giant theme park.

The theme park West also endangered and perverted the myth of the 'Old West'. As historic contributors to the 'imagining' process, past re-creation industries such as Wild West shows and rodeos shaped popular understandings of the American frontier. Amusement parks continued the process. Park designers cast the nineteenth-century frontier as pure entertainment. They played with history, narrowing the frontier experience in the process. Rendering the 'Old West' as fantasy playground, parks such as Disneyland threatened to turn the 'Old West' vision into childish fairytale. Furthermore, theme park Wests encouraged reverence for their new and discreet fairytales. As Eco identified, 'Disneyland not only produces the illusion, but – in confessing it – stimulates the desire for it'. The desire ran to ensuring the predictable behaviour of fake crocodiles and the majesty of a fake New Orleans, to a cogent 'wild West' representation of the West. If tourists believed what they saw, then the frontier myth was little more than entertainment.[14]

However, the theme park West of the late 1950s and early 1960s never fully blossomed. As simulations of the frontier West, theme park worlds betrayed remarkable flaws. Their purpose, to entertain by rides, automatically precluded any narrative depth or rigour. Few visitors took seriously the cartoon characters and jaunty stereotypes. Constantly reminded of Mickey Mouse and Pluto, visitors to Frontierland could not escape the reality of their presence in a Disney Corporation West, a consumer cartoon creation. The proximity of Frontierland to other clearly imagined worlds such as Fantasyland assured that tourists recognised the broader Disney canon as a fictional enterprise. It was unlikely that many people took the artifice of Frontierland as gospel. The extent of whimsy may even have backfired on the 'Old West' vision, showing instead its weaknesses and errors.

Amusement park neo-Turnerism also failed to match with life outside the berms. The White colonial narrative inside the park seemed socially irrelevant outside it. Frontierland resembled a true fantasy trip, at odds with the multi-ethnic, industrial and metropolitan West. The 'Old West' reverie struggled alongside a rising vision of the region as dominated by global, high-technology businesses. The values of 'frontier lands' appeared in conflict with the key issues of American society in the 1960s. Vietnam, Watergate, race riots and protest marked the demise of a 'black and white' world immortalised on the plastic frontier of Disney. The American Indian Movement of the 1960s and 1970s challenged problematic stereotypes of 'noble savages' that theme parks continued to indulge in. New Western history further questioned the pro-conquest narrative of the theme park West. The rise of realistic portrayals of the West posed a challenge to park fantasies and their frontier mythologies. Frontierland in the 1950s marked not only the apogee of the 'fantasy West', but also its last outpost.

Whether due to competition, real estate prices or a loss of appeal in the mythic West, a number of theme parks floundered only a couple of decades after opening. In 1980, Frontier Village hosted its final season, or, as television adverts span it, 'the last round up'. Rio Grande Industries, owner of the park since 1973, closed the business due to legal difficulties experienced while attempting to expand the enterprise. Sector competition from Marriot's Great America in Santa Clara also contributed. The holding company auctioned rides, furniture (including a Cigar Store Indian), and even sold off dirt as souvenirs (envelopes noted how 'Over seven million visitors have trodden over the souvenir soil contained in the attached packet'). CBS Evening Magazine covered the story, the reporter reminiscing how the park 'gave a lot of us urban dwellers a taste of what the Wild West was like'. The park's foremost ride, the Apache Whirlwind, resembled a dinosaur skeleton. A suburban development grew up on the parkland, fittingly named 'Frontier Village'. Two years later, Frontier Land in North Carolina closed. In 2007, Wild West World, based in Kansas, lasted only one season.[15]

The Disney Corporation updated rides in Frontierland to reflect shifting visions of the American West. Back in the 1950s, Walt Disney had anticipated that his park would mature and grow, as if the plastic trees would somehow bear fruit akin to their organic brethren in California citrus groves. The real process was more akin to pruning. Some changes reflected the desire to reduce the role of live animals within the park and thus better control unpredictable elements. Hence, the Stagecoach Ride along the 'Rivers of America' and across the 'Living Desert' lasted for only four years (1955–9), while mule train tides were phased out in the late 1960s and early 1970s. Other alterations were determined by concern for the Disney image. With its tepees, totem poles, impressive chiefs and 'authentic' ceremonial dances, Indian Village (1955–71) played to all the classic stereotypes of Native American behaviour. An animatronic 'Bear Country' replaced it, with the Country Bear Jamboree (sponsored by Pepsi-Cola) performing country songs. Most illuminating was the case of the Burning Settler's Cabin that could be seen from passing keelboats, canoes and trains in the 1950s. By the 1970s, the deadly Indian arrow had disappeared, with the cabin dweller the supposed victim of pirates. Rather than real flames, an artificial fire effect was used during the energy crisis of 1973. By the 1980s, the frontiersman was drunk from imbibing too much moonshine, rather than dead. In the 1990s, the cabin had accidentally caught fire, endangering a local (fake) eagle's nest. Over several decades, the message of the Burning Settler's Cabin had gone from the dangers of Indian aggression to forest fire prevention. Eliminating all references to Indians in the hope of avoiding controversy, Disney imagineers only reinforced the sense of the Western frontier as a White endeavour. This diverged considerably from modern academic takes on the westward experience. For Patricia Nelson Limerick, the frontier deserved to be seen as a 'multicultural common property, a joint-stock company of the imagination'. In terms of Frontierland, Disney seemed perilously out of touch with such sentiments. However, the mass appeal of any 'Disneyfied' product insulated the corporation from overt criticism.[16]

Competing Visions?

In the 1890s and 1900s, frontier nostalgia captured the dominant mood of the time, people performing in Buffalo Bill shows were themselves live Western heroes, and the Wild West myth carried a degree of social and material realism. By the 1950s, the fantasy no longer matched the material West, but the Wild West as a symbol of a great America suited the Cold War environment in its provision of patriotic home comforts to the anxious White middle classes. A century after the official closure of the frontier, the appeal of the Wild West myth should have dissipated. With the rise of New Western history, a new technological and post-industrial West, and the increasing flow of cross-border migration and global production lines, what could the old frontier myth possibly provide its new audience?

One answer was fantasy entertainment. The 'Old West' vision survived through a neo-frontier filter of technology, post-modernism and tourism, a successful synthesis with the new. Entertainment mediums ensured the persistence of mythology in popular culture, which in turn, boosted the regional tourist economy. For Francaviglia, Disney's 'romanticizing of the "Old West" helped lay the groundwork for the "New West" of amenity tourism and chic residence'. Consumers welcomed technologically sophisticated but narrative light re-creations of the past. Successive technologies recycled the frontier format, the 'Wild West' moving from paper and canvas to celluloid and theme park, even virtual expanse. Such presentations ended up underlining the old frontier as a 'relic' to be entertained by, something increasingly distant and exotic for most people. In the process, theme parks such as Disneyland became the last concrete bastions of the great Wild West illusion. Frontierland was a fantasy realm, an heroic geography, perfectly preserved within the berms of a theme park. Akin to a last survivor hiding inside a circle of wagons, outside its strictures were skyscrapers, crime, cars and confusion: the New West.[17]

Tourists seem supremely capable of navigating competing visions of the West. They drive seamlessly from Calico Ghost Town to bustling, neon-lit Las Vegas in the Mojave. They watch a simulated IMAX cinema performance of the Grand Canyon then sit on the South Rim of the national park taking pictures. The recreational West seems analogous to 'pick and mix' sweets, the visitors choose what they want to consume, then overspend and overeat. Few seem to suffer temporal confusion or simulation fatigue. Such impulses capture the rise of the post-modern West: a place where meta-narratives of old and new frontier myths have no dominant or rightful vantage.

At the same time, tourists are drawn to the West precisely because of its grand messages and powerful images. The old vision had these in spades: 'Go West' for adventure; strike it rich in the gold fields; find freedom from religious persecution; form a new life in the wilderness; help shape the direction of the nation. The 'New West' also shouts 'Go West' for play, strike it rich at casinos and silicon gold mines, find freedom from the metropolis, go hiking in the wilderness and build a new business-savvy, Hollywood-powered country. In fact, the competing visions share some things in common. Apart from racial and colonial dimensions, the two Wests partake in a similar theology. They both forward consumption, opportunism, individualism, movement, escapism and environmental motifs as key. A synthesis is possible. Part of the appeal of Disneyland was to both 're-enact the past', and practice the 'future'. It was no accident that Frontierland and Tomorrowland faced each other. Stuck together, they combined Western nostalgia with futurism. The Disney glue lay in melding together the two visions of the West (and America). Today at Pioneertown, tourists take snapshots of the frontier cabin with its chromed automobile and contemporary plastic chair outside. Not because of the oddity of the image, but because of its completeness. In a West of 'nostalgic retro' and the 'neo-frontier', Pioneertown endures as a prime symbol of a fantasy amalgam.[18]

Notes

1. LeRoy Ashby, *With Amusement for All: A History of American Popular Culture Since 1830* (Lexington: University of Press Kentucky, 2006), p. 81; David Louter, 'Glaciers and gasoline: the making of a windshield wilderness, 1900–1915', in David M. Wrobel and Patrick T. Long (eds), *Seeing and Being Seen: Tourism in the American West* (Lawrence: University Press of Kansas, 2001), p. 249; Michael A. Amundson, 'Yellowcake to singletrack: culture, community and identity in Moab, Utah', in Liza Nicholas, Elaine Bapis and Thomas Harvey (eds), *Imagining the Big Open: Nature, Identity, and Play in the New West* (Salt Lake City: University of Utah Press, 2003), p. 151.

2. Hal Rothman, *Devil's Bargains: Tourism in the Twentieth-Century American West* (Lawrence: University Press of Kansas, 1998), pp. 17, 10; Wrobel and Long (2001), p. 18.
3. Karal Ann Marling, 'Disneyland, 1955: just take the Santa Ana freeway to the American dream', *American Art*, 5/1–2 (Winter–Spring 1991), pp. 172, 170. On amusement parks, see Judith Adams, *The American Amusement Industry: A History of Technology and Thrills* (Boston: Twayne, 1991), and Russel Nye, 'Eight ways of looking at an amusement park', *Journal of Popular Culture*, 15/1 (Summer 1981), pp. 63–75. On Disneyland, see: Karal Ann Marling (ed.), *Designing Disney's Theme Parks: The Architecture of Reassurance* (Paris: Flammarion, 1997); Karen Jones and John Wills, *The Invention of the Park: From the Garden of Eden to Disney's Magic Kingdom* (Cambridge: Polity Press, 2005), Ch. 5; Michael Sorkin (ed.), *Variations on a Theme Park: The New American City and the End of Public Space* (New York: Hill & Wang, 1992); and Sharon Zukin, *Landscapes of Power: From Detroit to Disney World* (Berkeley: University of California Press, 1991), Ch. 8.
4. Owen Wister, *The Virginian* (1902), p. 41; Michael Steiner, 'Frontierland as Tomorrowland: Walt Disney and the architectural packaging of the mythic West', *Montana*, 48/1 (Spring 1998), p. 11.
5. On Coney Island, see: Woody Register, *The Kid of Coney Island: Fred Thompson and the Rise of American Amusements* (Oxford: Oxford University Press, 2001); and John Kasson, *Amusing the Million: Coney Island at the Turn of the Century* (New York: Hill & Wang, 1978).
6. Walt Disney, 'Frontierland', *True West* (May–June 1958), pp. 11, 10.
7. Richard Francaviglia, 'Walt Disney's Frontierland as allegorical map of the American West', *The Western Historical Quarterly*, 30/2 (Summer 1999), p. 158.
8. Details of train ride: 'Burning Settler's Cabin' at: www.yesterland.com/burning-cabin.html (accessed 21 June 2008).
9. Steiner (1998), p. 17.
10. Disney: quoted in Steiner (1998), p. 12.
11. Francaviglia (1999), p. 168.
12. Train ride: 'Frontier Village Railroad' at: www.frontiervillage.net/pages/trainspiel.html (accessed 21 June 2008); Princess Tenaya. 'Remembering Frontier Village stars and celebrities' at: www.frontiervillage.net/pages/stars.html (accessed 21 June 2008). Also, see Gary Singh, 'Silicon alleys: remembering Frontier Village', *Metro* (Silicon Valley), 21–7 September 2005.
13. Jean Baudrillard, *Simulations* (1983), pp. 23, 25.
14. Umberto Eco, *Travels in Hyperreality* (London: Picador, 1986), p. 44.
15. 'Final memories: Frontier Village', *CBS Evening Magazine* (September/October 1980).
16. Patricia Nelson Limerick, 'The adventures of the frontier in the twentieth century', in James R. Grossman (ed.), *The Frontier in American Culture* (Berkeley: University of California Press, 1994), p. 94.
17. Francaviglia (1999), p. 167.
18. Steiner (1998), p. 6.

Bibliography

Listed here are some useful works of scholarship that have appeared on the American West since 1945. It provides a guide for further reference rather than a comprehensive list of all sources used.

General Materials

Allmendinger, Blake, *The Cowboy: Representations of Labor in an American Work Culture* (New York: Oxford University Press, 1993).
Aquila, Richard, *Wanted Dead or Alive: The American West in Popular Culture* (Urbana: University of Illinois Press, 1998).
Barth, Gunter, *Fleeting Moments: Nature and Culture in American History* (New York: Oxford University Press, 1990).
Campbell, Neil, *The Cultures of the American New West* (Edinburgh: Edinburgh University Press, 2000).
Cawelti, John, *The Six-Gun Mystique* (Bowling Green: Bowling Green University Popular Press, 1975).
Cronon, William, George Miles and Jay Gitlin (eds), *Under an Open Sky: Rethinking America's Western Past* (New York: Norton, 1992).
Deverell, William (ed.), *A Companion to the American West* (Malden: Blackwell, 2004).
Findlay, John, *Magic Lands: Western Cityscapes and American Culture after 1940* (Berkeley: University of California Press, 1992).
Johnson, Michael, *New Westers: The West in Contemporary American Culture* (Lincoln: University of Nebraska Press, 1996).
Hine, Robert and John Mack Faragher, *The American West: A New Interpretive History* (New Haven: Yale University Press, 2000).
Limerick, Patricia Nelson, *Legacy of Conquest: The Unbroken Past of the American West* (New York: Norton, 1987).
Limerick, Patricia Nelson, *Something in the Soil: Legacies and Reckonings in the New West* (New York: Norton, 2000).
Matsumoto, Valerie and Blake Allmendinger (eds), *Over the Edge: Remapping the American West* (Berkeley: University of California Press, 1999).
Milner, Clyde II, Carol O'Connor and Martha Sandweiss (eds), *The Oxford History of the American West* (Oxford: Oxford University Press, 1994).

Nicholas, Liza, Elaine Bapis and Thomas Harvey (eds), *Imagining the Big Open: Nature, Identity, and Play in the New West* (Salt Lake City: University of Utah Press, 2003).
Nugent, Walter, *Into the West: The Story of its People* (New York: Vintage, 1999).
Reibsame, William (ed.), *Atlas of the New West: Portrait of a Changing Region* (New York: Norton, 1997).
Ronda, James (ed.), *Thomas Jefferson and the Changing West* (Albuquerque: University of New Mexico Press, 1997).
Rothman, Hal, *Devil's Bargains: Tourism in the Twentieth Century American West* (Lawrence: University Press of Kansas, 1998).
Slotkin, Richard, *Regeneration Through Violence: The Mythology of the American Frontier, 1600–1860* (Middletown: Wesleyan University Press, 1973).
Slotkin, Richard, *The Fatal Environment: The Myth of the Frontier in the Age of Industrialization, 1800–1890* (Middletown: Wesleyan University Press, 1985).
Slotkin, Richard, *Gunfighter Nation: The Myth of the Frontier in Twentieth-Century America* (New York: HarperCollins, 1992).
Smith, Henry Nash, *Virgin Land: The American West As Symbol and Myth* (Cambridge, MA: Harvard University Press, 1978 [1950]).
Solnit, Rebecca, *Storming the Gates of Paradise: Landscapes for Politics* (Berkeley: University of California Press, 2007).
West, Elliott, 'A longer, grimmer, but more interesting story', *Montana: The Magazine of Western History*, 40/3 (Summer 1990), 72–6.
White, Richard, *'It's Your Misfortune and None of My Own': A New History of the American West* (Norman: University of Oklahoma Press, 1991).

Chapter 1

Abbott, Carl, *The Great Extravaganza: Portland and the Lewis and Clark Exposition* (Portland: Oregon Historical Society, 1981).
Ambrose, Stephen, *Undaunted Courage; Meriwether Lewis, Thomas Jefferson, and the Opening of the American West* (New York: Simon & Schuster, 1997 [1996]).
Aron, Stephen, 'The afterlife of Lewis and Clark', *Southern California Quarterly*, 87/1 (2005), 27–46.
Buel, J. W., *Louisiana and the Fair*, vol. 3 (St Louis: World's Progress Publishing, 1804).
Coues, Elliot, *History of the Expedition under the Command of Lewis and Clark to the Sources of the Missouri River* (New York: Dover, 1964 [1893]).
DeVoto, Bernard (ed.), *The Journals of Lewis and Clark* (Boston: Houghton Mifflin, 1953).
Duncan, Dayton and Ken Burns (eds), *Lewis and Clark: The Journey of the Corps of Discovery* (New York: Knopf, 1997).
Jackson, Donald (ed.), *Letters of the Lewis and Clark Expedition with Related Documents, 1783–1854* (Urbana: University of Illinois Press, 1978).
Lang, William, 'Lewis and Clark and the American century', *Montana: The Magazine of Western History*, 48/1 (Spring 1998), 56–61.
Lavender, David, *The Way to the Western Sea: Lewis and Clark Across the Continent* (New York: Harper & Row, 1988).

Moulton, Gary E., *The Journals of the Lewis & Clark Expedition* (Lincoln: University of Nebraska Press, 1983–2001).
Norman, Dean, *On the Lewis and Clark Trail: Wally's Woods*, vol. 2 (Cleveland: Beaver Creek Features & Trafford Publishing, 2002).
Ostler, Jeffrey, *The Plains Sioux and U.S. Colonialism from Lewis and Clark to Wounded Knee* (New York: Cambridge University Press, 2004).

Chapter 2

Bennett, James D., *Frederick Jackson Turner* (Boston: G. K. Hall, 1975).
Billington, Ray Allen, *The Genesis of the Frontier Thesis: A Study in Historical Creativity* (San Marino: The Huntington Library, 1971).
Billington, Ray Allen, *Frederick Jackson Turner: Historian, Scholar, Teacher* (New York: Oxford University Press, 1973).
Billington, Ray Allen, *America's Frontier Heritage* (Albuquerque: University of New Mexico Press, 1974 [1963]).
Etulain, Richard (ed.), *Does the Frontier Experience Make America Exceptional?* (Boston: St. Martin's Press, 1999).
Grossman, James R. (ed.), *The Frontier in American Culture* (Berkeley: University of California Press, 1994).
Hofstadter, Richard, *The Progressive Historians: Turner, Beard, Parrington* (New York: Vintage, 1968).
Hofstadter, Richard and Seymour Martin Lipset (eds), *Turner and the Sociology of the Frontier* (New York: Basic Books, 1968).
Klein, Kerwin Lee, 'Reclaiming the "F" word, or being and becoming postmodern', *Pacific Historical Review*, 65 (May 1996), 179–215.
Taylor, George Rogers (ed.), *The Turner Thesis: Concerning the Role of the Frontier in American History*, 3rd edn (Lexington: D. C. Heath, 1972).
Turner, Frederick Jackson, *The Frontier in American History* (New York: Henry Holt, 1921).

Chapter 3

Bellesiles, Michael, *Arming America: The Origins of a National Gun Culture* (Brooklyn: Soft Skull, 2003 [2000]).
Brown, Bill (ed.), *Reading the West: An Anthology of Dime Westerns* (Boston: Bedford Books, 1997).
Brown, Richard Maxwell, *Strain of Violence: Historical Studies of American Violence and Vigilantism* (New York: Oxford University Press, 1975).
Courtwright, David, *Violent Land: Single Men and Social Disorder from the Frontier to the Inner City* (Cambridge, MA: Harvard University Press, 1996).
Davis, David, 'Ten-gallon hero', *American Quarterly*, 6/2 (Summer 1954).
Deconde, Alexander, *Gun Violence in America: The Struggle for Control* (Boston: Northeastern University Press, 2003).
Denning, Michael, *Mechanic Accents: Dime Novel Accents and Working-Class Culture in America* (London: Verso, 1987).
Dykes, J. C., 'Dime novel Texas; or, the sub-literature of the Lone Star State', *Southwestern Historical Quarterly*, 49/3 online edition.

Bibliography

Dykstra, Robert, *The Cattle Towns* (New York: Atheneum, 1976).
French, Warren, 'The cowboy in the dime novel', *Texas Studies in English*, 30 (1951).
Hofstadter, Richard and Michael Wallace, *American Violence: A Documentary History* (New York: Vintage, 1971).
Hollon, W. Eugene, *Frontier Violence: Another Look* (New York: Oxford University Press, 1974).
Hosley, William, *Colt: The Making of an American Legend* (Amherst: University of Massachusetts Press, 1996).
Johanssen, Albert, *The House of Beadle and Adams and its Dime and Nickel Novels: The Story of a Vanished Literature*, vol. 1 (Norman: University of Oklahoma Press, 1950).
Kohn, Abigail, *Shooters: Myths and Realities of America's Gun Cultures* (Oxford: Oxford University Press, 2004).
Kopel, David, *Samurai, the Mountie and the Cowboy: Should America Adopt the Gun Controls of Other Democracies?* (Buffalo: Prometheus, 1992).
McGrath, Roger, *Gunfighters, Highwaymen & Vigilantes: Violence on the Frontier* (Berkeley: University of California Press, 1987).
Stange, Mary and Carol Oyster, *Gun Women: Firearms and Feminism in Contemporary America* (New York: New York University Press, 2000).
Squires, Peter, *Gun Culture or Gun Control* (London: Routledge, 2000).
Wright, Will, *The Wild West: The Mythical Cowboy and Social Theory* (London: Sage, 2001).

Chapter 4

Barsness, John A., 'Theodore Roosevelt as cowboy: The Virginian as Jacksonian man', *American Quarterly*, 21/3 (Autumn 1969), 609–19.
Brown, Richard Maxwell, *Strain of Violence: Historical Studies of American Violence and Vigilantism* (Oxford: Oxford University Press, 1975).
Brown, Richard Maxwell, *No Duty to Retreat: Violence and Values in American History and Society* (Oxford: Oxford University Press, 1991).
Cannon, Lou, *President Reagan: The Role of a Lifetime* (New York: Touchstone, 1991).
Dellinger, Paul, 'From power to politics: the Western films of Ronald Reagan', *Under Western Skies*, 15 (July 1981), 5–7.
DeVoto, Bernard (ed.), *Mark Twain in Eruption* (New York: Harpers, 1940).
Fishwick, Marshall, 'The cowboy: America's contribution to world mythology', *Western Folklore*, 11/2 (April 1952), 77–92.
Hutton, Paul Andrew, 'Col. Cody, the Rough Riders and the Spanish American War', *Points West* (Autumn 1998), 8–11.
Keller, Alexandra, 'Historical discourse and American identity in Westerns since the Reagan era', in. John O'Connor and Peter Rollins (eds), *Hollywood's West: The American Frontier in Film, Television and History* (Lexington: Kentucky University Press, 2005), 240–60.
Lowitt, Richard (ed.), *Politics in the Postwar American West* (Norman: University of Oklahoma Press, 1995).
Lutz, Wayne, 'The cowboy in us all', *The Tocquevillian*, 30 November 2002.

Mulroy, Kevin (ed.), *Western Amerykanski: Polish Poster Art and the Western* (Los Angeles/Seattle: Autry Museum/University of Washington Press, 1999).
Price, B. Byron, 'Cowboys and presidents', *Convergence: Autry National Center Magazine*, (Spring/Summer 2006), 6–13.
Rogin, Michael, *Ronald Reagan, the Movie, and other Episodes in Political Demonology* (Berkeley: University of California Press, 1987).
Santina, Dan, 'Cowboy imagery and the American presidency', *Counterpunch*, 19 December 2005.
Smith, Hedrick, Adam Clymer, Leonard Silk, Robert Lindsey and Richard Burt, *Reagan the Man, the President* (New York: Macmillan, 1980).
Vaughan, Stephen, *Ronald Reagan in Hollywood: Movies and Politics* (Cambridge: Cambridge University Press, 1994).
Watts, Sarah, *Rough Rider in the White House: Theodore Roosevelt and the Politics of Desire* (Chicago: University of Chicago Press, 2003).
White, G. Edward, *The Eastern Establishment and the Western Experience* (Austin: University of Texas Press, 1989 [1968]).
Wills, Garry, *Reagan's America: Innocents at Home* (London: Heinemann, 1985).
Wills, Garry, *John Wayne: The Politics of Celebrity* (London: Faber & Faber, 1997).

Chapters 5 and 6

Anderson, Karen, 'Work, gender and power in the American West', *Pacific Historical Review*, LXI (1992), 481–99.
Armitage, Susan, 'Revisiting "the Gentle Tamers Revisited": the problems and possibilities of Western women's history – an introduction', *Pacific Historical Review*, LXI (1992), 459–62.
Armitage, Susan and Elizabeth Jameson (eds), *The Women's West* (Norman: University of Oklahoma Press, 1987).
Bakken, Gordon and Brenda Farrington, *Encyclopedia of Women in the American West* (Thousand Oaks: Sage, 2003).
Bartley, Paula and Cathy Loxton, *Plains Women: Women in the American West* (New York: Cambridge University Press, 1991).
Brown, Dee, *The Gentle Tamers: Women of the Old West* (London: Barrie & Jenkins, 1958).
Butler, Anne, *Daughters of Joy, Sisters of Misery: Prostitutes in the American West, 1865–1890* (Chicago: University of Illinois Press, 1987).
Butler, Anne, 'The way we were, the way we are and the way ahead', *Western Historical Quarterly*, 36 (Winter 2005), 423–7.
Carter, Sarah, Lesley Erickson, Patricia Roome and Char Smith, *Unsettled Pasts: Reconceiving the West through Women's Eyes* (Calgary: University of Calgary Press, 2005).
Castaneda, Antonia, 'Women of color and the rewriting of Western history: the discourse, politics, and decolonization of history', *Pacific Historical Review*, LXI (1992), 501–33.
Chow, Rey, *Women and Chinese Modernity: The Politics of Reading Between West and East* (Minneapolis: University of Minnesota Press, 1990).
Dufran, Dora, 'Low down on Calamity Jane' (Deadwood: Helen Rezatto, 1981).

Faragher, John Mack, *Women and Men on the Overland Trail* (New Haven: Yale University Press, 1979).
Faragher, John Mack, 'HBO's *Deadwood*: not your typical Western', *Montana: The Magazine of Western History*, 57/3 (Autumn 2007), 60–5.
Foote, Stella, *A History of Calamity Jane: America's First Liberated Woman* (New York: Vantage Press, 1995).
Holmes, Kenneth (ed.), *Covered Wagon Women: Diaries and Letters from the Western Trails, 1840–1890*, vol. 1: 1840–1849 (Glendale: Arthur H. Clark, 1983).
Jameson, Elizabeth, 'Towards a multicultural history of women in the western United States', *Signs*, 13/4 (Summer 1988), 761–91.
Jeffrey, Julie Roy, *Frontier Women: The Trans-Mississippi West, 1840–1880* (New York: Hill & Wang, 1979).
Jennewein, J. Leonard, *Calamity Jane of the Western Trails* (Rapid City: Dakota West Books, 1953).
Jensen, Joan M. and Darlis A. Miller, 'The gentle tamers revisited: new approaches to the history of women in the American West', *Pacific Historical Review*, XLIX (1980), 173–213.
Lemsink, Judy Nolte, 'Beyond the intellectual meridian: transdisciplinary studies of women', *Pacific Historical Review*, LXI (1992), 463–80.
Larson, T. A., 'Dolls, drudges and vassals: pioneer women in the West', *Western Historical Quarterly*, 3/1 (January 1972), 4–16.
Lucey, Donna M., *Photographing Montana, 1894–1928: The Life and Work of Evelyn Cameron* (New York: Alfred Knopf, 1990).
Luchetti, Cathy, *Women of the West* (St George: Antelope Island Press, 1982).
McClure, Andrew, 'Sarah Winnemucca: post-Indian princess and voice of the Paiutes', *Melus*, 24/2 (Summer 1999), 29–51.
McLaird, James, 'Calamity Jane's diary and letters: the story of a fraud', *Montana: The Magazine of Western History*, 45 (1995), 20–35.
McLaird, James, *Calamity Jane: The Woman and the Legend* (Norman: University of Oklahoma Press, 2005).
McMurtry, Larry, *Buffalo Girls* (New York: Simon & Schuster, 1990).
Modleski, Tania, 'A woman's gotta do ... what a man's gotta do? Cross-dressing in the Western', *Signs*, 22/3 (Spring 1997), 519–44.
Morrissey, Katherine, 'Engendering the West', in William Cronon, George Miles and Jay Gitlin (eds), *Under an Open Sky: Rethinking America's Western Past* (New York: Norton, 1992), 132–44.
Myres, Sandra, *Westering Women and the Frontier Experience, 1800–1915* (Albuquerque: University of New Mexico Press, 1982).
Parker, Jerry, 'The cult of true womanhood and the Western movement', *The Chico Historian* (Spring 1992).
Pascoe, Peggy, *Relations of Rescue: The Search for Female Moral Authority in the American West, 1874–1939* (Oxford: Oxford University Press, 1990).
Powell, Malea, 'Rhetorics of survivance: how American Indians *use* writing', *College Composition and Communication*, 53/3 (February 2002), 396–434.
Richey, Eleanor, *Eminent Women of the West* (Berkeley: Howell-North Books, 1975).
Riley, Glenda, 'Images of the frontierswoman: Iowa as a case study', *Western Historical Quarterly*, 8 (April 1977), 189–202.

Riley, Glenda, *The Female Frontier: A Comparative View of Women on the Prairie and the Plains* (Lawrence, University Press of Kansas, 1988).
Riley, Glenda, *Confronting Race: Women and Indians on the Frontier: 1815–1915* (Albuquerque: University of New Mexico Press, 2004).
Riley, Glenda and Richard Etulain (eds), *By Grit and Grace: Eleven Women who Shaped the American West* (Golden: Fulcrum, 1997).
Riley, Glenda, and Richard Etulain, *Wild Women of the Old West* (Golden: Fulcrum, 2003).
Rosen, Ruth, *The Lost Sisterhood: Prostitutes in America, 1900–1915* (Baltimore: Johns Hopkins University Press, 1982).
Rosinsky, Natalie, *Sarah Winnemucca: Scout, Activist, Teacher* (Minneapolis: Compass Point Books, 2006).
Ruoff, A. LaVonne Brown, 'Three nineteenth-century American Indian autobiographers', in A. LaVonne Brown Ruoff and Jerry W. Ward Jr (eds), *Redefining American Literary History* (New York: MLA, 1990), 251–69.
Scharff, Virginia, 'Else surely we shall all hang separately: the politics of Western women's history', *Pacific Historical Review*, LXI (1992), 535–55.
Scherer, Joanna Cohan, 'The public faces of Sarah Winnemucca', *Cultural Anthropology*, 3/2 (May 1988), 178–204.
Schlissel, Lillian, *Women's Diaries of the Westward Journey* (New York: Schoken Books, 2004 [1982]).
Sigerman, Harriet, *Land of Many Hands* (New York: Oxford University Press, 1997).
Tong, Benson, *Unsubmissive Women: Chinese Prostitutes in Nineteenth Century San Francisco* (Norman: University of Oklahoma Press, 1994).
Welter, Barbara, 'The cult of true womanhood', *American Quarterly*, XVIII (1966), 151–76.
West, Elliot, 'A longer, grimmer, but more interesting story', *Montana: The Magazine of Western History*, 40/3 (Summer 1990).
Yung, Judy, *Unbound Feet: A Social History of Chinese Women in San Francisco* (Berkeley: University of California Press, 1995).
Zanjani, Sally, *Sarah Winnemucca* (Lincoln: University of Nebraska Press, 2001).

Chapter 7

Adams, David Wallace, *Education for Extinction: American Indians and the Boarding School Experience* (Lawrence: University Press of Kansas, 1995).
Almaguer, Tomas, *Racial Fault Lines: The Historical Origins of White Supremacy in California* (Los Angeles: University of California Press, 1994).
Axtell, James, *Beyond 1492: Encounters in Colonial America* (New York: Oxford University Press, 1992).
Barta, Tony, 'Relations of genocide: land and Lives in the colonization of Australia', in I. Walliman and M. N. Dobkowski (eds), *Genocide and the Modern Age* (New York: Greenwood Press, 1987).
Bird, S. Elizabeth, *Dressing in Feathers: The Construction of the Indian in American Popular Culture* (Oxford: Westview Press, 1996).
Brown, Dee, *Bury my Heart at Wounded Knee: An Indian History of the American West* (London: Vintage, 1991 [1970]).

Bibliography

Castile, George Pierre and Robert L. Bee (eds), *State and Reservation: New Perspectives on Federal Indian Policy* (Tucson: University of Arizona Press, 1992).

Chalk, Frank and Kurt Jonassohn, *The History and Sociology of Genocide: Analysis and Case Studies* (New Haven: Yale University Press, 1990).

Charny, Israel W., 'Toward a generic definition of genocide', in George J. Andreopoulos (ed.), *Genocide: Conceptual and Historical Dimensions* (Philadelphia: University of Pennsylvania Press, 1994).

Churchill, Ward, *Fantasies of the Master Race: Literature, Cinema and the Colonization of American Indians* (Monroe: Common Courage Press, 1992).

Churchill, Ward, *Indians are US? Culture and Genocide in Native North America* (Monroe: Common Courage Press, 1994).

Churchill, Ward, *A Little Matter of Genocide: Holocaust and Denial in the Americas, 1492 to the Present* (San Francisco: City Lights Books, 1997).

Crosby, Alfred, *Ecological Imperialism: The Biological Expansion of Europe, 900–1900* (New York: Cambridge University Press, 1986).

Cutler, Bruce, *The Massacre at Sand Creek* (Norman: University of Oklahoma Press, 1997).

Deloria, Vine, *Custer Died for Your Sins: An Indian Manifesto* (Norman: University of Oklahoma Press, 1988).

Dippie, Brian, *The Vanishing Indian: White Attitudes and US Policy* (Lawrence: University Press of Kansas, 1982).

Drinnon, Richard, *Facing West: The Metaphysics of Indian-hating and Empire-building* (Norman: University of Oklahoma Press, 1997 [1980]).

Greene, Jerome and Douglas Scott, *Finding Sand Creek: History, Archaeology and the 1864 Massacre Site* (Norman: University of Oklahoma Press, 2004).

Hoig, Stan, *The Sand Creek Massacre* (Norman: University of Oklahoma Press, 1961).

Hoxie, Frederick, *Indians in American History* (Arlington Heights: Harlan Davidson, 1988).

Hoxie, Frederick, *Parading through History: The Making of the Crow Nation in America, 1805–1935* (New York: Cambridge University Press, 1995).

Hoxie, Frederick, *A Final Promise: The Campaign to Assimilate the Indians, 1880–1920* (Lincoln: University of Nebraska, 2001).

Jaimes, M. Annette (ed.), *The State of Native America: Genocide, Colonization and Resistance* (Boston: South End Press, 1992).

Kane, Kate, 'Nits make lice: Drogheda, Sand Creek and the poetics of colonial extermination', *Cultural Critique*, 42 (Spring 1999), 81–103.

Katz, S. T., *The Holocaust in Historical Context, vol. 1: The Holocaust and Mass Death Before the Modern Age* (New York: Oxford University Press, 1992).

Katz, S. T., 'The uniqueness of the Holocaust: the historical dimension', in A. S. Rosenbaum (ed.), *Is the Holocaust Unique? Perspectives on Comparative Genocide* (Boulder: Westview Press, 2001).

Killoren, John, *Come Blackrobe: De Smet and the Indian Tragedy* (Norman: University of Oklahoma Press, 1994).

Kuper, Leo, *Genocide* (New Haven: Yale University Press, 1981).

Lewy, Guenter, 'Were American Indians the victims of genocide?', *History News Network Magazine*, George Mason University, 22 November 2004.

Lopez, Barry, *Of Wolves and Men* (New York: Touchstone, 1978).

Madley, B., 'Patterns of frontier genocide, 1803–1910: the aboriginal Tasmanians, the Yuki of California and the Herero of Namibia', *Journal of Genocide Research*, 6 (2004), 167–92.
Moore, MariJo (ed.), *Genocide of the Mind: New Native American Writing* (New York: Nation Books, 2003).
Novack, George, *Genocide Against the American Indians: Its Role in the Rise of US Capitalism* (New York: Pathfinder, 1970).
Ortiz, Simon, *From Sand Creek* (Tucson: University of Arizona Press, 1981).
Perkin, Robert, *The First Hundred Years: An Informal History of Denver and the Rocky Mountain News* (New York: Doubleday, 1959).
Perry, Richard, *From Time Immemorial: Indigenous Peoples and State Systems* (Austin: University of Texas Press, 1996).
Power, Samantha, *A Problem from Hell: America and the Age of Genocide* (New York: Basic Books, 2002).
Sartre, Jean-Paul, *On Genocide, and a Summary of the Evidence and Judgements of the International War Crimes Tribunal* (Boston: Beacon Press, 1968).
Scott, Bob, *Blood at Sand Creek: The Massacre Revisited* (Caldwell: Caxton, 1994).
Stannard, David, *American Holocaust* (New York: Oxford University Press, 1992).
Stone, Dan (ed.), *The Historiography of Genocide* (Basingstoke: Palgrave, 2008).
Svaldi, David, *Sand Creek and the Rhetoric of Extermination: A Case Study in Indian–White Relations* (Boston: University Press of America, 1989).
Thornton, Russell, *American Indian Holocaust and Survival: A Population History Since 1492* (Norman: University of Oklahoma Press, 1987).
Thornton, Russell, *The Cherokees: A Population History* (Lincoln: University of Nebraska Press, 1990).
Utley, Robert, *Frontiersmen in Blue: The United States Army and the American Indian, 1848–1865* (Lincoln: University of Nebraska, 1967).
Utley, Robert, *The Indian Frontier of the American West, 1846–90* (Albuquerque: University of New Mexico Press, 2003).
West, Elliott, *The Contested Plains: Indians, Goldseekers and the Rush to Colorado* (Lawrence: University Press of Kansas, 2000).
Wilson, James, *The Earth Shall Weep: A History of Native America* (London: Picador, 1998).
Wooster, Robert, *The Military and United States Indian Policy, 1865–1903* (New Haven: Yale University Press, 1988).
Wynkoop, Edward and Christopher Gerboth, *The Tall Chief: The Unfinished Autobiography of Edward W. Wynkoop, 1856–1866* (Denver: Colorado Historical Society, 1994).

Chapter 8

Abbey, Edward, *Desert Solitaire: A Season in the Wilderness* (New York: Ballantine Books, 1968).
Abbey, Edward, *The Monkeywrench Gang* (Philadelphia: Lippincott, 1975).
Abbott, Carl, *The Metropolitan Frontier: Cities in the Modern American West* (Tucson: University of Arizona Press, 1993).
Aitchison, Stewart, *A Wilderness Called Grand Canyon* (New York: Gramercy, 1993).

Bibliography

Bowden, Charles, *Killing the Hidden Waters* (Austin: University of Texas Press, 1977).
Catlin, George, *North American Indians*, I (Philadelphia: Leary, Stuait, 1913).
Childs, Elizabeth, 'John Wesley Powell, art and geology at the Grand Canyon', *American Art*, 10/1 (Spring 1996), 7–35.
Chung, Su Kim, *Las Vegas: Then and Now* (San Diego: Thunder Press, 2002).
Davis, Mike, *Dead Cities* (New York: The New Press, 2002).
Douglass, William A. and Pauliina Raento, 'The tradition of invention: conceiving Las Vegas', *Annals of Tourism Research*, 31/1 (2004), 7–23.
Dunar, Andrew J. and Dennis McBride, *Building Hoover Dam: An Oral History of the Great Depression* (Reno: University of Nevada Press, 1993).
Ferrari, Michelle and Stephen Ives, *Las Vegas: An Unconventional History* (New York: Bullfinch, 2005).
Findlay, John, *People of Chance: Gambling in American Society from Jamestown to Las Vegas* (New York: Oxford University Press, 1986).
Fox, William, *In the Desert of Desire: Las Vegas and the Culture of Spectacle* (Reno: University of Nevada Press, 2005).
Fradkin, Philip, *A River No More: The Colorado River and the West* (Berkeley: University of California Press, 1995).
Franci, Giovanni, *Dreaming of Italy: Las Vegas and the Virtual Grand Tour* (Reno: University of Nevada Press, 2005).
Goodman, Robert, 'Still learning from Las Vegas: the new face of urban redevelopment in a scavenger economy', *Perspecta*, 29 (1998), 86–96.
Hausladen, Gary (ed.), *Western Places: American Myths* (Reno: University of Nevada Press, 2003).
Hays, Samuel P., *Conservation and the Gospel of Efficiency: The Progressive Conservation Movement, 1890–1920* (Pittsburgh: University of Pittsburgh Press, 1999 [1959]).
Hollon, W. Eugene, *The Great American Desert: Then and Now* (New York: Oxford University Press, 1966).
Holtorf, Cornelius, *From Stonehenge to Las Vegas: Archaeology as Popular Culture* (Walnut Creek: Alta Mira, 2005).
Hughes, J. Donald, *In the House of Stone and Light* (Grand Canyon: Grand Canyon Natural History Association, 1978).
McKibben, Bill, *The End of Nature* (New York: Random House, 1989).
McPhee, John, *Basin and Range* (New York: Farrar, Straus & Giroux, 1981).
Marx, Leo, *The Machine in the Garden: Technology and the Pastoral Idea in America* (London: Oxford University Press, 1964).
Nash, Roderick, *Wilderness and the American Mind* (New Haven: Yale University Press, 1982 [1967]).
Nicoletta, Julie, *Buildings of Nevada* (New York: Oxford University Press, 2000).
Nye, David E., *American Technological Sublime* (London: MIT Press, 1994).
Parkman, Francis, *The Oregon Trail* (Boston: Little, Brown, 1892).
Pisani, Donald J., *To Reclaim a Divided West: Water, Lawe and Public Policy* (Albuquerque: University of New Mexico Press, 1992).
Pyne, Stephen J., *How the Canyon Became Grand* (London: Penguin, 1998).
Reisner, Marc, *Cadillac Desert: The American West & its Disappearing Water* (London: Secker & Warburg, 1990).

Rothman, Hal, *The Culture of Tourism, The Tourism of Culture: Selling the Past to the Present in the American Southwest* (Albuquerque: University of New Mexico Press, 2003).
Rothman, Hal, *Neon Metropolis* (New York: Routledge, 2003).
Rothman, Hal and Mike Davis (eds), *The Grit Beneath the Glitter: Tales from the Real Las Vegas* (Berkeley: University of California Press, 2002).
Runte, Alfred, *National Parks: The American Experience* (Lincoln: University of Nebraska Press, 1979).
Schwartz, D., 'Ambient frontiers: the El Rancho Vegas and Hotel Last Frontier – Strip pioneers', *Electronic Journal of Gambling Issues: eGambling* (February 2001), online edition.
Shepperson, Wilbur S. (ed.), *East of Eden, West of Zion: Essays on Nevada* (Reno: University of Nevada Press, 1989).
Stegner, Page, *Marking the Sparrow's Fall: The Making of the American West* (New York: Henry Holt, 1998).
Stevens, Joseph, *Hoover Dam: An American Adventure* (Norman: University of Oklahoma Press, 1988).
Venturi, Robert, Denise Scott Brown and Steven Izenour, *Learning from Las Vegas* (Cambridge, MA: MIT Press, 1977 [1972]).
Weatherford, Gary and F. Lee Brown (eds), *New Courses for the Colorado River: Major Issues for the Next Century* (Albuquerque: University of New Mexico Press, 1986).
Webb, Walter Prescott, *The Great Plains* (New York: Grosset & Dunlap, 1931).
Wilson, Richard Guy, 'American modernism in the West: Hoover Dam', in Thomas Carter (ed.), *Images of American Land: Vernacular Architecture in the Western United States* (Albuquerque: University of New Mexico Press, 1997), 291–319.
Worster, Donald, *Rivers of Empire: Water, Aridity and the Growth of the American West* (New York: Oxford University Press, 1985).

Chapter 9

Anderson, Christopher, 'Jesse James, the bourgeois bandit: the transformation of a popular hero', *Cinema Journal*, 26/1 (Autumn 1986).
Basso, Matthew, Laura McCall and Dee Garceau (eds), *Across the Great Divide: Cultures of Manhood in the American West* (New York: Routledge 2001).
Buscombe, Edward and Roberta Pearson (eds), *Back in the Saddle Again: New Essays on the Western* (London: BFI, 1998).
Coyne, Michael, *The Crowded Prairie: American National Identity in the Hollywood Western* (London: I. B. Tauris, 1997).
Dellinger, Harold, *Jesse James: The Best Writings on the Notorious Outlaw and His Gang* (Guilford: Globe Pequot, 2007).
Dyer, Robert, *Jesse James and the Civil War in Missouri* (Columbia: University of Missouri Press, 1994).
Elkin, Frederick, 'The psychological appeal of the Hollywood Western', *Journal of Educational Sociology*, 24/2 (October 1950).
Etulain, Richard and Glenda Riley (eds), *The Hollywood West: Lives of Film Legends Who Shaped It* (Golden: Fulcrum, 2001).

Bibliography

McGee, Patrick, *From Shane to Kill Bill: Rethinking the Western* (Oxford: Blackwell, 2007).
McVeigh, Stephen, *The American Western* (Edinburgh: Edinburgh University Press, 2007).
Packard, Chris, *Queer Cowboys: And Other Erotic Male Friendships in Nineteenth-Century American Literature* (New York: Macmillan, 2005).
Patterson, Eric, *On Brokeback Mountain: Meditations About Masculinity, Fear, and Love in the Story and the Film* (Lanham: Lexington Books, 2008).
Platinga, Carl, 'Spectacles of death: Clint Eastwood and violence in "Unforgiven"' *Cinema Journal*, 37/2 (Winter 1998).
Proulx, Annie, Larry McMurtry and Diana Ossana, *Brokeback Mountain: Story to Screenplay* (London: Harper, 2005).
Rainey, Buck, *The Reel Cowboy: Essays on the Myth in Movies and Literature* (Jefferson: McFarland, 1996).
Rainey, Buck, *Western Gunslingers in Fact and on Film: Hollywood's Famous Lawmen and Outlaws* (Jefferson: McFarland, 1998).
Rollins, Philip Ashton, *The Cowboy: An unconventional History of Civilization on the Old-Time Cattle Range* (Albuquerque: University of New Mexico Press, 1936 [1922]).
Saunders, John, *The Western Genre: From Lordsburg to Big Whiskey* (London: Wallflower, 2001).
Seal, Graham, *The Outlaw Legend: A Cultural Tradition in Britain, America and Australia* (Cambridge: Cambridge University Press, 1996).
Stacy, Jim (ed.), *Reading Brokeback Mountain: Essays on the Story and the Film* (Jefferson: McFarland, 2007).
Stiles, T. J., *Jesse James: Last Rebel of the Civil War* (London: Jonathan Cape, 2003).
Tompkins, Jane, *West of Everything: The Inner Life of Westerns* (New York: Oxford University Press, 1992).
Walker, Janet (ed.), *Westerns: Films Through History* (New York: Routledge, 2001).
White, Richard, 'Brokeback Mountain: a Western', *Montana: The Magazine of Western History*, 56/2 (Summer 2006).

Chapter 10

Carter, A., *Buffalo Bill Cody: The Man Behind the Legend* (New York: Wiley, 2000).
Hendrew, Paul, 'The contradictory legacies of Buffalo Bill Cody's first scalp for Custer', *Montana: The Magazine of Western History*, 55/1 (Spring 2005).
Herman, Leonard, *Phoenix: The Fall and Rise of Videogames* (New Jersey: Rolenta Press, 1994).
Herz, Jessie Cameron, *Joystick Nation: How Videogames Ate Our Quarters, Won Our Hearts, and Rewired Our Minds* (New York: Little, Brown, 1997).
Jenkins, Henry and Justine Cassell (eds), *From Barbie to Mortal Kombat: Gender and Computer Games* (Cambridge, MA: MIT Press, 1998).
Johnson, Michael L., *Hunger for the Wild: America's Obsession with the Untamed West* (Lawrence: University Press of Kansas, 2007).
Jones, Steven G. (ed.), *Cybersociety: Computer-Mediated Communication and Community* (Thousand Oaks: Sage, 1995).

McLure, Helen, 'The wild, wild web: the mythic American West and the electronic frontier', *The Western Historical Quarterly*, 31/4 (Winter 2000), 457–76.
Moses, L. G., *Wild West Shows and the Images of American Indians, 1883–1933* (Albuquerque: University of New Mexico Press, 1999).
Poole, Stephen, *Trigger Happy: The Inner Life of Videogames* (London: Fourth Estate, 2000).
Provenzo, Eugene F., *Video Kids: Making Sense of Nintendo* (Cambridge, MA: Harvard University Press, 1991).
Rydell, Robert W., and Rob Kroes, *Buffalo Bill in Bologna: The Americanization of the World, 1869–1922* (Chicago: University of Chicago Press, 2005).
Warren, Louis S., *Buffalo Bill's America: William Cody and the Wild West Show* (New York: Random House, 2005).

Chapter 11

Ball, Howard, *Justice Downwind* (New York: Oxford University Press, 1986).
Coates, Peter, 'Project Chariot: Alaskan roots of environmentalism', *Alaska History*, 4/2 (Fall 1989).
Costandina Titus, A., *Bombs in the Backyard* (Reno: University of Nevada Press, 2001).
Fernlund, Kevin (ed.), *The Cold War American West* (Albuquerque: New Mexico University Press, 1998).
Hevly, Bruce amd John M. Findlay (eds), *The Atomic West* (Seattle: University of Washington Press, 1998).
Kirsch, Scott, 'Watching the bombs go off: photography, nuclear landscapes, and spectacular democracy', *Antipode*, 29/3 (1997).
Kuletz, Valerie L., *The Tainted Desert: Environmental and Social Ruin in the American West* (New York: Routledge, 1998).
Nash, Gerald D., *The American West Transformed: The Impact of the Second World War* (Bloomington: Indiana University Press, 1985).
Nash, Gerald D., *World War II and the West: Reshaping the Economy* (Lincoln: University of Nebraska Press, 1990).
O'Neill, Dan, *The Firecracker Boys* (New York: St. Martin's Press, 1994).
Rothman, Hal, *The Greening of a Nation?: Environmentalism in the United States Since 1945* (Orlando: Harcourt Brace, 1998).
Smith, Michael, 'Advertising the atom', in Michael J. Lacey (ed.), *Government and Environmental Politics: Essays on Historical Developments Since World War Two* (Baltimore: Johns Hopkins University Press, 1989).
Solnit, Rebecca, *Savage Dreams: A Journey into the Landscape Wars of the American West* (New Berkeley: University of California Press, 1994).
Wilson, Alexander, *The Culture of Nature: North American Landscape from Disney to the Exxon Valdez* (Cambridge: Blackwell, 1992).

Chapter 12

Adams, Judith, *The American Amusement Industry: A History of Technology and Thrills* (Boston: Twayne, 1991).
Ashby, LeRoy, *With Amusement for All: A History of American Popular Culture Since 1830* (Lexington: University of Press Kentucky, 2006).

Bibliography

Baudrillard, Jean, *Simulations* (New York: Semiotext(e), 1983).
Eco, Umberto, *Travels in Hyperreality* (London: Picador, 1986).
Francaviglia, Richard, 'Walt Disney's Frontierland as allegorical map of the American West', *The Western Historical Quarterly*, 30/2 (Summer 1999).
Jones, Karen and John Wills, *The Invention of the Park: From the Garden of Eden to Disney's Magic Kingdom* (Cambridge: Polity Press, 2005).
Kasson, John, *Amusing the Million: Coney Island at the Turn of the Century* (New York: Hill & Wang, 1978).
Marling, Karal Ann, 'Disneyland, 1955: just take the Santa Ana Freeway to the American Dream', *American Art*, 5/1–2 (Winter–Spring 1991).
Marling, Karal Ann (ed.), *Designing Disney's Theme Parks: The Architecture of Reassurance* (Paris: Flammarion, 1997).
Nye, Russel, 'Eight ways of looking at an amusement park', *Journal of Popular Culture*, 15/1 (Summer 1981).
Register, Woody, *The Kid of Coney Island: Fred Thompson and the Rise of American Amusements* (Oxford: Oxford University Press, 2001).
Rothman, Hal, *Devil's Bargains: Tourism in the Twentieth-Century American West* (Lawrence: University Press of Kansas, 1998).
Sorkin, Michael (ed.), *Variations on a Theme Park: The New American City and the End of Public Space* (New York: Hill & Wang, 1992).
Steiner, Michael, 'Frontierland as Tomorrowland: Walt Disney and the architectural packaging of the mythic West', *Montana*, 48/1 (Spring 1998).
Wrobel, David M. and Patrick T. Long (eds), *Seeing and Being Seen: Tourism in the American West* (Lawrence: University Press of Kansas, 2001).
Zukin, Sharon, *Landscapes of Power: From Detroit to Disney World* (Berkeley: University of California Press, 1991).

Index

9/11, 27, 29–30, 87, 110–11, 240

Abalone Alliance, 106, 108
Abbey, Edward, 203, 211, 222
Abilene, Texas, 69
African-Americans, 7, 80, 94, 95, 173, 210, 218, 239
agrarian ideal, 12, 51, 90, 292
agriculture, 4, 12, 42, 43, 69, 89, 106–7, 195, 204, 292
air pollution, 3, 202–3, 222
Alaska, 292
American Fur Company, 64, 67
American Indian Movement (AIM), 173, 319
A Night at the Museum (2006), 100
Apache, 237–8
Arapahos, 181–90
aridity, 195, 204, 221, 222–3
Assassination of Jesse James (2007), 88, 246–7, 254–6
Atari, 260
Atomic Energy Commission (AEC), 219, 288, 289–90, 298
Atoms for Peace, 289
Auditor (dog), 90
automobiles, 1, 194, 203, 217, 275, 276, 290, 306, 308
Autry, Gene, 1, 67, 88, 232, 310

Bannocks, 143
Barnum, P. T., 74, 309
Bartram, William, 48–9
Battle of the Little Big Horn, 188, 269–70

Battle of Wounded Knee, 89, 175–6, 179
Baudrillard, Jean, 31, 318
Beadle & Adams, 73–4
bears, grizzly, 16, 54, 56
Bierstadt, Albert, 197
Big Bus, The (1976), 294–5
Billington, Ray Allen, 40, 41, 51
Billy the Kid *see* William H. Bonney
bison, 16, 53, 64, 67, 70, 171, 176, 183, 189, 196, 198, 238
Black Hills, 151, 159
Black Kettle, 181, 183, 186, 187, 188, 189
Blackfeet, 18, 19, 30
Blood Bros. (1990), 263, 269
Bodie, California, 65
Bonney, William H., 62
Boone, Daniel, 13, 91, 312
Boot Hill, 70, 136
Boot Hill (1977), 262, 266–7
Bosque Redondo, 177
Boulder City, Nevada, 210
Brokeback Mountain (2005), 241–6
Brower, David, 202
buffalo *see* bison
Buffalo Bill *see* William Frederick Cody
Bureau of Reclamation, 205, 206, 208, 210
Bush, George W., 11, 27, 87, 88, 109–13, 240
Butte, Montana, 89–90

Calamity Jane, 68, 149–67
Calamity Jane (1953), 164–5, 310
Calico, California, 307, 311, 322

Index

California Gold Rush, 49, 64, 176
Call, Carrie, 123–30, 141
Cameron, Evelyn, 131–9
Campaign for Nuclear Disarmament (CND), 108
Carson, Kit, 62, 82, 177, 188
Catlin, George, 57, 71, 105, 196–7
cattle industry, 68–9, 72, 93,
Cattle Queen of Montana (1954), 103, 233
cattle towns, 69–71, 72
Charbonneau, Touissant, 16, 17
Chavez, Cesar, 7, 89
Cherokee, 177
Cheyenne, 181–90
Cheyenne (1984), 262, 264, 273
Chicago, 4, 51
Chinese-Americans, 65, 136, 171, 210
Chivington, John, 181–90
Church of Latter Day Saints of Jesus Christ *see* Mormons
Cimino, Michael, 104, 237
Civil War, 62, 63, 65, 74, 89, 247, 249
Clark, William, 11, 14, 18, 20, 23, 28
class, 74–5, 123, 135–6
Code of the West, 67, 93, 110
Cody, William Frederick (Buffalo Bill), 4, 6, 52–3, 66, 77, 82, 88, 94, 97, 121, 149, 159, 162, 232, 262–3, 305, 310
Cold War, 26, 105, 107–8, 219, 236, 284–5, 300, 301, 314–15, 321
Colorado River, 195, 199, 203–11, 224
Colt firearms, 62, 64, 65–6, 68, 71, 73
Colt, Samuel, 66, 71
Columbia River, 13
Columbine High School, Colorado, 271
Comstock, Anthony, 75
Coney Island, New York, 74, 135, 311–12
conservation, 99, 196–203
Coolidge, Calvin, 100–1
Cooper, James Fenimore, 50, 61, 76, 269
Corps of Discovery *see* Lewis and Clark Expedition
Costner, Kevin, 237–40
cowboys, 60–1, 68–9, 72, 76, 77–8, 83–4, 87–9, 92–4, 97–9, 101, 104, 107–8, 109–14, 240, 242–3, 244–6

Crazy Taxi (1999), 276
crime, 66–7, 75, 78–9, 232, 247–50
Crockett, Davy, 91, 296, 312
Crow, 67
Custer, George Armstrong, 5, 52, 97, 100, 151, 162, 189, 269–70
Custer's Revenge (1983), 261, 269–70, 280

Dakota Territory, 90, 97
Dances with Wolves (1990), 237–9, 247
Davy Crockett (TV series), 310, 315
Dawes Act (1887), 148, 177
Day, Doris, 164–5
Deadwood, South Dakota, 152–3, 156–7, 159, 161
Deadwood (2004–6), 167
Deadwood Dick, 74, 76, 80, 154–5
Death Valley Days, 103
Desperados (2001), 261, 277–8, 280
diaries, 53–7, 123–39
dime novels, 73–84, 92, 94, 153–5, 250, 263–4, 266
disease, 47, 176, 180
Disney, Walt, 4, 6, 43–4, 211, 310, 312
Disneyland, California, 4, 211, 218, 262, 293, 309–22
Dodge City, Kansas, 60, 62, 69–71, 110, 266–7
Donner Party, 126
Doom Town, Nevada, 219, 297
Dust Bowl, 42, 89

Earp, Wyatt, 66, 232
Earth First!, 89, 195, 211
earthquakes, 277
Eastwood, Clint, 236, 237–9, 264, 266, 268
Eco, Umberto, 318, 319
Eisenhower, Dwight, 101, 289
emigrant guidebooks, 55, 71–2, 124
environmental issues, 28–9, 195, 202, 211, 221, 224, 307
ethnicity, 5, 6, 28, 43, 89, 93–4, 135–6, 141–2, 239, 277–8, 319
Euro-Americans, 6, 39, 40, 43, 54, 94, 142, 263, 313

expansion, westward, 12–21, 23, 29, 45, 49, 182, 196, 197, 198, 273–4
Exploration of the Colorado River of the West (1875), 199

fallout, radioactive, 284, 295
Far Horizons, The (1955), 26
farming *see* agriculture
fashion, 88, 111, 127, 134, 144, 162, 165, 166
federal government, 90, 99–100, 106–7, 179, 180, 185–6, 188, 205, 210, 213–14
female suffrage, 123
feminism, 122, 151, 161–2, 164–5, 166
firearms industry, 63–6, 71–2, 73
Ford, John, 95, 232, 234, 262, 274, 307–8
Foreman, Dave, 195, 211
Forest Service, 99
Fremont, John Charles, 23, 142, 212
frontier
  as border, 53, 55
  closure of, 24, 39, 49, 56, 61, 94, 97, 157, 232, 235, 295
  descriptions of, 53–7
  as myth, 3–4, 6, 29, 43–4, 61, 63, 83–4, 87–8, 93–4, 99, 101–2, 103, 105–7, 110–11, 208, 221, 235, 279
  reopening of, 89, 291
  violence, 62–86, 92–4, 98, 110–11, 171–90, 265–71, 279
  as a word, 48–57, 66, 88,
frontier thesis, the, 4–5, 39–59, 105, 218, 221
  and Indians, 46, 50
  reception of, 41–5
  as socio-environmental theory, 45–8
Frontier Village, San Jose, California, 315–17, 319–20
Frontierland, 4, 43–4, 218, 309–22
fur trade, 13, 14, 15, 19, 64, 69, 123

gambling, 69, 70, 136, 213, 215, 217, 219
gangs, 65
genocide, 30, 63, 171–90
germ theory, 45–8
Geronimo, 98, 100
Ghost Dance, 4, 148

Gold Rush *see* California Gold Rush
Gore, Al, 111
Gore, Sir George, 67
government *see* federal government
Grand Canyon, Arizona, 3, 6, 99, 194–203, 207, 208, 209, 217, 220, 222, 223–4, 275–6, 322
Grants, New Mexico, 300, 306
Great Depression, 42, 213, 232, 252
Great Train Robbery, The (1903), 231–2, 264
Grey, Zane, 61, 203, 262
gun culture, 60–86, 107–8, 110
Gun Fight (1975), 261, 264, 266–7, 271, 272

Hanford, Washington, 291, 298, 299
Heaven's Gate (1980), 104, 237
Hickok, Wild Bill, 152–3, 159, 162, 215
High Noon (1952), 107, 236, 242–3, 264
hispanics, 5, 93, 308
historiography *see* West: historiography
Hohokam, 204
Hollywood, 1, 106, 286, 294–5; *see also* Westerns
Homestead Act (1862), 75, 133
homosexuality, 155–6, 166, 241–6, 254
Hoover Dam, 194–6, 203–11, 213–14, 220, 222, 223–4, 288
horses, 132, 133, 134, 231, 234
hunting, 64, 67, 90, 100, 131–9, 305
Hunting Trips of a Ranchman (1885), 93

Indian Removal Act (1830), 177
Indians *see* Native Americans
Ingraham, Prentiss, 73, 77, 82, 94
irrigation, 204–5
Iron Horse, The (1924), 232, 274

James, Jesse, 62, 92, 111, 246–56
Japanese-Americans, 7
Jefferson, Thomas, 12–15, 18, 22, 23, 51, 292
Jesse James (1939), 251–2
Johnson County Range War, 68
Johnson, Lyndon, 101

Index

Kennedy, John F., 43, 66, 88, 101
Knott's Berry Farm, California, 309, 311, 317

language, 78, 81–2
Las Vegas, 194–6, 211–24, 286, 287–8, 305
Last Frontier, Las Vegas, 217, 219
law enforcement, 62, 65–7, 71, 78, 87, 92, 110, 235, 248, 270
Law and Order (1953), 103, 104
Lee, Ang, 241–6
Leone, Sergio, 236
Lewis and Clark Expedition, 11–38
  and commemoration, 25, 27, 30–1
  and commerce, 13–14, 30–1, 32–3
  and Indians, 15–16, 19, 28, 30
  journey of, 15–18
  and natural history, 16–17, 19, 27–9, 273
  and popular memory, 21–31, 100
  significance of, 18–21, 305
Lewis and Clark Trail (1978), 34
Lewis, Meriwether, 11, 13, 16–17, 18, 20, 23, 28
Life and Adventures of Calamity Jane (1896), 151–3, 163–4
Life Among the Piutes: Their Wrongs and Claims (1883), 145–7
Limerick, Patricia Nelson, 5, 44, 49, 122, 131, 178, 321
Little Big Man (1970), 236
Little Bighorn Battlefield, 5
Little Missouri River Stockmen's Association, 92
Lodge, Henry Cabot, 90, 97
Lone Ranger, 234
Los Alamos, New Mexico, 288–9
Los Angeles, California, 3, 6, 89, 204
Los Angeles City Gun Club, 67
Louisiana Purchase, 14
Lum, Mrs Ah ('China Mary'), 136
Lummis, Charles, 98, 99, 200
lynching, 62, 66–7

MacKenzie, Alexander, 13
Man Who Shot Liberty Valance, The (1962), 95

Mandans, 12, 16, 30
Manifest Destiny, 20, 56, 101, 105, 124, 177, 195, 205, 233
Mann, Anthony, 61
Mann, Mary, 145
masculinity, 67–8, 79–80, 88–9, 90–4, 97, 98, 100, 102, 106, 111, 113, 121, 129, 133, 243, 245, 268
McCoy, Joseph, 94
Mexicans, 63
militias, 90
miners and mining, 64–5, 90, 182, 213
missions, Spanish, 177, 180
Moab, Utah, 306, 308
Montana, 131–9
Montana Freemen, 89
Monument Valley, 234, 307–8
Moran, Thomas, 105, 197, 276
Mormons, 89, 123, 171, 204, 212
Moulin Rouge, Las Vegas, 218
Mount Rushmore, 26, 100
Muir, John, 99, 202, 203
Mulholland, William, 4, 6
Museum of Jurassic Technology, Los Angeles, 309

National Park Service, 5, 190, 194, 297
national parks, 99, 196–203, 306–7, 308
Native Americans, 141–9, 171–90
  depictions of, 12, 16, 19, 46, 57, 129–30, 143, 144, 147, 175, 184–5, 196, 233, 238, 262, 269–70, 273, 308, 313, 317, 320–1
  and federal programs, 106
  and fur trade, 64
  and genocide, 63, 171–90
  and memorials, 5, 190
  and overland travel, 129–30
  and survivance, 6, 146–9, 178
  and war, 5
natural disasters, 1, 128
Navajo, 89, 177
Nevada Test Site, 219, 286, 290–1, 297–8
New Deal, 205–11
New Frontier, Las Vegas, 219, 220
New Western history, 5, 44–5, 49–50, 238, 285, 321

Nez Perce, 17, 18
Northwest Passage, 14, 15, 18, 20, 32
novels, 61–2, 83, 91, 155–6
nuclear energy, 43, 107–8, 178, 219, 284–301

Oakley, Annie, 68, 121, 151, 233
oil industry, 109
O'Keeffe, Georgia, 272
Open Range (2003), 239–40
Oregon Trail, 123
overland travel, 123–30

Pacific Gas and Electric Company (PG&E), 292
Paiute, 4, 142–9
Parkman, Francis, 50–1, 198
Pasteur, Louis, 47
Peabody, Elizabeth, 145, 147
Peckinpah, Sam, 236, 255
photography, 3, 92, 132, 134–9, 144, 157, 199–200, 307
Pinchot, Gifford, 204
Pioneertown, California, 1–3, 317, 322
Pitt, Brad, 254
Plainsman, The (1936), 162
poetry, 73
politics, 14–15, 87–117
Pony Express, 153
populism, 90
Porter, Edwin S., 231
Posse (1993), 239
Powell, John Wesley, 23, 46, 199, 204, 220
preservationism, 197, 203
progressivism, 90, 95, 99
Project Chariot, 292
prostitution, 136, 155, 161
Proulx, Annie, 113–14, 241–6

racism, 65, 80, 123, 136, 171, 175–6, 210, 218
railroads, 74, 99, 123, 142, 200, 201, 212–13, 273–4, 290, 306, 313, 317
Ranch Life and the Hunting Trail (1888), 93, 94, 103
ranchers and ranching, 68–9, 72, 90–1, 92, 111–13, 131–9

Reagan, Ronald, 88, 100–9, 113, 284, 310
Reclamation Act, 99
Red Dawn (1984), 295
Red River (1947), 246
Re-enactments *see* Wild West shows
religion, 53–4, 110, 146, 176–7
Remington, Frederic, 94, 95, 105, 262, 272
reservations, 142–9, 177, 180, 183
Richland, Washington, 291
Riley, Glenda, 44, 122, 129, 138, 141, 166
Rocky Flats, 284
rodeo, 94
Rogers, Roy, 1, 67, 232, 234
Romanticism, 197, 199
Roosevelt, Franklin D., 205, 206, 207
Roosevelt, Theodore, 21, 24, 50, 54, 88, 90–100, 101, 110, 113, 121, 181, 200, 204
Roswell, New Mexico, 309
Rough Riders, 95–7, 98, 100
Route 66, 300, 306
rural life, 89, 106, 131–9, 242, 245
Russell, Charles, 24–5, 52, 273

Sacagawea, 16, 17, 25, 28, 32, 100
Sagebrush Rebellion, 106
San Francisco, 65, 276, 277
Sand Creek Massacre, 172, 181–90
scalping, 129
schooling, 147–9, 177
Schwarzenegger, Arnold, 108
Seaman (dog), 14, 18, 28
Seattle World's Fair (1962), 293
Second Amendment, 62
Second World War, 43, 261
Shane (1953), 107, 233, 235, 238
Sheridan, Philip, 186, 189
Shootist, The (1976), 237, 264
Sierra Club, 29, 99, 202
Sim City (1987), 276–7
Simpsons, The, 32, 298, 300
Sioux, 16, 19, 30, 269
simulation (of West), 3, 31–2, 52, 211–24, 261–5, 305–22
Sitting Bull, 52
slavery, 40, 43

Index

Smith, Henry Nash, 21, 264
Smith, Will, 239
Smith & Wesson, 65
smog, 3, 202–3
social Darwinism, 45–8
Spanish, 12, 13, 199, 212; *see also* missions
Spanish–American War, 95, 97, 100
Spencer, Herbert, 46–8
Stagecoach (1939), 214, 232, 264, 268
Stanwyck, Barbara, 103, 233
Star Trek, 43
Star Wars (1977), 275
St Louis, 22
Sunset Riders (1991), 269

Taylor, Buck, 77, 94
technology (and West), 3, 11, 33–4, 43, 63–4, 71, 80–2, 206, 209–10, 260–80, 292, 309
Texas, 83, 109–10
Them! (1954), 286
theme parks, 309–22
Tombstone, Arizona, 78, 136
tourism, 67, 194–5, 199–203, 207, 211–24, 305–22
  Nuclear, 285, 286–8, 296–8, 300–1
  Old West, 1–3, 30–1
'Trail of Tears', 177
transport *see* automobiles, railroads
Treaty of Fort Laramie (1851), 179, 182
Trinity Site, New Mexico, 296–7
Triplett, Frank, 55, 56
Turner, Frederick Jackson, 4, 6, 24, 39–59, 61, 89, 121, 130, 172, 195, 218, 221, 234, 274, 301, 313–14, 319
Turner thesis *see* frontier thesis
Twain, Mark, 44, 98, 177

Unforgiven (1992), 238–9, 240, 247
United Farmworkers Union, 89
US Army, 5, 142–6, 151–2, 175–6, 179–80, 181–90
US Congress, 5, 64, 188
uranium rush, 292–3
urban growth, 4–5, 214–15, 222, 291

Vegas Vic, 215, 218–19
videogames, 108, 260–80
Vietnam War, 101, 173, 236
vigilantism, 66–7, 92–3, 270
violence *see* frontier violence
Virginian, The (1902), 61, 83, 94, 310

Wanted (1984), 268, 272
War of Independence, 62
Warhol, Andy, 100, 113, 246
water, 4, 6, 44, 194–224
Wayne, John, 89, 100, 101–2, 104, 111, 232, 234, 236, 237, 240, 245, 246, 264, 268
Webb, Walter Prescott, 195
West
  as creation story, 31, 39, 113
  and digital culture, 33–4, 50, 260–80
  as dumping ground, 260
  and East compared, 76, 91, 133
  and economics, 14, 19, 64–6, 72, 76, 88–9, 93, 106–7, 109, 135, 305–6
  as escape, 77, 91, 99–100, 215, 235, 240, 314–15
  and Europe compared, 62, 72, 131–2, 198, 207
  European interest in, 13–14, 41, 48, 52, 67, 107–8, 131, 263, 264, 278–9, 305
  historiography of, 4–5, 24, 26–27, 40, 41–5, 49–50, 121–3, 131, 141–2, 166, 285
  and politics, 87–117
  visions of/mythology, 3–6, 12, 18–21, 49, 51–3, 71, 72, 75, 76–7, 87–9, 90, 98, 104–6, 113–14, 121–2, 195–6, 214, 307, 321–2
West San Francisco Vigilance Committee, 66–7
western art, 24–5, 52, 57, 94, 95–6, 98, 100, 105, 113, 271–4
Westerns
  Hollywood, 4, 60–1, 83–4, 87, 101–3, 104, 107–8, 161–7, 231–56, 264, 310–11
  TV, 1, 103, 234
Westworld (1973), 113, 266–7
Wheeler, Edward, 76, 154–5

White, Richard, 5, 44, 90, 104, 263, 291
Whites *see* Euro-Americans
Wichita, Kansas, 69
Wild Bill Hickok *see* Hickok
Wild Bunch, The (1969), 236
Wild West shows, 3, 4, 52–3, 66, 75, 77, 94, 97, 121, 157–8, 231, 251, 262–3, 305, 311–12, 317, 318, 321
Wild, Wild West, The (1999), 239
wilderness, 12, 16–17, 28–9, 46–7, 54–5, 99–100, 127–30, 137, 298
Wilderness Hunter, The (1893), 93–4
Winchester, 60, 61, 65, 70, 87, 94, 97
Winchester '73 (1950), 60–1
Winnemucca, Sarah, 141–9
Winning of the West (1889–96), 21, 24, 93–4, 121

Wister, Owen, 61, 83, 93, 94, 100, 310
wolves, 54, 56, 94, 135, 137, 171, 238, 273, 308
women, 44, 52, 68, 79–80, 121–39, 141–67, 233, 243, 262
World Columbian Exposition, Chicago (1893), 4, 39–40, 50, 51–3
Worster, Donald, 44, 195, 210
Wovoka (Jack Wilson), 4, 6
Wyatt Earp (1994), 239
Wyoming, 123, 305

Yellowstone National Park, 157, 197, 217, 286, 288
Yosemite National Park, 99, 197, 198, 288, 306